BROTHER, CAN YOU SPARE A RHYME?

100 Years Of Hit Songwriting

by

Spencer Leigh

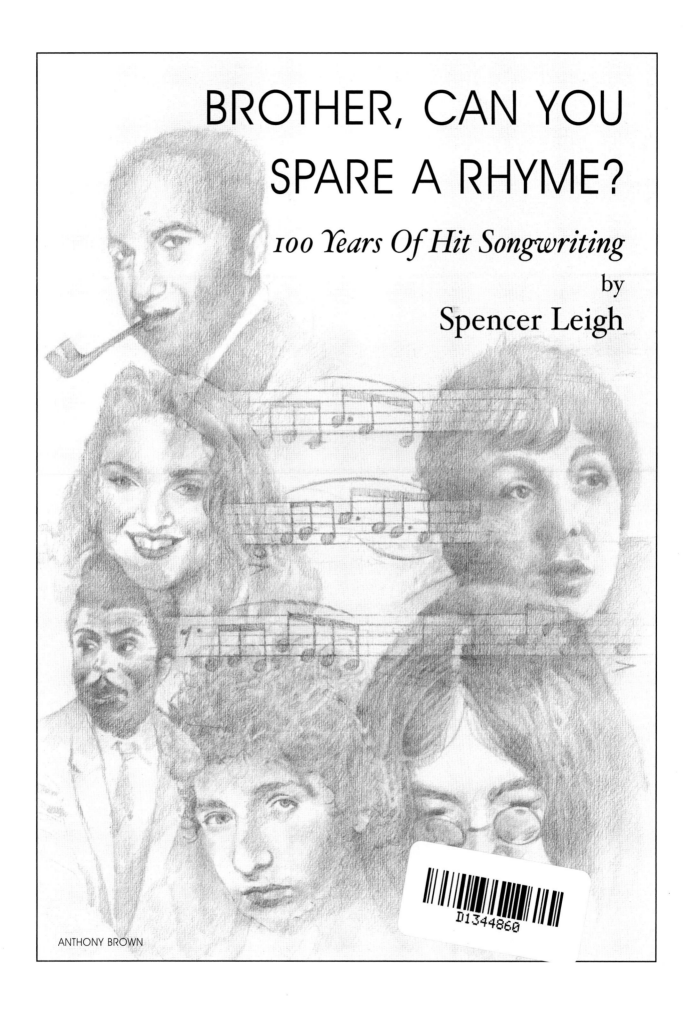

ANTHONY BROWN

First published in 2000 by
SPENCER LEIGH LIMITED
Registered in England and Wales. Registered number 3761499
Registered office - 42 Longcliffe Drive, Ainsdale, Southport, Merseyside, PR8 3PR.
England.

The text is © Spencer Leigh 2000.
Cover and book design by Tony Brown.
The illustrations are © Tony Brown 2000.
The photographic credits are given at the end of the book.

British Library Cataloguing-in-Publication Data.
A catalogue record for this book is available from the British Library.

ISBN 0 9538233 0 X

ABOUT THE AUTHOR

Spencer Leigh was born in Liverpool in 1945. His "On The Beat" programme has been broadcast on BBC Radio Merseyside for 15 years and he writes for several magazines including "Record Collector", "Now Dig This" and "Country Music People". He also writes obituaries for "The Independent", so when interviewing musicians, he is tempted to offer them a complete package!

Spencer Leigh's books include "Paul Simon - Now And Then" (1973), "Presley Nation" (1976), "Stars In My Eyes" (1980), "Let's Go Down The Cavern" (with Pete Frame) (1984), "Speaking Words Of Wisdom: Reflections On The Beatles" (1991), "Aspects Of Elvis" (edited with Alan Clayson) (1994), "Memories Of Buddy Holly" (with Jim Dawson) (US only, 1996), "Halfway To Paradise: Britpop 1955-1962" (with John Firminger) (1996), "Behind The Song" (with Michael Heatley) (1998) and "Drummed Out - The Sacking Of Pete Best" (1998).

This book is dedicated to my good friend, Bob Wooler, the former DJ at the Cavern, who, like me, is always looking for a good song.

Bob discussed his admiration for well-crafted songs with the young Merseyside bands, including the Beatles, and this must have raised the quality of their own songwriting.

ABOUT THE ARTIST

Anthony Brown was born in Liverpool on New Year's Day 1961. Following his initial art school education, his training as a graphic designer and illustrator led him through a large variety of opportunities including his work as an exhibiting artist and his hand-in-hand experiences as a composing, performing and recording musician.

His work is on display from Liverpool to New York (with a few stops in-between!) and his plans for the future include an exhibition of his recent paintings and drawings and his creation of a children's book.

He works from a studio at the Liverpool Academy Of Arts on Seel Street in Liverpool's city centre, which is an informal, ever changing gallery, showing his works. Feel free to visit the gallery whenever you are in the area.

CONTENTS

FOREWORD
By Dennis Locorriere

I'm a singer....I've been singing for as long as I can remember, whether I was the little boy in front of the TV set belting out "Santa Claus Is Comin' To Town" at the top of his lungs or the adult lead vocalist of a pretty successful pop group, delivering the hits to an audience halfway around the world.

I'm always ready to 'find' a great song....one that fills me with with so much emotion that I can't wait to sing it to someone else.

I also write songs, which I guess somewhat qualifies me to write this foreword....but when I write it's usually in an effort to come up with a good song for me to sing!

As I said, I'm a singer and it's as a singer I write this piece. I've only been around for slightly more than half the time covered in Spencer's wonderful book, but I can recall hearing the catchy little 'ditties' designed to reflect the upbeat times in post-war America.

I listened intently to the raw, exciting rock and roll of the Fifties, squeezing out of my tiny plastic transistor radio. I was more than willing to succumb to the charms of The Beatles. They captured the attention of the world with their funny haircuts and quirky sense of humour, but it was their words and melodies that worked their way into our hearts.

In the short seven years between the downbeat of "It Won't Be Long" and the missing last note of "Her Majesty", The Beatles managed to set a new standard and change the language of contemporary songwriting forever.

Every generation seems to grow up complaining that *"They just don't write 'em like they used to..."* but the truth is, they do! Oh sure, you're always gonna have the 'hacks'....the writers who will jump on a bandwagon in order to stay current, but there will also always be the ones who do it from the heart, write how they feel and damn the *trend du jour*. It's a century of that kind of artistry and dedication that is celebrated in this book.

Here's to the next hundred years of someone sitting at a piano, dreamily picking out a simple melody....or bent over a guitar, trying to find the right chord....you know....the one that makes the lyric really take off in the bridge!

Here's to the songs not yet written...After all, without them what would we singers do?

[signature]

June 26th 2000

AND STRICTLY ENTRE NOUS
Acknowledgments

Luckily, I have a large address book and there are scores of people that I have asked for information. My thanks to everyone who has added to my original lists or has given me some information for the text itself. In particular, I wish to thank Tim Adams, Stephen Barnard, Bryan Biggs, Terry Birkenhead, Stuart Booth, Mike Brocken, Lorraine Brown, Billy Butler, Steve Caddick, Trevor Cajiao, Bill Citrine, Alan Clayson, Frankie Connor, Ray Curry, Ossie Dales, Geoffrey Davis, Andrew Doble, Peter Doble, Peter Doggett, Davy Edge, Ron Ellis, John Firminger, Gillian Gaar, Clive Garner, Diana Gower, Roger Hill, Andrew Humphries, Patrick Humphries, Brian Jacques, Ed Jones, Anne Leigh, Mark Lewisohn, Nickie Mackay, Billy Maher, Lizzie-Anne Meachin, Eddie Mooney, Colin Morgan, Mick Ord, Mick O'Toole, Pierre Perrone, Al Peters, Jon Philibert and his colleagues at MCPS, Peter Spaull, Geoff Speed, Bill Tasker, Ian Whitcomb, David Williams, Steve Williams, Bob Wooler and Alex Young. Thanks to Bob Wooler for preserving those sheet music covers - and for buying them in the first place! I am also grateful for the use of the fine library at the Institute of Popular Music at the University of Liverpool.

My special thanks to Tony Brown for the cover illustration and many others throughout the book. He also designed the pages and has, I think, done a wonderful job. Whatever you think of the text, the book looks right. My thanks too to Steve Kinley at Ashley Printers and also to all at Tony Michaelides Promotions, especially Steve Dinwoodie for their help in publicising the book.

"Brother, Can You Spare A Rhyme?" started as a series of articles for "Record Collector" magazine and they appeared between May and August 1999. The four sections covering 1900 to 1999 are the backbone of this book. Also, the analysis of "Candle In The Wind" appeared in "Record Collector" in November 1997 and the one of "American Pie" in February 1999. My thanks to Peter Doggett and Andy Davis for permission to reprint all this, albeit in an amended and longer format. And that's one thing I would like to say about songwriting: if an article of mine is being reprinted, I can't resist the temptation to tinker with it. Okay, I should have got it right the first time, but how is it that songwriters so rarely revise their work? Paul McCartney told me (I'm posing here) that he would rather write a new song than revise an old one. Bob Dylan is the only major songwriter who updates his work - sometimes with a different tune - even then, many of his lyrics are still untouched.

Further thanks to "Country Music People" for permission to reprint my interview with Gordon Lightfoot and to "The Independent" for permission to reprint my obituary of Shel Silverstein. The Shel Silverstein obit was written in three hours - it had to be - and strangely in view of what I say above, I've hardly changed anything. Sometimes the gods are in your favour. "Imagine", in a very different form, originally appeared in Bill Harry's now defunct magazine, "Idols", which was an excellent concept that didn't find its market. The interviews with Sammy Cahn, Gordon Lightfoot, Elvis Costello, Sir Tim Rice and Jimmy Webb were broadcast on BBC Radio Merseyside at the time, but have never appeared in print.

I hope that I've not overlooked any great songs while putting this book together, but that's the joy of popular music - there's so much of it. As Noel Coward said, " How potent cheap music can be". Lou Reed commented, "But he didn't write any. If he'd said 'emotional', then I would say 'Absolutely'."

Maybe the songs hold the key to the 20th century. Ludwig van Beethoven wrote, "Music is a higher revelation than all wisdom and philosophy." Mind you, he was a musician.

SING ME AN OLD-FASHIONED SONG
Listing of pre-1900 hits

Billy Joel admitted "We Didn't Start The Fire", but his lyric only paid tribute to the 20th century. Many contemporary songs vanish from the memory the week they leave the charts, but many of of the best-known tunes and songs were written long before 1900.

In order to set the scene for this book, all the songs listed here were written before 1900 but, in some instances, the dates of composition can only be approximate and also the words and the music might be written decades apart. The message is clear: if you want your composition to last, write either a children's song or a hymn. Make it "All Things Bright And Beautiful" and you can't lose. Why did General William Booth, the founder of the Salvation Army, say that the Devil had all the best tunes? It's the hymns that have endured.

1240 -   SUMMER IS ICUMEN IN
            (A song about the cuckoo written by John
            of Fornsete, a monk at Reading. Well done,
            John, you wrote the world's first pop song.)

c1300 - O COME O COME IMMANUEL

c1400 - ADAM LAY YBOUNDEN
c1400 - IN DULCE JUBILO
            (Top 10 for Mike Oldfield, 1975)
c1400 - COME DOWN, O LOVE DIVINE
1529 -   A MIGHTY FORTRESS IS OUR GOD
            (Paul Simon wrote his first classic song

"American Tune", in 1529, a considerable feat considering he wasn't born until 1941.
He borrowed the tune of "A Mighty Fortress Is Our God", replacing Martin Luther's words with his own.)
c1540 - GREENSLEEVES
            (Mentioned by Shakespeare in "The Merry
            Wives Of Windsor". Allegedly composed by
            Henry VIII, but if you believe that...)
c1550 - SING A SONG OF SIXPENCE
1561 -   ALL PEOPLE THAT ON EARTH DO
            DWELL
1582 -   GAUDETE
            (Top 20 for Steeleye Span, 1973)

1591 -   COVENTRY CAROL
1592 -   WHILE SHEPHERDS WATCHED

c1600 - GOLDEN SLUMBERS
            (Words by playwright Thomas Dekker. Decca
            turned down Paul McCartney, but McCartney
            didn't turn down Dekker as he put his own
            melody to Dekker's words on "Abbey Road".)
c1600 - DING DONG MERRILY ON HIGH
c1600 - THE TWELVE DAYS OF CHRISTMAS

1620 -   POP GOES THE WEASEL
            (A singing game from the Pilgrim Fathers, later
            adopted by London hatters. Top 20 for
            Anthony Newley, 1961.)

1640 - GATHER YE ROSEBUDS WHILE YE MAY
(Original title, "To The Virgins"!)

c1650 - THE FIRESHIP
(A sea shanty that became "The Rakish Kind" and then the 1951 Guy Mitchell hit, "The Roving Kind".)

1666 - BARBARA ALLEN
(Must be earlier, but this is when Samuel Pepys noted it in his diary)

1680 - I GAVE MY LOVE A CHERRY
(Also called "The Riddle Song", melody used for "The Twelfth Of Never". Donny Osmond any one?)

1687 - AULD LANG SYNE (music)
(Robbie Burns added words in 1789, which Cliff swopped for Jesus's in 1999.)

c1700 - LOWLANDS LOW

c1700 - THE HOLLY AND THE IVY

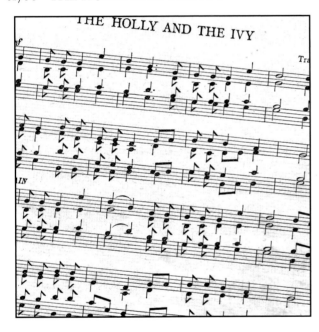

1707 - WHEN I SURVEY THE WONDROUS CROSS

1708 - JESUS CHRIST IS RISEN TODAY

1719 - O GOD, OUR HELP IN AGES PAST

1739 - HARK THE HERALD ANGELS SING (words)
(Charles Wesley wrote these words in 1739, but I've seen them © Hallmark Cards, 1991. Music is from 1840.)

1740 - RULE BRITANNIA

1741 - HALLELUJAH CHORUS
(Handel's greatest hit, from "The Messiah")

1745 - GOD SAVE THE KING
(Or Queen, as appropriate. Written as the battlecry of the House of Hanover and many of the xenophobic, bellicose words by Henry Carey are not appropriate today.)

1745 - MY BONNIE LIES OVER THE OCEAN
(About Bonnie Prince Charlie, "They call me 'The Young Pretender'.")

1746 - THE SKYE BOAT SONG
(About Bonnie Prince Charlie's escape after being routed at Culloden, which was the last battle to be fought on land in the UK. The Scots were so exhausted from marching that it was over in an hour.)

1747 - LOVE DIVINE, ALL LOVES EXCELLING
(Charles Wesley based this on a pop song of the day, "The Song Of Venus".)

1755 - OH HAPPY DAY
(Top 10 for the Edwin Hawkins Singers, 1969)

1761 - BOBBY SHAFTO

1765 - BAA BAA BLACK SHEEP

1770 - GOD REST YE MERRY GENTLEMEN
(This was written as "God Rest Ye Merry, Gentlemen" but no-one sings it like that now.)

1776 - ROCK OF AGES, CLEFT FOR ME
(Written by a Devon vicar with the impressive name of Augustus Montague Toplady. Today's tune was added in 1853 when it was a century ahead of its time through being a song with "Rock" in its title.)

1778 - TIS THE GIFT TO BE SIMPLE
(Shaker hymn: melody used for "Lord Of The Dance" by Sydney Carter)

1779 - AMAZING GRACE
(A slave-ship ran into a storm and its captain, John Newton, promised to give up the trade and dedicate his life to God if they survived. He became a clergyman and wrote this hymn about his experience.)

1783 - WE PLOUGH THE FIELDS AND SCATTER

1789 - AULD LANG SYNE (words)
(Great Robbie Burns lyric, music from 1687, and the song that brought in the Third Millennium.)

1790 - CHANSON DE MARIE ANTOINETTE
(Like "Greensleeves" with Henry VIII, it is said that Marie Antoinette wrote this tune. In 1950 it became "My Heart Cries For You" and won Guy Mitchell his first gold disc.)

1797 - O COME ALL YE FAITHFUL

c1800 - PLASIR D'AMOUR
(Written by organist, Giovanni Martini, and recorded in its original version by Joan Baez and Mary Hopkin. Melody used for Elvis Presley's "Can't Help Falling In Love".)

1806 - TWINKLE, TWINKLE, LITTLE STAR

1809 - A FROG HE WOULD A-WOOING GO
(With a roly-poly, gammon and spinach)

1812 - FRANKIE AND JOHNNIE
(Originally appeared in 1812 as "Françoise Et Jean")

1814 - STAR-SPANGLED BANNER
(Written the morning after the Americans had beaten the English at Fort McHenry, near Baltimore)

1815 - THE BATTLE OF NEW ORLEANS
(Once more the Brits are on the run. Originally called "The Eighth Of January")

1818 - SILENT NIGHT
(In 1818 a young Austrian priest, Joseph Mohr, visited a woodcutter's family and saw their new baby. Drawing comparisons with the birth of Jesus, he wrote "Song For Heaven", which became "Stille Nacht" and later "Silent Night". The church organist and village schoolteacher, Franz Grüber, set the poem to music, but as the church organ needed repair, the carol was scored for tenor, a baritone, a children's choir and a guitar. It was performed on Christmas Eve in the Church of St.Nikola in the small town of Oberndorf, near Salzburg. A few weeks later, a repairman, Karl Mauracher, came to fix the organ. Grüber played him "Silent Night" and Mauracher, completely enthralled, took a copy home to Zillertal. In 1831 Mauracher arranged the carol for four voices and had the Strasser children perform it at a reception for the King and Queen of Saxony. It became popular, but it wasn't translated into English until 1863, the wordsmith being Rev. John Freeman Young. The first known recording is by the Haydn Quartet in 1905.)

1823 - ANNIE LAURIE

1824 - SONG OF JOY
(When Beethoven ran a lottery, people would shout "Roll Over Beethoven".)

1825 - STEAL AWAY

1826 - THE WEDDING MARCH
(Mendelssohn. Elizabeth Taylor's favourite tune or, at least, she heard it more than any other.)

1830 - MAGGIE MAY
(means Maggie will)

1831 - ROCK OF AGES, CLEFT FOR ME
(Words written, 1776)

1833 - I SAW THREE SHIPS

1837 - WOODMAN, SPARE THAT TREE
("The Fallen Oak", in 1841, could be the world's first answer song.)

1839 - WHAT SHALL WE DO WITH A DRUNKEN SAILOR?

1839 - JOY TO THE WORLD

1840 - HARK THE HERALD ANGELS SING
(music) (Mendelssohn. See 1739.)

1840 - NEARER MY GOD TO THEE
(Allegedly played by the dance band on the Titanic as the ship was sinking, but who would really know?)

1844 - O FOR THE WINGS OF A DOVE
(Mendelssohn again.)

1847 - ABIDE WITH ME
(A busy day for Rev. Henry Francis Lyte. He preached a sermon, wrote this hymn and died.)

1848 - ALL THINGS BRIGHT AND BEAUTIFUL
(Words 1848, melody 1887.)

1850 - DE CAMPTOWN RACES
(The writer, Stephen Foster, noticed that Negro communities often lived in shacks and tents on the outskirts of towns, hence "Camptown". The word, "doodah", comes from this song.)

JOAN BAEZ

1852 - WAY DOWN UPON THE SWANEE RIVER
(Foster again and he'd never seen the Swanee River. He simply chose a name that sounded right. It was almost "Way Down Upon The Pedee River".)

1854 - I DREAM OF JEANNIE WITH THE LIGHT BROWN HAIR
(Foster wrote this tender love song about his wife, Jane McDowell, but they had an unhappy marriage due to his drinking. Foster's lager?)

1854 - D'YE KEN JOHN PEEL
(Written for the funeral of a master huntsman and, in years to come, might be used at the funeral of a master DJ.)

1855 - WHAT A FRIEND WE HAVE IN JESUS

1855 - LONDONDERRY AIR

1856 - COME INTO THE GARDEN, MAUD
(Words by Tennyson)

1857 - WE THREE KINGS OF ORIENT ARE

1857- JINGLE BELLS
(In 1857 a Boston teacher, James Pierpont, wrote "The One-Horse Open Sleigh" for a Christmas entertainment to be performed by Sunday schoolchildren. The song became "Jingle Bells", and most performers avoid Pierpont's badly-written second verse:

"The horse was lean and light
Misfortune was his lot.
We got into a drifting bank
And we became upsot."

"Upset" didn't rhyme, so what else could he do? As far as I know, Jerry Jeff Walker is the only songwriter to rewrite the verse. Anyone fancy a gangsta rap about "slaying in the snow"?)

1859 - I WISH I WAS IN DIXIE
(Written by a Unionist, Dan Emmett, who was furious when the South took up his song: "If I'd known that, I never would have written it.")

1860 - ETERNAL FATHER STRONG TO SAVE

1860 - LAND OF MY FATHERS

1861 - THE BATTLE HYMN OF THE REPUBLIC
(Julia Ward Howe wrote stirring words to the tune of "John Brown's Body" during the American Civil War, receiving $4 from a publisher for its outright sale. This call to arms was written by a pacifist and it is God, and not the soldiers, that she sees marching on.)

1861 - AURA LEE
(Melody used for Elvis Presley's "Love Me Tender", 1956)

1861 - WE PLOUGH THE FIELDS AND SCATTER

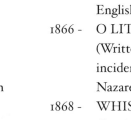

ELVIS PRESLEY

1862 - BLAYDON RACES
(Written and performed by crippled ex-collier, George Ridley)

1864 - SHALL WE GATHER AT THE RIVER?

1865 - ONWARD CHRISTIAN SOLDIERS
(Who says books of song lyrics don't sell? "Hymns Ancient And Modern" has sold 70 million copies.)

1866 - WHEN YOU AND I WERE YOUNG, MAGGIE
(A schoolteacher, George Johnson, wrote the song about his child bride, Maggie Clarke, who died young.)

1866 - HOW GREAT THOU ART
(Written by a Swedish minister and then translated into German. A Russian version was heard by a missionary and it was translated into English.)

1866 - O LITTLE TOWN OF BETHLEHEM
(Written in Bethlehem on Christmas Day. Why, incidentally, do we always call him Jesus of Nazareth?)

1868 - WHISPERING HOPE
(Septimus Winner, a versatile musician, published his hymn under his mother's maiden name, Alice Hawthorne, because he thought its sentiments were more feminine than masculine.)

1868 - TOM DOOLEY
(True story: Tom Dula killed his girlfriend for giving him a sexually transmitted disease. Top 10 for both the Kingston Trio and Lonnie Donegan in 1958.)

1869 - LITTLE BROWN JUG
(Joseph Winner was jealous of his brother's success with "Whispering Hope" and determined to write a song with more lasting appeal. Luckily for him, Glenn Miller liked it.)

1870 - SHENANDOAH
(A trader who fell in love with the daughter of an Indian chief wrote this song. The 19th cenury's "Running Bear".)

1872 - SWING DOWN, SWEET CHARIOT
(Sarah Sheppard was talked out of suicide and so wrote a song about dying. Negro slave workers had visions of chariots swinging down from the sky and taking them to Heaven. Also known as "Swing Low, Sweet Chariot".)

1875 - MY GRANDFATHER'S CLOCK

1875 - I'LL TAKE YOU HOME AGAIN, KATHLEEN
(Written by Tom Wetendorff whose wife, Jennie, was in New York, but "Kathleen" sounded better and added its Irish quality.)

1876 - DANCE OF THE HOURS
(Melody for Allan Sherman's 1963 hit, "Hello Muddah, Hello Faddah".)

1880 - GREEN GROW THE RUSHES-O
(Sung by American forces in Mexico, giving rise to the term, "Gringos".)

1881- CLEMENTINE
(Original manuscript says it is to be performed "with mock seriousness". Is that how Huckleberry Hound sings it?)

1882 - THE 1812 OVERTURE
(Tchaikovsky: that's what comes of seeing Glenda Jackson naked in a railway carriage.)

1884 - ROCK-A-BYE BABY

1885 - WILLOW, TIT-WILLOW
(Gilbert and Sullivan as opposed to Gilbert O'Sullivan)

1886 - GOODNIGHT IRENE

1888 - AMERICA THE BEAUTIFUL
(Originally a poem, music added 1895)

1888 - WHERE DID YOU GET THAT HAT?
(Originally sung by the music-hall performer, J.C.Heffron, and based on his catch-phrase.)

1889 - AVE MARIA
(Schubert, a maths teacher, wrote songs and symphonies in his spare time.)

c1890 - HE'S GOT THE WHOLE WORLD IN HIS HANDS
(US No 1 for 14 year old London lad, Laurie London, in 1958.)

1890 - THE WHIFFENPOOF SONG
(Written by a university student and based on a Rudyard Kipling poem, "Gentleman Rankers". It was adopted by the Whiffenpoof Society of Yale University and its potential as a hit song was first realised by Rudy Vallee in 1936.)

LONDON LAD, LAURIE LONDON

1891 - AMERICAN PATROL
(Glenn Miller hit)

1891 - TRA-RA-RA-BOOM-DE-AY
(Written by the tour manager of the Tuxedo Girls who had heard the tune in a German brothel. One Tuxedo Girl danced to it so wildly that she collapsed and died.)

1892 - DADDY WOULDN'T BUY ME A BOW-WOW
(Music hall song that Vesta Victoria performed with innuendo.)

1892 - THE NUTCRACKER
(Nut Rocker anyone?)

1892 - DAISY BELL
(Also known as "A Bicycle Built For Two" and written about the craze for tandems)

1892 - AFTER THE BALL
(Chas Harris wrote this after seeing a couple arguing at a dance. He turned down $10,000 for the copyright, marketed it himself, and the song effectively started Tin Pan Alley. Also, in 1892, Coca-Cola stopped advertising their product as an "uplifting medicine".)

1893 - MY OLD DUTCH
(London music-hall performer, Albert Chevalier, wrote this on the back of a cigarette packet while strolling from Oxford Street to Islington one foggy night.)

1893 - HAPPY BIRTHDAY TO YOU
(In 1893 the sisters and kindergarten teachers, Mildred and Patty Hill, wrote "Good Morning To You" for their school. Along the way someone changed the words to "Happy Birthday To You". In 1934 Western Union started Singing Telegrams and the first was sent to Rudy Vallee on his birthday. Western Union were sued for breach of copyright and reverted to "For He's A Jolly Good Fellow" for future telegrams.)

1895 - WALTZING MATILDA

1895 - GUANTANAMERA
(Verses written by Cuban poet, Jose Marti : the music, an old Cuban melody, was added in 1949.)

GLENN MILLER

1896 - WHEN THE SAINTS GO MARCHING IN

1896 - SHE'LL BE COMING ROUND THE MOUNTAIN
(Sung by American railway workers, the "she" being a train, and pretty well the same tune as "The Saints".)

1896 - ALSO SPRACH ZARATHUSTRA
(Alias "2001: A Space Odyssey")

1897 - THE STARS AND STRIPES FOREVER!
(John Philip Sousa; the source of the football chant, "Here we go, here we go, here we go.")

1898 - LILY OF LAGUNA
(Just as well that the Southport - born songwriter, Leslie Stuart, didn't visit Laguna as it was a mosquito-ridden swamp.)

1899 - MAPLE LEAF RAG
(I'm going to cheat here and have this as my song for 1900.)

WHAT'S ANOTHER YEAR?
Songs with the 20th century in their titles

This is a true century of song. Each song mentions a year, a decade or the century in the title. Undoubtedly and predictably, 1984 was the most popular year for songwriters, but no work on the list rivals "The 1812 Overture" in quality or popularity.

Titles such as "Candle In The Wind 1997" have not been included. The multiple entries for Robert Fripp arise through his 1987 album, "Let The Power Fall", where each track was named after a year. Herbie Flowers and Kenny Pickett's No 1 song for Clive Dunn, "Grandad" (1970), is, remarkably, one of the few songs that contains an overview of the century. Another is Ian Campbell's "Old Man's Song" and for 1950 onwards, try Billy Joel's "We Didn't Start The Fire".

20th CENTURY - BRAD
20th CENTURY - COLD CHISEL
20th CENTURY BLUES - NOEL COWARD
20th CENTURY BLUES - ROBIN TROWER
20th CENTURY BOY - T.REX
20th CENTURY DRIFTER - MARTY ROBBINS
20th CENTURY FOX - THE DOORS
20th CENTURY FOX - NORMAN GREENBAUM
20th CENTURY MAN - KINKS
20th CENTURY MAN - ROY HARPER
20th CENTURY VAMPIRE - THE SCREAMING DEAD

LIVING IN THE 20th CENTURY - STEVE MILLER BAND

JIM MORRISON

TURN OF THE CENTURY -DAVID GRISMAN AND TONY RICE
CHANGE OF THE CENTURY - ORNETTE COLEMAN
1900 YESTERDAY - LIZ DAMON'S ORIENT EXPRESS
1900 - ENNIO MORRICONE
DAYTON, OHIO, 1903 - RANDY NEWMAN
1903-70 - IDLEWILD
THE YEAR 1905 (SHOSTAKOVICH'S SYMPHONY NO 11.)

SPRING OF 1912 - BROTHERHOOD OF MAN
1913 MASSACRE - WOODY GUTHRIE
ENGLAND 1914 - RALPH McTELL
1916 - MOTORHEAD
1917 - DAVID OLNEY / LINDA RONSTADT AND EMMYLOU HARRIS
PARIS 1919 - JOHN CALE
1919 MARCH - PETE ALLEN / SAVOY JAZZMEN
1919 RAG - KID ORY AND HIS CREOLE JAZZ BAND / LU WATTERS AND HIS YERBA BUENA JAZZ BAND
/ KENNY BALL AND HIS JAZZMEN / DUTCH SWING COLLEGE BAND / MONTY SUNSHINE

THE ROARING TWENTIES - DOROTHY PROVINE
1921 - THE WHO
ACAPULCO 1922 - KENNY BALL
LOUISIANA 1927 - RANDY NEWMAN
1927 KANSAS CITY - DAVID SOUL
THE 1927 FLOOD - LONNIE McINTORSH
1929 - MERLE HAGGARD
YEAR OF '29 -LOWELL FULSON

THE WHO

1930 MAMA - CLARA BURSTON
RESOLUTIONS FOR 1932 - CAVAN O'CONNOR
1932 - HENSON CARGILL
1932 VINCENT BLACK LIGHTNING - RICHARD THOMPSON
'34 BLUES - CHARLEY PATTON
(Charley Patton hopes 1934 will be a better year. It turned out to be the year he died.)
THE LAST DAY OF JUNE 1934 - AL STEWART
1935: BIRTH OF A LEGEND - JIMMY CARR (Elvis tribute)
1937 PRE-WAR KIMBALL - NANCI GRIFFITH
1938 CANADIAN THREE STEP - JIMMY SHAND AND HIS BAND
'39 - QUEEN
CLASS OF '39 - BENNY GOODMAN
LAUGHING INTO 1939 - AL STEWART
JULY 12, 1939 - CHARLIE RICH

CHARLEY PATTON

1941 - NILSSON
NEW YORK MINING DISASTER 1941 - THE BEE GEES
SUMMER OF '42 - BIDDU
'43 - LEVEL 42
SUMMER OF '43 - MICHEL LEGRAND
1944 - ROGER WHITTAKER
BRIDE 1945 - PAUL SIEBEL
TEXAS - 1947 - GUY CLARK
'48 CRASH - SUZI QUATRO
1948ISH - ROY HARPER
SUMMER OF '48 - BARRY MANILOW
DECEMBER '48 - ROYAL HUNT
CHILDHOOD 1949 - BOBBY GOLDSBORO
JANUARY 11th 1949 BLUES - LUTHER STONEMAN

BARRY MANILOW

CHILD OF THE FIFTIES - THE STATLER BROTHERS
FIFTIES CHILD - BARCLAY JAMES HARVEST
I WAS A PART OF THE 50's - PAUL EVANS
BORN IN THE 1950s - THE POLICE
1950 BLUES - TAMPA RED
1951 - MARC 'BASS' JOHNSON
1951 - "TOMMY" SOUNDTRACK
THE WAY IT WAS IN '51 - MERLE HAGGARD
1951 BLUES - LUTHER HUFF
PARKER '51 - STAN GETZ (Great title!)
THIS IS 19 AND 52 BABY - JOHN LEE HOOKER
1954 BOOGIE BLUES - CAPTAIN AND TENNILLE
NINETEEN FIFTY-SIX - YOUNG RASCALS
CITY AND UNITED 1956 - LORD KITCHENER
BACK IN '57 - AMERICAN FLYER
CLASS OF '57 - STATLER BROTHERS
'57 CHEVROLET - BILLIE JO SPEARS
1958 BLUES - LITTLE SAM DAVIS
BORN LATE '58 - MOTT THE HOOPLE
1959 - JOHN ANDERSON
1959 - PATTI SMITH
1959 - SISTERS OF MERCY
SUMMER LOVE '59 - SHADOWS
CLASS OF '59 - BOB LUMAN

STAN GETZ

ONE THOUSAND NINE HUNDRED AND WHEN - ROBB STORME AND THE WHISPERS
SO SIXTIES -   LINDA LEWIS
THE SIXTIES - T-BONE BURNETTE
WAY BACK IN THE 1960s - INCREDIBLE STRING BAND
60s MAN - SWEET
1960-SOMETHING SONGWRITER OF THE YEAR - TENNESSEANS
1960 - AMERICA
BACK IN '60 - BAD MANNERS
1961 - THE GOLDENTONES
1961 - NICK HEYWARD
SUMMER OF '61 - FRANKIE AVALON
GIRL FROM 1962 - THE HEADCOATS
1963 - NEW ORDER`
NOVEMBER 22, 1963 - JACE ALEXANDER & VICTOR GARBER (From Sondheim musical, "Assassins")
DECEMBER '63 (OH WHAT A NIGHT) - FOUR SEASONS
QUEEN OF 1964 - NEIL SEDAKA
BACK IN '64 - THE RUTLES
BACK IN '65 - GIDEA PARK
CLASS OF '65 - JOE WALSH
(I WISH IT COULD BE) 1965 AGAIN - THE BARRACUDAS
1966 AND ALL THAT - HALF MAN HALF BISCUIT
1967 - ADRIAN BELEW
JUNE 15 1967 - GARY BURTON

SUMMER '67 - FAMILY
AUGUST 1967 - HOLY MODAL ROUNDERS
BACK IN '67 - AVERAGE WHITE BAND
1967 (SO LONG AGO) - TOM ROBINSON
SOMEDAY, AUGUST 29, 1968 - CHICAGO
68 GUNS - THE ALARM
SUMMER '68 - PINK FLOYD
BORN IN '69 - ROCKET FROM THE CRYPT
EASTER RISING 1969 - EASTERHOUSE
SUMMER OF '69 - BRYAN ADAMS
1969 - IGGY POP AND THE STOOGES
1969 - ROSS HANNAMAN
CROSEO '69 - DAFYDD IWAN (A cynical view of the Prince of Wales' investiture)
MADONNA W/CHILD, CA. 1969 - GUY CLARK
'69 ANNEE EROTIQUE - SERGE GAINSBOURG AND JANE BIRKIN

IGGY POP

LIVING IN THE '70s - SKYHOOKS
70s CHILDREN - THE FISH COMPANY
1970 - THE STOOGES
1971 - PERRY BLAKE
KENTUCKY FEB 27 '71 - TOM T. HALL
OCTOBER 4th, 1971 - BUDDY GRECO
SANTA DOG 1972 - THE RESIDENTS
73 - ADAM F.
'73 HEB FLARES - TYNAL TYWYLL (Welsh rock: the title translates as "'73 Without Flares".)
APRIL '73 - CIRKUS
1974 - AMY GRANT
1974 BLUES - EDDIE HARRIS
TEENAGE LAMENT '74 - ALICE COOPER
1975 OVERTURE - IRON BUTTERFLY
1976 - GRAND FUNK RAILROAD
SPIRIT OF '76 - THE ALARM
1977 - THE CLASH
1977 - ASH
MARCH 18, 1977 - STEVE FORBERT
SUMMER OF '77 - BURT BACHARACH
AUGUST 16, 1977 - RAY SMITH
1978 - RODNEY JONES
'78 STYLE - JON SPENCER BLUES EXPLOSION
ST. VALENTINE'S DAY 1978 - KATE AND ANNA McGARRIGLE
SUMMER OF '78 - BARRY MANILOW
THE YEAR 2003 MINUS 25 - WAYLON JENNINGS AND WILLIE NELSON
SEPTEMBER 1979 - BILL BARRON
1979 - SMASHING PUMPKINS
1979 - MEAT BEAT MANIFESTO
JULY '79 - CHRIS HUNTER
WINTER OF '79 - TOM ROBINSON BAND

ALICE COOPER

80s LADIES - K.T. OSLIN
1980 - HERB ALPERT

1980 - EASTSIDE BAND

1980 - STEEL LOCKS

1980 - AFTER THE FIRE

1981 - JIMMIE MASION

HIGHLIGHTS OF '81 - JOHNNY PAYCHECK

SUMMER OF '81 - MONDO ROCK

AUGUST 14, 1981 - RICK SPRINGFIELD

1982 - SONS OF CHAMPLIN

1982 - RANDY TRAVIS

1982 BLUES - JIMMIE DAVIS

SUMMER OF '82- FUN BOY THREE

1983 - LUCIO DALLA

1983 - LINDISFARNE

1983 (A MERMAN I SHOULD TURN TO BE) - JIMI HENDRIX EXPERIENCE

1984 - DAVID BOWIE

1984 - GEOFF LEAHY

1984 - MAXINE

1984 - ROBERT FRIPP

1984 - SPIRIT

1984 - VAN HALEN

1984 - RICK WAKEMAN

1984 - CRAIG DILLINGHAM

1984 - SWEET ROCK

1984 - RAY WHITLEY (Recorded 1968)

SEXCRIME (1984) - EURYTHMICS

ANOTHER 1984 - BILLY SQUIER

1985 - PAUL McCARTNEY AND WINGS

1985 - ROBERT FRIPP

SUMMER '85 - ALTERNATIVE RADIO

JULY 13th 1985 - JOHN WESLEY HARDING

AUGUST '85 - THE MOONLIZARDS

1986 - ROBERT FRIPP

1987 - ROBERT FRIPP

'87 AND CRY - DAVID BOWIE

1988 - ROBERT FRIPP

OCTOBER 17, 1988 - KEITH JARRETT

1988 AKTIVATOR - STEVE HILLAGE

POP SONG '89 - R.E.M.

1989 - ROBERT FRIPP

JIMI HENDRIX

DAVID BOWIE

ROBERT FRIPP

THE 90s - SAGA
1990 - TEMPTATIONS
1990 - A NEW DECADE - SOUL II SOUL
1991 - BILLY THORPE
1991 - JOHN BRUNNING BAND
TIMEWARP 1991 - MEMBRANES
IN 1992 - BIG BILL CAMPBELL AND THE ROCKY MOUNTAINEERS (Recorded 1935)
1993 - BOZ SCAGGS
CHRISTMAS EVE 1993 - BIG JOE LOUIS AND HIS BLUES KINGS

NAZIS 1994 - ROGER TAYLOR
1995 - ELEANOR RIGBY
1996 - MARILYN MANSON
EURO '96 - Y TYSTION
ROTTERDAM '97 - ALAN CLAYSON
1999 - DAVE SAMPSON
1999 - PRINCE
1999 - NIRVANA
1999 - PAUL BRETT
1999 - SEVENTH WAVE
1999 - SEAHORSES
1999 A.D. - THE VENTURES
NYC 1999 - PUSSY GALORE
SPACE 1999 - KILDOZER

KRIS KRISTOFFERSON

THE TWENTIETH CENTURY IS ALMOST OVER - JOHNNY CASH
END OF THE CENTURY - WILCO
SLOUCHING TOWARDS THE MILLENNIUM - KRIS KRISTOFFERSON
MILLENNIUM - ROBBIE WILLIAMS
MILLENNIUM - KILLING JOKE
MILLENNIUM BUG - ROD PAUL
NEW MILLENNIUM - DREAM THEATER
MILLENNIUM CONCERTO SUITE - YNGWIE MALMSTEEN
SONG FOR THE MILLENNIUM (MULETA) - JAN AKKERMAN
FAMOUS IN THE LAST CENTURY - STATUS QUO

STATUS QUO

ANTHEM FOR THE YEAR 2000 - SILVERCHAIR
THE YEAR 2000 - O'JAYS
2000 AD - REZILLOS
DISCO 2000 - PULP
2000 BLACK - ROY AYERS
2000 MAN - ROLLING STONES
2000 MAN - KISS
ATOMIC MOOG 2000 - COLDCUT
21st CENTURY - BLONDIE
21st CENTURY BOOGIE - PADDY MILNER
21st CENTURY STANCE - MARC BOLAN
21st CENTURY JESUS - FEAR FACTORY
21st CENTURY POEM - LEFTFIELD
21st CENTURY SCHIZOID MAN - KING CRIMSON
ALSO SPRACH ZARATHUSTRA (2001) - DEODATA

Thinking ahead:
YEAR 2001 - 1910 FRUITGUM COMPANY
2010 - ANDY SUMMERS
APRIL 2031 - WARRANT
ACID PRIEST 2088 - THE FALL
2112 - RUSH
IN THE YEAR 2525 - ZAGER AND EVANS
3000 - DR. OCTAGON
YEAR 3000 BLUES - TEN YEARS AFTER
YEAR 40080 - KITARO
THE FUTURE - LEONARD COHEN ("I've seen the future, brother, it is murder.")

MARC BOLAN

LEONARD COHEN

ANDY SUMMERS

21

AS TIME GOES BY
Introduction

A hundred years is a long period of time - it is, after all, a lifetime if you're lucky - but it is only just over 5,000 weeks, which doesn't seem nearly as long. Those weeks between 1900 and 2000 have seen radical changes in the way we live and work. With the help of extraordinary advances in technology, the ways in which we both perform and listen to music have been transformed. In 1900, we gathered around the piano for amateur recitals in the parlour; now we can hear brilliant performances at the push of a button.

The central part of this book, "As Time Goes By", is in four parts and covers the key songs of each year of the 20th century. By and large, I've opted for the great singalong songs, so hits like "Duke Of Earl", "Twist And Shout", "I Love You Love Me Love" and "Smells Like Teen Spirit" are not included as they rely on great performances rather than being great songs. In any event, it would be impossible to sing along with "Smells Like Teen Spirit" as nobody can decipher the words.

I thought that I'd have difficulty in finding songs that everyone would know from the first decade but not a bit of it. I'd swop the key songs of the last decade for those of the first any day! And the first decade was every bit as innovative as the last - electricity, telephones, the cinema and all manner of transport were coming into being. I am sure these songs will sound in your mind as soon as you see the titles. You can sing the majority of these early songs down at your local and be sure that many people would join in. Will we be able to say the same for today's music in 2100?

The dates refer to the years when the songs were actually written which are not necessarily the years that they became popular. And before we start, an assessment from Hunter S. Thompson, "The music business is a cruel and shallow money trench, a long, plastic hallway where thieves and pimps run free, and good men die like dogs. There's also a negative side."

AS TIME GOES BY
Part One - 1900 - 1924

1900 -   MAPLE LEAF RAG (Scott Joplin)

> Relief of Mafeking - Trade union delegates
> establish the Labour party, which wins two
> seats - Death of Oscar Wilde - Sigmund Freud
> writes "The Interpretation Of Dreams" -
> Birmingham University, "Daily Express", the
> Davis Cup and the Queen Mother are born
> with the century

At a theatre in Coney Island, New York, a member of an audience was transfixed by hearing a pianist deliberately missing beats in his music. He shouted, "Play that ragged tune again!" and thus, ragtime got its name.

Scott Joplin, who was born in 1868, developed his musical talent in the honky-tonks and brothels of St. Louis and Chicago, although his own music sounds stately and introspective. Encouraged by friends, he studied at a college in Missouri and played at the Maple Leaf Club in Sedalia, Missouri: there were many maple trees in Sedalia. Joplin wrote "Maple Leaf Rag" in 1899 and although a publisher was impressed, he thought the piece was too difficult to publish. Joplin disagreed and returned with a 14 year old who played the piece perfectly.

"Maple Leaf Rag" became a success throughout America and was played at New Year parties for the turn of the century. The song's success enabled Joplin to become a full-time composer and teacher. In 1902 he wrote another famous rag, "The Entertainer", and he completed his opera, "Treemonisha", in 1911. The opera's failure disappointed Joplin so much that it prompted his early death in 1917. His music found new popularity when it was used to superb effect in the Robert Redford film, "The Sting".

Puccini wrote his famed opera, "Tosca", in 1900 and the songs of the year were "Goodbye Dolly Gray", "A Bird In A Gilded Cage" and Leslie Stuart's "Soldiers Of The Queen", which became "Soldiers Of The King" within a year.

When Count Zeppelin's dirigible crashed, he recorded a message seeking finanical help for his airships. 300 copies were sent to wealthy people throughout the world. His recording is more valuable than anything by Led Zeppelin.

1901 -   O SOLE MIO
(Giovanni Capurro - Eduardo di Capua)

> Death of Queen Victoria, aged 81: Edward
> VII becomes King - President McKinley
> assassinated - First British submarine -
> Inauguration of Nobel prizes - Use of finger
> prints for detection - Australia becomes self-
> govening.

The Italian aria, "O Sole Mio", which means "My Sunshine", was written in 1901 and was famously recorded by Enrico Caruso in 1916. In 1949 Tony Martin recorded an English version with the title, "There's No Tomorrow". Elvis Presley was very fond of "O Sole Mio", but when his publishers, Hill and Range, couldn't reach a deal over "There's No Tomorrow", they asked four writing teams for new lyrics. The best was by Aaron Schroeder and Wally Gold and Elvis brought Mario Lanza's record of "O Sole Mio" to the session so he knew what he had to match. "It's Now Or Never" became a transatlantic No 1 in 1960 and is the record that marked Elvis' change from rock'n'roll singer to adult entertainer. Pavarotti often performs "O Sole Mio" and the melody is also known with its more recent lyric, "Just One Cornetto".

You might still hear "The Honeysuckle And The Bee" at a barn dance and "Trotting To The Fair" in an Irish pub. Other classics from the year are "Just A-Wearyin' For You" and Josef Locke's favourite, "Blaze Away!".

1902 - LAND OF HOPE AND GLORY
(Edward Elgar - Arthur Benson)

Lord Salisbury retires as PM (the last PM from the House of Lords) and is replaced by his nephew, Arthur Balfour - Edward VII is crowned - Telegraphy applied to ships - "The Hound Of The Baskervilles" and "Peter Rabbit" published.

Edward Elgar was a church organist and music teacher who wrote "The Enigma Variations" (1899) and "The Dream Of Gerontius" (1900). He lived in Malvern and found inspiration as he cycled round the countryside: he liked the cycle of the seasons (sorry about that). In 1898, he wrote to a friend, "I hope someday to do a great work - a sort of national thing, that my fellow Englishmen might take to themselves and love."

Starting in 1901 the world's first easy rider wrote his marches, "Pomp And Circumstance", and he was so pleased with his melody for the first that he even thought of turning it into a symphony. When Henry Wood conducted the first performance of the march, "the people simply rose and yelled. Merely to restore order, I had to play the march three times." Elgar was persuaded to make a song out of it and Arthur Benson supplied the words, turning it into "Land Of Hope And Glory". It was played at King Edward VII's coronation and His Majesty commented, "That tune will go round the world." He was right.

EDWARD ELGAR

The songwriter, Ron Shields, wrote for vaudeville singer, Joe Palmer, notably "In The Good Old Summertime", but Palmer was struck down by multiple sclerosis. He developed an act based around himself in a wheelchair and featuring a young Al Jolson.

Other songs of the year include "The Entertainer", "Bill Bailey, Won't You Please Come Home" and "Oh Didn't He Ramble". The composer of the operatic ballad, "Because", Guy D'Hardelot, was in reality Mrs Helen Rhodes, as it was not considered proper for ladies to write songs.

1903 - WE SHALL OVERCOME
(Charles Tindley - Frank Hamilton - Pete Seeger - Guy Carawan - Zilphia Horton)

Russian massacre of Jews at Kishinyov - Irish landlords bought out - Emily Pankhurst founds suffragette movement - British road speed limit increased to 20 mph.

Pete Seeger recalls that the Civil Rights anthem, "We Shall Overcome" has its origins in 1903. He told me, "A black preacher in Philadelphia around 1903 writes a song,

'I'll overcome someday,
I'll overcome someday,
If in my heart I do not yield,
I'll overcome someday.'

"The song became well-known in black churches, but Afro-African people carry on a great tradition which says that a song in a book is just a basis to start improvising, and down in the Deep South they started changing it. It got a new tune and the words changed slightly. In 1926 tobacco workers in Charleston, Carolina went out on strike and some pickets who were walking up and down and singing old hymns changed it still further. Instead of being 'I will overcome', it was

'We will overcome,
We'll get higher wages,
We'll have higher pay,
We will overcome someday.'

"They taught this song to a white friend, an organiser of the union, who taught it to me and I taught it to others up North and I made up the extra verses. I taught it to Guy Carawan who was about 30 years old at the time, and he took it down South in 1960 and taught it to the students who were sitting down in restaurants and demanding a cup of coffee, no matter what colour their skin. They'd go to jail, and in jail they'd do a lot of singing. In two or three months this song went across the South and everybody realised that it was the theme song of the Civil Rights Movement.

"What the kids did to it, incidentally, was add the Motown beat, the soul rhythm, I'm not sure that the tobacco workers had it that way. I'm sure my union organiser friend, Zilphia Horton didn't sing it that way. I tried singing it in various ways and was never satisfied with it. I'm sure when Guy Carawan taught it to the students in 1960, they said, 'Oh, you've got a good song but you've got the beat wrong.' and changed it.'"

Before sick animals, it was wounded soldiers. Rolf Harris recalls, "'Two Little Boys' was written by an American songwriting team about the American Civil War, the ranks of blue referring to the Union forces and the ranks of grey being the Confederates from the Southern States. It was sung to me by a guy in Australia who had learnt it from his mother when he was young and had never forgotten it. He said, 'It's a great song and it's a great story, and children learn it instantly.' He was right. Blokes enjoyed it as they could whistle it down the street, women liked the emotion of it, and it's just a marvellous song.

Harry Lauder was a Scottish comic who laughed at his own jokes and wrote a new song for each of his pantomimes in Newcastle, including "Roamin' In The Gloamin'" (1901), "A Wee Deoch An Doris" (1902) and, in 1903, the cheerful and romantic "I Love A Lassie". Lauder wrote outstanding comic songs but he could also be serious and he wrote "Keep Right On To The End Of The Road" after his son was killed in the First World War. In 1919, he became the first music hall entertainer to be knighted and he died in 1950. Anticipating the video generation, Lauder made short films based on his hit songs.

Other familiar songs of 1903 include "Ida! Sweet As Apple Cider!" and "Mother O'Mine" with words by Rudyard Kipling. The barber-shop favourite, "Sweet Adeline" was written by a post office clerk, Richard Gerard, who proudly had a visiting card printed saying he had written the song. Number 97, a fast mail train, ploughed into a mountain in 1903 and that led to "The Wreck Of The Old 97", a best-seller in 1924 for Vernon Dalhart.

1904 - THE TEDDY BEARS PICNIC
(John W. Bratton - Jimmy Kennedy)

Licence plates compulsory - Russia at war with Japan - Silicone discovered - Rodin's "The Thinker" - Football's ruling body, FIFA, is established.

In 1904 American Presidents preferred outdoor activities, but Theodore (Teddy) Roosevelt became a figure of fun when he went bear-hunting. John Bratton wrote an instrumental called "The Teddy Bear's Picnic", but it wasn't until 1932 that an Irish lyricist, Jimmy Kennedy put words to it. He passed it to Henry Hall and his Orchestra and the record still appears on children's compilations today.

George M. Cohan was born on 3rd July 1878, but being a patriot, he told everyone he was born on Independence Day. His parents were vaudeville artists but he joined the family act, the Four Cohans, with little interest. He was more ambitious so he toured with own show, "Little Johnny Jones", which included "I'm A Yankee Doodle Dandy" and "Give My Regards To Broadway". He called himself the Yankee Doodle Boy and he would wrap himself in the American flag. In 1942, he was played by Jimmy Cagney in the Hollywood bio-pic, "Yankee Doodle Dandy". Cohan admitted, "I only know four chords but they're all good ones."

The songs of the year include "Meet Me In St. Louis, Louis", "Fascination" and the novelty, "The Preacher And The Bear", which has been recorded by the Big Bopper and Jerry Reed. Puccini's "Madam Butterfly" was staged in 1904 and J. M. Barrie wrote his children's play, "Peter Pan". When asked why his later works hadn't matched the success of that play, he commented, "Some peter out and some pan out."

1905 -   FREIGHT TRAIN (Elizabeth Cotton)

> Russia, now weakened after defeat by
> Japan, has first revolution - Sinn Fein party
> formed - Herbert Austin builds car - Aspirin
> goes on sale - Albert Einstein develops his
> theory of relativity.

Elizabeth Cotton was a black singer-guitarist who was born in 1893 and raised in Chapel Hill, North Carolina. When she was 12, she wrote "Freight Train", although she did not copyright it. She was one of the first people to play the guitar left-handed and, as she had no-one to show her, she developed her own technique. That is, until the church deacons told her to put down the guitar and serve the Lord, advice she followed until she was 50.

Her break came when she worked as a daily help for Charles Seeger, part of the folksinging Seeger family. Mike and Peggy Seeger appreciated her talent and her songs, particularly "Freight Train". The song became a hit during the skiffle boom for Chas McDevitt and Nancy Whiskey, and she went to court to establish her rights.

SOPHIE TUCKER

"Freight Train" is one of many songs written about the symbol of the new century, the railway. Most, including "Wabash Cannonball" and "Rock Island Line", cannot be dated as precisely as "Freight Train" and their authorship is obscure. "I'm Alabama Bound" is about the Negroes who left their farms and wandered around, looking for work and hoping to escape racial prejudice. "Midnight Special" relates to the Southern Pacific train which passed the Sugarland penitentiary: if its light shone on an inmate, he would supposedly receive a pardon. Trains marked a revolution in transport, replacing the covered wagon for travelling across America. There is also something romantic about train songs that is lacking in plane songs, possibly the feeling of watching the world go by in trains, while planes are soulless. I'd rather have "Freight Train" by the Chas McDevitt Skiffle Group with Nancy Whiskey than "Luton Airport" by Lorraine Chase.

Other songs of 1905 include "Mary's A Grand Old Name", "My Gal Sal", "Daddy's Little Girl", "In The Shade Of The Old Apple Tree", "I Wouldn't Leave My Little Wooden Hut For You" and "Wait 'Til The Sun Shines, Nellie", which Buddy Holly recorded. Debussy wrote "Claire De Lune". An undated song from around these times is "The Boll Weevil Song" about the bug which attacks cotton crops. Times change and a century later, it's the millennium bug.

1906 -   SOME OF THESE DAYS
(Shelton Brooks)

> Liberals win General Election - Mount Vesuvius
> erupts - Mr Rolls and Mr Royce form a
> company - San Francisco earthquake -
> Play about appalling conditions in
> Ireland, "The Playboy Of The Western
> World" - SOS becomes international
> distress signal.

Throughout the century, songs have been based on snippets of conversation. The ragtime pianist, Shelton Brooks, in a Cincinnati restaurant, heard a couple arguing. One said, "You'd better not walk out on me, honey, for some of these days, you're going to miss me." Shelton quickly wrote "Some Of These Days" and started performing it. His songs, "Some Of These Days" and "Darktown Strutters Ball", were sheet music successes, and then "Some Of These Days" was taken up by Sophie Tucker, later called the Last of the Red Hot Mamas. She was very ambitious and her prayer was "Lord, make me a millionaire." When she died in 1966, her final words were "Where's Teddy?", asking for her pianist.

A record was released about an earthquake, "The Destruction Of San Francisco", by the Columbia Band. In 1906 you could also hear "Waiting At The Church (My wife won't let me)", "Chinatown, My Chinatown" and "Keep On The Sunnyside" for the first time. Not to mention that mawkish homily by Max Ehrmann, "Desiderata", a Top 10 hit for US TV talk show host, Les Crane, in 1972, although "Be gentle with yourself, many fears are born out of fatigue and loneliness", is good advice. In 1970 King Crimson, thinking the poem dated back to the 17th century, used it to advertise their "Lizard" album.

In April 1906, the daredevil Irish-American traindriver, Casey Jones, was killed when his train, the Cannonball Express, came off the rails at an S-bend as it was leaving Memphis. Wallace Saunders, a labourer who helped to clear the site, wrote "Po' Jimmy Jones, The Good Old Porter".

Songs about Casey have appeared over the years including "Casey Jones", a 1910 song recorded by Johnny Cash, "Casey Jones Was His Name" (Hank Snow), "Casey Jones The Miner" and "Casey Jones The Union Scab". Not to mention the Grateful Dead's Casey Jones who was "riding that train / high on cocaine." Many of these songs are inaccurate but Wallace Saunders' original interestingly depicts Casey's widow as uncaring:

> *"Mama, mama, have you heard the news,*
> *Papa got killed on the CB&Q's,*
> *Quit crying, children, and don't do that,*
> *You got another papa on the same durn track."*

CB&Q stood for the Cincinnati, Burlington and Quincy Railroad.

JOHNNY CASH

1907 - I DO LIKE TO BE BESIDE THE SEASIDE (John A. Glover-Kind)

Discovery of blood groups and inventions include the electric washing machine and refrigerators - Start of Territorial Army - Picasso and Braque evolve Cubist movement ("Paint not what you see but what you know is there") - Official recognition of taxis in UK - House of Commons begins process to curb the power of the Lords, but the Lords refuse to pass the legislation until 1911.

Just as there are comic annuals now, Feldmans published collections of comic songs. They began in 1896 and one of their regular composers was John Glover-Kind (1881-1918). His most famous song, associated with the Blackpool organist, Reginald Dixon, is "I Do Like To Be Beside The Seaside", and it was so popular that he wrote a follow-up, "I Don't Like To Be Beside The Seaside". Glover-Kind's sheet music has alternative words for Blackpool and Brighton. His other songs include "By The Beautiful Silvery Sea", "Let's Wait And See The Pictures" and, intriguingly, "Let's Have Free Trade Amongst The Ladies". Many of his songs were performed by Mark Sheridan, who also sang "All The Ducks Went Quack, Quack, Quack", "At The Football Match Last Satuday" and "You Can Do A Lot Of Things At The Seaside That You Can't Do At Home".

His style was continued by George Formby and George's father, also called George Formby, was a miserable, consumptive man who, nevertheless, enjoyed singing comic songs. His best known song is "Standing At The Corner Of The Street" and if he spluttered during the performance, he would say his catchphrase, "Coughing better, tonight?"

Also from the year are "She's A Lassie From Lancashire", "On The Road To Mandalay" (words by Rudyard Kipling), "Budweiser's A Friend Of Mine" and Irving Berlin's first published lyric, "Marie From Sunny Italy". Cecil Spring-Rice, the Ambassador to Washington, wrote "I Vow To Thee, My Country", but died a month later. The hymn was used at Charles and Diana's wedding in 1981.

The Tariff Commission reported that the average British workman was becoming indolent : he was "less thrifty, takes less interest in his work, is fonder of outdoor amusements, is more addicted to drink and generally is more interested in the next football match and the nearest public house than he is in his work." No wonder "I Do Like To Be Beside The Seaside" was popular.

1908 - DOWN BY THE OLD MILL STREAM
(Tell Taylor)

Baden-Powell sets up Scout movement -
Model T's in production - "The Wind In The
Willows" published - Olympic Games in
London - England's first international football
match, beating Austria 6-1.

Tell Taylor, a Broadway writer and performer, was on holiday back in his hometown of Findlay, Ohio. He went fishing and, remembering a past girlfriend, wrote "Down By The Old Mill Stream". He gave the song to the barber-shop quartet, the Orpheus Comedy Four, and the sheet music became so popular that it sold 200,000 in St. Louis alone. Tell Taylor died in 1937, just as Hollywood was putting a bio-pic into production. The film was never made - wish it had been, I'd love to know if people really sang in barbers' shops.

Other classic songs from the year are "Shine On Harvest Moon" and the tongue-twisting "She Sells Sea Shells On The Sea Shore". Al Jolson brought some dignity to the ridiculous "Where Did Robinson Crusoe Go With Friday On A Saturday Night?" "The Black And White Rag", a terrific title for a piano solo, was written by the ragtime composer, George Botsford, and became a 1952 hit for the entertainer, Winifred Atwell. Winnie lost much of her popularity to Russ Conway but this record found new popularity as the theme for BBC 2's snooker coverage from 1969 to 1984.

1909 - I WONDER WHO'S KISSING HER NOW
(Harry Orlob - William Hough - Frank Adams -
Joseph Howard)

Pensions for the over 70s - Woman's suffrage
becomes militant - Did Peary reach the
North Pole? - Bleriot makes first cross-Channel
flight.

How did these four people write one song? The answer is, They didn't, and it took a court case to establish that Harry Orlob was a sole composer who was being cheated out of his royalties. The song came from the musical, "The Prince Of Tonight", which was staged in Chicago in 1909. It became known to a wider public through performances by Ada Reeve and Harry Woodruff. Sam Costa started the DJs' joke, "That was so and so with such

and such, and I wonder who's kissing her now on the backside."

Other songs of the year are "By The Light Of The Silvery Moon", "Meet Me Tonight In Dreamland" and "All The Nice Girls Love A Sailor". John Galsworthy's "Strife", the first play to seriously tackle the collision course between the workers and the capitalists, was first staged in 1909.

1910 - ALEXANDER'S RAGTIME BAND
(Irving Berlin)

Edward VII dies, accession of George V -
Portugal declared a republic - Crippen
arrested on board ship, the first capture of a
criminal through radio - Not to be outdone,
Lady Baden-Powell starts the Girl Guides -
Death of Florence Nightingale

Irving Berlin wanted to convey the colour and excitement of the ragtime era, although "Alexander's Ragtime Band" was more of a march and lacked the syncopation of ragtime music. He played it as an instrumental for Jesse Lasky, Samuel Goldwyn's brother-in-law, who was developing a cabaret show, "Folies Bergères", which means "mad shepherdesses", in New York. He played it three times and then asked, "Do you think it's good?" "I wouldn't go as as far as that," said Lasky, "but I may use it."

It was tried for one performance and then dropped, with Berlin regarding it as a failure. Berlin worked on another show, "Ziegfield Follies", and when that was successful, he wrote ragtime lyrics to his troublesome song. It was included in a new revue in 1910, "The Happy Whirl", but when that folded, it looked as though the song was destined for obscurity. However, when other performers picked up on the song, the publishers' 75 song-pluggers were instructed to promote the song and within a year, almost a million copies of the sheet music had been sold.

"Alexander's Ragtime Band," was performed nightly by Al Jolson. The minstrel days of blackface performers were drawing to an end, but Al Jolson went on to superstardom. Jolson started wearing blackface because his Negro dresser had told him, "You'd be much funnier, boss, if you blacked your face like mine. People always laugh at the black man." At the time, nobody thought that was offensive.

Another song from 1910 was "When You Were Sweet Sixteen" and Jolson later said, "I'll never forget the thrill one rainy night when I first heard James Thornton play his song, 'When You Were Sweet Sixteen'. All the years in between haven't dimmed the thrill of that moment, because whenever I sing that song, I'm a young kid again staring out there on 14th Street in the rain."

The year also saw "Joshua" (sweeter than orange squash you are!), "Mother Macree", "Ah, Sweet Mystery Of Life", "Steamboat Bill", "I'm Henry VIII, I Am", and "I'm Shy, Mary Ellen, I'm Shy". The hymn called "A Perfect Day" was published, by a songwriter who was crippled, widowed and bankrupt!

IRVING BERLIN

1911 - TORNA A SORRENTO
(Ernesto de Curtis - Claude Aveling)

Revolution in China - Strikes in UK - Trolley buses in Leeds - MPs given a salary (£400pa) - Mona Lisa stolen (recovered 1913) - A Model T Ford is driven up Ben Nevis to show its capabilities.

The Italian ballad, "Torna A Sorrento" has been sung by tenors from Caruso to Pavarotti. Well, it sure beats "Live Like Horses". In 1947 it was given an English lyric, "Come Back To Sorrento", and this has been recorded by several artists including Gracie Fields, Josef Locke and Dean Martin. In 1960 the melody was given a second English lyric by Doc Pomus and Mort Shuman and as "Surrender", it was a No.1 for Elvis Presley.

Other songs of the year are "Let Me Call You Sweetheart", "Oh You Beautiful Doll", the Freudian "I Want A Girl Just Like The Girl Who Married Dear Old Dad", and "The Spaniard That Blighted My Life", a gold disc for Al Jolson.

I have never checked the truth of this anecdote as I would be so disappointed were it not so. When a Liverpool theatre wanted to book Caruso, they discovered that his fee was £600, a tremendous amount, although these days you'd be lucky to get change from £100,000 for one of the Three Tenors. A businessman who lived in Huskisson Street said he would pay half the fee if Caruso would entertain his friends afterwards at his house. Caruso agreed and so played Liverpool.

1912 - IT'S ALL IN THE GAME
(Charles Gates Dawes - Carl Sigman)

Coalminer's strike - First parachute descends from aircraft - Titanic, supposedly "unsinkable", sinks - Piltdown skull discovered, but exposed as a hoax in 1953 - Scott dies in the Antarctic (and Amundsen had beaten him to the Pole) - Schizophrenia diagnosed.

Charles Dawes was a banker and a politician, who helped stablise the nation's finances after the First World War and was awarded the Nobel Peace Prize in 1925. He was the Vice-President to Calvin Coolidge from 1925 to 1929 and then became the US Ambassador to Great Britain.

He also played the flute and, in 1912, he wrote a tune which he called "Melody In A Major". It wasn't until 1951 that the tune was given a lyric, namely, "It's All In The Game" by Carl Sigman. Louis Armstrong and Nat "King" Cole recorded the song, and it became a transatlantic No.1 for Tommy Edwards in 1958.

The first Royal Command Performance took place in 1912 and Queen Mary was appalled to see the male impersonator, Vesta Tilley, on the bill. She instructed the ladies in her party to look away as a female in trousers was not very ladylike.

Jack Judge, a music hall singer of Irish descent from Oldbury, Worcestershire, was appearing at the Grand Theatre, Stalybridge in January 1912. He bet some friends five shillings (25p) that he could compose and then perform a new song the following night. On the way back to his digs, he heard someone asking for directions and getting the response, "It's a long way." Jack added the name of an Irish town and the next day he gave the new lyric to his conductor, Harry Williams, to write the music. While he performed "It's A Long, Long Way To Tipperary", some performing seals kept time with their flippers. The song is about Paddy leaving Molly and yearning to return home, but it took on a new dimension as a marching song in the First World War.

LOUIS ARMSTRONG

Other well-known songs from the year are "Waiting For The Robert E Lee", "My Melancholy Baby", "Row, Row, Row", "Who Were You With Last Night?", "When Irish Eyes Are Smiling", "When The Midnight Choo-Choo Leaves For Alabam", "They All Walk The Wibbly Wobbly Walk" and "Moonlight Bay". Like so many classical pieces, Frederick Delius based his atmospheric "On Hearing The First Cuckoo In Spring" on a folk song, this one from Norway.

Much publicity was given to the Titanic's maiden voyage, but it sank. (I hope I haven't spoilt the ending of the film for you.) Many ballads were composed about the disaster and the first person to record a tribute was Robert Carr.

1913 - DANNY BOY (Frederic Weatherly)

Woodrow Wilson becomes US President - Zip fastener invented - Charlie Chaplin's first film - D. H. Lawrence writes "Sons And Lovers" and Proust "Swann's Way", the first volume of "A La Recherche Du Temps Perdu"

A criminal lawyer and part-time lyricist, Fred Weatherly, was sent the music of "The Londonderry Air" by his sister-in-law. She sensed that he could put words to it and he exceeded expectations with the sad, reflective story of a mother mourning her son, "Danny Boy". It has been recorded by Bing Crosby, Roy Orbison and the Glenn Miller Orchestra and Fred's other lyrics have included "The Holy City" and "Roses Of Picardy". In 1959, "Danny Boy" became a rock'n'roll hit for Conway Twitty. His version could not be released in the UK because the lyric was still in copyright and permission could not be obtained. Twitty resourcefully wrote his own words to "The Londonderry Air", "Rosaleena", and released that instead. "Danny Boy" was recorded by Elvis a year before he died and the song was played at his funeral.

"You Made Me Love You" is also from 1913 and it was subsequently sung by Judy Garland to a photograph of Clark Gable. Other successes include "An Irish Lullaby", "The Sunshine Of Your Smile", "Now Is The Hour" (based on a Maori chant heard by an American tourist), "Marcheta" (Karl Denver's first hit), "The Old Rugged Cross", "If I Had My Way" and the new dance craze, "Ballin' The Jack". Then there's that Laurel and Hardy favourite, "The Trail Of The Lonesome Pine". Al Bryan and Fred Fisher wrote "Peg O' My Heart", but composers didn't line up to work with Bryan who insisted that he wrote his best songs in the nude.

Gustav Holst, fascinated by astronomy, started "The Planets", which he completed in 1916. The middle theme of "Jupiter" became the music for the hymn, "I Vow To Thee My Country". Parisians were shocked by Stravinsky's "The Rite Of Spring". An Anglo-French music hall performer, Harry Flagson, was shot dead by his own father, shades of Marvin Gaye.

1914 - ST. LOUIS BLUES
(William Christopher Handy)

Assassination of Archduke Franz Ferdinand of
Austria sparks World War I - First Zeppelin raid -
Christmas truce in no-man's-land - James
Joyce writes "Dubliners".

One of the most thrilling records you can buy is "Louis
Armstrong Plays W.C. Handy", a 1954 LP which has been
issued on CD with bonus tracks and, most surprisingly, an
interview with old man Handy talking about another
great composition, "Careless Love" (1921). W.C. Handy,
who was born in 1873, was a composer, bandleader
and cornet player, known as "The Father Of
The Blues". He had been cheated out of his
royalties for "Memphis Blues" in 1912, and
he determined not to make the same
mistake with "St Louis Blues", which is
really a woman's song. "St Louis Blues"
is unquestionably a masterpiece, and
was the title of a film biography of his
life, starring Nat "King" Cole.

1914 was a classic year for songs which
have endured: "Play A Simple Melody",
"They Didn't Believe Me", "Twelfth Street
Rag" (words, 1919), "Under The Bridges Of
Paris", "Till The End Of Time", and 'Aba Daba
Honeymoon', a hit for Debbie Reynolds in 1951. Al
Jolson sang "I'm Glad My Wife's In Europe" and he
wished she was. Geroge Bernard Shaw wrote his comedy,
"Pygmalion", which became the 1956 musical, "My Fair
Lady".

German operettas like "The Merry Widow" (1905) lost
their popularity when the war started, and, starting Tin
Hat Alley, Ivor Novello offered "Keep The Home Fires
Burning". A few years ago the Rhos Male Voice Choir
were in concert with Tom O'Connor and the theatre
manager rang Tom O'Connor and asked him where the
conjuror was going to appear on the bill. "There's no conjuror," said Tom, "Only me and the Rhos Male Voice
Choir." "Oh no," said the manager, "I have the poster
here - 'Tom O'Connor and the Rhos Male Voice Choir
with the magic of Ivor Novello'."

And what about Kenneth Alford, the pseudonym of
Major F.J. Ricketts, who was the bandmaster of the
British second battalion, Argyll and Sutherland

W.C. HANDY

Highlanders? He composed the march, "Colonel Bogey",
now known as "Hitler has only got one ball".

1915 - PACK UP YOUR TROUBLES IN YOUR
OLD KIT-BAG
(Felix Powell - George Powell)

World War I - Women urged to volunteer for
war work - Lusitania sunk - The foxtrot is the new
dance craze - Rasputin's rise in Russia

No doubt about it - war is good for songwriters. "Pack
Up Your Troubles In Your Old Kit Bag" was a
popular music hall song, written by the singer
George Powell and his brother, Felix, a
pianist with the Sundown Pierrots. They
introduced the song on their residency
at the Bridge Pavilion in Ilkley,
Yorkshire.

Another popular music hall song was
the satirical "Burlington Bertie From
Bow", performed by Ella Shields, while
the musical, "Chu Chin Chow", started
its run of 2,300 performances at Her
Majesty's Theatre, London. Two more
standards from the year: "Paper Doll",
revived by the Mills Brothers in 1942, and "I
Ain't Got Nobody". Jelly Roll Morton's "Jelly Roll
Blues" becomes the first jazz composition to be copyrighted. "The piano," he said, "should always be an imita-
tion of a jazz band." You can hear that in his intricate and
embellished arrangments.

JELLY ROLL MORTON

How about this tongue-twisting lyric for "Mother's Sitting Knitting Little Mittens For The Navy" by Bob Weston and Herman Darewski:

> *"Mother's sitting knitting little mittens for the Navy.*
> *Bertha's busy bathing baby Belgium refugees.*
> *Sarah's shaming shirkers making Guernseys for the*
> *Ghurkahs.*
> *Oh, such busy bees a-buzzing, oh so busy.*
> *Maggie, Mol and Maud are making muffins for*
> *Marines,*
> *While Minnie winds the wool when they begin.*
> *Sister Cissy's knitting socks and Susie's sewing shirts for*
> *soldiers,*
> *Still, poor Papa props his pants up with a pin."*

Why couldn't poor Papa repair his own pants? Well, this was 1915, remember.

1916 - IF YOU WERE THE ONLY GIRL IN THE WORLD
(Clifford Grey - Nat D. Ayer)

World War I - Easter uprising in Dublin - Lloyd George becomes Prime Minister - Blood transfusion service starts - Rasputin assassinated - D. W. Griffith directs the first epic film, "Intolerance" - Dadaism ("Dada Wouldn't Buy Me A Bauhaus"?).

The American songwriter, Nat D. Ayer, came to London during the ragtime era and, surprisingly, stayed while the war was on. He adjusted to the locale and wrote "I'm Going Back To Dear Old Shepherd's Bush" and "That Ragtime Suffragette". He also wrote "Oh You Beautiful Doll". His revue, "The Bing Boys Are Here", starred George Robey, known as "The Prime Minister Of Mirth" and knighted in 1954, and included "If You Were The Only Girl In The World", a duet with George and Violet Loraine. The armed forces sang an amended version, "If you were the only Boche in the trench, And I had the only gun."

"Roses Of Picardy", "What Do You Want To Make Those Eyes At Me For" and "Pretty Baby" are some more songs of the year, but my selection was nearly "Jerusalem". The visionary writer, William Blake, wrote his poem in 1808, which, let's face it, is as incomprehensible as "A Day In The Life". Possibly he's saying that by living together in the Lord, we build Jerusalem in 'England's green and pleasant land", but who knows what he was taking at the time. It was set to music by Sir Hubert Parry in 1916 and first performed at a Votes For Women concert. It is now associated with The Last Night of the Proms and Euro 2000 and is effectively another national anthem.

Spare a thought for Basil Hallam, a good-looker with little acting or singing ability, the Fabian of his day. He became a West End star because so many young actors were away fighting. He had been rejected for service because of a bad foot, but, after being called a coward, he was determined to be accepted and he died when his parachute failed to open. His final record was "Goodbye Girls, I'm Through".

1917 - FOR ME AND MY GAL
(Ray Goetz - Edgar Leslie - George Myer)

World War I - British royal family renounces German names and they become the Windsors - RSPCA's first animal clinic - Lenin seizes power in Russia.

The recent long-running West End musical, "Me And My Girl", was not a revival of an old show, but a celebration of songs published by Noel Gay including "For Me And My Gal". The song originated from a little-known American musical from 1917, "The Bells Are Ringing", but it is associated with Al Jolson.

The Original Dixieland Jass Band introduced "Tiger Rag", and there was also "Love Will Find A Way", "Give Me The Moonlight" and "The Bells Of St. Mary". Noël Coward's "Forbidden Fruit", published when he was only 17, shows a cynicism beyond his age.

ORIGINAL DIXIELAND JASS BAND

The novelty songwriters, Bob Weston and Bert Lee, wrote "Good-bye-ee!", lovingly parodied by Peter Cook and Dudley Moore, and "Paddy McGinty's Goat", forever associated with Val Doonican. Bob Weston also wrote "The End Of Me Old Cigar" and "What A Mouth", later revived by Tommy Steele to prove to his dad that he was as good as the Two Bills of Bermondsey. George S. Cohan wrote the stirring "Over There!" the day that President Wilson signed the declaration of war. It states, "I won't be coming back 'til it's over over there" and was recorded by Caruso.

1918   SWANEE (George Gershwin - Irving Caesar)

Armistice - Women over 30 given right to vote, while men can vote at 21 - RAF created - Worldwide flu epidemic with 20 million deaths.

In 1918 Al Jolson opened in the musical, "Sinbad", in New York and found the fans were screaming for his two new hits, "Rockabye Your Baby With A Dixie Melody" and "Swanee". "Swanee" was written by a 19 year old George Gershwin and it earned George $10,000 in one year. When Jolson followed Caruso in a charity concert for the end of the war, he shouted, "Folks, you ain't heard nothin' yet." And he was right - his biggest hits, and the first talkie, "The Jazz Singer", were still to come.

GEORGE GERSHWIN

The war with its dreadful toll was ending and bright, breezy songs were in vogue - "Somebody Stole My Gal", "After You've Gone" and "I'm Always Chasing Rainbows", which was based on a Chopin melody. "I'm Always Chasing Rainbows" had new found popularity in 1945 when it was revived by Dick Haymes and Helen Forrest.

The most memorable song title of the year has to be "Would You Rather Be a Colonel With An Eagle On Your Shoulder Or A Private With A Chicken On Your Knee?"

1919 -   A PRETTY GIRL IS LIKE A MELODY
(Irving Berlin)

Lady Astor becomes first woman MP - Jack Dempsey, world heavyweight boxing champ - Great year for flying records including Alcock and Brown making the first non-stop transatlantic flight.

Irving Berlin loved "A Pretty Girl Is Like A Melody" which he wrote for "The Ziegfield Follies Of 1919". He called it the "best individual song written for a musical", but he was given to declarations like this. Because beauty contests have become unfashionable, the song has gone out of favour as it is associated with the "Miss World" broadcasts. Right from an early age, Irving Berlin realised the potential of his work and had his own company, Irving Berlin Limited.

"I'm Forever Blowing Bubbles" from the US musical, "Passing Show", is still sung by West Ham supporters because one of their players resembled "Bubbles" in Millais' sentimental painting. Other key songs of the year are "Don't Dilly On The Way", "If You're Irish, Come In To The Parlour", "Let The Rest Of The World Go By", "Ja-Da", "Say It With Flowers", "Dardanella" and a comment on American servicemen abroad, "How Ya Gonna Keep 'Em Down On The Farm After They've Seen Paree?" Leslie Henson recorded a P.G Wodehouse lyric, "Motoring", which told of his 22 girlfriends and their 22 cars, not to mention his wife's Ford.

The original Dixieland Jass Band from New Orleans had done much to popularise jazz and they came here for West End appearances. George Robey was so annoyed to find these upstarts getting more applause than himself that he insisted they be dropped from the show. As the revue depended on him, the jazzers went elsewhere and found greater success at the London Palladium.

1920 - I'LL BE WITH YOU IN APPLE BLOSSOM TIME
(Albert Von Tilzer - Neville Fleeson)

All Russian factories with more than 10 workers nationalised - Martial law in Ireland - Sir Geoffrey De Havilland founds aircraft company - Joan of Arc canonised - Agatha Christie publishes her first whodunnit, "The Mysterious Affair At Styles".

"I'll Be With You In Apple Blossom Time" was introduced by Nora Bayes, who also sang "Has Anybody Here Seen Kelly". Albert Von Tilzer also wrote "Give Me The Moonlight" and "Put Your Arms Around Me, Honey", while his brother Harry came up with "A Bird In A Gilded Cage", "Down At The Old Bull And Bush" (based on the German "Down Where The Würzburger Flows") , "I Want A Girl Just Like The Girl That Married Dear Old Dad" and "Wait 'Til The Sun Shines, Nellie".

Other songs of the year include "Alice Blue Gown", "Margie", "Whispering", "The Cuckoo Waltz", "Just A Song At Twilight" and "Look For The Silver Lining". The music hall comedian from Bradford, Jack Pleasants, introduced his song, "Twenty-One Today", around this time - he also wrote "I'm Shy, Mary Ellen, I'm Shy". The spiritual, "Amen", was first heard in America.

JACK PLEASANTS

In 1920, the minimalist French composer, Erik Satie coined the phrase, "furniture music", which was music "that would be a part of the surrounding noises". In another word, Muzak. He saw his compositions as "meshing with the clatter of knives and forks without drowning it completely and without imposing itself." Around the same time John Philip Sousa objected to "canned music" on the radio.

1921 - MAMMY
(Sam Lewis - Joe Young - Walter Donaldson)

Fascists in Italian parliament and rise of Mussolini - Irish Free State founded - Unemployment in UK passes 1m - First Austin 7 and first Hercule Poirot - Dr Marie Stopes opens birth control clinic and HMV opens first all-music store, both in London - Footprints of Yeti discovered in Himalayas

By 1921, Al Jolson was regarded as the World's Greatest Entertainer and much has since been written about a Jew putting on black face to perform. Bill Frawley was the first to sing "Mammy", but the vaudevillian was upstaged by Jolie who added the song in a revival of his musical, "Sinbad". When he was performing nine one-hour shows a day for the troops during the Second World War, he commented, "I almost wore the knees out of my pants singing 'Mammy'."

This exceptionally strong year also included "Second Hand Rose" (Fanny Brice and then Barbra Streisand), "Ma, He's Makin' Eyes At Me", "I'm Just Wild About Harry", "Toot Toot, Tootsie" (another train song, performed by Al Jolson) and "April Showers" (Jolie again). Two novelties surfaced in 1921 - "Delaney's Donkey" (later made popular by Val Doonican) and "The Sheik Of Araby", a George Harrison favourite and written to accompany Rudolph Valentino's silent films. The character actor, Will Fyffe, was harangued by a drunk at Glasgow railway station, who said to him, "I belong to Glasgow". Cue for a song.

1922 - LOVESICK BLUES (Irving Mills - Cliff Friend)

BBC established: licence fee, ten shillings (50p) - Howard Carter discovers Tutankhamun's tomb - Irish leader, Michael Collins, assassinated - T. S. Eliot writes "The Waste Land" and James Joyce "Ulysses".

Cliff Friend, a test pilot and a vaudeville pianist from Cincinnati, wrote the melody for "Lovesick Blues" with the lyricist, Irving Mills. It was for a long-forgotten musical about lovesick pilots called "O-oo Ernest". Mills, who became Duke Ellington's publisher, realised the song's potential and bought out Friend's interest.

The song was recorded by Elsie Clark in 1922 but "The Minstrel Man from Georgia", Emmett Miller, added the yodel in 1925. Then in 1939, Rex Griffin recorded "Lovesick Blues" and became known for that and "The Last Letter".

Rex Griffin and Hank Williams, both drunks, played shows together. Hank Williams could only record songs published by Acuff-Rose and so Hank told Fred Rose that he had purchased the rights of "Lovesick Blues" from Rex Griffin, which, in any event, were not his to sell. Hank Williams' record was a smash hit - he got seven encores when he sang it on the "Grand Ole Opry" radio show - and Acuff-Rose had to contend with an irate Irving Mills. In 1962 Frank Ifield followed his No 1 "I Remember You" with a yodelling, twisting "Lovesick Blues" that was also a chart-topper.

The jaunty "Way Down Yonder In New Orleans" was a hit in 1922 and its composer, Turner Layton, was delighted when Freddie Cannon revived it in 1959. If New Orleans was not to your liking, you could travel to "Chicago" (later revived by Sinatra and just what is a "toddling town"?) or visit "Carolina In The Morning". Arthur Wood wrote "Barwick Green" as part of his suite, "My Native Heath": since 1950, it has been the signature tune for "The Archers".

HANK WILLIAMS

1923 - WHO'S SORRY NOW?
(Bert Kalmar - Harry Ruby - Ted Snyder)

Stanley Baldwin becomes Prime Minister - Devastating earthquakes in Tokyo and Yokohama - Massive inflation in Germany - Crossword puzzles devised.

The New York songwriters, Bert Kalmar and Harry Ruby wrote "I Wanna Be Loved By You", "Nevertheless" and Groucho Marx's theme song, "Hooray For Captain Spaulding". "Who's Sorry Now" was introduced by the vaudeville duo, Van and Schenk, in 1923 although several cover versions quickly followed. The song was revived by Harry James in 1946 and was then sung by Gloria De Haven in "Three Little Words", the 1950 bio-pic about Kalmar (Fred Astaire) and Ruby (Red Skelton). During the mid-1950s, Connie Francis cut unsuccessful singles until her domineering dad suggested that she revive "Who's Sorry Now", which became an international hit. After that, she cut several of her dad's favourite songs.

The Temperance Seven had hits with two songs from 1923 - "You're Driving Me Crazy" and "Pasadena" and also recorded the dance craze, "The Charleston" (1925). Jelly Roll Morton introduced "Wolverine Blues", and there's "Last Night On The Back Porch", "Mexicali Rose" and the most ridiculous of novelty songs, "Yes, We Have No Bananas", not to mention the first song George Harrison learnt on the guitar, "That Old Gang Of Mine". Its composer, Harry Woods, also wrote a song called "Here Comes The Sun" in 1930. Coincidence?

Jo Stafford won a gold disc in 1954 for "Make Love To Me", a song with eight composers. It was originally an instrumental from 1923, "Tin Roof Blues", and the composers were the first members of the New Orleans Rhythm Kings, together with their publisher, Walter Melrose. Bill Norvas and Alan Copeland wrote the lyric, "Make Love To Me", in 1953, hence it took eight men to make love to Jo Stafford.

1924 - ROSE MARIE (Otto Harbach - Oscar Hammerstein II - Rudolf Friml)

First Labour government with Ramsey Macdonald as PM - Lenin dies - Quantum theory - Loudspeakers invented - E. M. Forster writes "A Passage To India" - Eric Liddell's Olympic gold, later the subject of "Chariots Of Fire".

The 1920s operettas feature cardboard cutouts acting Mills and Boon romances. "Rose Marie", about how a Canadian mountie always gets his woman, was staged on Broadway in 1924 and two songs became instant successes, the title song and "Indian Love Call". It was filmed with Joan Crawford (1928 - a silent musical!), Nelson Eddy (1935) and Howard Keel (1954). The country singer, Slim Whitman, at his wife's suggestion, had success with both of the songs with "Rose Marie" topping the UK charts for 11 weeks. Also from a 1924 operetta comes "The Drinking Song" (Sample lyric: "Drink, drink, drink") from "The Student Prince". You can imagine Father Jack singing that.

At the time of his death in 1924, Giacomo Puccini was working on an opera about a Chinese princess whose cruelty is overturned by love. The key aria, "Nessun Dorma", was written by Puccini but the opera was completed after his death by Franco Alfano.

George Gershwin had a marvellous year - "Fascinating Rhythm" was a most infectious song, while his "Rhapsody In Blue", for piano and orchestra, brought jazz into the concert hall. For some unknown reason, he also accepted a commission to write a West End musical, "Primrose", with a British lyricist, Desmond Carter.

The ultra-witty "Hard Hearted Hannah" is now performed on stage with great relish by George Melly. Melly brings out the sado-masochism in the song, which is highly unusual for Tin Pan Alley in 1924.

"Leather's tough but Hannah's heart is tougher
She's the gal who likes to see men suffer.
To tease 'em and thrill 'em,
To torture and kill 'em
Is her delight they say."

Another couplet says:

"Making love to Hannah in a big armchair
Is like strolling through Alaska in your underwear."

Quite a contrast to "Oh Rose Marie, I love you."

The sexually-named Jelly Roll Morton, was experimenting with piano rolls in which the notes are reproduced on perforated, thick paper and played back on a piano-player. His famed instrumentals included "King Porter Stomp" (1923) and "Shreveport Stomp" (1924).

Eddie Cantor made America sing with "It Had To Be You" and other great melodies of the year include "I Want To Be Happy", "Tea For Two", "I'll See You In My Dreams", and "What'll I Do". Considering the reference to "my pretty little poppy" in "Amapola", some group could revive it as a pro-drugs song. Al Jolson was saying "California Here I Come", while the silliest song of the year was "Does Your Chewing Gum Lose Its Flavour On The Bedpost Overnight?", which became an international hit for Lonnie Donegan 35 years later.

LONNIE DONEGAN

WRITERS' BLOCK
Tin Pan Alley

If you're in London, you may go to Foyle's in Charing Cross Road. Cross over and you will see a short, narrow street ahead of you. That is Denmark Street, once Britain's Tin Pan Alley. Though there are still some music publishers and instrument shops there (not to mention a music book shop, Helter Skelter, which wasn't there before), the street is only a shadow of its former self. Up until the Beatles led the revolution for performers writing their own songs, performers and their managers would trudge up and down the street, picking up manuscripts everytime they entered a poky office and hoping that they had found the elusive hits.

The origins of Tin Pan Alley and, indeed, the original Alley itself are in New York, a musical city if there ever was one. During the later part of the 19th century, the music publishing companies had been clustering on West 28th Street between Broadway and Sixth Avenue. The booking agencies for the theatres and music halls were also based in New York City. The new, enterprising publishers would encourage vaudeville artists to perform their songs: they might tour all year and then return to Tin Pan Alley for new material, some of which might be specifically written for them. This is the start of performers wanting songs to suit their personalities.

The publishers would also distribute sheet music to American stores, where they would be sold, usually for home piano use. Family sing-songs are rare today, but it was then a major source of entertainment, and clearly, proportionately more people could read and play music. For many years, the public preferred to buy sheet music to records, perhaps thinking that DIY was better than something that had been previously made. Even in the 1950s, many homes still had piano stools stuffed with music. It wasn't just cheerful, matey songs that would be sung around the piano. In the Victorian era, both tear-stained ballads and hymns were very popular.

The presentation of the sheet music changed very little with the years. Usually, it was a simple four page document, the front page contained the title, the composers and an illustration, and the remaining three gave you the music. The artist pictured on the cover might not be the one most associated with the song: for example, the British sheet music for Buddy Holly's "That'll Be The Day", showed Larry Page, who had recorded a cover version. A love for that sheet music comes across in Dennis Potter's imaginative TV serial, "Pennies From Heaven", in 1978. The play takes place in the mid-1930s and Bob Hoskins as a sheet music salesman, dreams of the perfect happiness that he finds in songs like "Painting The Clouds With Sunshine", "There's A Goldmine In The Sky" or "I Only Have Eyes For You".

The street realised the value of marketing when Chas Harris both wrote and published a very popular song, "After The Ball", in 1892. He did everything he could to encourage performers to sing his songs. Through his efforts, everything became less genteel and by the turn of the century, there was a bustling trade. The publishers hired pianists who would write with lyricists at their uprights or would play potential successes to visiting performers. There was no sound-proofing or air conditioning, so the windows would be open and a stroller would hear a cacophony, which resembled tin pans being clashed together. The phrase, "Tin Pan Alley", was first used by the songwriter, Monroe Rosenfeld, in an article in 1899, although he may not have coined it.

From then on, Tin Pan Alley reigned supreme. Sheet music sales boomed, and around ten songs a year sold over a million copies in the first decade of the 20th century. The songwriters were nothing if they couldn't write to order - if "coon songs" (and that is what they were called) were wanted, then the writers would grind them out. If it was ragtime, they would switch to ragtime, and so on. With no trouble at all, the songwriters showed their patriotism by writing songs for the First World War (not, of course, called the "First World War" at the time as nobody had any idea that there would be another.).

Music publishing became a legitimate trade, and it became even more lucrative after legislation. The publishers received two cents a copy on sheet music following the Copyright Law of 1909. Then the American Society of Composers, Authors and Publishers (ASCAP) was formed in 1917. As a test case, they sued a restaurant for playing their members' music without payment. They won, and some years later, scored similar victories against cinemas, radio stations and record companies. Cylinders were replaced by flat discs from 1897, but it wasn't until the 1920s they merited enough sales to attract Tin Pan Alley.

MORT SHUMAN (AT PIANO) WITH DOC POMUS.

Most of the early songwriters were hacks and they did not need to be good musicians as special pianos enabled them to switch keys by pressing levers. Irving Berlin, the first major songwriter to come out of Tin Pan Alley, used such a piano as he could only play in F sharp. By the 1920s, the Alley was attracting more literate and sophisticated writers like George Gershwin, Jerome Kern and Cole Porter, and the standard of the work dramatically improved. Irving Berlin's compositions could match anyone's but he must have felt inferior when George Gershwin, a concert pianist, was around.

With the popularity of Broadway musicals, Tin Pan Alley moved to a street off Times Square and then came the "talkies" from Hollywood. "The Jazz Singer" with Al Jolson was an awe-inspiring start but the Depression reduced cinema audiences. In 1933, "42nd Street", with a score by Harry Warren and Al Dubin, became a major success, and one Hollywood musical followed another. It was a California Gold Rush for songwriters: some moved east and others supplied their songs from New York.

Tin Pan Alley during the 20s and 30s can be summed up as rhythm and Jews. The majority of the songwriters, and indeed the publishers, were male Jewish immigrants, whose parents may have come from Russia or Poland. Some of this can be attributed to peer pressure and to the fact that the offices were close to the Jewish communities in New York, but that doesn't explain why they were able to write so well. Quite possibly, many of their families had had to learn English as a second language, and the wordsmiths became entranced with the use of words and their meanings. (The whole subject is most intriguing: an American writer has recently written a book, "When Boxing Was A Jewish Sport", so it is not just songwriting.)

Some writers wrote alone, but most songs were written by two man teams with a distinctive demarcation between words and music. Some had exclusive relationships, but most writers were willing to try new partners. There were very few female composers and it was not until the 1960s that one became nationally known, namely, Carole King. I have never found a satisfactory explanation of this: why was songwriting so male dominated? Lots of women wrote novels at home, so why couldn't they write songs?

The British version of Tin Pan Alley developed in the 1920s with the publishers, Francis Day and Hunter, Feldman's and Lawrence Wright, among others. At first, the publishers had been taking their songs from America and indeed, Americans wrote many of the familiar British music hall songs. Then the British composers, Ivor Novello and Noël Coward, showed themselves to be as able as their US counterparts. Because Denmark Street is so short, the success of the publishing companies and then the record companies' own publishing companies led to premises in Charing Cross Road and New Bond Street. However, Denmark Street is regarded as the spiritual, if not physical, home of the UK's Tin Pan Alley.

CAROLE KING

The record producer, Wally Ridley, was born in 1913: "I started work at Feldman's when I was 15, and Feldman's, Francis Day and Hunter, and Chappell's were the main publishers. I learnt to fill inkwells and do the chores but I also had the opportunity to play for very great talents, people like Sophie Tucker, whose piano player, Ted Shapiro, taught me a great deal about accompaniment. We used to publish ten songs a week every week of the year, the film songs of Harry Warren and Al Dubin and Johnny Burke all came through us. I used to play them first in the written key, and then I would transpose them, up a semitone, down a semitone, and so on, so that I could play them in any key. If anybody came in to hear new songs, I could play them in their key, which is enormously important as a singer can't get to grips with a song if he has to sing it in a key which is unsuitable. It has to be in the right key and in the end, I could transpose anything on sight."

Once the singer had agreed to perform the song, orchestrations had to be supplied. The film composer, Ron Goodwin, recalls his early years: "I was working for a music publisher in London and the hit song when I went there was 'Whispering Grass'. The publisher would persuade all sorts of people to broadcast it, and then orchestrations would have to be made for whatever orchestra they were singing it with. I was the lowly copyist who copied the parts for the musicians from that score. You do it one instrument at a time. First of all you copy the first flute part, and then you copy the second one, and so forth. It's really just copying in a neat hand for the orchestra to be able to play what the orchestrator has written on the score. One of the orchestrators was a wonderful chap called Harry J. Stafford. Harry was prone to taking extended lunches, you know propped up against a bar somewhere, and he would come back a little the worse for wear. One day the manager said, 'Where's that bloody orchestration I wanted?' Harry drew himself up with the full dignity of alcohol, picked up the copy of 'Whispering Grass', put it on tne floor, stood on it and said, 'I'm on it now'."

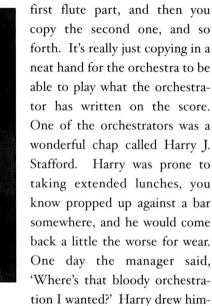

The music publisher, Freddy Bienstock, describes the American scene during the 1940s: "I had a cousin in New York who had a job as a song-plugger at Chappell Music and he would visit all these glorious bandleaders like Benny Goodman and Tommy Dorsey and persuade them to play Chappell's songs on their radio broadcast. This seemed the most heavenly thing one could possibly do, but when I asked him about a job he said that I was too young. I had to wait until I was 16. In 1943, he told me that he had a job for me at Chappell's, starting in the stock room. It was only $16 a week, but nevertheless, I came to New York and started to work in their stockroom. I got great satisfaction in 1984 when I bought Chappell's." Lucky man.

With much laughter, Freddy recalled his first day at Chappell. "This man was being sacked and he said to the great Max Dreyfus who was sacking him, 'Mr Dreyfus, my fate is in your hands.' He said, 'How can you say a thing like that? Don't you know your fate and my fate are in the hands of God?' I thought, 'My god, he's firing him and he's passing the buck to God'."

Fortunately, Max Dreyfus didn't sack Freddy Bienstock. "I was there for ten years. I had two years in the stock room and worked my way up to become a song-plugger. My job was to see the various bands who had airtime from the Waldorf Hotel, the Commodore and the like and ask them to play the songs that I was assigned to promote. Chappell were promoting the songs of Jerome Kern and Cole Porter so it was a lovely, easy, glamorous existence. I didn't have to be at the office before 11 o'clock in the morning and I would visit radio stations for daytime programming, and at night I would go from one nightclub to another. I would get paid for it and I had an expense account, so it was marvellous.'

The songs were often plugged by the composers themselves. The US singer, Jerry Wayne, who is the father of Jeff Wayne of "The War Of The Worlds" fame, recalls, "I remember a composer calling me up and saying, 'I have a new song that I would love you to hear', and as we didn't have cassettes, I had to go in and hear it. I said, 'Yeah, lovely song', and so I was the first to record 'Room Full Of Roses'. I used to go from publisher to publisher and even Frank Loesser and Jule Styne worked as rehearsal pianists. You could go in and rehearse a programme you were doing. They would do it for free but they would expect you to perform one of their songs."

Wally Ridley, back in London: "I used to teach most of the singers who were recording and broadcasting in those days. Sam Browne, who was the vocalist with Ambrose, would rush into Feldman's and say to me, 'Wal, go through these songs with me please. I've got a recording session in an hour.' He would put up four different songs, which I would teach him, and then he would get into a cab and dash round to the studio to make his money, which he would then bet on the horses."

The main haven for songwriters was the Brill Building, a faceless office block at 1619 Broadway in Manhattan, and I like to think that 'Brill' may be short for 'Brilliant'. Freddy Bienstock: "The Brill Building was the home of all the main music publishers and a songwriter might start on the penthouse floor where we had our office and if we didn't take his songs, he would go to the 11th floor and so on until they found a home.

There's a legend around Walter Donaldson who was always betting on racehorses and always needed money. He would sell a song like 'My Blue Heaven' to three different publishers and then they would have to sort out their interests. Of course the publishers should have been furious with him but they weren't as they wanted his next songs. He was a great writer." (Fats Waller was also known to sell songs many times over in order to pay for his wild lifestyle.)

The Brill Building songwriters could write whatever you wanted - love ballads, show tunes, sambas, fox-trots and novelties - but they had difficulties in the mid-1950s in coming to terms with rock'n'roll. Most of the older songwriters detested the music, and this typical remark about Elvis Presley came from Billy Rose, who wrote "Happy Days And Lonely Nights": "Not only are most of his songs junk, but in many cases they are obscene junk, pretty much on a level with dirty comic magazines. It's this current climate that makes Elvis Presley and his animal posturings possible."

Rock'n'roll songwriter, Paul Evans, recalls: "They were disgusted with us, with what we were writing, and the tragedy is that some of us bought into that. They kept telling us that we were writing garbage, that we would be very lucky if we ever had a hit, and that no-one would ever hear of the songs again. They thought rock'n'roll writers couldn't write standards but they were wrong. I'm doing very well with my old rock'n'roll songs!"

Part of their antipathy is because rock'n'roll changed the market, reducing the demand for sheet music and increasing it for records. However, the genesis of the new songs in the rock'n'roll era was precisely the same. You shut yourself in a tiny cubicle and hoped for inspiration. Doc Pomus was a blues songwriter, who turned to rock-'n'roll: "When I decided to become a full-time songwriter, I thought the best way to survive was to write an extraordinary number of songs. I realised that if I wrote by myself there was no way I could write an extraordinary number of songs, so the best thing would be to find a co-writer. My cousin knew Mort Shuman, who knew a lot about young people's songs. I locked him up in a room with me everytime we wrote, and right from the beginning, every time I wrote I would give him a little piece of the song. This went on for the longest while and as he contributed more and more, I gave him larger percentages of the songs. Then one day I said to him, 'Mort Shuman, you are my full partner.'"

Paul Evans wrote a transatlantic smash, "When", for the Kalin Twins: "I would write with one co-writer in the morning and then I would move over and write with another one. We wrote every day at prescribed hours. It wasn't, 'I've got a great idea, let's get together', it was always 'Let's get together Monday, Wednesday and Friday and see if we can come up with some songs.' I was very lucky as it was much easier than it is now. There were a lot less writers, and the artists were not writing much of their own material. There was a need for songs, and I knew that if I wrote three or four songs a week, maybe more, most of them would get recorded."

Sometimes the songs came together very quickly. Paul Evans: "I was at a recording session and Al Byron came in with the lyric for 'Roses Are Red' and said he would like me to write the music to it. I made a joke and said, 'I'll stop the session and write this in two minutes.' I wrote the melody straightaway and spent all weekend trying to write a better one, and I couldn't do it."

CYNTHIA WEIL AND BARRY MANN

Some people wrote so many songs that they thought they had better use pseudonyms. British songwriter, Bunny Lewis: "I worked a lot with Norrie Paramor. He was the head of A&R at Columbia and a lot of people wouldn't record his songs on other labels if they knew he'd written them. To get round this, he had 34 pseudonyms. Eventually, the Performing Right Society issued an edict to the effect that no one could have more than five."

Norman Newell: "Of course I would liked to have my own name on my song successes but it was considered wrong to write your own songs if you were a producer. It was unfair on the artist, who might find it difficult to say no to the person who is running his career. Also, another producer might think, 'If Norman Newell thinks this is a good enough song, then why doesn't he record it himself?' Today it is such a different world - the producer and the artist write all the songs. I never thought it was possible when I was a record producer to have an album that contained all new songs. I thought you had to have some that the public knew, so it's quite amazing the way the world has changed."

I asked Norman Newell if he stuck to his rules. Didn't his artists ever know what they were recording? "Well, I told them afterwards if the song was a success! It was a difficult situation, and Matt Monro didn't know that 'Portrait Of My Love' was my song at first. I didn't think it would be a hit as I thought it was too sophisticated by talking about Michelangelo. I thought hit songs were things that people sang in pubs!"

Despite what you read in books, the Brill Building was not the home of rock'n'roll. That was over the road at 1650 Broadway. In 1958, the songwriter and publisher, Don Kirshner, created his own songwriting teams: Carole King and Gerry Goffin, Barry Mann and Cynthia Weil, and Neil Sedaka and Howard Greenfield among them, and most coming from the same area of Brooklyn. They were talented songwriters, who, very naturally, were at one with the young audience, and so their songs hit the right emotional spots. By 1962, Aldon employed 18 writers and the oldest was only 26. It was a positive, competitive atmosphere and so successful that Kirshner set up a second office on the West Coast, thus supplying songs for the surfing bands. The 1996 film, "Grace Of My Heart", was loosely based on Carole King's life and gives a very good picture of the teen factory.

Cynthia Weil recalls her first hit song, written with Barry Mann: "The first chart record that we had was 'Bless You' for Tony Orlando, who was 16 at the time. Tony was signed to the same company as us and so everybody in the office went home to write for him. I had the title and we wrote the song, which we thought was perfect for him. We did have cubicles in which we could write, and we sometimes wrote there and we sometimes wrote at home. One of the advantages of writing in the cubicles was that you had everybody around you, and it was a turn-on to hear what everybody else was doing. It was so inspirational and competitive that it got you all jazzed up to work harder and write faster and do more. There were friendly rivalries between the writers but as we matured, the rivalries disappeared and the friendships continued."

Paul Evans: "There were two restaurants in the Brill Building where the writers hung out. The older ones would be in Dempsey's and the younger ones in The Turf. I was in The Turf when the news about the Big Bopper, Buddy Holly and Ritchie Valens came through. The place cleared out as they were all racing to pianos to write songs about the plane crash."

So the younger writers were, in some ways, like the older ones. They could write to order and they could be astonishingly prolific. Paul Evans continues: "Barry Mann is one of the great pop writers of all-time, usually writing with his wife Cynthia Weil. When we were kids in New York, he was racing down the street out of breath and I said, 'Stop, Barry, congratulations!', and he said, 'Paul, what are you congratulating me for?' I said, 'You have three songs in the Top 10, congratulations!' and he said, 'Paul, they're all on the way down!', and he was off to write another song."

MIKE STOLLER, ELVIS PRESLEY & JERRY LEIBER.

In a sense the sound became as important as the song. Neil Sedaka: "The 'sha la la''s became a Neil Sedaka trademark. When Howie and I ran out of lyrics, we used to sing 'sha la la' and 'dooby doo'. We did it in 'Breaking Up Is Hard To Do', 'Happy Birthday Sweet Sixteen' and yes, it's part of the song, absolutely. It's part of the lead sheet, right there on the manuscript, absolutely."

Every songwriter wanted to have Elvis on his CV, and that was organised back in the Brill Building by Freddy Bienstock: "Elvis had contracts to make three motion pictures a year, and to be honest, there was never enough time to score them properly. I was given the script and we always managed to find a title song.

The scripts never indicated where the songs should be, and I had to mark up where songs were possible. I would then distribute 12 scripts to 12 different teams, and tell them to work on songs for certain situations. I would get four or five songs for each situation and I would take them to Elvis who would select the songs. Both the mass production and the fact of being tied down to titles like 'Kissin' Cousins', 'Wild In The Country' and 'Harum Scarum' made everything very difficult. It was difficult to get hit songs, and the quality of his songs suffered. Of course, there are exceptions - 'Return To Sender' was a marvellous song."

Mort Shuman: "The minute Elvis had a film or anything like that, all the writers were put on call and they started working like crazy. About a block and a half away from the Brill Building, there was an eight track recording studio called Associated Recording where they made Tin Pan Alley demos. It was going 24 hours a day and the publishers were sending these demos out to Nashville, Hollywood and Memphis. They were usually made with three or four studio musicians and if the writer could sing passably, as it was my case, he would do the vocals. Loads and loads of demos would be made for Elvis. The songs I did for Elvis are great fun to listen to because I was trying to impersonate him."

So why, in the 1960s, did Elvis record such poor material? Can these really be the best songs from hundreds of demos? The reason is that Elvis was restricted to the Brill Building writers, many of whom hated what they were doing, and Elvis couldn't get his hands on Aldon songs. Because of this, the British songwriter, Bunny Lewis, found his luck was in. "I met Elvis in Hollywood when he was recording the score to some ghastly film for Hal Wallis. I said to someone who worked for Colonel Parker, 'I'm very impressed with Elvis in the recording studio because he knows what he wants, but these songs are awful rubbish.' I was told it had to be that way as the Colonel took slices of the royalties and many writers wouldn't accept that. He didn't just want the publishing, which was a foregone conclusion, but half of the writer's royalties as well. I said, 'Is there any chance of me writing a song for Elvis?' and as they said, 'Yes', I thought of his capabilities and what brought out the best in his voice.

I wrote 'The Girl Of My Best Friend', which was released as a B-side, but the American jocks turned it over and made it a hit. That was just fortuitous."

Although Otis Blackwell wrote "Don't Be Cruel", "All Shook Up" and "Paralyzed" by himself, the label says "Blackwell - Presley". Elvis, it appeared to me, was doing nothing new: Al Jolson used to claim credits on songs he didn't write. Freddy disagreed: "It's not quite the same thing. In the early days, Elvis would show dissatisfaction with some lines and he would make alterations, so it wasn't just what is known as a 'cut-in'. His name did not appear after the first year, but if Elvis liked the song, the writers would be offered a guarantee of a million records and they would surrender a third of their royalties to Elvis."

On the other hand, the New York manager, Doug Yeager, tells me, "I've heard many of the original demos by Otis Blackwell and I know that Elvis would record them note for note and also inflection for inflection from the way Otis sang them."

For 12 years, nearly every song that Presley recorded went through Freddy Bienstock. "He had only had limited education, but he had been to high school and he was very street smart. He was clever in that respect. You couldn't fool him and he had a terrific song sense. I once played a song for him and after eight bars he took it off and said, 'That's not for me.' I was sure that it was a good song for him so I put it aside, and about nine months later, I thought I would resubmit it. I put it on and he listened to the first eight bars and then said, 'I didn't like it the first time and I don't like it now.' I was stunned that he would have remembered those eight bars. I was embarrassed about that."

THE MONKEES

In 1963 Don Kirshner sold Aldon to Screen-Gems Columbia for $2m, although he was still running the day to day operations. It was an astute move at the time as no-one could have predicted the true value of these copyrights due to reissues, revivals, tribute bands and commercials. In 1964 Kirshner thought he had done well as the upsurge of the Beatles and Bob Dylan encouraged performers to record their own material and there was not such a demand for Screen-Gems material. It was not hip to have your songs written by some third party. Some writers found a lifeline with the Monkees and then the Archies, both groups being manufactured (in very different ways) by Kirshner.

Barry Mason, who wrote "Delilah" and "The Last Waltz", recalls, "When I was doing really well, I met a guy in a pub and he was pestering me. A publisher pulled me to one side and said, 'Ignore that guy. His name's Michael Carr. He was a big songwriter twenty years ago, but he's now a drinker. He's always bugging people to write with him and he's a bit of a pest.' Anyway, I got talking to him and he told me that he had written 'South Of The Border' which was the first song that I had ever sung in my life. I was lost in admiration as he had written some wonderful songs".

"I said, 'Michael, I'd love to write a song with you', never expecting it to be anything good. I just thought it would be an experience to talk to him and listen to the stories of the past. We left the pub, both of us had had some drinks, and we walked down Denmark Street, looking for an office that was still open and we found a room with a piano. I can see it now with the little light on the piano, and Michael played me the beginning of this idea that he'd had, and I loved it, and in the early hours of that morning we finished '1-2-3 O'Leary'. It was Michael's title and it was a children's game that he knew from Ireland. Des O'Connor cut it and it was an instant hit, but the tragedy was that Michael died before he could see Des give him his comeback hit."

One day in 1962, 10 Brill Building writers including Neil Diamond got together and wrote "Ten Lonely Guys", which was recorded by Pat Boone. They are all given namechecks in the lyric. This must top the list for a multiple composing credit, unless of course, the 101 Strings wrote something in a recording break.

NEIL DIAMOND

The Brill Building is still functioning - Paul Simon has maintained an office there for over 30 years - but there are now major publishers in other American cities. Indeed, there are probably more songwriters in Nashville than New York, and not all are writing country. Intriguingly, the Nashville publishers usually insist that writers co-write their songs - not one lyricist and one music man, but two songwriters. The publishers therefore have their risks reduced by having the wagon pulled by two horses instead of one.

Recently, as an experiment (presumably in money-making), some key Nashville and New York songwriters have been working together. However, they are unlikely to match the astonishing success of Dianne Warren, who writes both words and music and runs her own publishing company, Realsongs. Her many hits include "I Don't Want To Miss A Thing" and "How Do I Live", and both Johnny Mathis and Patti LaBelle have recorded albums of her songs.

Freddy Bienstock: "Everything was done on a much more personal basis at that time - now it all about money and guarantees and so forth. I also think that the quality of the songs was higher. A song was presented to a publisher and it was discussed and then given to an artist, who had some input into it, and so by the time Tony Bennett, Frank Sinatra or Perry Como recorded the song, the song had been fashioned into something that was quite right. The standards fell with the advent of albums as so many more songs were needed and it was difficult to cherrypick in the same way. Very often the performer or his advisers thought they could write them themselves. That is why we have so few new standards nowadays."

One great Tin Pan Alley story is that songs had to pass the Old Grey Whistle Test. If the doorman could remember it after one hearing, it stood a chance of being a hit. Mitch Murray: "If you look at my songs, they only have four or five chords maximum as that's all I know. That may sound amateurish but it forces me to write very melodic songs. I can't rely on clever chords to make them sound beautiful, and today's writers can really fool you with their chords. At the end of it, they won't stand up as songs you can whistle. Nowadays, they are record writers. In my day, the songs were often hits despite the records but you can't say that now. They have to be good records."

HERE'S ONE I MADE EARLIER
Same title, different songs

The songwriter Sammy Cahn criticised modern songwriters for not even bothering to come up with original titles. Here are some well-known songs with distinctive titles, only someone else had thought of the title first. As Dr John says, "You can't copyright the blues and you can't copyright a title."

I've ignored some of the more obvious duplicates - for example, six different songs called "Always" have made the UK charts. I'd have thought that there would have been hundreds of songs called "True Love" but the title doesn't appear to have been used until Cole Porter wrote a song for Bing Crosby and Grace Kelly in 1956. Since then, Joan Armatrading, Glenn Frey and Joe Longthorne have recorded different songs called "True Love". In the early 60s, the Dave Clark Five recorded two songs called "Because" and then Dave wrote and produced a new song called "Because" for Julian Lennon from the West End musical, "Time" (1985). In-between there was the Beatles' "Because" on "Abbey Road".

Title	*First song*	*Second song*
ABSOLUTE BEGINNERS	Jam (1981)	David Bowie (1986)
ACHY BREAKY HEART	George Jones (1962) (As "Aching, Breaking Heart")	Billy Ray Cyrus (1992)
ALL AROUND THE WORLD	Little Richard (1956)	Jam (1977) *Third song:* Lisa Stansfield (1989), *Fourth song*: Jason Donovan (1993), *Fifth song*: Oasis (1998)
ALL THE WAY	Frank Sinatra (1957)	Robert Cray (1999)
ALL YOU NEED IS LOVE	Beatles (1967)	Holly Johnson (1999) (As "All U Need Is Love")
ALWAYS SOMETHING THERE TO REMIND ME	Sandie Shaw (1964)	Housemartins (1988) (As "There Is Always Something There To Remind Me")

ANGEL EYES	Frank Sinatra (1958) (song written in 1953)	Abba (1979), *Third song*: Roxy Music (1979)
BAND OF GOLD	Don Cherry (1955)	Freda Payne (1970)
BANG BANG	Cher (1966)	B.A. Robertson (1979)
BARCELONA	Musical: "Company" (1970)	Freddie Mercury (1987)
THE BEST IS YET TO COME	Tony Bennett (1959)	Scootch (2000)
BLUE EYES	Don Partridge (1968)	Elton John (1982)
BLUE MONDAY	Fats Domino (1956)	New Order (1983)
CALL ME	Petula Clark (1965)	Blondie (1980), *Third song* - Go West (1985), *Fourth song* - Spagna (1987)
CANDY MAN	Roy Orbison (1961)	Sammy Davis Jr (1972)
CHAINS	Cookies (1962)	Tina Arena (1995)
C'MON EVERYBODY	Eddie Cochran (1958)	Elvis Presley (1964)
CONGRATULATIONS	Cliff Richard (1968)	Traveling Wilburys (1988)
COUNTRY BOY	Fats Domino (1960)	Head Hands And Feet (1971)
CRAZY	Patsy Cline (1961)	Mud (1973), *Third song* - Seal (1990), *Fourth song* - Eternal (1994), *Fifth song* - Mark Morrison (1995), *Sixth song* - Lucid (1999)
CRY BABY CRY	Larry Clinton (1938)	Beatles (1968)
DANCING IN THE DARK	Fred Astaire (1931)	Kim Wilde (1983), *Third song* - Bruce Springsteen (1984)
DEVIL WOMAN	Marty Robbins (1962)	Cliff Richard (1976)
DONNA	Ritchie Valens (1958)	10cc (1972)
DON'T BE CRUEL	Elvis Presley (1956)	Bobby Brown (1988)
DON'T PLAY THAT SONG	Ben E. King (1962)	Nicki French (As "Don't Play That Song Again") (2000)
DON'T GO BREAKING MY HEART	Burt Bacharach (1965)	Elton John and Kiki Dee (1976)
DON'T LET THE SUN CATCH YOU CRYING	Ray Charles (1959)	Gerry and the Pacemakers (1964)
DRIVE MY CAR	Beatles (1965)	David Crosby (1989)
FIRE	Crazy World Of Arthur Brown (1968)	Pointer Sisters (1979)
FROM THIS MOMENT ON	Writer: Cole Porter (1950), later a success for Frank Sinatra	Shania Twain (1998)
HAVE I TOLD YOU LATELY THAT I LOVE YOU	Gene Autry (1946), then Elvis Presley (1957)	Van Morrison (1989), then Rod Stewart (1993)
HEARTBEAT	Ruby Murray (1954)	Buddy Holly (1958)

HEARTBREAK HOTEL	Elvis Presley (1956)	The Jacksons (1980) *Third song* : Whitney Houston (1998)
HELP YOURSELF	Tom Jones (1968)	Julian Lennon (1991)
HERE COMES THE SUN	Vincent Lopez (1930)	George Harrison (1969)
HEY GOOD LOOKIN'	Ethel Merman (1942) (written by Cole Porter)	Hank Williams (1951)
HOMEWARD BOUND	Harry Cooper (1917)	Simon and Garfunkel (1966)
HOW DO YOU DO IT	Show, "Ballyhoo Of 1932", co-written by Yip Harburg	Gerry And The Pacemakers (1963)
I CAN'T STOP LOVING YOU	Don Gibson (1958), Ray Charles (1962)	Leo Sayer (1978)
I FORGOT TO REMEMBER TO FORGET	Elvis Presley (1955)	Travis Wammack (1973)
I STAND ACCUSED	Jerry Butler (1965)	Merseybeats (1966)
I'LL NEVER FALL IN LOVE AGAIN	Johnnie Ray (1959)	Lonnie Donegan (1962), then Tom Jones (1967), *Third song* - Bobbie Gentry (1969)
I'LL SAIL MY SHIP ALONE	Moon Mullican (1950)	The Beautiful South (1989) ("I'll Sail This Ship Alone")
IF	Perry Como (1950, written 1934)	Bread (1971)
IF I RULED THE WORLD	Harry Secombe (1963)	Kurtis Blow (1986)
I'M DOWN	The Beatles (1965)	The Hollies (1974)
IT'S OVER	Roy Orbison (1964)	Jimmie Rodgers (1966)
IT'S SO EASY	Buddy Holly & Crickets (1958)	Andy Williams (1970)
JUST THE WAY YOU ARE	Gordon Macrae (1950)	Billy Joel (1977)
KEEP THE HOME FIRES BURNING	Ivor Novello (1914)	Bluetones (2000)
KNOCK ON WOOD	Dooley Wilson (1942)	Eddie Floyd (1966)
LET ME ENTERTAIN YOU	Show "Gypsy" (1959)	Robbie Williams (1998)
LONELY BOY	Paul Anka (1959)	Andrew Gold (1977)
THE LOOK OF LOVE	Dusty Springfield (1965)	ABC (1982)
LOVE ME DO	Beatles (1962)	Badfinger (1970)
LUCILLE	Little Richard (1957)	Kenny Rogers (1977)
MARIA	From "West Side Story" (1957)	Blondie (1999)
MISS YOU	Rudy Vallee (1929)	Rolling Stones (1978)
MOTHER	John Lennon (1970)	The Police (1983)
THE MOST BEAUTIFUL GIRL (IN THE WORLD)	Rodgers and Hart for Broadway musical, "Jumbo" (1935)	*Second song* - Charlie Rich (1974) *Third song* - Prince (1994)

MY LOVE	Petula Clark (1966)	Paul McCartney (1973)
MY WAY	Eddie Cochran (1959)	Frank Sinatra (1969)
NEW ORLEANS	Elvis Presley (1958)	U. S. Bonds (1960)
NINE TO FIVE	Sheena Easton (1980)	Dolly Parton (1980)
NO REGRETS	Tommy Dorsey & His Orchestra (1936)	*Second song* - Shirley Bassey (1965), originally French song, "Non, Je Ne Regrette Rien". *Third song* - Tom Rush (1967), then Walker Brothers (1976).
NO MATTER WHAT	Badfinger (1971)	Boyzone (1998)
OH CAROL	Neil Sedaka (1959)	Smokie (1976)
ONE FINE DAY	From "Madam Butterfly" (1904)	Chiffons (1963)
ONLY THE LONELY	Frank Sinatra (1958)	Roy Orbison (1960)
ONLY YOU	Platters (1954, new version a hit in 1955)	Yazoo (1982), *Third song* - Praise (1991)
PAPA DON'T PREACH	Betty Hutton (1947) (As "Poppa Don't Preach")	Madonna (1986)
PEEK-A-BOO	Cadillacs (1958)	New Vaudeville Band (1966)
PERFECT DAY	Writer, Carrie Jacobs Bond (1910)	Lou Reed (1972), star-studded charity version (1997)
A PICTURE OF YOU	Joe Brown (1962)	Boyzone (1996)
THE POWER OF LOVE	Frankie Goes To Hollywood (1984)	Huey Lewis & News (1985), *Third song:* Jennifer Rush (1985)
P.S. I LOVE YOU	Writers: Johnny Mercer - Gordon Jenkins (1934), US hit for Hilltoppers	Beatles (1962), *Third song:* Curtis Mayfield (1976)
RIP IT UP	Little Richard (1956)	Orange Juice (1983)
ROCK AROUND THE CLOCK	Hal Singer (1950)	Bill Haley (1954)
RUNAWAY	Del Shannon (1961)	Janet Jackson (1995), *Third song:* The Corrs (1995)
SAVE THE LAST DANCE FOR ME	Arthur Tracy (1931)	Drifters (1960)
SCHOOLDAY	Writers: Will D.Cobb, Gus Edwards, ("Schooldays") (1907)	Chuck Berry (1957)
SHAME SHAME SHAME	Jimmy Reed (1963)	Shirley And Company (1975)
SHIP OF FOOLS	World Party (1987)	Second song - Erasure (1988), *Third song* - Tansads (1994).
SINGING THE BLUES	Bix Beiderbecke (1927)	Marty Robbins (1956), then Guy Mitchell and Tommy Steele
THE SPIDER AND THE FLY	Fats Waller (1938)	Rolling Stones (1965)
STAIRWAY TO HEAVEN	Neil Sedaka (1960)	Led Zeppelin (1972)
STAND BY ME	Ben E. King (1961)	Oasis (1997)

STAY	Maurice Williams (1961)	Shakespears Sister (1992)
SUCH A NIGHT	Clyde McPhatter & Drifters (1954)	Dr John (1973)
TEARS ON MY PILLOW	Little Anthony And The Imperials (1958)	Kylie Minogue (1990)
TIME AFTER TIME	Writers: Sammy Cahn - Jule Styne (1947)	Cyndi Lauper (1984)
TWO OF US	Emmie Joyce (1926)	Beatles (1969)
THE VERY THOUGHT OF YOU	Ray Noble (1934)	Bob Dylan (Unreleased 1984)
VENUS	Frankie Avalon (1959)	Shocking Blue (1970)
WALK ON BY	Leroy Van Dyke (1961)	Dionne Warwick (1964)
WATERLOO	Stonewall Jackson (1959)	Abba (1974)
WHAT IN THE WORLD'S COME OVER YOU?	Jack Scott (1960)	Rockin' Berries (1964)
WHY WORRY	Donald Peers (1951)	Dire Straits (1985)
WISHING WELL	Free (1973)	Terence Trent D'Arby (1987)
WOMAN	Paul McCartney for Peter and Gordon (1966)	Mike McGear (1972) *Third song:* John Lennon (1980)
WONDERWALL	George Harrison (1968)	Oasis (1995)
WOMAN IN LOVE	Frankie Laine (1956)	Three Degrees (1979), *Third song* - Barbra Streisand (1980)
YESTERDAY	Fred Astaire (1935) ("Yesterdays")	Beatles (1965)
YOUNG AT HEART	Frank Sinatra (1954)	Bluebells (1984)
YOUNG BLOOD	Coasters (1957)	Rickie Lee Jones (1979)
YOU'VE GOT A FRIEND	James Taylor (1971)	Big Fun and Sonia (1990)
YOU WIN AGAIN	Hank Williams (1952)	*Second song* - "So You Win Again" by Hot Chocolate (1977) *Third song* BeeGees (1987)

Most songwriters, if confronted with an earlier song, deny having heard it. Robin Gibb told me that he had never heard Hank Williams' "You Win Again" and when I challenged that, he said that he didn't listen to country music.

Similarly, Gerry Marsden denies having heard Ray Charles' "Don't Let The Sun Catch You Crying" despite the fact that Mersey groups were pillaging R&B repertoires for songs to cover. That may be true, but the publishers of the original song demanded £7,000 compensation and the song's title is now written as "Don't Let The Sun (Catch You Crying)". Gerry and the Pacemakers were unlucky because as said earlier, you can't copyright a title.

It's refreshing to come across Clive Gregson who freely admitted he had borrowed the Who's title, "Tattoo", or Holly Johnson, who said his "All U Need Is Love" was a tribute to the Beatles. "I'm not like Oasis," he contended, "At least I come from Penny Lane."

AS TIME GOES BY
Part 2 - 1925 - 1949

1925 - ALWAYS (Irving Berlin)

Colour bar legal in South Africa - George Bernard Shaw wins Nobel prize - Books include "The Great Gatsby", "The Trial" and "Mein Kampf".

Irving Berlin had a secretary, Arthur Johnston, who helped with the transcription of his songs. One day Irving was chatting to Johnston's girlfriend and she asked if he would write a song about her sometime. Always one for showing off, he said, "Why not now?" and dashed off "I'll Be Loving You, Mona". Arthur dutifully jotted it down, but they thought little of it at the time. Some months later, Irving Berlin came across the song - he couldn't recall writing it and Arthur was no longer dating Mona. With slight adjustments, the song became "Always". Irving Berlin was getting married, so he assigned the copyright to his bride as a wedding present. This is an unparalleled act of generosity in Berlin's life, although he was still keeping it in the family.

Al Jolson was also feeling generous. His new stage musical, "Big Boy", featured him on horseback, and he didn't care for one of the songs. He passed "If You Knew Susie" to Eddie Cantor, which became his biggest hit. Years later in a radio broadcast, he told Eddie, "If I'd known the song was that good, I'd never have given it to you."

The songwriter Jack Yellen gave Sophie Tucker a gift of "My Yiddisher Mama", with both English and Yiddish lyrics. The wacky Charleston was the dance craze of the year and many songs had "Charleston" in their titles - like "The Twist", the best-known is "The Charleston". Other 1925 songs are "Sweet Georgia Brown", "Dinah", "Yes, Sir, That's My Baby", "Girls Were Made To Love And Kiss", "On Mother Kelly's Doorstep", "Pal Of My Cradle Days", "Tea For Two" and a striking homage to New York from Rodgers and Hart, "Manhattan".

*"We'll have Manhattan
The Bronx and Staten
Island too."*

Wordplay doesn't come any finer.

1926 - ARE YOU LONESOME TONIGHT?
(Roy Turk - Lon Handman)

Princess Elizabeth born, later Queen Elizabeth II - First General Strike in UK in support of miners (Chant of the year: "Not a penny off the pay, Not a minute on the day") - "Winnie The Pooh" is published and "Ben Hur" excites cinemagoers - Hirohito becomes Emperor of Japan.

"Are You Lonesome Tonight?" is Al Jolson's great lost recording. I've never seen it on CD and yet it is one of his best performances. The song was written by two Tin Pan Alley songwriters, who included a narration based on Jacques' speech from "As You Like It". Jolson's recording was quickly followed by one from Vaughn Deleath, who was the first woman to sing on radio.

Outside of publishing deals, "Are You Lonesome Tonight?" is the only song which Colonel Parker asked Elvis to record. Elvis copied Jolson's arrangement note for note and word for word, and he recorded it late at night with the lights out in order to increase his emotional feelings. It became a transatlantic No 1 in 1960, and his laughing version, caught in concert in 1969, is taken by some as evidence that he was perpetually high and by others that he had a wonderful sense of humour.

Another Elvis favourite, "Hawaiian Wedding Song", also dates from 1926 and other songs include "Baby Face" (a novelty song transformed by Little Richard), "Mountain Greenery" (its melody was "borrowed" by

Lionel Bart for "Fings Ain't Wot That Used T'Be"), "Bye Bye Blackbird", "The Black Bottom" (a dance of the day), "Side By Side", "When The Red, Red Robin Comes Bob-Bob-Bobbin' Along", and the jazz standard, "Muskrat Ramble". The Bachelors plundered 1926 for "Diane", "Ramona" and "Charmaine", which is also associated with Mantovani's cascading strings. (Mantovani's sound can be attributed to an arranger with the distinctive name of Ronald Binge.)

"Tango Tzigane" by the Danish violinist, Joseph Gade, was a continental hit and given a lyric, "Jalousie". In 1938 Patience Strong, who wrote sentimental homilies for the "Daily Mirror", had her finest hour when she wrote the English lyric, "Jealousy". Joseph Gade died in a concentration camp during the Second World War, but the songwriter, Harry Ralton, who wrote "I Remember The Cornfields", was luckier. He was imprisoned in Auschwitz and was spared by a German commandant who liked his songs.

Seeing poverty in America, Bud Flanagan wrote "Underneath The Arches", which he later made famous with Chesney Allen. More optimistically, there are the Gershwins' "'S Wonderful" and "Someone To Watch Over Me" and Irving Berlin's "Blue Skies", which was introduced by Belle Baker in the musical, "Betsy". Irving was sitting in the front row and when Belle forgot the words, he shot to his feet, gave her a prompt and joined her in the song.

1927 - OL' MAN RIVER
        (Jerome Kern - Oscar Hammerstein II)

Charles Lindbergh flies solo from New York to Paris - Stalin expels Trotsky from Communist party - Al Jolson stars in the first "talkie", "The Jazz Singer" - Trotsky publishes "Problems Of Everyday Life".

"Show Boat", a musical about life on the Mississippi, contained several well-known songs, "Make Believe", "Can't Help Lovin' Dat Man", "Bill" and, most successful of all, "Ol' Man River". At the last minute, Hammerstein had felt the show needed a song about the Mississippi itself but Kern was too busy as he had accepted other work. Hammerstein told him not to worry: if he slowed down the banjo music in Act One, he would have the tune he needed. Hammerstein wrote about the changelessness of

PAUL ROBESON

he river but it is now regarded as a protest song, largely because of its association with the civil rights activist, Paul Robeson. The word "niggers" is usually replaced by "natives" today.

Sometime later, an admirer told Mrs Kern how much he admired "Ol' Man River". Mrs Hammerstein, who happened to be there, corrected him: "Mr Kern wrote 'Dum-dum-dum-dum'," she said, "My husband wrote 'Ol' Man River'." Having said that, for some years, Kern demanded that his name be larger than Hammerstein's on the sheet music, which must have been very demeaning for Hammerstein. Kern's ego reached its peak in 1942 when he received a full screen credit for "You Were Never Lovelier" while his co-writer, Johnny Mercer, had to share a screen with others.

Ironically, ol' man river was misbehaving and Charley Patton, a Mississippi blues musician who played the guitar behind his head, wrote about the flood of 1927 in "High Water Everywhere".

During the year, Gene Austin was looking down that "Lonesome Road", and other good songs were "The Best Things In Life Are Free", "Among My Souvenirs" and two songs everybody knows, "Bless This House" and "Seven Drunken Nights". Fats Waller revived "I Ain't Got Nobody (And There's Nobody Cares For Me)", which is described on the sheet music as a "Slow Drag".

1928 -   SONNY BOY
          (Buddy DeSylva - Lew Brown - Ray Henderson)

          The Thames bursts its banks, flooding parts of
          London - Voting age for women lowered to
          21 - Alexander Fleming discovers penicillin -
          First Mickey Mouse cartoon.

Al Jolson was following his very successful film, "The Jazz Singer", with "The Singing Fool". In one scene, he has to cope with the loss of his young son. The only way he could handle this was through song and so he rang some songwriting friends in New York and asked for one. They could not take the commission seriously and laughed their way through the schmaltzy "Sonny Boy". Al Jolson laughed too but he realised that audiences everywhere would be reaching for handkerchiefs. "Sonny Boy" sold three million copies, the biggest-selling record to that time.

The same three composers also wrote "Together" in 1928 and other hits of the year were "Love Me Or Leave Me", "St James Infirmary" (with Louis Armstrong and arguably about a hospital in Bristol), "Lover, Come Back To Me", "I Wanna Be Loved By You" (now associated with Marilyn Monroe) and "My Baby Just Cares For Me", which found a new lease of life in 1987 when Nina Simone's recording was used on a TV ad for Chanel perfume. In 1928, there was also a competition to complete Schubert's "Unfinished Symphony", but as it is still regarded as unfinished, the entries can't have been impressive.

The German playwright, Bertolt Brecht, worked with a classical composer who loved jazz, Kurt Weill. Their best-known work, "The Threepenny Opera (Dreigroschenoper)", opened in Berlin in 1928 starring Weill's wife, Lotte Lenya, and was based on John Gay's play, "The Beggar's Opera" (1728). The avant-garde musical satirised post-war Germany, and "Mack The Knife" is about a gangster, Macheath, who is always around but never caught. The song's German title, "Mordtat", translates as "murder deed". Weill moved to America to escape persecution from the Nazis and he wrote with Ira Gershwin, Ogden Nash and Alan Jay Lerner.

An intriguing CD which puts Brecht and Weill's music in context is Ute Lemper's "Berlin Cabaret Songs", released in both English and German versions in 1997. I'd never heard these 1920s songs before and the subject matter includes lesbianism, gay rights and political satire. Hitler soon put a stop to that.

Country music was a new force to be reckoned with via the Carter Family's "Wildwood Flower" and Jimmie Rodgers' "Blue Yodel No.1", better known as "T For Texas". Eddie Cantor, every bit as mannered as Al Jolson, recorded "Makin' Whoopee" (later recorded by Nilsson and Ray Charles), and Cole Porter wrote the cleverest lyric of the year with the innuendo-laden "Let's Do It". Porter regularly updated his lyric and his friend, Noël Coward, also performed his own version. I have even heard it revised for Y2K, starting with "Blairs do it."

1929 -   STARDUST
          (Hoagy Carmichael - Mitchell Parish)

          Labour government comes to power under
          Ramsey MacDonald - St Valentine's Day
          Massacre - Securities on the New York Stock
          Exchange collapse.

Hoagy Carmichael lived in Bloomington, Indiana and, in his adolescence, played the piano in a coffee-house, The Book Nook. He returned there in 1927 and as he remembered his girlfriend, Dorothy Kelly, the melody for "Stardust" came to him. He persuaded the proprietor not to close until he had completed it. He played it to a friend, Harry Hostetter, and a few days later, he was surprised to find Harry playing it himself. Harry said, "Oh, it's just in case you forgot it." In 1929 "Stardust" was an instrumental success, and some brilliant, poetic lyrics by Mitchell Parish were added in the same year. Both of Hoagy Carmichael's autobiographical books took their title from his song, "Sometimes I Wonder" and "The Stardust Road".

FATS WALLER,

54

Other great songs were that Sting favourite, "Spread A Little Happiness", "Without A Song", "With A Song In My Heart", "If I Had A Talking Picture Of You" (how topical can you get?) and two Fats Waller gems, "Honeysuckle Rose" and "Ain't Misbehavin'". Noël Coward wrote a romantic waltz, "I'll See You Again" and Irving Berlin was "Puttin' On The Ritz". Gus Cannon introduced the catchy "Walk Right In" and the Cuban composer, Ernesto Lecuona, wrote "Andalucia Suite", one of whose movements became "Malagueña".

The sentimental "Tears", which was recorded by Rudy Vallee, was popular but the song did not become a phenomenon until 1965 when Ken Dodd's singalong treatment became the biggest selling record of the year, even outstripping the Beatles.

"Happy Days Are Here Again" was written for a film about World War I, "Chasing Rainbows", but the composers gave it to the bandleader, George Olsen, who introduced it the night the stock market collapsed. All the diners at the Hotel Pennsylvania were in a state of shock, but when George said, "Sing it for the corpses", they brightened up. "Happy Days Are Here Again" became the theme song for the Democratic Party. Avoid the painfully slow interpretation by Barbra Streisand.

1930 - MOOD INDIGO
        (Duke Ellington - Irving Mills - Barney Bigard)

        Ninth planet discovered and named Pluto -
        Gandhi encourages civil disobedience
        in India - First World Cup with Uruguay
        beating Argentina 4-2.

Born in 1899, Edward Ellington acquired his nickname, Duke, when he was just a child and from his teens, he worked as a pianist and then a bandleader. His band had a residency at the Cotton Club in Harlem and became well-known for both orchestrated and improvised jazz. In time, he wrote concertos, sacred music and symphonies as well as straight jazz.

DUKE ELLINGTON

He recorded "Mood Indigo" in 1930 under the title of "Dreamy Blues". He said that it was "a story about a little girl and a little boy. They are about eight and the girl loves the boy. They never speak of it, but she just likes the way he wears his hat. He comes to her house everyday and she sits in her window and waits. One day he doesn't come. 'Mood Indigo' tells how she feels."

Duke wrote the main theme for "Mood Indigo", while his clarinetist, Barney Bigard, helped with the melody for the verse. Mitchell Parish wrote the lyric but missed out on the credit, being usurped by Irving Mills, who took a composing credit as well as all the publishing. Ellington fell out with Mills when he asked him to buy a $5,000 coffin for his mother's funeral and Irving bought a cheap one and pocketed the balance.

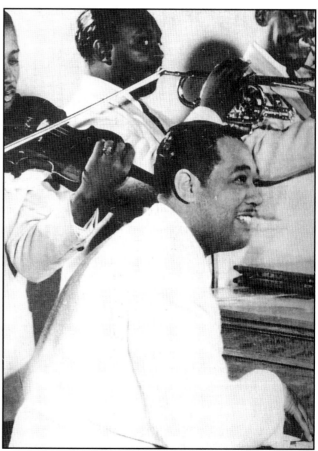

DUKE ELLINGTON AT THE PIANO

Hoagy Carmichael wrote "Georgia On My Mind", but was it about a girlfriend or the State? Then there are the syncopated "I Got Rhythm" (introduced by Ethel Merman), "I'm Confessin' (That I Love You)", "They All Laughed", "But Not For Me" and the controversial "Ten Cents A Dance" - when the song was filmed, the "pansies and rough guys" in the original became "dandies and rough guys".

George Gershwin's musical, "Strike Up The Band", was a controversial satire on war and diplomacy. Ira Gershwin wrote the lyric for the opening marching song and subsequently changed them for America's entry into World War II. He later revised them for UCLA, which ensured him a season ticket to their ball games.

"Falling In Love Again" came from the film, "The Blue Angel", which was filmed in both English and German and made a star of Marlene Dietrich. Eric Coates' idyllic "By The Sleepy Lagoon" is still used to introduce "Desert Island Discs". Jelly Roll Morton's "If Only Someone Would Love Me" could easily have inspired Tommy Reilly's theme music for "Dixon Of Dock Green".

1931 -   AS TIME GOES BY
           (Herman Hupfeld)

Oswald Mosley forms UK fascist party - First Highway Code published - National government saves UK from economic disaster - Boris Karloff stars in "Frankenstein" and Charlie Chapin makes "City Lights", which contains no dialogue.

In 1931 Herman Hupfeld wrote "As Time Goes By" for a Broadway revue, "Everybody's Welcome", where it was sung by Frances Williams. It was recorded by Rudy Vallee who also sang a controversial song of Hupfeld's the following year, "Let's Put Out The Lights And Go To Bed". The BBC banned this record and the song was changed to "Let's Put Out The Lights And Go To Sleep".

The making of the 1942 film, "Casablanca" is a book in itself. Ronald Reagan was replaced by Humphrey Bogart, and the principals were not told how the story would develop. It contains the memorable line, "Play it, Sam, play 'As Time Goes By'", which is invariably misquoted as "Play it again, Sam". The singer-pianist Sam is played by Dooley Wilson.

MORNING HAS BROKEN
Words by
ELEANOR FARJEON
Musical Arrangement by
CAT STEVENS

Also from the year are "Don't Put Your Daughter On The Stage, Mrs. Worthington", "Mad Dogs And Englishmen" (both Noël Coward), "Dancing In The Dark", "Dream A Little Dream Of Me", "Lazy River", "I Apologise", "On The Sunny Side Of The Street" and "River, Stay 'Way From My Door". The Street Singer, Arthur Tracy, had success with an English version of a Cuban song, "Marta". Another Cuban composition, "El Manisero", became "The Peanut Vendor". Someone, quite inappropriately, added lyrics to Mendelssohn's "Songs Without Words".

Suppose you read Psalm 118, verse 24:

"This is the day which the Lord hath made; we will rejoice and be glad in it."

Would it inspire you? Maybe not, but the children's author, Eleanor Farjeon, wrote a poem, "Morning Has Broken", around that verse. She thought little of it at the time and sold it for $3. It was set to a Gaelic tune from 1888, but Cat Stevens wrote a new melody in 1971.

The "Daily Mirror" published a poem, "Love Letters In The Sand", which was set to music. It was recorded by Russ Columbo, becoming his first major success. Columbo scored a succession of hits, writing "Prisoner Of Love" himself, but he was killed in 1934 when a friend struck a match on an antique pistol on his desk, not knowing it was loaded. Another of Russ Columbo's hits: "You Call It Madness".

Also, Cab Calloway sang "Minnie The Moocher", the "hi-de-hi, hi-de-ho" song, which was stacked with drug references. Marijuana was regarded as a harmless craze and the songs of the period include "Smokin' Reefers" and "Chant Of The Weed". Louis Armstrong, who is said to have smoked marijuana every day of his working life, recorded his paean to the drug, "Muggles" in 1928.

The lyrics of Cole Porter's "Love For Sale" were considered too disgusting for British ears so Al Bowlly hummed the tune with Roy Fox and his Band. Quite possibly, the song was more a comment on the Depression than on prostitution. There was no doubting the intention of the union anthem, "Which Side Are You On?", written by a Kentucky coal-miner's daughter, Florence Reese, while her father was on strike.

Gracie Fields's first talkie, "Sally In Our Alley", included "Sally". In her final Royal Variety Performance in 1978 at the age of eighty, she said, "I've been singing a man's song all my life."

1932 - TRY A LITTLE TENDERNESS
(Harry Woods - James Campbell - Reginald Connelly)

Eamon de Valera becomes President of the Irish Free State - Amelia Earhart flies solo across Atlantic - Hunger marchers fight police in Hyde Park - King George V makes first Christmas Day broadcast - Aldous Huxley publishes "Brave New World", which contains a definition of "muzak", "The world was continuously alive with gay, synthetic melodies".

OTIS REDDING

The songwriter Harry Woods (1896 - 1970) wrote "Paddlin' Madeline Home" (1923), "When The Red, Red Robin Comes Bob-Bob-Bobbin' Along" (1926), "I'm Looking Over A Four Leaf Clover" (1927) "River Stay 'Way From My Door" (1931) and "What A Little Moonlight Can Do" (1934). He was born with no fingers on one hand and yet he managed to work out his melodies on the piano. His songs were often novelties, but "Try A Little Tenderness" is a very sensitive song about relationships. The definitive version to some is by Frank Sinatra and to others, by Otis Redding.

Otis changes "the same old shabby dress" to "the same old shaggy dress", and I wonder why. Harry's songs were published by Campbell, Connelly & Co Ltd, which explains the co-writers.

Despite only having one playing hand, Harry Woods worked at a tough bar in Times Square. One night he got into a fight and repeatedly banged his opponent's head on the bar with his good arm. Two people were sitting there and one said to the other, "That's Harry Woods, the man who wrote 'Try A Little Tenderness'."

Other songs of the year include "How Deep Is The Ocean", "I'm Getting Sentimental Over You", "The Sun Has Got His Hat On", "Ain't It Grand To Be Bloomin' Well Dead?", "I've Told Every Little Star", "Don't Bring Lulu", Maurice Chevalier's "Louise" and "Brother Can You Spare A Dime", which is covered in the next chapter. Duke Ellington's "It Don't Mean A Thing (If It Ain't Got That Swing)" is the first song to mention "swing".

Noël Coward's show tune, "Mad About The Boy", was about the love of four people for a worthless film star, but is now regarded as a message on his own sexuality. The other musical showman of the West End, Ivor Novello, was also at pains to hide his sexuality, and his female admirers had no idea about his private life. His songs have not aged as well as Coward's but he wrote a succession of West End hits including "Glamorous Night" (1935), "Careless Rapture" (1936), "Crest Of The Wave" (1937) and "The Dancing Years" (1939).

Cole Porter's stage musical, "The Gay Divorce", starred Fred Astaire, and Porter wrote a song, "Night And Day", that would both help the dancer regain his breath and not tax his pleasant, but limited, vocal range. Speaking on "Breakfast With Frost" in January 2000, Spike Milligan chastised the music of today ("all this crap now") and added, "All these kids have never heard a tune like 'Night And Day'."

1933 - STORMY WEATHER
(Harold Arlen - Ted Koehler)

Adolf Hitler becomes Chancellor of Germany and orders boycott of Jewish businesses - Bodyline bowling by England in Australian test series - Prohibition ends in America.

1934 - ANYTHING GOES (Cole Porter)

Bonnie and Clyde ambushed and killed - Hitler expels suspected traitors from Nazi party in "the night of the long knives" - Driving tests made compulsory - Belisha beacons invented.

Harold Arlen and Ted Koehler (pronounced "Cola") wrote the Cotton Club revues, and "Stormy Weather" was introduced by Ethel Waters, who recalled the night in her autobiography: "When I got out there in the middle of the Cotton Club floor, I was singing the story of my own misery and confusion, the story of the wrongs and outrages done to me by people I had loved and trusted. I sang 'Stormy Weather' from the depths of my private hell in which I was being crushed and suffocated." Must have been one hell of a performance.

Other songs of the year include "Smoke Gets In Your Eyes", "Easter Parade", "Hold Me", "Blue Moon", "Don't Blame Me", "My Happiness", and the song that gave country music a bad name, "Old Shep". "Old Father Thames" was London's answer to "Ol' Man River" and its writer Betsy O'Hagan was a pseudonym for the publisher, Lawrence Wright.

COLE PORTER

In April 1933 the country singer, Jimmie Rodgers, travelled by sea from San Antonio to New York for RCA recording sessions, knowing that he was so ill that he would not return alive. He had several new songs that he wanted to record and a bed was brought to the studio so that he could rest between takes. On May 24th 1933 he recorded his final song, "Fifteen Years Ago Today", and the next day he lapsed into a coma, dying on the 26th at the age of 35.

1934 was Cole Porter's year as his musical, "Anything Goes", had a stupendous score, including three famous 'list' songs, "I Get A Kick Out Of You", "You're The Top" and the title song. Even Cole Porter himself called it "a perfect show - a show that needed no tinkering after the opening night." The show did not have a title when the rehearsals began and when the leading man, William Gaxton, was asked to delay his entrance, he said, "Okay. Anything goes." Cole Porter loved the expression and rushed home to complete a song, returning with it the next day. The show was daring, suggesting the decadence of the 1930s, and "sniffing cocaine" in "I Get A Kick Out Of You" would not have been allowed had it been a Tin Pan Alley rather than a show tune.

Cole Porter originally wrote "I Get A Kick Out Of You" with amusing references to the aviator, Charles Lindbergh and his wife. When their infant son was kidnapped and then murdered, he substituted the offending lines and in so doing, came up with the most glorious multiple rhyme in popular music:

*"**Flying** too **high** with some **guy** in the **sky***
*Is **my i**dea of nothing to do,*
*But **I** get a kick out of you."*

Sometimes, though, Cole Porter was too clever for his own good, and his worst couplet has to be in "Let's Not Talk About Love":

"Honey, I suspect you all
Of being intellectual."

The Sussex-born conductor and arranger, Ray Noble lived from 1903 to 1978 but he only published 50 songs. He had a high success rate, scoring with "Goodnight Sweetheart" (1931), "Love Is The Sweetest Thing" (1932), "The Very Thought Of You" (1934) and "Cherokee" (1936).

Shirley Temple was "On The Good Ship Lollipop" in the film "Bright Eyes", which is about a 'plane, not a boat, called Lollipop. "With Her Head Tucked Underneath Her Arm" was a far wittier novelty song. The ballads included "I Only Have Eyes For You" and "I Don't Know Why". The trumpeter, Wingy Manone, wrote "Isle Of Capri", and he had lost an arm as a child in a tram accident in New Orleans. Every Christmas Bing Crosby gave him one cufflink, so presumably Bing bought his presents every other year.

The country music hits included "Tumbling Tumbleweeds" and "Cattle Call", which is normally sung so badly that it curdles the milk. "Winter Wonderland" was a seasonal hit.

A Mexican song, "Cuando Vuelva A Tu Lado", became "What A Diff'rence A Day Made". The Czechoslovakian "Skoda Lasky" was given an English lyric, "Lost Love", although it is now better known as an instrumental, "Beer Barrel Polka"!

The stage musical, "The Gay Divorce", was turned into a film tour de force for Fred Astaire and Ginger Rogers under an amended title, "The Gay Divorcée". A fifth of the film was taken up with a sensational, 18 minute production number, "The Continental", written by Con Conrad and Herb Magidson. The song won the first Oscar for Best Song.

SIDNEY POITIER &
DOROTHY DANDRIDGE
'PORGY AND BESS' (1959)

1935 - SUMMERTIME
(George Gershwin - DuBose Heyward)

Radar invented - Speed limit of 30 mph for built-up areas - Germany passes laws legitimising the persecution of Jews and "Negro or Jewish" music is banned from German radio - Alcoholics Anonymous formed - Launch of Penguin Books - Garbo appears in "Anna Karenina".

Both Jerome Kern and George Gershwin had plans to turn the stage play, "Porgy" by DuBose Heyward, into a musical. Kern planned to use Al Jolson in blackface, but Gershwin was more sophisticated and less patronising, insisting that the parts should be played by Negroes. This stipulation continues to this day. Although Gershwin had written several hits, "Porgy And Bess" only had limited success and Gershwin died in 1937, at the age of 38, not realising how popular it would become.

"Porgy And Bess" uses Afro-American rhythms to stunning effect with the score including "I Got Plenty O' Nuttin'", "Bess, You Is My Woman Now" and "Summertime". George's brother, Ira, wrote, "He takes two simple quatrains of DuBose's, studies the lines, and in a little while a lullaby called 'Summertime' emerges - delicate and wistful, yet destined to be sung over and over again."

Al Dubin and Harry Warren won an Oscar for "Lullaby Of Broadway" from the film, "Gold Diggers Of 1935". Al Dubin is a fascinating, unpredictable character who lived for food and fun. He weighed over 20 stone and he wrote his lyrics on menus. Harry Warren was publicity shy and the studio boss, Jack Warner, told him that he had won the Oscar in order to get him to attend the ceremony. It worked, but Warner's plan could have backfired as the other nominees were Irving Berlin's "Cheek To Cheek" (from "Top Hat") and Jerome Kern's "Lovely To Look At" (from "Roberta").

Big Joe Williams introduced the blues song, "Baby Please Don't Go" and many artists picked up on "Milkcow Blues Boogie". Fats Waller had fun with "My Very Good Friend The Milkman" and "I'm Gonna Sit Right Down And Write Myself A Letter". Seven-year-old Shirley Temple sang "Animal Crackers In My Soup" with sixty orphans in her 30th film, "Curly Top" - and no, that's not a mistake: no-one could work a child so hard nowadays. Then there's "Red Sails In The Sunset", "Cool Water", "I'll Never Say 'Never Again' Again", "I'm In The Mood For Love" and the Cole Porter standard, "Just One Of Those Things". Porter also defied convention with a sensual look at a South American dance, "Begin The Beguine", which he wrote on a cruise somewhere between Kalabahi and the Fiji Islands.

Like 1977, it was also a year of a Silver Jubilee and Betty Driver, later a "Coronation Street" actress, recorded "Jubilee Baby".

1936 -   ORANGE BLOSSOM SPECIAL
           (Ervin T. Rouse)

           George V succeeded by Edward VIII -
           German troops enter the Rhineland - Civil
           war in Spain - GPO introduces a talking clock,
           "Tim" - Jarrow march - Edward VIII abdicates
           and George VI becomes King.

Ervin, Gordon and Earl, the Rouse Brothers, were a country band from Florida, and Ervin would entertain audiences with a fiddle piece that "was a little bit crazy". The Rouse Brothers played it to simulate a train coming, and their manager, Lloyd Smith, convinced a railway company that it would be the perfect music to promote their new Miami to New York service. He would even name the tune after the train, "Orange Blossom Special". The Rouse Brothers were delighted but then they didn't know Smith had copyrighted the song in his own name. "Orange Blossom Special" became popular and it took a year for Ervin Rouse to establish his composing credit and hence, royalties. In 1939 he thought that the song needed a lyric and he wrote one about the train itself. Bill Monroe and Bob Wills started playing the tune and it has become a country cliché, although good musicians can still make it exciting. The Hellecasters play a 25 minute instrumental version in concert, which is fantastic.

A close second for my song of the year is "These Foolish Things (Remind Me Of You)", which, according to record labels, is written by Holt Marvell, Jack Strachey and Harry Link. The song has an American sophistication, but it is British with Holt Marvell being a pseudonym for the BBC employee, Eric Maschwitz. He hid his identity because he feared that his employer would not approve. Frank Sinatra included the song on one of the world's first albums, "The Voice" (1945) and his reflective performance of this song about lost romance is definitive. James Brown converted it to a soul ballad in 1963 and it was the title track of a best-selling album by Bryan Ferry ten years later. The most poignant version in recent years has been by Aaron Neville in 1993.

Other gems from 1936 include "The Way You Look Tonight", "The Music Goes Round And Round", "Goody Goody", "It's A Sin To Tell A Lie", "Beyond The Sunset", "Pennies From Heaven", "Is It True What They Say About Dixie?" and "In The Chapel In The Moonlight". The humorist from 'The New Yorker', Dorothy Parker, wrote a plaintive song "I Wished On The Moon", with Ralph Rainger.

Then there's the ultimate death disc, "Gloomy Sunday", an Hungarian song which had to be withdrawn as many Hungarians, on hearing the song, leapt out of windows and topped themselves. Paul Robeson's version was in keeping with the sombre mood of the times in America. Five years later came the best-known version by Billie Holiday, but as far as I know, the Americans stayed resolutely alive.

No such problems in the UK as George Formby was cleaning windows, although that too was banned. The BBC didn't give the saucy song airplay until the 1950s:

> *"Pyjamas lying side by side,*
> *Ladies' nighties I have spied,*
> *I've often seen what goes inside*
> *When I'm cleaning windows."*

1936 was also the year in which the young Ruth Jones said to the bandleader, Lionel Hampton, "I don't care what you call me so long as you give me a job." He named her Dinah Washington.

GEORGE FORMBY

1937 -   MY FUNNY VALENTINE
           (Richard Rodgers - Lorenz Hart)

Germans bomb Guernica - Frozen foods on sale - Edward marries Mrs Simpson - Air-raid shelters built in UK cities - Billy Butlin opens first holiday camp at Skegness - Japan bombs Shanghai - J.R.R. Tolkien publishes "The Hobbit".

Lorenz Hart hated his size (just five foot tall), his looks, his homosexuality and his drunkenness. He was disorganised but he could work fast, usually because he wanted to get to the bar, and one dazzling lyric followed another. Despite Lorenz Hart's problems, Richard Rodgers was spoiled as his second partner, Oscar Hammerstein, laboured over his words. In 1937, for example, Rodgers and Hart wrote "My Funny Valentine", "Where Or When" and "The Lady Is A Tramp". "My Funny Valentine" contains autobiographical touches and despite its tenderness, you can sense the self-loathing below the surface. When Hart died in 1943, his final words were "What have I lived for?"

In recent years, I have been working with Bob Wooler, the former DJ at the Cavern, on his autobiography. Bob often sends me letters with his views on various musical topics and, apropos of nothing, he sent me his comments on Sarah Vaughan's interpretation of "My Funny Valentine". "I consider this to be a monstrous mistreatment of a lovely song, a classic example of how not to interpret a song. There is a complete and high-handed departure from the tune, which the composer must have sweated over to perfect for the sentiment of the song. This is purely and simply an excuse for vocal histrionics and unadulterated showing-off. Sarah Vaughan can't be a true artist to take such liberties with someone else's efforts. It is ugly and gross and horrible and these remarks are being kind to her - I could have resorted to a torrent of four-letter words." It is great that some people can still be passionate about this wonderful music.

In the 1937 film, "Feather Your Nest", a singer has difficulty in recording "Leaning On A Lamppost", and so he asks a technician to sing it for him, hoping that no-one will notice the difference. It is one of the few romantic songs in George Formby's repertoire.

It was a good year for novelty songs - the Seven Dwarfs sang "Whistle While You Work" and everybody was dancing "The Lambeth Walk", actually on the south side of the Thames. Allan Jones, the father of Jack, sang "The Donkey Serenade". Then there's the gospel song, "Farther Along", Duke Ellington's "Caravan", Irving Berlin's "I've Got My Love To Keep Me Warm", Bob Hope's theme song "Thanks For The Memory" and a song associated with Dinah Washington, "September In The Rain".

A Portuguese composition, "Lisbon, Antigua", was recorded but it didn't find American success until Nelson Riddle's version in 1956, which was used in the Ray Milland film, "Lisbon". An instrumental recorded by Tommy Dorsey, "Dancing With You", was quickly given lyrics and became the standard, "Once In A While". Gene Krupa became the first drummer to play an extended solo on a record, namely, "Sing, Sing, Sing".

Cole Porter admired a French song and when he realised that its title translated as "I've Got You Under My Skin", he set about using the phrase himself. Fanny Brice made the song popular and once again, it was full of sensuality and innuendo. Cole Porter was also asked to write the title song, "Rosalie", for a Nelson Eddy film. Louis B. Mayer rejected six of his melodies so in the end, he slung together some musical clichés and thereby wrote a No 1 song. The film also included a Cole Porter standard, "In The Still Of The Night". It was, however, a dreadful year for him as a horse fell on his legs and he was in appalling pain for the rest of his life.

COLE PORTER

1938 -   GOD BLESS AMERICA (Irving Berlin)

Germany annexes Austria - Chamberlain signs "Peace in our time" deal with Hitler - Orson Welles' radio broadcast of "The War Of The Worlds" creates havoc.

In 1918 Irving Berlin wrote the patriotic "God Bless America", but he felt it was too solemn and wasn't surprised when it was rejected for his show, "Yip! Yip! Yaphank". He put it in his files and forgot about it. Twenty years later, with the world on the brink of a second world war, he decided to write a great peace song. He toyed with several ideas and then realised that "God Bless America" was perfect. He passed it to Kate Smith for an Armistice Day broadcast. It was an instant hit and despite Berlin's intentions, it became a rallying cry when America went to war. Now it is as close to an American national anthem as you can get.

Noël Coward parodied the British peerage in "The Stately Homes Of England", some sixty years before Tony Blair started reforming the House of Lords. No wonder he only received his knighthood towards the end of his life. He wrote in his 1970 diary, "During lunch, the Queen asked me whether I would accept Mr Wilson's offer of a knighthood. I said, 'Yes, ma'am.' Apart from that, my seventieth birthday was uneventful."

Kurt Weill, now in America and working with Maxwell Anderson, wrote the stage musical, "Knickerbocker Holiday", which included the peg-legged Peter Stuyvesant character as a satire on Roosevelt. Walter Huston agreed to play the role providing he had a tender song, "a moment for the old son of a bitch to be charming". Weill sent him a telegram asking for his vocal range and Huston wired back, "No range, no voice". Challenged by this, they wrote a reflective piece about growing old, "September Song". The very phrase, "The days grow short", says it all. "September Song" became a hit for Bing Crosby and then Charles Coburn performed it in the film of "Knickerbocker Holiday". Huston's version was used in the 1951 film, "September Affair".

This fine year also produced the cheerfulness of "You Must Have Been A Beautiful Baby" (once cheekily sung by Maurice Chevalier to the Queen Mother), "My Prayer", "I've Got A Pocketful Of Dreams", "Two Sleepy People", "Me And My Girl", "Love Walked In", "San Antonio Rose" and, wait for it, "Knees Up Mother Brown".

Ella Fitzgerald asked the songwriter, Van Alexander, to do something with a nursery rhyme that she liked and he wrote the standard, "A-Tisket, A-Tasket". On a higher plane, Samuel Barber's "Adagio For Strings" has become one of the world's best-known classical pieces following its use in the film, "Platoon", and the Old Spice ads.

1939 -   OVER THE RAINBOW
(Harold Arlen - E.Y. Harburg)

Spanish Civil War ends with victory to fascists under General Franco - Germany occupies whole of Czechoslovakia - Germany and USSR sign non-aggression pact - Germany and the USSR both invade Poland and divide the country between them - Start of Second World War - Books include "The Grapes of Wrath" (John Steinbeck) and "Old Possum's Book Of Practical Cats" (T. S. Eliot)

Bad move. Shirley Temple's agent turned down "The Wizard Of Oz" and the role went to Judy Garland. Garland was a seasoned 16 year old playing 12, and so she could bring a maturity to the songs. The lyricist, Yip Harburg, rejected one of Harold Arlen's melodies, thinking it more suited to Nelson Eddy than a young girl from Kansas. Arlen discussed the problem with Ira Gershwin, who suggested a quicker tempo, and Harburg then wrote about rainbows and lemon drops. He said, "The girl from Kansas had no colour in her life. The only thing colourful would be a rainbow." The producers disliked the song at first but fortunately it wasn't removed from the print, as happened to some sequences, and the song won an Oscar. Garland, for some reason, was given a special Oscar: if she had competed normally, would she have beaten Vivien Leigh in "Gone With The Wind" as best screen actress?

JUDY GARLAND

"Over The Rainbow" became Judy Garland's signature tune and when her own life was tormented, she turned the song into one of hope. In her final performances, she would say, "I'm still looking for those bluebirds", and perform the song with tears in her eyes.

There was "Deep Purple", "Scatterbrain", "Jeepers Creepers", "Day In, Day Out", "South Of The Border", the wartime "Run Rabbit Run", Glenn Miller's exhilarating "In The Mood", and two of America's greatest gospel songs - "Peace In The Valley" and "Take My Hand, Precious Lord". The bandleader, Kay Kyser recorded the infuriatingly catchy "Three Little Fishes" and it was so insidious that an inmate of the Kansas State Penitentiary killed another convict who kept singing it.

Glenn Miller was so impressed with "Stardust" that he asked its lyricist, Mitchell Parish, to write the words for "Moonlight Serenade". He also picked up "In The Mood" after Artie Shaw failed to record it. Andy Razaf was paid a flat $200 to write the lyric and although better known as an instrumental, it has been recorded by Bette Midler.

The songwriter Ross Parker was told by his publisher to write a patriotic British song to rival "God Bless America". He asked a serviceman about the motto on his cap, "Semper fidelis", which meant "Always faithful". This led to "There'll Always Be An England" and a few months later he wrote "We'll Meet Again". Was World War Two was started by Vera Lynn's agent?

FATS DOMINO

1940 - YOU ARE MY SUNSHINE
(Jimmie Davis - Charles Mitchell)

Second World War - Churchill becomes Prime Minister - Rationing in UK - Hitler invades Netherlands, Belgium and France - Churchill says of Battle of Britain pilots, "Never was so much owed by so many to so few." - Britain blitzed - Chaplin satirises Hitler in "The Great Dictator".

Jimmie Davis was a country singer who recorded risqué songs in the early 1930s such as "Tom Cat And Pussy Blues". He turned to more conventional material and he wrote "Nobody's Darlin' But Mine", "It Makes No Difference Now" with Floyd Tillman, and, in 1940, "You Are My Sunshine", with his steel guitarist, Charles Mitchell. It was sung by Tex Ritter in the film, "Take Me Back To Oklahoma", and became a pop and country success. Davis had undertaken political work in Shreveport and in 1944, he stood as the Democratic candidate for the Governorship of Louisiana. His opponents paraded his early recordings as proof that he was unfit to hold office, but he used "You Are My Sunshine" as his campaign song and won. He later became a gospel singer, finding a third use for his most famous song as "Christ Is My Sunshine". Davis celebrated his 100th birthday in September 1999 (although this was three years early according to some encyclopedias!) and he is still performing.

The first ever record sales chart was published by "Billboard" in July 1940. Tommy Dorsey was at No 1 with "I'll Never Smile Again" and also at No 8 with "Imagination". His brother Jimmy, was at No 2 with "The Breeze And I", with Glenn Miller at No 3, also with "Imagination"

"Blueberry Hill" became a No.2 US hit for the Glenn Miller Orchestra, while Gene Autry sang it in the 1940 western, "The Singing Hills". Both Fats Domino and Louis Armstrong had success with "Blueberry Hill" in 1956. Glenn Miller also recorded an instrumental based around the telephone number of a hotel in which he was staying, "Pennsylvania 6-5000".

Eric Coates wrote "Calling All Workers" for his wife who was working for the Red Cross. It became the signature tune for "Music While You Work" and it was thought that its rhythms caused cows to produce more milk.

Lorenz Hart wrote a brilliant, provocative lyric, "Bewitched, Bothered And Bewildered", for the Rodgers and Hart musical, "Pal Joey". The contentious lines included:

> *"Vexed again, perplexed again,*
> *Thank God I can be oversexed again -*
> *Bewitched, bothered and bewildered am I."*

That all-embracing love song, "All The Things You Are", comes from 1940 and so also do "When You Wish Upon A Star" (from Walt Disney's "Pinocchio"), "Whispering Grass", "That's When Your Heartaches Begin", "When The Swallows Come Back To Capistrano" (all three recorded by the Ink Spots), "So Long It's Been Good To Know You" (Woody Guthrie), and an uplifting song for wartime England, "A Nightingale Sang In Berkeley Square", another song from Eric Maschwitz. Ornithologists have pointed out that nightingales never sang in Berkeley Square, but you've got to have some poetic imagination.

1941 - LONDON PRIDE (Noël Coward)

> Royal Navy sinks the Bismarck - Hitler conquers Yugoslavia and Greece - Rudolf Hess imprisoned - Germany invades Russia and Soviet forces drive Germans back - Japan bombs Pearl Harbour, bringing America into the war - Orson Welles is the star, writer and director of "Citizen Kane".

Noël Coward had seen the street sellers with their bunches of lavender, begging passers-by to buy some "London pride". Some of them sang an age-old song, "Who'll Buy My Violets", and Coward was intrigued to find the tune had been appropriated by the Germans for "Deutschland über Alles". Time he thought to return the tune back to London where it belonged.

All this came together in "London Pride", which is a brilliant song and not just a pious hymn. It is witty and lively and reading the lyrics, you can see how skilfully Coward captured the bulldog spirit:

> *"Ev'ry blitz your resistance toughening,*
> *From the Ritz to the Anchor and Crown,*
> *Nothing ever could override*
> *The pride of London town."*

The Brits themselves weren't above pilfering. "Lili Marlene" by the cabaret performer, Lale Andersen was the first German record to sell a million, with the words written in 1915 and melody, 1939. It was given an English lyric, and so, amazingly, this song was sung by the troops on both sides. Vera Lynn sang her clarion call, "The White Cliffs Of Dover", which is an American song, while "Bless 'Em All" soon had ribald lyrics. Richard Addinsell's "The Warsaw Concerto" was featured in the war film, "Dangerous Moonlight". "I Don't Want To Set The World On Fire", "Perfidia", and, God help us, "I Came, I Saw, I Conga'd" were also among the year's successes.

1942 - WHITE CHRISTMAS (Irving Berlin)

> US recaptures Pacific islands taken by Japanese - Montgomery defeats Rommel at El Alamein - Germans reach Stalingrad - Magnetic recording tape invented.

The film, "Holiday Inn", is about a rich, lazy hotelier, who only opens for the holidays. Irving Berlin was commissioned to write holiday songs and he had "Easter Parade" (1933) in the bag. Although a cantor's son, Berlin realised that Christmas was the most important holiday and so his song had to be great and not just very good. He kept "White Christmas" as simple as possible as a few images can speak volumes, but his introduction about being in the heat of Los Angeles is rarely performed. (The Carpenters have recorded it.) Irving Berlin appeared in his office the next day and said, "Not only is this the best song I have written, it is the best song that anybody has ever written." When Bing Crosby took the song from the excited composer, he said coolly, "You don't have to worry about this one, Irving."

That year Irving Berlin was asked to present the Oscar for the Best Song, and he became the only person in the whole history of the Academy Awards to present himself with an Oscar. Not that it would have bothered him. He would have been mortified if he'd had to hand over the statuette to a competitor. In 1957, Irving was so annoyed when Elvis Presley recorded a playful, mocking, rocking "White Christmas" that he phoned radio stations and begged them not to play it.

No song could rival "White Christmas" for the song of the year, but "That Old Black Magic", "I Remember You" (both by Johnny Mercer), "Happiness Is Just A Thing Called Joe" and "Born To Lose" are all excellent. You could be stunned by "Sabre Dance" and you could dance to "Chattanooga Choo Choo" or "The Cokey Cokey", now better known as "The Hokey Cokey". "Deep In The Heart Of Texas" was so infectious that the BBC banned it from daytime listening as workers were using their tools for banging the machinery to keep time with the song.

Bette Davis starred in the cruising romance, "Now, Voyager" and when she learnt that her lover was married, she said, "Oh, Jerry, we have the stars, let's not ask for the moon." Max Steiner's score won an Oscar, and words were added to the theme music to create a hit record for Dick Haymes, "It Can't Be Wrong", the following year. Many years later the song was revived by US protesters for the gay cause, who put a new interpretation on the line, "Would it be wrong to kiss?".

JOHNNY MERCER

1943 -   OH WHAT A BEAUTIFUL MORNIN'
(Richard Rodgers - Oscar Hammerstein II)

German forces in Stalingrad surrender - German U-boats withdraw from North Atlantic - Red Army tanks defeat the Germans at Kursk - Mussolini flees and Italy surrenders.

"Oklahoma!" was a trendsetting musical as it didn't open with a chorus line (it opened with this ballad), had a serious plot (including a death), and included a ballet. It was the first Rodgers and Hammerstein musical and the score included "People Will Say We're In Love", "The Farmer And The Cowman", the rousing "Oklahoma!" (which has become the State's official song) and "Oh What A Beautiful Mornin'", which is now associated with Howard Keel. Hammerstein sweated six weeks over the lyric for "Oh What A Beautiful Mornin'" and then he rang Rodgers to say he had the lyric he wanted. Rodgers noted it down and called him back an hour later with the melody. Rodgers found it difficult to give compliments and even Hammerstein's best efforts only raised the response, "It's adequate".

The rhythmic "Beat Out Dat Rhythm On A Drum" and the novelty "Pistol Packin' Mama" are other hits of the year. Well in keeping with the times was Noel Coward's "Don't Let's Be Beastly To The Germans", although its humour was misunderstood by many.

"Don't let's be beastly to the Germans
When our victory is ultimately won,
It was just those nasty Nazis
who persuaded them to fight
And their Beethoven and Bach are really
far worse than their bite."

Following a union dispute, a recording ban by American musicians began. To circumvent this, Dick Haymes recorded new songs with only vocal accompaniment by the Song Spinners. The songs, "It Can't Be Wrong" and "You'll Never Know", were smash hits.

WOODY GUTHRIE

1944 -   THIS LAND IS YOUR LAND
(Woody Guthrie)

Allies bomb Nuremberg - First prefab homes
- Huge seaborne invasion against the
Germans - Paris liberated.

Woody Guthrie was a left-wing radical, endlessly cam-
paigning for the rights of workers and the common man.
He wrote sharp, pithy lyrics but he plundered existing
ballads for his tunes - "Pastures Of Plenty" used "Pretty
Polly", and "Roll On Columbia" resembled "Goodnight
Irene", but "So Long, It's Been Good To Know You" and
"Reuben James" appear to be original melodies.

Like many left-wingers, Guthrie hated the jingoism of
Irving Berlin's "God Bless America". Why should God
bless America and nowhere else? Why should politics be
interwoven with religion? Why should Americans feel
that they need do nothing because God has blessed them?
How he hated the song and, in 1940, he wrote a parody,
"God Bless America (For Me)", to the tune of a Baptist
hymn, "Oh My Lovin' Brother". Four years later, he
amended his lyric to "This Land Is Your Land". Woody
never sought commercial acclaim for his songs, but this
became popular as the theme for his weekly show on a
New York radio station. Even if you knew nothing of
Woody's politics, this was a marvellous song about the
beauty of America.

The songwriter Scott Wiseman was being visited in hospital by his wife and before she left, she whispered, "Have
I told you lately that I love you". Despite being ill, he
started writing the song and once recovered, he passed it
to the cowboy singer, Gene Autry, who recorded it in
1946.

Brilliant ballads surfaced in "Love Letters" (Ketty Lester,
Elvis Presley, Alison Moyet) and Cole Porter's "Ev'ry

Time We Say Goodbye" (underrated at the time but taste-
fully revived by Ella Fitzgerald). This gives the lie to the
oft - repeated view that Cole Porter wrote nothing decent
after his accident. Sy Oliver delivered a distinctive instru-
mental but inspiration ran out with the title, a simple
"Opus One". Cheerful novelties alleviated the gloom of
the war including "Maizy Doats And Dozy Doats",
"Maybe It's Because I'm A Londoner", "Swingin' On A
Star", "The Trolley Song" (about a tram) and "Ac-Cent-
Tchu-Ate The Positive". The jazz bandleaders, Duke
Ellington and Harry James, merged their talents to write
"I'm Beginning To See The Light", another apt comment.

1945 -   YOU'LL NEVER WALK ALONE
(Richard Rodgers - Oscar Hammerstein II)

Bombing of Dresden - Mussolini captured
and shot - Hitler commits suicide - Germany
surrenders - USA drops atomic bombs on
Hiroshima and Nagasaki, and Japan surrenders - United Nations formed - George Orwell
publishes "Animal Farm" and biros and
Tupperware come into being.

Richard Rodgers and Oscar Hammerstein wrote
"Carousel" in 1945, the score containing "June Is Bustin'
Out All Over" and "If I Loved You". Their inspirational
ballad, "You'll Never Walk Alone", was unusual in that the
title only occurred in the final line. Frank Sinatra was the
first to record it. Some rock'n'roll performers sang it,
notably Gene Vincent, Roy Hamilton and Conway
Twitty. In 1963 Gerry and the Pacemakers completed
their hat-trick of No 1's with their recording. The song
was taken up by the Kop choir at Liverpool FC and is now
the city's anthem. In 1985 Gerry led a new, all-star recording for the Bradford City fire appeal.

"You'll Never Walk Alone" touched the optimism that
people felt now that the war was ending. Ivor Novello's
"We'll Gather Lilacs" from his lavish, stage musical,
"Perchance To Dream", was written with that in mind.
Other songs of the year were "Laura", "Long Ago And Far
Away", "Since I Fell For You" and "The More I See You",
and jazz musicians were experimenting with the
polyrhythms and improvisation of bebop. Benjamin
Britten wrote his famed opera, "Peter Grimes".

In July 1945, Lou Preager and his Dance Orchestra were featured in a new BBC radio contest, "Write A Tune", which boasted £1,000 prize money for the best song submitted. It was so much money that the BBC was inundated with songs - 73,853 to be precise. The winners were Eily Beadell and Nelly Tollerton with "Cruising Down The River On A Sunday Afternoon", which was sung and then recorded by Paul Rich. It became a standard and it was the title song of the 1953 US film, "Cruising Down The River", featuring Dick Haymes and Billy Daniels. Incidentally, the BBC's prize money came from the Hammersmith Palais, an early example of radio sponsorship and almost certainly flaunting the BBC's rules.

1946 -   THERE'S NO BUSINESS LIKE SHOW
         BUSINESS (Irving Berlin)

         IBM introduces the first computer - Churchill
         warns of the Iron Curtain and recommends
         reconciliation of France and Germany - US
         report suggests link between cigarette
         smoking and lung cancer - The first bikinis.

Jerome Kern had been contracted to write a musical about the western heroine, Annie Oakley called "Annie Get Your Gun". When he died, Irving Berlin was asked to take over the score and he decided, typically, that it should be a musical about show business rather than hillbillies. Within a few days, he had written rough versions of "Doin' What Comes Naturally", "Anything You Can Do", "You Can't Get A Man With A Gun", "They Say It's Wonderful" and the tour de force, "There's No Business Like Show Business". The song is associated with Ethel Merman and it was also the title song of a 1954 film starring Marilyn Monroe and Johnnie Ray. Irving Berlin disliked the film of "Annie Get Your Gun" so much that he stipulated in his will that it was not to be shown publicly again, so you won't catch it on TV.

Walt Disney's version of the Uncle Remus stories, "Song Of The South", began with Uncle Remus strolling down a country lane and singing "Zip-A-Dee-Doo-Dah". Everything was satisfactul with this song as it was transformed into a Phil Spector classic by Bob B. Soxx and the Blue Jeans in 1962. Two great ballads also surfaced in 1946, "You Always Hurt The One You Love" and "Come Rain Or Come Shine".

In the early 1940s the jazz singer Mel Tormé formed a songwriting partnership with the lyricist Bob Wells. They wrote title songs for the films, "Abie's Irish Rose" and "Magic Town". In the summer of 1945, Mel went to Bob's house in the San Fernando Valley. It was unlocked so he let himself in and found that Bob had left a lyric on the table:

> "Chestnuts roasting on an open fire,
> Jack Frost nipping at your nose,
> Yuletide carols being sung by a choir
> And folks dressed up like Eskimos."

When Bob returned, he told Mel that it was so hot that he'd been thinking of Christmas to cool himself down. Mel was impressed with the lyric and they completed the song, simply called "The Christmas Song", that afternoon. Mel was not yet recording himself so in 1946, his publisher, Johnny Burke, asked Nat "King" Cole to record it as a Christmas single. Nat sang, "To see if reindeers really know how to fly". Mel was furious and told him that the plural of "reindeer" was "reindeer" and that he'd ruined a perfect take. Nat dutifully sang the song again. Nat should have looked in a dictionary and told him to get lost - most dictionaries give both spellings. Shortly afterwards, Mel Tormé recorded the song himself and his is the only version I've heard with an introductory verse and, of course, no "reindeers" in sight.

Nat 'King, Cole is also associated with another song from 1946, "(Get Your Kicks On) Route 66": American place names, "Flagstaff, Arizona, Don't Forget Winona" have a romanticism about them.

NAT "KING" COLE

1947 - GOOD ROCKIN' TONIGHT (Roy Brown)

         Coal industry nationalised - India achieves
         independence - British government bans
         midweek sporting events "to keep workers
         from getting tired" - Dead Sea Scrolls
         discovered - First Edinburgh festival.

The New Orleans songwriter, Roy Brown had something more intimate than dancing in mind when he wrote "Good Rockin' Tonight". He introduced his earthy song as an occasional vocalist with the Wynonie Harris band. Harris recorded it himself, and both performers had success with the song.

When Elvis Presley recorded the song in 1954, he sensibly dropped the references to the hits of the day, "Sweet Lorraine" and "Sioux City Sue", and this verse is rarely sung now. The phrase, "good rockin' tonight", has passed into common currency and was the title for an autobiographical musical about the TV producer, Jack Good, in 1992. It is also the name of some high-profile US record auctioneers.

Merle Travis' "Sixteen Tons" and Tex Williams' "Smoke! Smoke! Smoke! (That Cigarette)" were adult novelties: Travis made a serious point about workers being paid in tokens that they could only use at their bosses' stores but Tex Williams had no idea of the damage that cigarettes could cause. Willie Nelson was to have success with "Blue Eyes Crying In The Rain" and Edith Piaf introduced her most famous song in 1947, "La Vie En Rose".

Tennessee Williams' groundbreaking play, "A Streetcar Named Desire", subsequently became a major film with Marlon Brando and Vivien Leigh. Dylan Thomas in a letter amusingly referred to it as "A Truck Named Fuck".

eden ahbez

1948 - NATURE BOY (eden ahbez)

Gandhi assassinated - GCEs replace the School Certificate - Jews in Palestine proclaim the state of Israel, and Arabs attack - National Health Service established - Morris Minor launched and everyone wants to play Scrabble - George Orwell writes "1984", reversing the final two digits of the current year - Christopher Fry wrote the play, "The Lady's Not For Burning".

eden ahbez - no capitals as he felt only the deity deserved them - was the first hippie. His real name was Alexander Aberle. He had a straggly beard and lived as a hermit under the Hollywood sign. His only possessions were a sleeping bag, some wooden flutes and a bicycle. He wrote the gentle "Nature Boy" about himself, and he thought Nat "King" Cole could do it justice. As it happened, Cole wanted to break into the more lucrative white market and was looking for the right song. Dressed in rags, ahbez turned up at the stage door, passed over his music and left without leaving a forwarding address.

He returned a week later by which time Cole had put the song into his act, which is a wonderful testimony to unsolicited material. "Nature Boy" became a standard and although ahbez passed songs to other artists and even made an album himself, he never surpassed "Nature Boy". This very strange enchanted boy was writing up to his death when he was over 80 years old.

Charles Trenet, became an aural Renoir when he wrote his evocative song about seaside resorts, "La Mer". He imagines white horses and heavenly angels out on the sea and he comments on what he sees in the reflections. The song became less imaginative when it was given an English lyric by Jack Lawrence, "Beyond The Sea", but nonetheless it won Bobby Darin a gold disc.

The poet Jacques Prevert wrote "Les Feuilles Mortes (Dead Leaves)" with the musician Joseph Korma. An executive at Capitol Records heard a French version and asked Johnny Mercer to write an English lyric. Jo Stafford and then Bing Crosby recorded "Autumn Leaves", but it was not a substantial hit until Roger Williams' piano instrumental in 1955, which cleverly duplicated the falling leaves with falling notes. Nat "King" Cole's version was put on the soundtrack of a 1956 film called "Autumn Leaves", starring Joan Crawford. The piece has also been recorded by such jazz luminaries as Miles Davis and Cannonball Adderley.

The narrative, "Deck Of Cards", was written and recorded by T. Texas Tyler but the song is a cheat. If you count the number of spots on a deck, it has to be divisible by 4, so how can it possibly be 365? Another country artist, Pee Wee King, had been performing "No Name Waltz" for years and it became "Tennessee Waltz" when his songwriting friend, Redd Stewart said, "Why is it that no one has written a waltz about Tennessee?" It is now the official state song of Tennesse although, having said that, they also have five others!

"Nice To Know You Care" by Norman Newell and the London club pianist, Leslie Baguley, deserves to be revived. It was originally recorded by Leslie Hutchinson (Hutch) and covered by Tommy Dorsey, the Dallas Boys and Tony Brent. Norman Newell was the godfather to Leslie Baguley's son, Craig, who owns and edits "Country Music People".

1948 was also the year of the first great doo-wop hit, "It's Too Soon To Know", a superb ballad written by Dorothy Chessler for the Orioles, not to mention Frank Loesser's "On A Slow Boat To China", who was on a slow boat to cancer as he smoked 80 cigarettes a day. And talking of Frank Loesser...

1949 - BABY IT'S COLD OUTSIDE (Frank Loesser)

Clothes rationing lifted - NATO established - German Democratic Republic set up in Soviet-occupied Berlin - China becomes a Communist country.

Frank Loesser and his wife had been performing a novelty duet, "Baby It's Cold Outside", at Hollywood parties for five years, but the public first heard it when it was performed by Red Skelton and Betty Garrett in the 1949 film, "Neptune's Daughter". The song deservedly won an Oscar - humorous duets are very hard to write - but some mean-spirited rivals complained that the award should be returned as it was not a new song. The numerous duet recordings include Ray Charles and Betty Carter, Ella Fitzgerald and Louis Jordan, Oliver Reed and Joyce Blair, and Tom Jones and Cerys Matthews from Catatonia.

Rodgers and Hammerstein had "South Pacific" up and running with its hit songs, "Some Enchanted Evening" and "Younger Than Springtime", while Ivor Novello was still writing new shows for the West End, this time "King's Rhapsody". Kurt Weill and Maxwell Anderson wrote a musical about apartheid in South Africa, "Lost In The Stars".

Hank Williams was at his saddest and most creative with "I'm So Lonesome I Could Cry", and another country standard came from the blind singer, Leon Payne, with "I Love You Because". It was also a year for bombastic, frontier songs - "The Cry Of The Wild Goose", "Ghost Riders In The Sky" and "Mule Train".

Pete Seeger, then with the Weavers, recalls, "In 1949 Lee Hays sent me four brief verses and said, 'Pete, do you think you can make up a tune?'. Like the old gospel hymns, only one word changed and you had a new verse. If I had a hammer, if I had a bell, if I had a song, etc. I put a tune to it but it wasn't as good a tune as it should have been, because the song never really went anywhere until three young people changed my tune. They kept the basic idea but they changed some of the notes, and their version went around the world. When I go round the world now, I have to laugh because most people sing it as Peter, Paul and Mary sing it and some, a few, may sing it as I wrote it. I change it still further. I decided that it must be a good song because it can be handled in so many different ways".

In 1939 a mail-order publisher in the US sent out a short story for Christmas. It was about Rudolph the Red-Nosed Reindeer and it was by Robert L. May, a man who missed out on royalties. Ten years later, Johnny Marks wrote a song based on the story and it became an international hit with over 500 recorded versions. Gene Autry was first, but he had to be persuaded by his wife, Ina, who thought it a clever variant on "The Ugly Duckling". The arranger, Dick Jacobs, agreed to take no fee if it was a flop, but double union rates if it was successful. As it happens, he got a handsome bonus as the drawling Autry topped the US pop and country charts in 1949 and the following year, it also made the Top 5.

"Blue Christmas" was also a seasonal hit and, for a sparkling end to this chapter, how about "Diamonds Are A Girl's Best Friend", written for the stage musical, "Gentlemen Prefer Blondes", by Leo Robin and Jule Styne. It was originally sung by the vivacious Carol Channing, who found fame in "Hello, Dolly!" and had a notable row with Elton John at a Royal Command Performance. She didn't land the film role, however, where the song was performed so gleamingly by Marilyn Monroe in 1953. I'm not sure about the premise, "gentlemen prefer blondes", but Elton certainly preferred that blonde as he wrote a song about her.

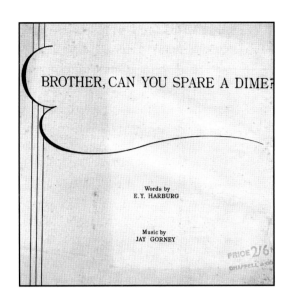

BROTHER, CAN YOU SPARE A DIME?
The story of the song

The pre-war Tin Pan Alley and Hollywood songs are not regarded as radical or reforming: those songs were written elsewhere by Woody Guthrie or can be found in the blues. There is, however, one major exception with the lyricist, Yip Harburg, who wrote "Brother, Can You Spare A Dime?", arguably the most significant song of the century.

Edgar Yipsel Harburg was born in New York on 8th April 1896: some books say 1898 but his centenary was celebrated in 1996. He was born into an immigrant family of Russian Jews on Manhattan's Lower East Side. His father worked in a clothes factory and his mother made hairpieces, and times were hard. From time to time they were evicted and Yip said, with hindsight, that his early life was far more exhilarating than his years in Hollywood.

As a teenager, Yip worked in a pickle factory and after that, was lighting and extinguishing street lamps for $3 a week. He was a bright lad and he was offered a place at City College, where he obtained a degree. His best friend was Ira Gershwin and together they wrote parodies and poems, which were well received.

In 1921 Harburg went into partnership with a college friend, selling electrical goods. He agreed to devote his time to the company and not publicise his verses. Although he didn't enjoy the work, the business built up well and by 1929, it was worth $250,000. Then came the Stock Market Crash and, like many other businesses, it fell to nothing. Ironically, it was the best thing that could have happened to Harburg. Ira Gershwin, now an established songwriter, sent him a rhyming dictionary with the inscription, "Start rhyming." He also introduced him to a possible collaborator, the pianist, Jay Gorney.

Harburg sold watches during the day, or at least tried to, and during the evening he would work with Gorney. They placed songs in revues, but the audiences for variety shows were dwindling with the Depression.

The Depression transformed American society. In 1925 only 3% of the nation's workforce was unemployed. By 1930, it was 9% and by 1933, it was 25%, which represents 13 million potential workers. Furthermore, millions of workers agreed to wage cuts in order to keep their jobs.

In 1931 Jay Gorney came to him with a completed song, "Big Blue Tears", but he did not care for the lyric he had been given:

> *"I will go on crying big blue tears*
> *'Til I know that you're true.*
> *I will go on crying big blue tears*
> *'Til all the seas run blue."*

Harburg appreciated the sadness in its melody and set about writing a more appropriate lyric. He later commented, "It was a terrible period. You couldn't walk along the street without crying, without seeing people standing in breadlines." The beggars simply asked for a dime, and that dime might have to keep them going until the next day.

Harburg did not want to write a maudlin lyric about someone who was down on his luck. He wanted to write about someone who had worked and fought for his country, and couldn't understand why he was being repaid in this way. "Brother, Can You Spare A Dime?" is a song of bewilderment.

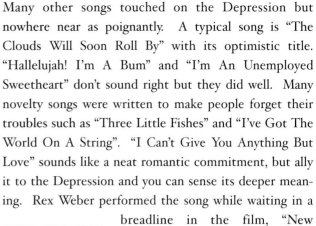

YIP HARBURG

> *"Once I built a railroad, now it's done,*
> *Brother, can you spare a dime?"*

The "brother" was a masterstroke. It was so much better than the "Mister" or the "Buddy" that performers sometimes mistakenly sing. It stressed kinship, fellowship, solidarity, that everyone was a part of the same family.

Jay Gorney liked the new lyric and the song was shown to the Broadway impresarios, the Shubert brothers, who weren't speaking to each other. One was for it, one against, but it was included in the 1932 show, "Americana".

"Brother, Can You Spare A Dime?" was recorded by Bing Crosby and the song became an immediate hit, the anthem of the dispossessed. It encapsulated the Great Depression as no-one could grasp what had happened and it was as much a protest song as anything Bob Dylan ever wrote. It was also recorded by Rudy Vallee and Al Jolson, although, admittedly, record sales were not high during the Depression years.

Many other songs touched on the Depression but nowhere near as poignantly. A typical song is "The Clouds Will Soon Roll By" with its optimistic title. "Hallelujah! I'm A Bum" and "I'm An Unemployed Sweetheart" don't sound right but they did well. Many novelty songs were written to make people forget their troubles such as "Three Little Fishes" and "I've Got The World On A String". "I Can't Give You Anything But Love" sounds like a neat romantic commitment, but ally it to the Depression and you can sense its deeper meaning. Rex Weber performed the song while waiting in a breadline in the film, "New America", in 1932.

Yip Harburg, realising his own good fortune at having his work recognised, threw himself into one project after another. In the next two years, he wrote, amongst others, "April In Paris" and "It's Only A Paper Moon", both of which became romantic standards. Jay Gorney, on the other hand, discovered the five-year-old Shirley Temple and thus helped to develop one of the 1930's biggest stars.

Yip Harburg often worked with Harold Arlen and their most famous work is their score for the film, "The Wizard Of Oz" (1938). You can twin "Brother, Can You Spare A Dime?" with "Over The Rainbow" as that, in its veiled way, is also a song of social concern:

> *"Birds fly over the rainbow,*
> *Why then, oh why, can't I?"*

Almost as imaginative as "The Wizard Of Oz" was "Finian's Rainbow", a 1947 stage musical written with Burton Lane and featuring "How Are Things In Glocca Morra?" The answer was probably "Not too good" as the Communist witch-hunt was starting in America, and many actors and writers found themselves blacklisted. The Senate objected to a musical he had written about the rights of women and Negroes, "Bloomer Girl", and Harburg found himself on the list. "I didn't mind," he later said, "I'm a rebel by birth. I contest anything that is unjust, that causes suffering for humanity. My feeling about that is so great that I couldn't live with myself if I weren't honest."

Yip was back in business after a few years and he wrote more direct, political material such as "Leave The Atom Alone" (1957). He gave a superb lyric to Pete Seeger about man's potential for destroying his own world, "Odds On Favourite", but Pete only set it to music recently, recording it on his 1999 CD, "Headlines And Footnotes". In addition to political songs, he has written the classic ballad, "Happiness Is Just A Thing Called Joe" and that hilarious Groucho Marx standby, "Lydia The Tattooed Lady".

"Brother, Can You Spare A Dime?" has been recorded by numerous folk artists including the Weavers, Spanky and Our Gang, Peter, Paul and Mary, and Odetta. There is also the sophisticated balladry of Barbra Streisand and Mel Tormé, and the jazz improvisations of Dave Brubeck.

Mel Tormé

Paul Simon tells how the composer, Leonard Bernstein, called him "Al" by mistake at a cocktail party, thus leading to his song, "You Can Call Me Al". That may be true, but is it merely coincidence that "Brother, Can You Spare A Dime?" says,

> *"Say, don't you remember they called me Al,*
> *It was Al all the time."*

Harburg updated his lyric for the Watergate era:

> *"Once we had Depression, but with a dime*
> *A guy wasn't out of luck.*
> *Now we've got inflation, drugs and crime,*
> *Brother, can you spare a buck?*
> *Once we had a Roosevelt, praise the Lord,*
> *Life had meaning and hope,*
> *Now we're stuck with Nixon, Agnew, Ford,*
> *Brother, can you spare a rope?"*

With "Big Issue" salesmen on the streets of our cities and the homeless holding out paper cups for change, "Brother, Can You Spare A Dime?" says as much about the civilised world now as it did then. George Michael wisely selected it as his opening song on his CD, "Songs From The Last Century", and his vocal to a big band arrangement makes it one of his best recordings.

Harburg died in a car accident in March 1981 and his family have set up the Harburg Foundation to support his causes. He is being recognised with a commemorative US postage stamp in 2002. He once said, "I have tried to write songs that are rhymed chronicles of a crazy but exciting world spinning aimlessly around a small, unimportant galaxy."

Yip was married to Jay Gorney's former wife. She would tell her friends, "I only marry men who have written 'Brother, Can You Spare A Dime?'"

I'VE HEARD THAT SONG BEFORE
Interview with Sammy Cahn

Sammy Cahn is a superb example of the Tin Pan Alley songwriter, writing to order and producing, for the most part, first class work. He is a contender for the lyricist of the century and I was very pleased to interview him when he came to London in 1987 to present his anecdotal show, "Words And Music", at the Duke of York's. The two hours that I spent with him represent two of the best hours of my life. The interview was condensed to a one-hour special for BBC Radio Merseyside and, outside of a few extracts, it has never appeared in print. It is entirely fitting that the whole text of the interview should appear in "Brother, Can You Spare A Rhyme?", which is essentially about the best-crafted songs of the 20th century.

It's a familiar story - the poor Jewish kid from the New York slums who makes good. Indeed, most of the key Tin Pan Alley songwriters were the sons of immigrant parents. The fact that their parents had to learn a new language might have rubbed off on them and so they became very adept with the English language and its rhymes and phrases. None more so than Sammy Cahn.

Sammy Cahn was born into a Polish immigrant family in on the Lower East Side in New York on 18th June 1913. His mother encouraged him to play the violin but he later switched to piano. In his teens, he played violin in a theatre orchestra and wrote his first song, "Like Niagara Falls, I'm Falling For You", at the age of 16. He collaborated with the orchestra's pianist, Saul Chaplin, and they had their first success in 1935 with "Rhythm Is Our Business" for Jimmie Lunceford.

In 1937 the Andrews Sisters topped the US charts with "Bei Mir Bist Du Schön" and from then on, Sammy Cahn has written hundreds, if not thousands, of songs. Many were written with Jule Styne, starting with "I've Heard That Song Before" in 1942 and including the Oscar-winning "Three Coins In The Fountain" (1954). The story behind this song was Sammy's first act finale and includes his poignant line, "You ask which comes first, the words or the music. I will tell you, the phone call." Because of studio deals, he says that when you hear "Make it mine, make it mine, make it mine", remember that only one-third of the song is his.

Another major collaborator was Jimmy Van Heusen and their many songs for Sinatra include "All The Way" (1957) and "High Hopes" (1959), both Oscar winners, as well as the title songs for the albums, "Come Fly With Me", "Come Dance With Me" and "No One Cares". They also won an Oscar for the song, "Call Me Irresponsible" in 1963. Sammy Cahn has also written with Nicholas Brodszky ("Be My Love", "Because You're Mine", both for Mario Lanza), Gene DePaul ("Teach Me Tonight") and many others. I had the feeling that if I'd said to Sammy, "I write music", we would have written a song on the spot.

Sammy Cahn's singing voice was rudimentary, but he was a splendid raconteur with a flair for self-promotion, whether on stage, on TV (with Michael Parkinson) or in print (his autobiography, "I Should Care"). He loved telling his carefully-honed anecdotes and if you've heard some of the stories in our conversation before, it doesn't matter. They are still great stories and they offer a tremendous insight into how the great popular songs of the 20th century were written.

It's a long interview but there's so much more that I would have liked to have asked him. Indeed, when I met up with again, briefly, after his show at the Duke of York's, he said, "You like Elvis. I should have told you about writing the comeback special for him and Frank in 1960." Indeed.

Sammy Cahn had opinions on all manner of subjects and when he was vice-president of ASCAP, he hosted a reception to honour the 50th anniversary of Muzak. He told the gathering, "I wish I could tell you how many times I have been in an elevator with a great big smile. All the passengers would have wondered who the idiot with the big smile was, but I was the writer of the song being played. I was earning money during that elevator ride, thanks to ASCAP! Suffice it to say, I love Muzak!"

The title of this chapter 'I've Heard That Song Before" comes from a song Sammy wrote with Jule Styne in 1942. Styne played him a melody and he responded with "I've heard that song before", "What are you", said Styne, "a tune detective?"

I think this interview reads well. I've never known an interviewee to sing so much - he appears to be able to recall every lyric he's written! - and I cherish the "special lyrics" that he kept singing. Sammy Cahn died in his 80th year on 15th January 1993 and I can imagine that his idea of heaven would be talking, endlessly talking, about his songs and, of course, writing new ones.

Would you like an ID?

> "Hello, this is Sammy Cahn
> And I am on
> With Spencer Leigh
> For BBC"

- so, you see, it all rhymes.

I'd like to talk about your background first. You heard Jewish music in your youth and I wonder if that influenced your songwriting.

I wouldn't think so, but Cole Porter said to me one time, "I envy you where you were born. Had I been born there,

I would have been a true genius." If you listen carefully to Cole Porter's melodies, they are often Hebraic in the minor tones. (Sings) "I love Paris in the springtime, I love Paris in the spring", "What is this thing called love?" They are both beautifully and melodically constructed on the minor chords, so if you want to write a really lovely melody with great passion, you could try the deep minor chords, the Hebraic tones.

You're a lyricist, but have you used them yourself?

Not regularly. The only one I can think of was "Bei Mir Bist Du Schon", which was totally on the minor chords. (Demonstrates) I went to the Apollo Theatre and heard two black boys singing "Bei Mir Bist Du Schön" in the original Yiddish. (Laughs). I wrote the English lyric.

That was in 1937, but you'd had a few successes before that.

Oh yes, I'd had "Until The Real Thing Comes Along", I'd had "Please Be Kind", and I'd had a song for Louis Armstrong called "Shoe Shine Boy". I also had another song for Louis Armstrong called "You're A Lucky Guy". Louis Armstrong had always been like a myth to me, a voice on a record that you listened to late at night, and he was the most astonishingly inventive singer and instrumentalist. When I was called one day and told that I was going to do the Cotton Club Revue, I said, "Who am I writing for?", and I was told, "Louis Armstrong". I said, "Louis Armstrong!" The Cotton Club was then on 47th Street on Broadway, which later became the Latin Quarter, and I walked into his dressing-room. The first thing he said to me was, "When were you born?" I said, "June 18th." He had a book full of birthdays and on the page for June 18th were all the celebrities who had been born on that day. He said, "Here. Sign your name."

It's said that Louis Armstrong didn't know when he was born so he picked July 4th 1900 for himself as it sounded perfect.

I didn't know that, but I started to work on his Cotton Club show and by a happy coincidence, the orchestra backing him was led by Jimmie Lunceford. The Jimmie Lunceford band was for me the single best band in all of music, and I say this with the knowledge that there was also Chick Webb, Count Basie and Duke Ellington. The single best band both to watch and to listen to was Jimmie Lunceford's. It had Sy Oliver's arrangements, and Tommy

Dorsey was bright enough to take Sy Oliver, an incredibly talented man, away from Jimmie Lunceford. The Sy Oliver arrangements had a vast, vast effect on the Tommy Dorsey Orchestra.

I know Sy Oliver, I know Tommy Dorsey, but I don't know Jimmie Lunceford.

Well, you listen to his records! I wrote their theme song, (Sings)

> *"Rhythm is our business,*
> *Rhythm is what we sell,*
> *Rhythm is our business,*
> *And business sure is swell.*
> *If you want rhythm on your radio,*
> *Write in and let us know,*
> *Rhythm is our business,*
> *Rhythm is what we sell."*

Willie Smith was singing:

> *"He's the drummer man in the band,"*

Crawfie [Jimmy Crawford] plays on those drums in the band, and Willie Smith was singing. You know, one of the greatest arrangements of all-time is the Sy Oliver arrangement of "Ain't She Sweet" for Willie Smith and the Lunceford band. If you play these things, you will find that they are just priceless. When he went to Dorsey, he had a tremendous effect with his trumpet challenges. I loved him. At the Cotton Club, we had a song,

> *"You're a lucky guy,*
> *When you consider*
> *The highest bidder*
> *Can't buy the gleam in your eye,*
> *You're a lucky guy."*

JIMMY LUNCEFORD

Ted Lewis, the man who used to say "Is everybody happy?", used to do a song called "Me And My Shadow", and his shadow was a little black boy. We wanted to have a little black boy in the show with Louis Armstrong and we said, "How do we get a little black boy in there?" At the end of the show, a little black boy came walking through the tables and went up to the stage where he said, "Shine, Mr Armstrong", and that's when Louis sang,

> *"Shoe shine boy,*
> *You work hard all day,*
> *Shoe shine boy,*
> *Got no time to play,"*

And this stamps the period of the song:

> *"Every nickel helps a lot..."*

A nickel for a shine!

Were you working with a collaborator at that stage in your career?

Oh yes, all those songs were written with Saul Chaplin. This was my rhythm period - I wrote "Rhythm Is Our Business", "Rhythm In My Nursery Rhymes" and a whole lot more. (Sings)

> *"I could learn my ABC's*
> *Bring home A's instead of D's,*
> *And my mom and dad I'd please*
> *If I had rhythm in my nursery rhymes."*

Just recently I got a call from Tommy Tune who is doing a Broadway show called "Steppin' Out" and he wanted to use an old tune of mine in his show called "Wrap Your Cares In Rhythm And Dance". I said, "That's fifty years old. Can't I interest you in something else? Saul Chaplin and I wrote a rhythm song that might be useful. (Sings)

> *"I could be a great singer,*
> *But I haven't a chance,*
> *Cause every vocal teacher I go to*
> *Tells me I ought to dance."*

I said to him, 'Why don't you use that?'" He said, "No, we'd like to use 'Wrap Your Cares In Rhythm And Dance'." So I went to see "Steppin' Out" at the Golden Theatre in New York City.

The song wasn't in the first act, but in the interval, I heard Harold Nicholas, one of the two Nicholas Brothers, singing. They were in a lot of those tremendous 20th Century Fox musicals. They did "Chattanooga Choo Choo" and they were just incredible. Anyway, during the interval, I hear him singing:

"If you're feeling lowdown
'Cause the skies are grey
Just wrap your cares in rhythm and dance
And dance your cares away."

I thought, "This is amazing. Did they buy this song just to have him sing it in the interval? What is going on?" Of course they hadn't and at the end of the show, I found that the finale was "Wrap Your Cares In Rhythm And Dance".

You're known for all the songs that you wrote for Frank Sinatra. Were you a friend of his before you wrote for him?
.

Yes, my relationship with Frank begins with Axel Stordahl, who was an arranger along with Paul Weston for Tommy Dorsey. Having written "Rhythm Is Our Business", I was established as a band writer, so Axel took me round to meet Tommy Dorsey and I met him and likewise, I met Frank Sinatra. I have met each and every one of the band leaders - Glenn Miller, Glen Gray, Charlie Spivak, Harry James - but Tommy Dorsey was to me the most impeccably trained orchestra leader. I would go to the Paramount Theatre and see the pit rise, and Tommy Dorsey starting off (Wordless vocalising on "I'm Getting Sentimental Over You") as the pit was coming up. They would go into "Marie", the Irving Berlin song, which again was down to the genius of Sy Oliver: Tommy Dorsey playing "Marie" and the band playing licks behind it. After that would come Connie Haines and then Jo Stafford and the Pied Pipers. Then Dorsey would feature Ziggy Elman on

trumpet, Buddy Rich on drums and himself on trombone. When all these showstoppers had finished, out stepped a young feller, thinner than my pinkie, and that was Frank Sinatra. He sang "South Of The Border" and he topped everything that had gone before. He was incredibly talented.

Did you immediately want to write for him?

Well, it wasn't a question of me writing for him. I was writing for the Dorsey band and he was singing the songs. He was so important and if you ask me why I maintain an allegiance to him, listen to this. In 1944, when Frank made it to Hollywood to do a multi-million dollar musical, "Anchors Aweigh", he walked into Louis B Mayer's office and they asked him who he wanted to do the songs. Did he want Rodgers and Hart? Did he want the Gershwins? Did he want Jerome Kern? He said, "None of them. I want Sammy Cahn." They said, "We don't mind hiring him, but who is he?" He said, typically, "Since you're not going to sing the songs, don't let it concern you. I know who he is and I want him to write for me." This caused a brouhaha and the eminent Lou Wasserman of MCA said to me, "Sammy, tell Frank to lean back because if he insists on you, we're going to blow this picture." I went to Frank and I said, "Look, Frank, yesterday nobody knew me and today they all hate me. Why not wait? There will be other pictures." Frank said, "If you're not there Monday, I won't be there Monday." And that is what separates Frank from the rest of them.

I did the songs for "Anchors Aweigh" and the one I love the most is "I Fall In Love Too Easily", which he sang at the Hollywood Bowl at the piano. I also love the song he does with Gene Kelly at the start of the film, "I Begged Her", and then there's "What Makes The Sun Set"

Did Frank have an incredible range?

This was his violin period. He went from violin to viola to cello, (Laughs) and when he got to Nelson Riddle, he had his bass sound. It takes genius to project in front of the Nelson Riddle band blasting away, but Frank could do it. He's an amazing feller.

You're a master of rhyme, and I love the way you rhyme "time" with "I'm" in "Time After Time".

Well, I have learnt all the feasible rhymes and I am not the first one to rhyme "time" with "I'm". Ira Gershwin wrote, (Sings)

> *"I'm bidin' my time*
> *'Cause that's the kind of guy I'm."*

With Jule Styne the tunes came first most of the time. (Sings)

> *"Time after time*
> *I tell myself that I'm*
> *So lucky to be loving you"*

I followed the musical line and the song leads me more than I lead it. (Sings)

> *"So lucky to be*
> *The one you run to see*
> *In the evening*
> *When the day is through.*
> *I only know what I know*
> *The passing years will show*
> *You've kept my love so young so new*
> *So time after time*
> *I tell myself that I'm*
> *So lucky to be loving you."*

The song is writing me more than I am writing it. I'm starting at top and I don't know where the lyric is going. Johnny Burke used to start from the bottom - he had his key idea and he would work backwards from that.

Did you go and sing your new songs for Sinatra?

To me, the greatest thrill of songwriting is the demonstration of the completed song. I always liked to do it myself. I would stand right in front of Sinatra and I would

sing it to him. It was an amazing thing to be doing. When I sang to one singer,

> *"And when we kiss, that isn't thunder, dear,*
> *It's only my poor heart you hear*
> *And it's applause,*
> *Because you're mine"*

he said, "How do you say 'Thunder, dear'?", but there was none of that was Sinatra. "Weatherwise, it's such a lovely day" - he knew instinctively how to do it. It was very easy to write for Sinatra.

Have you any other examples?

When I sang "Come Fly With Me" for Frank, I sang,

> *"Come fly with me,*
> *Let's fly, let's fly away.*
> *If you can use some exotic views,*
> *There's a bar in far Bombay."*

I said "views" instead of "booze". When he had finished recording, I said, "When you sing the song in Vegas or a night club, you should sing 'booze'." He said, "Call the band back, I want another take." Jimmy Van Heusen was angry with me as he thought that the word "booze" would get the record banned, which gives you an idea as to how far censorship has moved. But that's what makes Sinatra different. He said, "No, I'm going to sing 'booze'."

Do you have a favourite session with Frank Sinatra?

Yes, I loved demonstrating the songs for "Our Town" with him. It was a TV production with Paul Newman as the boy and Eva Marie Saint as the girl. It was at twilight at his home in Carrowood Drive, Hornby Hills, California. He just sat there and we sang,

"You will like the folks you meet in our town,
The folks you meet on any street in our town.
Pick out any cottage, large or small,
You'll find they're appealing
With that lived-in feeling."

He had his thumb on his lower lip, just kneading the lip and listening. He heard all the songs, every song, and then he looked at me and nodded. He's not too demonstrative and it was the most incredible experience. "Our Town" went on the air in Los Angeles at 6pm, to be shown in New York simultaneously at 9pm, and it was a 90 minute broadcast, live, with Nelson Riddle and his Orchestra. Nelson was a block away, watching the monitor and conducting. Sinatra was singing for the angels that night, he has never sung better in his life - (Sings)

"Love and marriage,
Love and marriage".

He was just incredible, and I won an Emmy for that song.

You got your first Oscar with a song that was performed by Sinatra, "Three Coins In The Fountain". Did you write the song around the script?

Not at all. I never saw the film and I never read the script. Someone came to see me and he said, "Three girls go to Rome and they throw coins in a fountain", and then he left. We wrote the song from that. I won't tell you the rest of the story as you'll see it on stage and it's really, really funny.

Well, it's not Christmas so "The Christmas Waltz" won't be in your show. What's the story behind that?

Jule Styne used to limber up with two songs, a Viennese waltz and a tango. He said to me one day, "Frank wants a Christmas song." I said, "A Christmas song after 'White Christmas'. What's the point? We're not writing a Christmas song."

He said, "Frank WANTS a Christmas song." I said, "Slow down that Viennese waltz" and then we had (Sings),

"It's that time of year
When the world falls in love"

So "The Vienna Waltz" became "The Christmas Waltz". Around Christmastime, I'll put it back into the show.

I was intrigued by what you said about "booze" and "views" in "Come Fly With Me", and Sinatra often sings different words on stage. I've heard several different sets of lyrics for "The Lady Is A Tramp".

When he came to London to play the Royal Albert Hall in 1980, he asked me to write him some new lyrics to Cole Porter's "Let's Do It", as I had previously done some for Las Vegas. He called me and said, "Sam, you did some lyrics for Vegas. Could you change them for London?" I said, "Sure. When do you want them?" He said, "Now." I said, "Why didn't you call me from the stage?" I picked the phone and called Jackie Collins, who lives in Beverly Hills, and I said, "Jackie, I need some information about England." She gave me some information and some names and I put them into the lyric, and it was incredibly well received. I have a cassette of it and I will give it to you. (Sammy goes into his bedroom, looks in a suitcase and comes out with a cassette, which he gives to me. As he gives me the tape he starts to sing.)

"Birds do it, bees do it,
History proves a few MPs do it,
Let's do it ,let's fall in love.
And likewise,
Lords do it, earls do it,
Boys with boys and girls with girls do it,
Let's do it, let's fall in love.

"And Margaret Thatcher I hear does it
And the Prime's in her prime,
With cool veneer does it
When does she find the time?"

I included some TV personalities and also had Mrs Whitehouse in there.

It must also have been remarkable that he learnt the song especially for the occasion.

Well, he knows "Let's Do It" of course, but he didn't learn the new lyrics. It didn't even start the way I had intended. (Sings)

> *"Let's fall in love,*
> *Why shouldn't we fall in love,*
> *People are doing it all of the time*
> *And it's easy to rhyme..."*

And then...

> *"And it's easy to rhyme,*
> *Ba-ba-ba-ba,*
> *And that's why,*
> *Birds do it, bees do it..."*

He pulled the paper out of his pocket and he did it cold, but it didn't matter. When he hears the laughter coming at him, he is stunned because he didn't know who Mrs Whitehouse was. He sings, "And Mrs Whitehouse alone does it", and it gets a roar and you'll hear his reaction. It's fascinating. (It certainly is.)

What's on the other side of this cassette?

Frank called me one time and said, "Ringo Starr's getting married and his bride is my No 1 fan and is also having her birthday, and I want you to write something that I could sing to her." So I wrote special lyrics for Ringo's bride, Maureen. This is Sinatra singing to her, with special lyrics by me. (Plays cassette and Sinatra sings, missing a couple of notes. "It was early the morning and Sinatra was a little tired," says Sammy. No matter, it's great.)

> *"There's no one like her,*
> *But no one at all,*
> *And as for charm,*
> *Hers is like wall to wall.*
> *She married Ringo*
> *And she could have had Paul,*
> *That's why the lady is a champ.*

> *"Creates excitement*
> *Whenever it's dull,*
> *She just appears*
> *And there goes the lull.*
> *She merely smiles*

> *And you're out of your skull,*
> *That's why the lady is a champ.*

> *"The folks who do and don't meditate*
> *Agree she's great,*
> *They mean*
> *Maureen,*
> *I've got more lyrics right after this vamp,*
> *Because the lady is a champ.*

> *"Though we've not met*
> *I'm convinced she's a gem,*
> *I'm just F S*
> *But to me she's Big M,*
> *Mainly because she prefers to me to them,*
> *That's why the lady is a champ.*

> *"I've lots of fans, well, at least one or two,*
> *But Peter Brown called me to tell me it's true,*
> *She sleeps with Ringo but she thinks of you,*
> *That's why the lady is a champ.*

> *"But I can boast, boast as much,*
> *As much as I please,*
> *The fact is that she's*
> *His wife,*
> *But that's life,*
> *But it's her day so I whistle and stamp,*
> *Because the lady, the charming lady, Mr Ringo's lady, is a champ."*

> *"May I toast you all the way*
> *Lift my glass and softly say*
> *I have thoughts for you this day*
> *But beautiful.*
> *Thoughts for you and for your Ringo*
> *That I must express*
> *With the warm and deep affection of F S.*
> *Would you kindly ask the guys*
> *If they'd grab a glass and rise*
> *'Cause I think we'd harmonise*
> *But beautiful.*
> *May your birthdays and birthday candles*
> *Softly gleam and glow*
> *For that would be*
> *But beautiful I know."*

They were just thrilled. This is what I do most of the time now, special lyrics for special occasions.

Did you write those new words for Frank's version of "Mrs Robinson"?

Yes, I did "You'll get yours, Mrs Robinson" and all that. Jilly is Frank's friend and Jilly's bar was a swinging place in New York City on 52nd Street.

Did Paul Simon mind?

Well, I didn't do it to be disrespectful. I really admire the Beatles and Jimmy Webb and Paul Simon. A lot of bad songs were written in the 30s and 40s - a lot of "moon and June" mush, and these are good songwriters. I love "Everybody's Talkin'" but Fred Neil could have improved it. "Going where the weather suits my clothes" is okay but "climate" would be better. You get the alliteration with "clothes" and it sings better too.

PAUL SIMON

Do any other "special lyrics for special occasions" spring to mind?

Yes. Many years ago Frank Sinatra was going to do a special television programme with Ethel Barrymore, the legendary Ethel Barrymore. She had an incredible face, and Sinatra's face and hers would look great together. I said, "It would be marvellous if you sang 'I've Grown Accustomed To Her Face', so why don't you call Alan Jay Lerner and ask him to write a special lyric for you." He called Alan and he said, "C'mon, Frank, don't bother me with this. Let Sammy do a special lyric for you." So that's what I did and I rather like: (Sings)

> *"You're all the lovely things I've known*
> *And that is why I've grown*
> *Accustomed to your face."*

Frank can call me any time, day or night, and I'll do special lyrics for him.

What was your last job?

Ah, that was in Washington DC and we were at the Ford Theatre to honour Mrs Reagan. Don Johnson came out and said, "Mrs Reagan, we're here to honour you, and we want to honour you with a special song, and when you want a special song, you call Mr Sammy Cahn." I came on stage and he continued, "And when you have a special song, you need a special dancing partner, and here is Mr Mikhail Baryshnikov." He then came on stage and he walked into the audience. He took her from Mr Reagan, "With your permission, sir", and brought her onto the stage and I sang,

> *"Pardon him please,*
> *If he feels ill at ease,*
> *With a real live girl.*
> *Nancy by name*
> *With the First Lady's fame,*
> *And a real live girl.*
> *Grand ballerinas as you might suppose,*
> *He understands when they're up on their toes,*
> *But here tonight*
> *He is awed by the sight*
> *And the glow that you feel*
> *With a real live girl."*

Then I turned to Don Johnson and I sang,

> *"Baryshnikov*
> *Can be shy as a dove*
> *With a real live girl,*
> *He won't amaze*
> *With those wild tourjetés*
> *With a real live girl.*
> *And Mrs Reagan is floating on air,*
> *He thinks she's Ginger*
> *And he's Fred Astaire,*
> *But here tonight he is awed by the sight*
> *And the glow that you feel*
> *From a real live girl."*

The two of us joined her and they handed her the Ford Theatre Award which was a beautiful gold plaque. It was a lovely, lovely evening and that is why more than anything else, I write special lyrics for special occasions. I went to Washington when they wanted money for the restoration of the Blair Home for the visiting dignatories.

It was $10,000 a couple for the evening. You had a reception at the White House and you went to the State Department with George Schultz and I sang these special lyrics,

"You know Blair's been standing there,
A hundred years or more,
It's been a long, long time."

To see President Reagan and George Schultz singing the song at my command is a very, very rewarding experience for me.

I've read somewhere that you wrote a special lyric to honour Cary Grant.

Ah yes, that was at the Friars Club in New York City. There are very few songs that are written for men to sing about men. The only love song from a man to a man is "My Buddy" where one soldier has lost his buddy. (Sings),

"Days are long since you went away,
I think about you all through the day,
My buddy.
My buddy, nobody quite like you."

It's a love song from a man to a man. At the Friars Club, I said, "There is only one song that fits this gentleman and it's written about a girl", but he'll forgive me the change,

"The most beautiful man in the world
Isn't me, no,
Isn't Dino,
But as we know
It's the man that we honour tonight.

"The most talented man in the world
Not John Gielgud
Though he's real good
Would he feel good
With a Friar to his left and a Friar to his right.

"Cary stands alone,
Nicest man we've known,
And that great physique
You would have to say is most unique.

"The most beautiful man in the world
Counting tall men,
Counting small men,
Counting all men
Counting men with a talent they cannot supplant
Is the one and only wonderful Cary Grant."

You mentioned Dean Martin in that special lyric and I presume he lends himself to parody because of his stage image.

Yes, I wrote lots of funny one-liners for him.

"The girl that I marry
Will have to be
A nympho who owns a distillery."

"You made me love you,
You woke me up to do it."

"I didn't know what time it was,
I drank my watch."

"Kiss me once and kiss me twice
And kiss me once again,
It takes a long, long time."

"I looked under Jordan and what did I see?
Mrs Jordan."

Funny thing about his drinking, that drinking is a crutch. Dean is not a heavy drinker, but he would come on stage and he would down a glass of apple juice and the audience would go, "Look what he's doing." It was to give the impression that he was loose and free. He has had more hits than Sinatra and his list of hits is incredibly important. (Sings)

"Return to me,
Oh my darling, I love you,
Hurry back, hurry back."

Wonderful songs! When he sings, he's doing Bing Crosby, and Perry Como is also doing Bing Crosby. Vic Damone is doing Frank Sinatra, but Dean Martin is doing Bing Crosby when he sings and Cary Grant when he acts. (Laughs)

One of the songs that you wrote for Sinatra is "All The Way", and that was for a film about the nightclub comic, Joe E Lewis.

That song was written for a film with the working title of "The Joker Is Wild", and I said to Jimmy Van Heusen, "They'll never call a film, 'The Joker Is Wild', it sounds too much like a poker game. Let's think of a song that they can use for the title instead." We came up with "All The Way", which was to establish a big, dramatic point. When Joe E Lewis was young, he was a singer (Sings)

"When somebody loves you,
It's no good unless he loves you..."

Big notes...

"All the way."

Later in the film the boy's in Chicago and the hoodlums cut his throat and leave him to die. He recovers and he tries to sing again but this time it's like this,

"When somebody loves you, It's no good unless he loves you..."

DEAN & FRANK

And he can't do those big notes. He realises that he is never going to hit those notes again and he becomes a singing comedian. That's the power of that song, it was written for dramatic effect. They still called the film, "The Joker Is Wild", though.

We could go on forever, but I know you're performing tonight and will want to save your voice. Just a couple more. What about "The Second Time Around"?

"The Second Time Around" is one of the most important songs I've written, because when people say to me, "You've written my song", they invariably mean "The Second Time Around". It is a hymn of hope for failed romance or whatever. That song was written for the film,

"High Time", in which Bing Crosby plays a widower who has achieved everything in life. He goes back to college - it's the same plot as Rodney Dangerfield's "Back To School" - and he meets a French teacher who's a widow. I said to Van Heusen, "What are we going to write for a widower and a widow? 'I'm glad that you're dead, You rascal you.' 'You'll be the death of me'." We kicked around some funny titles and I said to him, "Are we going to be the only team that couldn't come up with a ballad for Bing Crosby? "What do you think of the title, 'The Second Time Around'? 'Love is wonderful the second time around, Just as beautiful with both feet on the ground.'" He said, "No, 'Love is lovelier the second time around, Just as wonderful with both feet on the ground." The song was then written very quickly. We sang it to Bing Crosby and he just nodded. The great, great artists know that you are doing your part, so it is very simple to write for them.

You won an Oscar for "High Hopes", which is really a children's song.

Oh yes, but that was a unique song. (Sings)

"Just what makes that little ol' ant
Think he'll move a rubber tree plant,
Anyone knows that an ant
Can't
Move a rubber tree plant."

The song is very infectious and people love to sing it. At the theatre tonight, you'll see, people love to sing along: it's a very, very interesting song. You see, originally I only had the idea for the title. "High hopes, High hopes, High apple-pie-in-the-sky hopes", that was all I had and then Van Heusen came back with some music. (Sings the chorus to the melody of "It's Going To Be A Great Day") Something like that, and I said, "No, no, maybe we should write this from the viewpoint of the animals." I realised that I had made a faux pas as he had written the best animal song ever in "Swinging On A Star". We were in a bungalow at 20th Century Fox and I looked around and I saw a stream of ants. I said, "No, I don't mean animals. I mean insects. Those ants have a sense of fulfilment, going up and down all day. Feller gets a sock on the jaw and as he falls to the ground, a stream of ants goes past his nose." What makes the song funny for me is that I have never seen an ant near a rubber tree plant, but when you say,

"Just what makes that little ol' ant
Think he'll move a..."

It can't be anything but "rubber tree plant". You can't say "acacia" because the architecture of the song calls for "rubber tree plant". When we sang the song to Sinatra, he laughed, and the song became a smash, smash hit.

Is it true that you reworked the song for JFK?

Yes, and that's the real miracle and the true adventure of songwriting. When we had to write a campaign song, the word "Kennedy" didn't fit into "High Hopes", although the title was right. Van Heusen said, "All right, Big Mouth, what are you going to do now?" I said, "There's always a way. Supposing we spell it." He said, "Spell it?" I said, "Remember 'H-A-double R-I-G-A-N spells Harrigan'." He said, "We're trying to elect Kennedy." I said, "I know who we're trying to elect but listen to this." I had,

"Just what makes that little ol' ant..."

and it became,

"K-E-double N-E-D-Y,
Jack's the nation's favourite guy.
Everyone wants to back Jack,
Jack is on the right track."

That's the great fun of writing special lyrics.

Your fourth Oscar song was with "Call Me Irresponsible".

That song was written for Fred Astaire to sing in the film, "Papa's Delicate Condition", but he never made the film. He never recorded the song and that is one of the disappointments of my life. The greatest thrill of my entire life was standing in front of Fred Astaire and doing the song. I came to the lines,

"Do my foolish alibis bore you,
Well, I'm not too clever,
I just adore you"

FRED ASTAIRE

and Astaire said, "Stop!" Van Heusen almost fell off his piano bench as this had never happened before. Astaire said, "That is one of the best songs I've ever heard." I said, "That is one of the best half-songs you've ever heard. May I finish it?" He said, "That's a great, great song. Would you like to know how you got this job?" I said, "Yes, I would." He said, "Johnny Mercer wasn't available." I said, "I consider that a high compliment." He said, "No, I'll give you the high compliment now. The next time Mercer leaves town, I won't worry."

Are contemporary performers doing your songs?

What gives me a great deal of pleasure is that Al Jarreau has just made another smash out of "Time After Time", which has been a hit any number of times. Our songs seem to gain more and more importance by the deluge of one-hit wonders. I am on the board of directors for ASCAP, which is equal to your PRS here, and there was a reception for Bob Dylan, and I knew him because I had inducted him into the Songwriters Hall Of Fame.

He said to me, "I've done one of your songs." I said, "YOU have done one of MY songs?" He said, "Yes" and I expected him to say something like "Teach Me Tonight", but he said, "It's 'All My Tomorrows'." Now this song was in the same film as "High Hopes", "A Hole In The Head", and it was sung by Sinatra and the girl: (Sings)

> *"Today I may not have a thing at all,*
> *Except for just a dream or two,*
> *But I've got lots of plans for tomorrow,*
> *And all my tomorrows belong to you."*

Pia Izadora did it with the London Philharmonic Orchestra and Dinah Shore has done it, so all of a sudden everyone is doing "All My Tomorrows". It proves what Jimmy Van Heusen said, "Write the best song you know how and don't worry about it."

How does Bob Dylan appeal to you as a lyric writer? In one song, "Señor", he rhymes "Armageddon" with "heading".

If he says "headin'" and "Armageddin'", I could buy it, but "heading" and "Armageddon", no. My problem with the new writers is that they don't respect title. If I'm going to write a song about Chicago, I know that there is a song called "Chicago". (Sings)

> *"Chicago, Chicago,*
> *That toddlin' town."*

I will not write a song called "Chicago", so I wrote,

> *"My kind of town,*
> *Chicago is..."*

Stephen Schwarz wrote "Day By Day" for "Godspell", and yet I have a song called "Day By Day". Cyndi Lauper did

SAMMY CAHN WITH FRANK SINATRA

a song called "Time After Time" and she has diminished both titles. PRS and ASCAP have monitors who listen to what radio stations are playing. They write down "Day By Day" or "Time After Time", but who can say which it is. The younger songwriters should respect title. That's my only complaint.

How high do you rate Lennon and McCartney?

I am the president of the Songwriters Hall Of Fame, a presidency bequeathed to me by Johnny Mercer, who was the first president, and we've just put them into the Songwriters Hall of Fame. They were the first recipients of an international award. They wrote words and they wrote music that will be here forever. "Yesterday" is wonderful but "Here, There And Everywhere" is an absolutely marvellous composition, and it has great words and great music. Paul McCartney and I share the same birthday and we exchange greetings on June 18th.

Does it surprise you that Lennon and McCartney were able to write all those great songs, although they were not musically trained?

No. Mr Irving Berlin had no musical talent whatsoever. Jerome Kern said to him, "Irving, you must learn how to write. You gotta be able to sit down and write your notes." Irving Berlin respected Jerome Kern so he started very laboriously to study music. (Sings) "A, B, C, D, E, F, G." After a month, he said, "Why, that son of a bitch. While I was learning how to write, I could have written twelve songs." (Laughs)

Sammy Cahn, thank you very much.

My great pleasure, Spencer.

AS TIME GOES BY
Part 3 - 1950-1974

1950 - MONA LISA (Jay Livingston - Ray Evans)

Start of Korean War - DNA determines how genes are passed from parents to children - Legal Aid introduced - Death of Kurt Weill - First episode of "The Archers".

"Captain Carey, U.S.A." is an espionage film set in Italy and starring Alan Ladd and Russ Tamblyn. A song is used to herald danger and the songwriter, Ray Evans, came up with "Mona Lisa". For authenticity, an Italian lyric was needed, and so the song is never heard in English during the film. When Nat 'King' Cole was asked to record an English version, he said that the title, "Mona Lisa", was too highbrow, a poor title for a song. He was persuaded to sing it, but it was only released as a B-side. The DJs picked up on the song and it won an Oscar. In 1959 both Carl Mann and Conway Twitty recorded rock'n'roll versions of the tune. In 1986 it was used as the title for a British film starring Bob Hoskins and Cathy Tyson.

In 1950 the folksinger, Ed McCurdy, was asked to write a song about peace for a women's magazine. He had no inspiration but after a night of heavy drinking, an idea came to him in a hotel room in Toronto. With a pen in one hand and a bottle in the other, he wrote "Last Night I Had The Strangest Dream", one of the 20th century's most enduring songs. "We met Ed McCurdy in New York," recalls Hughie Jones of the Spinners, "His song refers to 'Swords and guns and uniforms' being scattered all around, and I told him that as swords and guns were the same thing, 'Flags and guns and uniforms' would be much better. He wasn't at all impressed as he was an American patriot."

The producer, Mitch Miller, wanted Frank Sinatra to record "The Roving Kind" and Percy Faith's "My Heart Cries For You". "I don't sing this crap," said Sinatra, leaving Mitch Miller with a problem. Rather than cancel the session, he asked the up and coming Guy Mitchell to step in, and both songs made the US Top 10. Sinatra did okay by reviving "Nevertheless (I'm In Love With You)", but the following year he made his worst record, "Mama Will Bark" with Dogmar.

Frank Loesser adapted some short stories by Damon Runyon under the title of "Guys And Dolls", and his brilliant score included "Luck Be A Lady", "Sit Down, You're Rockin' The Boat", "If I Were A Bell" and "The Oldest Establised (Permanent Floating Crap Game)". "Fugue For Tinhorns", in which three men discuss the day's betting, sets the mood magnificently. Frank argued that his ballads should be reprised in the second half of the show: he lost the argument but it was the Loesser of two evils as he punched the soprano, Isobel Bigley, for not singing "I'll Know" correctly.

"Cerisier Rose Et Pommer Blanc" was a French pop song by Jacques Larue and Louiguy (the pseudonymn of Louis Guiglieml), given an English lyric by Mack David in 1951. It became an international hit when it became a mambo instrumental as "Cherry Pink And Apple Blossom White" for Perez Prado and his Orchestra and was featured in the Jane Russell film, "Underwater", in 1955.

Frankie Laine was very impressed with Fred Darien's demo of a new song, "Jezebel". "If they'd released that" he told me, "I never would have recorded it as it was so terrific". Laine's version was an international hit, but it was recorded for the French market by Edith Piaf with a lyric by Charles Aznavour. When I asked Aznavour how many songs he had written for Piaf, he said, "six and a half".

Other 1950 hits include "Shotgun Boogie" (a 1947 Merle Travis composition with "Tennessee" Ernie Ford close to inventing rock'n'roll), "Cold, Cold Heart" (Hank Williams having another dig at his wife, Audrey), "Be My Love", "It Is No Secret" and "I'm Movin' On" (written en route to a recording session by Hank Snow). The most ridiculous novelty of the year was "I Said My Pajamas (And Put On My Prayers)", recorded by Tony Martin and Fran Warren.

MERLE TRAVIS

1951 -   CRY (Churchill Kohlman)

Festival of Britain - Burgess and Maclean flee to Soviet Union - Zebra crossings introduced - J.D. Salinger's "The Catcher In The Rye" and Graham Greene's "The End Of The Affair" - Start of "The Goon Show" - First use of the word, "discotheque".

Churchill Kohlman was a nightwatcher at a drycleaners in Werners, Pittsburg. He wrote two songs, "Cry" and "Appreciation", for a talent contest. "Appreciation" made the finals but Johnnie Ray heard "Cry" on an obscure single by Ruth Casey and wanted to record it. His melodramatic performances made the song a million-seller and he became known as the Cry Guy and the Prince of Wails. His British agent, Ken Pitt, recalls, "When Johnnie Ray came over, I watched him very closely and I am certain that his crying was absolutely genuine, and that he could do it to order, twice nightly. I put it down to the fact that he was a very emotional boy. He was very lonely and he often went back to his hotel room and cried."

Other new songs of 1951 include "Mockin' Bird Hill" (with new, multi-tracking techniques from Les Paul and Mary Ford), "Blue Velvet" (a UK Top 10 hit for Bobby Vinton in 1990) and "Come-On-A My House" (based on an Armenian folk song and written by an Armenian, David Seville, who later created the Chipmunks). "They try to tell us we're too young," sang Nat "King" Cole, then aged 32.

Hank Williams's "Hey Good Lookin'" had a rock'n'roll vocabulary with references to hot rods and soda pops, while his original lyric (never recorded!) to "I Can't Help It (If I'm Still In Love With You)" began:

"Today I passed you on the street
And I smelt your rotten feet,
I can't help it if I'm still in love with you."

JOHNNIE RAY IN CONCERT

Pee Wee King and his Golden West Cowboys climbed high in the US country charts with "Slow Poke" but this was too colloquial for the UK. The UK label showed the revised title of "Slow Coach", although the recording itself wasn't changed.

Pete Seeger, then with the Weavers, recalls, "'Kisses Sweeter Than Wine' was made up about 1951. We had a job at a big fancy night club in Texas and wanted to make a record and Lee Hays was saying that we needed some new songs. I leafed through a notebook and came up with the chorus of 'Kisses Sweeter Than Wine'. I'd thought of the chorus but hadn't been able to go any further. I'd put new words to an Irish melody that Leadbelly had developed. Lee said, "Hey, let me see what I can do with that," and the next day he came back with seven or eight verses. We pared them down to four or five and we recorded it."

Alan Jay Lerner and Burton Lane wrote the songs for the Fred Astaire and Jane Powell film musical, "Royal Wedding", with Powell replacing an ailing Judy Garland. The amusingly titled "How Could You Believe Me When I Said I Loved You When You Know I've Been A Liar All My Life?" was an infuriatingly catchy duet for the stars.

Alan Jay Lerner continued with a Broadway musical about the Californian gold rush, "Paint Your Wagon", which was written with Fritz Loewe. The score included "I Talk To The Trees", "They Call The Wind Maria" and the growlers' favourite, "Wand'rin' Star". The theme of "Paint Your Wagon" owed something to "Oklahoma!" but Rodgers and Hammerstein had turned to Siam for "The King And I", creating standards with "Getting To Know You" (excellently turned round by James Taylor), "Shall We Dance?", "I Whistle A Happy Tune" and "Hello Young Lovers", although the plot seems skimpy and politically incorrect today. A parody in "That Was The Week That Was" was "Hello young lovers, you're under arrest."

1952 - HIGH NOON (DO NOT FORSAKE ME)
(Ned Washington - Dimitri Tiomkin)

Death of George VI - Last London tram - UK tests atomic bomb and US the H-bomb - Smog in London - Agatha Christie's "The Mousetrap" ensnares its first customers in the West End - Ernest Hemingway writes "The Old Man And The Sea".

One of the best of all western songs is the theme from "High Noon", starring Gary Cooper and Grace Kelly. Gary Cooper knows that the killers are coming to town at the very time he is getting married and he cannot get the townsfolk to help him. (If the role had been played by Clint Eastwood, he wouldn't have even considered help!) At the first screening, the executives thought the film was too miserable. The composer, Dimitri Tiomkin, thought a strong theme song would change everything and his song is performed by Tex Ritter over the credits, although, admittedly, it does give the plot away. The theme recurs throughout the film to clever effect. Tex Ritter didn't want to record the song for a single, but realised his mistake when Frankie Laine took it into the charts.

A couple of 1952 songs became famous during the rock-'n'roll era a few years later, namely, "Hound Dog" and "Lawdy Miss Clawdy". It was a strong year for country music with the standards - "The Wild Side Of Life", "(Now And Then, There's) A Fool Such As I", "Half As Much" (written by Curley, and not Hank, Williams) "Your Cheatin' Heart" (Hank Williams) and "Jambalaya (On The Bayou)", which was written by Hank Williams and Moon Mullican and which, like so many cajun songs, was about food.

Doris Day sang "When I Fall In Love", Kay Starr was on the "Wheel Of Fortune", and Mario Lanza belted out "Because You're Mine", parodied as "Big horse, you're mine". It was hello, brolly to Gene Kelly and his athletic dancing in the title sequence of "Singin' In The Rain", although the song was written in 1929. Frank Loesser wrote a delightful score for Danny Kaye's film biography, "Hans Christian Andersen", which included "The Ugly Duckling" and "Wonderful Copenhagen". A favourite with both children and their parents was "I Saw Mommy Kissing Santa Claus".

Vera Lynn showed she could score peacetime hits with "Auf Wiederseh'n Sweetheart", which was recorded with "The Soldiers, Sailors and Airmen of Her Majesty's Forces". What, all of them? Surprisingly, Vera Lynn did not record "You Belong To Me", which was taken as a ballad for servicemen overseas. Still, the competition was strong with versions by Alma Cogan, Joni James, Dean Martin, Patti Page, Dickie Valentine, Jimmy Young and the winner, Jo Stafford.

1953 - ROCK AROUND THE CLOCK
(Jimmy Myers - Max C. Freedman)

Death of Hank Williams in the back of a car on New Year's Day - Mau Mau uprising in Kenya - Stalin dies - Conquest of Everest - Millions buy TVs for the coronation of Queen Elizabeth II - Korean War ends - The first James Bond novel, "Casino Royale", is published.

The words "rock'n'roll" had been a sexual euphemism in black music for some years, but "Rock Around The Clock" suggested that this could be the name for a new teenage music. The song was first recorded by Sunny Dae and the Arcades in 1953, and Jimmy Myers recorded it himself as Jimmy DeKnight and his Kings of Rhythm. Meanwhile, the co-writer, Max Freedman had approached Bill Haley and his Comets. Their version, recorded in 1954, was initially released as "a foxtrot" but it became a youth favourite and then a smash hit following its use in the film, "The Blackboard Jungle".

The 3D sci-fi epic, "It Came From Outer Space", was a big film in 1953, and the title could just as easily have applied to rock'n'roll. No-one over 25 understood what was going on and "Rock Around The Clock" spearheaded the revolution. The phrase, "rock around the clock", passed into the language and, despite its nursery rhyme lyric, it has been recorded by numerous performers. Bill Haley's own version has been in the UK charts on nine separate occasions, including an appearance on a Jive Bunny mastermix.

In 1953 the songwriter and producer, Buck Ram, recorded a session with the doowop group, the Penguins, who had scored with "Earth Angel". He asked the musicians if they could stay on for a record with the Platters, but the pianist had already left. Buck could only play triplets, but no matter, he played them on the original version of his song, "Only You (And You Alone)". He was to make a new recording in 1955 and the song bridged the gap between the existing popular music and rock'n'roll. Buck Ram said that the key to success was "simple melodies, simple lyrics and no over-production", and what can be simpler, and more effective, than "Only you can make the world seem right"?

There's no clear winner in 1953 for the song of the year. How do you choose between "Rock Around The Clock" and "I Believe", which are in total-ly different styles, and "Only You" which is somewhere in-between? The religious ballad, "I Believe", has yawning gaps in its lyric - how often does a singer "see a new born cry" unless, of course, he is also a doctor or a nurse? Still, it con-tains powerful imagery, and Frankie Laine has said, "It accom-plished an awful lot in its day because it said all the things that need to be said in a prayer, and yet it didn't use any of the holy words - Lord, God, Him, His, Thine, Thou. It said it all and it changed the whole spectrum of faith songs."

FRANKIE LAINE

Frankie should know as he was also in trouble for record-ing "Answer Me". It opened with an organ and Frankie singing as reverently as he could:

> *"Answer me, Lord above,*
> *Just what sin have I been guilty of,*
> *Tell me how I came to lose your love,*
> *Please answer me, oh Lord."*

That was dynamite in 1953. The record was banned throughout the States and in the UK, thus enabling Nat "King" Cole to clean up with an amended "Answer Me, My Love". Frankie himself recorded the revised lyric for South Africa.

"Crying In The Chapel" was another popular religious ballad and other songs of the year include "Vaya Con Dios" (Les Paul and Mary Ford), "O Mein Papa" (Preston-born Eddie Calvert grew to hate his No 1 hit, likening it to a six-inch nail being drilled into his head), "Where Did My Snowman Go?" (Petula Clark with children from Dr Barnardo's Homes), "Rags To Riches" and the novelty "Little Red Monkey", recorded by the "Take It From Here" team of Jimmy Edwards, Joy Nichols and Dick Bentley as well as by Rosemary Clooney, the mother of George. Jerry Leiber and Mike Stoller wrote a vignette about prison life, "Riot In Cell Block No 9" for the Robins, who became the Coasters. One of the most recorded songs of the year was "Hold Me Thrill Me Kiss Me", and, somewhat surprisingly, the UK honours went to the little-known Muriel Smith. The song returned to the Top 20 in 1994 for Gloria Estefan.

Three notable songs appeared in films. They were "Moulin Rouge", known as "Where Is My Heart?", "April In Portugal", based on a Portuguese fado called "Coimbra" and now an exotica classic, and "Limelight", written by Charlie Chaplin. Vocal versions of "Limelight", known as "Eternally", were also available from Vic Damone and Jimmy Young. Chaplin had been criticised during the McCarthy era and he was refused re-entry into America after a visit to the UK for the British premiere of "Limelight. As a result of this abominable behaviour by the US government, Chaplin's film was not screened there until 1972. His score then won an Oscar.

Lita Roza secured the first of 50 No 1 hits by Liverpool performers with a children's song, "How Much Is That Doggie In The Window?", but she was far from happy. "Dick Rowe had an American hit by Patti Page that he wanted me to cover for the British market. When I got to the studio and heard the song, I said, 'I'm not record-ing that rubbish, I hate it!' and he said, 'Oh, Lita, it's going to be a big hit.' He persuaded me to sing it through once, and I said, 'I'm never going to sing that again, ever - and I never have.'"

Its composer, Bob Merrill, wrote many of Guy Mitchell's hits, including 1953's "She Wears Red Feathers", "Look At That Girl" and "Chicka Boom". He said, "The secret of composing popular songs is to fall in love with clichés."

Dean Martin was wary of the lyrics by the Liverpool-born Jack Brooks for "That's Amore" as he thought he was being mocked for his Italian origins - "When the moon hits your eye like a big pizza pie, That's amore". He had to be persuaded to sing it for the film, "The Caddy". The record was very successful and thus contributed to the rift with his partner, Jerry Lewis.

"Ebb Tide" was a shimmering instrumental written by Robert Maxwell and given lyrics by Carl Sigman. Maxwell adorned his harp with multi-coloured lights which he controlled by foot pedals. He also wrote TV themes for Jackie Gleason and Ernie Kovacs and he never became a newspaper proprietor. Odd though that his best-known composition should be about the sea.

1954 -   RELEASE ME (Eddie Miller - Dub Williams)

Launch of nuclear submarine, The Nautilus - Roger Bannister runs four-minute mile - Rationing ends - First Wimpy bar - UK rabbits almost wiped out by myxomatosis - Publication of *The Lord Of The Rings"* (J.R.R. Tolkien) and *"Lord Of The Flies"* (William Golding).

The country music songwriter, Eddie Miller was in a bar in San Francisco and he heard two people arguing. The wife said, "If you'd release me, we wouldn't have any problems and everything would be all right." Miller thought it was an intriguing way to ask for a divorce and wrote "Release Me" with his partner, Dub Williams, whose real name was W.S. Stevenson. They gave the song to Jimmy Heap and the Melody Makers and it was covered by Ray Price and Kitty Wells, who all made the US country charts in 1954. In 1962 it was an R&B hit for Esther Phillips and then in 1967 an international one for Engelbert Humperdinck.

Irving Berlin was disturbed when he heard Eddie Fisher was going to record one of his songs as he knew Fisher had a poor memory. He sent a secretary to the session with the printed lyric who then ensured that Fisher sang them correctly. Berlin was so pleased that he warmed

to Fisher and gave him "Count Your Blessings (Instead Of Sheep)" for a banquet to commemorate the arrival of the first Jews in America.

"This Ole House" was written after the songwriter, Stuart Hamblen, found the body of a prospector in a rundown hut, miles from anywhere. Surprisingly, both "I Left My Heart In San Francisco" and "My Ding-A-Ling" were first recorded in 1954. So were the torch ballads, "The Man That Got Away" and "Secret Love" and the more light-hearted "Little Things Mean A Lot", "Mr Sandman", Cole Porter's "I Love Paris" and "Gilly Gilly Ossenfeffer Katzenellen Bogen By The Sea". The latin dance songs, "Sway (Quien Sera)" (Dean Martin, 1954: Smooth 2000), and "Mambo Italiano" (Rosemary Clooney, 1954: Shaft, 2000), are still played today. Eric Coates wrote the rousing theme for "The Dam Busters", a World War II film about Barnes Wallis, the inventor of the "bouncing bomb", and Wing Commander Guy Gibson, who carried out Wallis' orders.

A cheesy musical about worker's rights, "The Pajama Game", was a Broadway hit and the subsequent London production starred Max Wall. The 1957 film musical starred Doris Day and John Raitt and then, in 1999, it was revived in the West End with Ulrika Jonsson in the Doris Day role. Ulrika in jimjams was a tremendous marketing gimmick, though not as much as Kathleen Turner in the nude for "The Graduate". Richard Adler and Jerry Ross' show included "Hey There!" and the tango "Hernando's Hideaway".

"I now pronounce you - men and wives" is the memorable line from the film, "Seven Brides For Seven Brothers", which, unusually, was not based on a stage musical. The film starred Howard Keel and Jane Powell and the hit songs included "Bless Your Beautiful Hide" and "Sobbin' Women" as well as great barn dance sequences. If it was remade today, one of the brothers would have to be gay.

Errol Garner recorded his jazz instrumental, "Misty", in 1954. A lyric was added by Johnny Burke, but Burke became seriously ill and it was his last major song. "Misty" was passed to Johnny Mathis and it won him a gold record in 1959. In 1971 it was used to heighten the tension in "Play Misty For Me" where Clint Eastwood is terrorised by a psychotic fan.

Edith Piaf recorded "La Goualante Du Pauvre Jean" in 1954. It was passed to Capitol Records in America, who misheard the title, writing down "gens" for "Jean". Hence, it was given an English title and lyric as "The Poor People Of Paris", a UK No 1 for Winifred Atwell.

1955 - UNCHAINED MELODY
(Hy Zaret - Alex North)

Churchill resigns and is succeeded by Eden - First East-West summit in Geneva - Ruth Ellis is last women to be executed in UK - State of emergency in Cyprus - ITV starts, first ad is for Gibbs SR - Teddy Boy violence - Blue jeans imported to UK - Vladmir Nabokov writes "Lolita", but UK publication delayed until 1959.

You may have wondered why "Unchained Melody", is so called as it has nothing to do with the lyric. The answer is that the song was written for a long-forgotten prison drama, "Unchained", starring Elroy Hirsch and Barbara Hale. Todd Duncan sang it in the film but the hit versions came from the blind balladeer, Al Hibbler, and instrumentally from Les Baxter. It was a UK No.1 for Jimmy Young, who suffered stomach pains whilst recording the song and had to be rushed to hospital - after he'd finished the recording, y'understand. There is an hilarious, frenzied doowop version by Vito and the Salutations from 1963. It was recorded by the Righteous Brothers in 1965, whose recording was revived for the pottery-in-motion scene in "Ghost" in 1990. It should be retitled "Ghost Melody" now. Elvis Presley loved Roy Hamilton's recording of the song and, in 1977, he took to playing it himself on stage with his own piano accompaniment.

Another ballad, "Stranger In Paradise", was based on a melody from Borodin's 1888 opera "Prince Igor". A French song called "Je T'Appartiens" made its first

CHUCK BERRY

appearance in 1955 and a few years later, it was given an English lyric, "Let It Be Me". Although the title sounds archaic, "Love Is A Many Splendored Thing" was only written in 1955 and was the title song of a film starring William Holden and Jennifer Jones. The song was turned down by Tony Martin, Frank Sinatra, Doris Day and Nat "King" Cole, but the Four Aces appreciated its potential. When they made the charts, the artists who had rejected the song changed their minds and recorded their own versions!

Frank Loesser added "A Woman In Love" to the score of "Guys And Dolls", but surprisingly, this wonderful ballad was "sung" by Marlon Brando and not Frank Sinatra. Sinatra did not warm to Brando calling him "Mumbles" on the set and openly criticising him as "the most overrated actor in the world". Although Sinatra didn't get "A Woman In Love", he scored with "Love And Marriage", which he sang in a live TV musical based on Thornton Wilder's "Our Town".

All the above are great songs, but 1955 marked the start of rock'n'roll proper, especially at Chess Records in sweet home Chicago. Marshall Chess told me of Chuck Berry coming to audition for his father, Leonard: "Chuck Berry was a beautician who wanted to be a blues singer, and he had done time for robbing a gas station when he was a teenager. He wrote some songs and made a demo tape and came to Chicago. Being a blues fan, he went to see Muddy Waters and after the set, he told Muddy that he had a tape and asked what he could do with it. Muddy sent him to my father. There were two tunes on the tape, 'Wee Wee Hours' and 'Ida Red'. My father wasn't blown away by 'Wee Wee Hours', but he heard something different in the rhythm of 'Ida Red'. He didn't like the lyric and he told Chuck to write a new one and come back the following week. When Chuck came back, it had turned into 'Maybellene'."

That song about a car race, "Maybellene", gave Chuck Berry a gold record first time out, and I asked Marshall to explain the songwriting credit of Chuck Berry and the rock'n'roll DJ Alan Freed. "Not any more, his name has been taken off it now. My father recorded 'Maybellene' and he went on a road trip to the East Coast. Alan Freed was one of the most important disc-jockeys, and my father threw some payola at him, and some friendship too. Even though he gave people payola, some of them were also his friends. On the way back, he stopped in Pittsburg and called my uncle. My uncle said, 'You'd better come back, we're getting thousands of orders from New York because Alan Freed is playing 'Maybellene'. It's going to be a monster, our first big crossover hit.' I was 13 and I remember being with my dad when the record was on a big, white radio station, WIND, in Chicago. He was so proud that they were playing his record that he bought me a new bicycle."

Not content with discovering Chuck Berry in 1955, Leonard Chess also signed Bo Diddley. His earthy, "shave-and-a-haircut" rhythm can be heard throughout his music and also on Buddy Holly's "Not Fade Away" and Elvis Presley's "His Latest Flame". Bo Diddley felt he had been ripped off and did Marshall Chess appreciate his argument? "No, the sound came from some African rhythm that was passed along in the folk music tradition. It's like I know Robert Johnson didn't invent a lot of his riffs. A lot of them were prior to him, but you never hear about that. I feel sorry for Bo as he's always saying he was cheated on his record royalties and that everybody has been cheating him. It's not just Chess Records, he doesn't like George Michael either! I saw him five years ago at The Rock And Roll Hall Of Fame and I said, 'If you would let go of this and forgive everyone, you'd become much more creative. Your energy is being zapped in bitterness.' He patted me on the head like I was still a little boy."

"Bo Diddley" became a national hit and Bo was invited onto "The Ed Sullivan Show". Sullivan was horrified that someone should be singing about himself and ordered him to sing "Some Enchanted Evening" instead. On the broadcast, Bo played the opening notes, and then launched into "Bo Diddley". Many of Bo's subsequent songs are plays on his name - "Bo Diddley's A Gunslinger", "Diddley Daddy", "Bo Meets The Monster" and "Hey Bo Diddley". He's a one-trick pony to be sure, but what a trick.

In 1955 Big Joe Turner recorded the original version of "Shake, Rattle And Roll", although its lyrics were bowdlerised by Bill Haley. Haley tinkers with the whole lyric but -and this is 1955, remember - he is happy with the chauvinistic opening couplet: Joe has her in the kitchen with the pots and pans and Haley has her making breakfast. It is the erotic poetry of Jesse Stone's lyrics that Haley had to change for airplay on white radio stations. Turner sings:

> *"You wear those dresses, the sun keeps shining through,*
> *I can't believe my eyes, all the mess belongs to you."*

which Haley dilutes to,

> *"You wear those dresses, your hair done up so nice,*
> *You look so warm but your heart is cold as ice."*

Haley can do nothing with the oral sex in this couplet and deletes it completely:

> *"I'm going over the hill and way down underneath,*
> *You make me roll my eyes and then you make me grit my teeth."*

Another rock'n'roll song full of sexual innuendo was "Whole Lotta Shakin' Goin' On", which was recorded by Big Maybelle, its writer Roy Hall, and Dolores Fredericks before Jerry Lee Lewis. In this case, Lewis adds a swagger and cockiness which makes it far more suggestive, especially where he suggests you stand in one spot and wiggle around a little bit! Popular music would never be the same again.

JERRY LEE LEWIS

92

1956 - FEVER (Otis Blackwell - Eddie Cooley)

Khrushchev denounces Stalin - President Nasser nationalises Suez Canal - Suez War starts - Uprising in Hungary against the Soviet Union - Playgoers are waiting for Godot.

Otis Blackwell is the unsung hero of rock'n'roll writers with "All Shook Up", "Great Balls Of Fire" and "Fever" to his credit. (Otis put his stepfather's name, John Davenport, on "Fever" as he was moonlighting.) Little Willie John's rhythmic, small-band arrangement of "Fever" took six hours of studio time to perfect. A paranoid, argumentative man, Little Willie John was jailed for manslaughter and died in prison in 1968 as a result of fever, in his case pneumonia. By then, "Fever" was internationally known through Peggy Lee's stark version with bass, drums, fingersnapping and revised lyrics about historical figures. It has been recorded by Elvis Presley, Madonna, Etta James and, surprisingly, Doris Day. You can tell from the lyrics whose version they have been listening to.

John Osborne's "Look Back In Anger" saw the advent of the Angry Young Man, but its ill-tempered protagonist, Jimmy Porter, was devoted to jazz. Had Osborne written his play a year later, Porter might have been a Teddy Boy passionate about rock'n'roll. It was roll over Beethoven indeed as rock'n'roll was coming through with "Heartbreak Hotel", based on a newspaper story, "Blue Suede Shoes", the title being suggested to Carl Perkins by Johnny Cash, and "Singing The Blues" by Melvin Endsley, a crippled, polio victim who made his way to Nashville and pitched the song to Marty Robbins.

As well as recording "Roll Over Beethoven", Chuck Berry wrote and recorded "Brown Eyed Handsome Man", renaming the Venus De Milo as the Milo De Venus. Marshall Chess told me, "Neither Chuck nor my father would have known any better! Also, you didn't have overdubbing or multi-tracking in the 1950s and if you had a take that was perfect except for that, you would never go back and change it. You would have to do everything again." But, I asked, wouldn't Chuck Berry have been embarrassed about it later? "I doubt it, knowing him. He would have thought it was funny, he wouldn't have been embarrassed."

A strong MOR standard was "The Twelfth Of Never" while Don Gibson's "Sweet Dreams" is a great country ballad, recorded by Patsy Cline and Elvis Costello. Johnny Cash told us of "Folsom Prison Blues" with its memorable line, "I shot a man in Reno just to watch him die." Jester Hairston wrote a seasonal calypso in "Mary's Boy Child", which is now sung as a carol in churches. Everyone loved "Memories Are Made Of This" and the phrase passed into the language, while Buck Ram came up with the poser's favourite for the Platters, "The Great Pretender". Eddie Cochran's "Twenty Flight Rock" was perfomed as an Elvis parody in "The Girl Can't Help It", but the song is as structured as anything from Tin Pan Alley. Cochran did not write any of the song but received a cut - in. The real composer, Nelda Bingo, used a pseudonym, Ned Fairchild. Wonder why?

RAY CHARLES

Doc Pomus wrote "Lonely Avenue" for Ray Charles, and Ray himself was very adept at converting gospel songs to R&B classics, naturally claiming the songwriting credit along the way. "This Little Light Of Mine" became "This Little Girl Of Mine" (1955), "You Better Leave That Liar Alone" was transformed into "Leave My Woman Alone" (1956), and "Talkin' 'bout Jesus" was reworked as 'Talkin' 'bout You" (1958). Even Ray's classic "I Got A Woman (way cross town)" (1955) is a rewrite of "I Got A Saviour (way cross Jordan)", and another hit, "Hallelujah I Love Her So" (1956) was "Hallelujah I Love Him So", with the "Him" being Jesus. Ray disassociated himself from rock-'n'roll saying, "My music is more serious, filled with more despair than anything you'd associate with rock'n'roll."

Alan Jay Lerner and Frederick Loewe wrote the stage musical, "My Fair Lady", whose score included Vic Damone's No 1, "On The Street Where You Live" and which cleverly made a virtue of the fact that Rex Harrison couldn't really sing. It is a rare example of a hit musical without a title song. The powers-that-be couldn't agree on a title for the show and eventually they picked the title that everyone disliked the least, "My Fair Lady".

Bing Crosby, Frank Sinatra and Louis Armstrong starred in Cole Porter's dazzling film musical, "High Society", but its simple, tender ballad, "True Love", stole the public's imagination. Bing sang the song with his concertina and a little help from Grace Kelly. Much to Cole's annoyance, it didn't win an Oscar, being pipped by "Whatever Will Be, Will Be". However, the title of another song from "High Society", "Who Wants To Be A Millionaire?", became the key phrase of 1999 as Chris Tarrant's TV series became as popular as the National Lottery. At the time of writing, the title has a hollow ring as no-one, except possibly Chris Tarrant, has become a millionaire through the show.

1957 - MARIA
(Leonard Bernstein - Stephen Sondheim)

Macmillan becomes PM after Eden resigns - Common Market established - ERNIE picks out first premium bond winners - USSR launches first Sputnik and puts a dog, Laika, into orbit - Train disaster in fog at Lewisham.

This was the year that Leonard Bernstein (music) and Stephen Sondheim (lyrics) wrote an unprecedented, faultless musical about gang life in America, "West Side Story", which was loosely based on "Romeo And Juliet". They excelled with rhythmic songs ("Something's Coming"), witty songs ("I Feel Pretty", "Gee Officer Krupke!") and social comment ("America" and "Gee Officer Krupke!" again). However, it is the ballads ("Somewhere", "Maria" and "Tonight") that everyone remembers.

The director, Jerome Robbins, asked Sondheim what the hero, Tony, was doing during "Maria":

"Well, he's standing outside her house and hoping she'll appear on the balcony."
"Yeah, but what he is doing?"
"He's standing there and singing the song."
"You mean, he's just looking at the audience."
"Yes."
"Well then, you direct it."

Although "Maria" is magnificent, the controversial "Gee Officer Krupke!" shows Sondheim's lyrical ingenuity as it mocks criminal psychology.

*"Our mothers all are junkies,
Our fathers all are drunks
Golly, Moses, naturally we're punks."*

"Maria" is associated with Johnny Mathis, but both "Somewhere" and "Maria" were UK hit singles for P.J. Proby, whose croaking vocal style was a combination of Dinah Washington and Billy Eckstine. The 1996 recording of "West Side Story" was panned, but unfairly so. Aretha Franklin does "Somewhere" magnificently and the rap version of "Gee Officer Krupke!" from Salt-n-Pepa, Def Jef and Lisa "Left Eye" Lopes works very well and shows that the lyric was ahead of its time. All, however, are dwarfed by Little Richard's ultra-ultra-camp "I Feel Pretty".

Mike Todd's wide-screen epic "Around The World In Eighty Days" has not lasted with the years, but its theme song, Victor Young's "Around The World", was a Top 20 hit for Bing Crosby, Ronnie Hilton, Gracie Fields and Mantovani. The Music Man, Robert Preston, found fame with his bombastic "76 Trombones" and Frank Sinatra sang the poignant ballad, "All The Way", which is beautifully effective in the film "The Joker Is Wild".

In 1957 the country singer Bobby Helms had an international hit with the ballad, "My Special Angel". While he was working in Canada, his producer, Paul Cohen, sent him a demo of "Jingle Bell Rock", but Helms didn't care for it. He improved the lyric, added a high-pitched middle eight and recorded it with top country musicians at Bradley's Barn in Nashville. The song went to No.6 in the

US and also made the Top 40 in 1958 and 1960. In the UK, a cover version by Max Bygraves made the Top 10 here, and the song is now a seasonal standard.

Teenagers were becoming a marketeer's dream, and so many songs were written about young love including, well, "Young Love". Debbie Reynolds had international success with the theme song from "Tammy", the Everly Brothers had their first hit with "Bye Bye Love", written by the husband and wife team, Boudleaux and Felice Bryant, and Paul Anka longed for his former babysitter in "Diana". The Coasters parodied private eyes in Leiber and Stoller's "Searchin'" and sang about watching the girls go by in "Young Blood", which started with a title from Doc Pomus.

In 1957 the rock'n'roll manager, Joe Rock, was driving across Pittsburgh to see his protégés, the Skyliners. He watched the plane carrying his girlfriend to a new life in Oklahoma and he thought of the opening lines of a song,

THE EVERLY BROTHERS

> *"I don't have planes and schemes,*
> *I don't have hopes and dreams,*
> *I don't have anything,*
> *Since I don't have you."*

He scribbled them down at a red light, and by the time he reached the Skyliners and stopped at several more lights, he had the complete lyric. Within a day, their lead singer Jimmy Beaumount, had the melody, and another standard had been born.

Rock'n'roll was making celebrities of unlikely people. Screamin' Jay Hawkins was as theatrical as he was musical with skulls, severed hands and explosions as part of the act. He appeared on stage in a coffin (the Drifters nailed him in one night, and he beat them up afterwards!), and in the 60s, his act included the tortuous "Constipation Blues". In 1956, his girlfriend had had enough of his nonsense and threw her keys on to the stage.

NINA SIMONE

When he returned home, he found that she had scrawled "Goodbye" in scarlet lipstick on the bedroom mirror. Jay bellowed and from that roar, came his greatest song, "I Put A Spell On You". Everyone got drunk at the recording session as Jay groaned and growled his way through the song. The record was banned by many US radio stations for being "suggestive and cannibalistic", but undeterred, Jay drove around New York, sitting up in a coffin and drinking wine. This infuriated the National Casket Association which instructed its members to sell no more coffins to Screamin' Jay Hawkins. Nina Simone removed Hawkins' excesses and turned "I Put A Spell On You" into a standard. It has also been recorded by the Crazy World Of Arthur Brown, Creedence Clearwater Revival and Bryan Ferry. Similarly, many artists have recorded Muddy Waters' slice of voodoo, "Got My Mojo Working", a mojo being a sexual talisman.

Because of restrictions from the McCarthy era, Ewan MacColl was not allowed to play folk clubs and concerts in America with Peggy Seeger. While she returned to her homeland, he wrote "The First Time Ever I Saw Your Face", a US No 1 for Roberta Flack in 1971 and in April 2000, a hit for Celine Dion. Peggy Seeger recalls, "He never sang it except for that once to me. It was made for me and given to me and I sang it from then on. I first recorded it in 1963 and then the Kingston Trio and Peter, Paul and Mary did it. The last verse which says 'The first time ever I lay with you' was too much for some of them, and they changed it to 'danced with you'. The tune has been changed even more. Roberta Flack did it very differently in 1971. Ewan used to say that Elvis' version was like Juliet at the top of the Post Office Tower with Romeo at the bottom."

The PM, Harold Macmillan, asked Flanders and Swan, how they could hold an audience for two hours when he couldn't hold the Commons' attention for more than 20 minutes. At the drop of a hat, Flanders replied, "Try singing to them".

1958 - IT'S ONLY MAKE BELIEVE
(Conway Twitty - Jack Nance)

Crash at Munich Airport of plane carrying Manchester United team - Church of England supports family planning - Parking meters installed - Race riots in Notting Hill - First months of the Common Market - First life peerages - First stretch of motorway (M6 in Lancashire) opens - First edition of "Blue Peter".

Conway Twitty was trying to make it as a rock'n'roll singer, but his records were dying on their feet. He and his band were playing at the Flamingo Lounge in Hamilton, Ontario, and in-between their sets, his drummer Jack Nance was playing a piano in an empty room. Before one set, he said, "Hey, Conway, I've got something." As soon as they'd finished, they went to the piano and within 20 minutes, they had written the tense ballad, "It's Only Make Believe". Jack Nance said, "There was real good chemistry between Conway and I. The chord changes on 'It's Only Make Believe' were changes that Conway couldn't have come up with on his own, but he had a real good feel for words." Possibly the song had come quickly because of its similarity to an oldie, "All Of A Sudden My Heart Sings", which Paul Anka had covered. The publishers sued Twitty and Nance but as the matter was settled out of court, we will never know the truth of the matter.

CONWAY TWITTY

The Everly Brothers were the hottest act in Nashville, and Boudleaux Bryant told me, "We had about ten or twelve new songs for them to look at. They were getting songs from all over town and over 100 songs would be screened for each session." When Phil Everly heard one song, he stopped in his tracks. "I first heard 'All I Have To Do Is Dream' on an acetate and it was just Boudleaux and his guitar. I said, ' You could put that out and it would be a hit.'" The simple words of the lyric are enhanced by the phrase, "gee whiz". "I can't explain why I put 'gee whiz' in there," said Boudleaux, "It was just a lucky rhyme."

Paul Evans, who co-wrote the Kalin Twins' "When" with Jack Reardon, recalls: "It was right after the Everly Brothers hit big and every label was looking for country-sounding pop duets. Decca had signed the Kalin Twins, and we sent the song to the Kalins' producer, who didn't like it much. He put it among the rejects, but when the Kalins got to his office, he wasn't there and they played those demos by mistake. They loved 'When' and their producer was too embarrassed to tell them that he had rejected it. It had a thrilling arrangement by Jack Pleis that really helped the record."

Don Gibson's country ballad, "I Can't Stop Loving You", would become a No 1 hit for Ray Charles in 1962, while Chuck Berry's "Johnny B. Goode" contained the riff that inspired a million guitarists. Surprisingly, Chuck Berry only had one UK Top 20 hit in the 1950s and that was "Sweet Little Sixteen", also in 1958. As Marshall Chess of Chess Records says, "He was energised by the 1950s in America and he must have known a lot of young white girls as his songs are so attuned to that booming teen culture."

Buddy Holly recorded Paul Anka's song, "It Doesn't Matter Anymore" and his own ballad, "True Love Ways". Phil Spector wrote "To Know Him Is To Love Him" after seeing the words on his father's tombstone and he recorded it as part of the group, the Teddy Bears. Eddie Cochran sang of teenage problems in "Summertime Blues" and so did the Coasters in "Yakety Yak". Another Coasters song, "Sorry, But I'm Gonna Have To Pass" meant little at the time, but it returned them to the charts in 1994 after being used on a TV ad. An excellent Coasters song, "Hey Sexy", was considered too racy for its time and it wasn't released until 1992. Slim Dusty was the archetypal Aussie in "A Pub With No Beer", which he has sung with many new verses over the years. By way of contrast, Cliff Richards "Move It!" only has one verse, which is repeated, because the songwritter Ian Samwell couldn't think of anything else.

Nobody remembers the song that won the 1958 Eurovision Song Contest, "Dors, Mon Amour", for France, but the Italian entry, which came second, has become a standard. Domenico Modugno sang "Volare (Nel Blu Dipinto Di Blu)" or, in English, "To Fly (The Blue Painted In Blue)", which was inspired by a picture on a packet of cigarettes. The next year he was back with "Ciao Ciao Bambino", another standard, and this time he was sixth. Something wrong somewhere.

The Poni-Tails scored with "Born Too Late", with its intriguing songwriting credits of Fred Tobias and Charles Strouse. Eight members of the Tobias family worked on Tin Pan Alley songs. There were the three brothers Harry, Charles and Henry, the wives of Harry and Charles, and three of their sons! The three brothers wrote "Miss You" (for Rudy Vallee in 1929). Harry wrote "Sweet And Lovely" and "Sail Along Silv'ry Moon", Charles wrote "Don't Sit Under The Apple Tree" and "The Old Lamplighter", and Henry had success with "If I Had My Life To Live Over" and "Katinka" for Mae West. Charles' son, Fred, also has his name on "Good Timin'" (1960), "Johnny Will" (1961) and "Blue River" (1963). Its co-writer, Charles Strouse, wrote the musicals, "Bye Bye Birdie" (1960), "Annie" (1976) and several others, but he has never had another song as big as "Born Too Late".

CHUBBY CHECKER

1959 - THE TWIST (Hank Ballard)

> Death of Buddy Holly, Ritchie Valens and the Big Bopper in a plane crash - Fidel Castro seizes power in Cuba - English Channel crossed by hovercraft - USSR spaceship reaches the moon - Postcodes introduced - Duty free shops established.

A gospel group, the Sensational Nightingales, had the original idea for the twist, but because they didn't perform secular material, they passed it to the R&B singer, Hank Ballard. He reworked the song and released it as "The Twist". The DJ Dick Clark liked his record but preferred a teenage artist performing the song and demonstrating the dance on his "American Bandstand" programme. Hence, the clean-cut Chubby Checker, whose record started a world craze and whose name was a play on the name Fats Domino. Domino himself cut the

extremely infectious "Be My Guest" in 1959, which was the inspiration for Van Morrison's "Precious Time" 40 years later. Chubby Checker's version of "The Twist" topped the US charts in 1960 and led to numerous twist songs (including "The Peppermint Twist", "Let's Twist Again", "Twistin' The Night Away", "Twist And Shout", "Ya Ya Twist", "The Oliver Twist" and, flashing forwards to 1983, "Twisting By The Pool") and other dance records ("The Locomotion", "Pony Time", "Limbo Rock", "The Fly", "The Mashed Potato", "The Wah-Watusi" and "Hanky Panky"). Everybody could twist, but few of the other dances were known in the UK, although the records themselves may have done well.

Chuck Berry wrote a hundred great lyrics and two good tunes. His records sound similar but his wordplay on "The Promised Land", "Nadine" and "Too Much Monkey Business" make him the poet of rock'n'roll. Chuck liked a Muddy Waters song about a telephone conversation, "Long Distance Call" (1951), and set about writing one himself. Most of his songs were about teenage problems, but this was about a man wanting to see his six-year old daughter now that he and her mother had split up. The song, "Memphis, Tennessee".

Towards the end of one of his bookings, Ray Charles told his band, "I'm just gonna fool around and y'all follow me." He played a riff that was floating in his head and it felt so good that he kept going. He improvised lyrics around the phrase, "Tell me what'd I say", and then grunted and groaned sounds of sexual ecstasy which he wanted the Raelets to repeat. He refined the song in subsequent performances and then he recorded it as "What'd I Say", working with the newly-invented Wurlitzer electric piano. It was the 1950s "Sexual Healing" and as Eric Burdon said, "His whole message was 'Take your old lady home and make love to her'." When you read Ray Charles' autobiography, you realise Eric Burdon was right, although in Ray's case, it wasn't just his old lady.

Bobby Darin, who would cut a tribute album to Ray Charles, wrote and recorded "Dream Lover". Frank Sinatra sang "High Hopes" and Billy Eckstine serenaded "Gigi". Martin Denny created an exotica classic in "Quiet Village", while the theme music for the Greek film, "Never On Sunday", was very distinctive. Jerry Leiber and Mike Stoller had a remarkable year with the Coasters writing "Charlie Brown" (banned by the BBC for using the delinquent word "spitball" for a pea-shooter), "Three Cool Cats" (with some Cuban rhythms), "Along Came Jones" (a parody of TV westerns), "I'm A Hog For You" (the best of the nursery rhyme rock'n'roll songs) and "Poison Ivy" (arguably about VD), amongst others.

The Belgian singer-songwriter, Jacques Brel, introduced a pleading, obsessive ballad, "Ne Me Quitte Pas" which, with a Rod McKuen lyric, would become "If You Go Away". McKeun wrote:

> *"I'd have been the shadow of your dog*
> *If I thought it might have kept me by your side."*

He says, "I only used one line of Brel's in 'If You Go Away' and that was the line about being 'the shadow of your dog'. However, only Frank Sinatra and I have ever sung that song right. Everybody else sings 'I'd have been the shadow of your shadow', which is wrong.'" But just as good.

The critics dismissed Rodgers and Hammerstein's "The Sound Of Music" as sickly and sweet, but it told the true life story of the Trapp's escape from the Nazis. The score included "My Favourite Things", "Do-Re-Mi", "Edelweiss" and "Climb Ev'ry Mountain". Hammerstein was very ill when he wrote the musical and he died shortly after the Broadway opening. The 1965 film version with Julie Andrews works as a sentimental story, a great musical - and a camp classic. Recently, some cinemas have been encouraging audience participation nights, clearly supposing it has a similar appeal to "The Rocky Horror Show".

1960 - SAVE THE LAST DANCE FOR ME
(Doc Pomus - Mort Shuman)

Princess Margaret marries photographer, Anthony Armstrong-Jones - Francis Chichester sails across the Atlantic - Laser beams invented - Conscription abolished - Trial of "Lady Chatterley's Lover": "Is it a book you would wish your wife or your servant to read" - Harold Pinter writes "The Caretaker".

A new generation of songwriters were working in cubicles in or around the Brill Building. Doc Pomus, a crippled blues songwriter in his thirties, teamed with a younger writer, Mort Shuman, to write teenage love songs. Doc used to take his beautiful wife dancing and he would allow her to dance with other men, provided she returned at the end of the evening, got hold of him and his sticks and guided him across the floor. From this experience came "Save The Last Dance For Me". If you listen to the song knowing this fact, you realise that it is about voyeurism, the singer enjoys seeing his woman dancing with other men.

Opposite the Brill Building at 1650 Broadway, Gerry Goffin and Carole King wrote their first hit of real significance with "Will You Love Me Tomorrow", again a song with a double dimension. The Shirelles sang it as teenage angst, but Carole King, by slowing it down on "Tapestry", related it to a broken marriage. Shirley Alston of the Shirelles recalls, "When I first heard it, I didn't think it was the right song for the Shirelles. The way that Carole King had presented it to us was more on the country side, she did it very laid back on the piano. There was nothing wrong with the way she was singing it but we wanted to be more into R&B, rather than being considered a pop act. Our producer, Luther Dixon, said, 'Just do it as a favour to me.' As soon as I went to the session and started to hear the music, I heard the life come into it and I thought it was beautiful. I was crying on that session. It's a beautiful song and a lot of people thought it was risqué It's all about 'Will you respect me in the morning?', so they were right."

Other excellent pop songs were Roy Orbison's "Only The Lonely", Jack Scott's "What In The World's Come Over You" and what, ironically, became Eddie Cochran's final record, "Three Steps To Heaven". Elvis Presley, now back on Civvy Street, sang "Stuck On You" and Mort Shuman told me about the writers: "John Leslie McFarland was more than eccentric, he was mad, totally round the bend. He escaped from prison and went to an airfield, flew off in a plane and landed it without ever having flown a plane before! We wrote 'Little Children' together and he wrote 'Stuck On You' with Aaron Schroeder. Aaron Schroeder looks like the head of an insurance company, a really dapper business man and it's hard to imagine him writing with this totally spaced-out lunatic. John Leslie made a couple of years of my life worthwhile."

Eric Spear wrote the theme for "Coronation Street", Bernard Herrmann was wonderfully sinister with his spine-tingling music at the Bates Motel in "Psycho" and Edith Piaf sang the Georges Moustaki song, "Milord". Translating Continental hits was specialist work undertaken by a few key lyricists such as Norman Newell: "'Sailor' was a tremendous hit in Germany, and the publisher phoned me one Friday and asked me to do the lyric over the weekend. He said he would send someone round to pick it up on Monday morning and I said I would have it ready - and something I will never, ever understand is that I completely forgot about it. I was astonished when I saw his messenger boy and I told him to go for a cup of coffee while I wrote the lyrics, which I did in ten minutes. I wondered if it was good enough, as you do when something comes quickly, but it became a tremendous hit, thank heavens. Petula Clark, Anne Shelton and the Andrews Sisters all did well with it."

The big country hit was the ridiculous "He'll Have To Go" - the singer wants the girl to whisper sweet nothings down the phone while she has a man by her side. Brian Hyland told of the girl with the "Itsy Bitsy Teenie Weenie Yellow Polka Dot Bikini". "Goodness Gracious Me" was a cleverly worded novelty hit, lyrics by Herbert Kretzmer, for Peter Sellers and Sophia Loren. The Coasters largely narrated "Shoppin' For Clothes", which was much more than a novelty, brilliantly conveying life in a black community. In his ethnic way, Andy Stewart told of "A Scottish Soldier", which was based on "The Green Hills Of Tyrol".

East-ender Lionel Bart, who had written the pop hits "A Handful Of Songs" (1957), "Living Doll" (1959) and "Do You Mind?" (1960), wrote the musical, "Oliver!" based on "Oliver Twist". "Charles Dickens wrote 'Oliver Twist' as a serial," Lionel Bart told me, "and that's why there are so many sub-plots. I had to condense a lot of that, and in addition, Fagin was only a two-dimensional villain. I had to give him a third dimension so I took the mickey out of myself to do that." The key song, "As Long As He Needs Me", became a career record for Shirley Bassey. "She hated 'As Long As He Needs Me'. This was before she'd had her voice trained and she couldn't hit the top note. She got so mad that she threw her wig at me."

DEAN MARTIN'S HIT, "THATS AMORE", EDDIE COCHRAN AND JIM REEVES WHO HAD A HIT WITH "HE'LL HAVE TO GO".

1961 - CRAZY (Willie Nelson)

Yuri Gagarin becomes the first man in space - Abortive Bay of Pigs invasion of Cuba - MOT tests for cars introduced - Start of Vietnam War - Joseph Heller writes "Catch 22".

Willie Nelson has said, "If a song had more than than three chords in it, there was a good chance it wouldn't ever be called country, and there was no way you could make a record that wasn't called country in Nashville at that time. I had problems because 'Crazy' had four or five chords in it. Not that it's real complicated, it just isn't your basic hillbilly song."

After several years of struggling, Willie Nelson had written a country No 1, "Hello Walls" (1961) for Faron Young, and everyone wanted his songs. Billy Walker sang Willie's demo on "Funny How Time Slips Away" and the song was intended for Patsy Cline. However, Billy's record label, Columbia, heard his demo and rescheduled a session to cut it as a single. Cline, a quick-tempered woman, was furious that Walker had stolen her song, and told Nelson to give her another one that had better be as good. Willie had written "Crazy", a reflective, conversational song inspired by leaving his family to sell songs in Nashville, and Cline was unimpressed.

When Patsy returned home, she found that her husband, Charlie Dick, had also got a copy of Willie's demo, and he loved the song. Her record producer, Owen Bradley, also said that it was uncommonly good. Cline agreed, but converted it to her style so that she could sing more of the lyrics. Ironically, this made the session more difficult as she had problems in reaching the notes. She was recovering from a car accident and she had a fractured hip and head injuries. Owen Bradley asked her to return a week later and he cut a new vocal, which was perfect. The song became a country classic and Willie has said that her version is "the favourite of anything I ever wrote."

A radio DJ and sports commentator, Ray Winkler, was a friend of Jim Reeves, but he couldn't interest Jim in his songs. Jim told him, "I wouldn't record a song, even if it was written by my own grandmother, if I didn't think it would sell and be a good song for my career." Eventually, in 1961, Ray gave Jim Reeves the song he wanted, "Welcome To My World". Jim recorded it for his album, "A Touch Of Velvet", but it was two years before it was issued as a single and became an international hit.

Jacques Brel wrote a reflective chanson about a man on his deathbed, "Le Moribund", and this has been a UK No 1 twice as "Seasons In The Sun", first for Terry Jacks in 1974 and then for Westlife in 1999. Roy Orbison sang two highly emotional ballads of his own, "Crying" and "Running Scared", as well as having a great B-side with Boudleaux Bryant's "Love Hurts". Taking a leaf from Ray Charles' book, Ben E. King updated an old gospel song and it became "Stand By Me": "I took it from an old spiritual that the Soul Stirrers did, (sings) 'Oh Lord, stand by me' but in the end my tune was nothing like that. Many, many times I have heard my song, 'Stand By Me', being done by gospel groups, which is very pleasing to me. The song bounced back into life when it was used as the title for a movie in 1987, and it gave me a whole new audience of young kids to sing to."

WILLIE NELSON

Acker Bilk played "Stranger On The Shore" (which he now introduces as "Strangler On The Floor"). "I called it 'Jenny' at first," says Acker, "because my daughter had been born around that time. A BBC producer was making a TV series called 'Stranger On The Shore' and he thought 'Jenny' would make a good theme tune. Columbia said, 'We'd better call it "Stranger On The Shore", so poor Jenny was done out of her tune."

Anthony Newley and Leslie Bricusse included "What Kind Of Fool Am I" and "Gonna Build A Mountain" in their musicial, "Stop The World, I Want To Get Off", and Newley admitted, "It was a very slight piece, even for the 60s, but it had a good score." If ever a song was made by one cryptic phrase, it was "Moon River": what did "my huckleberry friend" mean? Johnny Mercer wrote the words and Henry Mancini the music, and the song was featured in the Audrey Hepburn movie, "Breakfast At Tiffany's".

The Coasters sang of their love for a stripper in "Little Egypt", which was subsequently recorded by Elvis Presley, and. talking of strippers, "Wheels Cha Cha" is now used for comic male nude dances with balloons. Elvis sang "Can't Help Falling In Love" in his beach movie, "Blue Hawaii": it was a hit for him and then in a faster version by Andy Williams in 1970. Elvis used the song as his way of thanking an audience and it became his closing number night after night in the 70s.

1962 - SOFTLY AS I LEAVE YOU
(Hal Shaper - Tony de Vita)

"Sunday Times" introduces the first colour supplement - Telstar satellite launched - Death of Marilyn Monroe - Macmillan sacks seven ministers and Harold Wilson calls him "Mac The Knife" - US discovers Soviet missile bases in Cuba and imposes a naval blockade - James Hanratty executed - Anthony Burgess writes "A Clockwork Orange" and first James Bond film, "Doctor No" is released.

Some people don't look right for their role. Matt Monro could have been up there with Frank Sinatra and Andy Williams, but he still looked like a London busdriver on a posh night out. He brought out the best in British writers, being the first to record standards by Cyril Ornadel and Norman Newell ("Portrait Of My Love", 1960), Leslie Bricusse ("My Kind Of Girl", 1961) and John Barry and Don Black ("Born Free", 1966). His greatest moment came in 1962 with "Softly As I Leave You".

The lyricist Hal Shaper recalls, "I was in Italy in 1961 and Tony de Vita was playing me a symphony in three movements that he had written. I loved the melody in the second movement and I brought it back to England. I made a piano demo and gave it to Matt Monro. About three months later, he said, 'I've been playing that tune endlessly. We're going to record it. Can you let George Martin have the lyrics by 10.30 tomorrow morning?' I said, 'Fine' and went home and tried to remember the tune. Luckily, I came up with a lyric and Matt recorded it. The lyric wasn't all that wonderful on paper but Johnnie Spence's arrangement rolled down, Matt did one take and we all looked at one another and said, 'Well, that's it.'

The song was a UK hit for Matt Monro, and then moved to America. Hal Shaper: "The song started slowly in America, although it was a Top 40 record. Then Doris Day recorded it, followed by Andy Williams and Brenda Lee. In those days, if you had a hit with a ballad, a number of wonderful singers would include it on their next album, which doesn't happen anymore. Then, in 1964, Frank Sinatra recorded the song, which kicked it off into glory, although I've never heard anybody sing it better than Matt. I love his version."

Songs can take on a meaning of their own. Hal Shaper again: "Elvis had gone to Las Vegas where Jerry Vale was singing 'Softly As I Leave You', and Jerry told Elvis a story about a man scribbling down this note on his deathbed. Elvis, who was psychically and mystically involved in everything, believed it to be true, and the song became a great favourite of his. When Elvis did it on stage for a live album, he said that I wrote the song on my deathbed."

Gerry Goffin and Carole King's songs were just as well-crafted as the earlier occupants of the Brill Building, and this is perfectly illustrated in "Up On The Roof", a song about living in the city and wanting to get away from it all. Gerry Goffin's lyric contains internal rhymes (stairs / cares) and the use of the word "drift" is magical. Rudy Lewis, the Drifters' new lead singer, was well up to the song and the production was sensitively handled by Jerry Leiber and Mike Stoller, superb songwriters themselves. Another great Carole King song from the same year is "Crying In The Rain" for the Everly Brothers, this time with a lyric from Howard Greenfield.

CAROLE KING

Nat "King" Cole sang that curious ballad, "Let There Be Love", with George Shearing's accompaniment. What other hit song contains a reference to chilli con carne, which sounded exotic at the time? David Rose recorded his percussive and sleazy composition, "The Stripper", which is now used by strippers everywhere. Booker T and the MG's created the insidious "Green Onions", which would also suit strippers, I think. Monty Norman wrote "The James Bond Theme" for "Doctor No", and the TV theme from "Maigret" is still known today. Gilbert Becaud introduced "Et Maintenant" which became "What Now My Love", which I prefer to punctuate as "What! Now, my love?"

A feature-length Italian documentary about human eccentricities, "Mondo Cane", was a controversial success, but Norman Newell put lyrics to its romantic theme music by Riz Ortolani and renamed it "More". Norman Newell recalls, "The Assistant MD at EMI had been offered the soundtrack of the film and he asked me to write lyrics for the main theme. It was a beautiful tune and it gave me trouble in one part only. The section that goes 'Laughing, weeping' took me three weeks to get right. Danny Williams recorded the lyric first and then Andy Williams, and there have been over a thousand different recordings. Because of this, it should be the lyric that I am most proud of but I prefer 'Portrait Of My Love'."

1962 was a scary year and anyone who was alive then is lucky to have survived. Statisticians have determined that the chance of a full scale nuclear war was 1 in 5 - shorter odds than dying when playing Russian Roulette. Pete Seeger recalls, "I wrote down three lines:

'Where are the flowers, the girls
have plucked them,
Where are the girls, they've all taken
husbands,
Where are the men, they're all in the army.'

Read them in a book, 'And Quiet Flows The Don' by Mikhail Sholokhov, the Soviet author. He describes the Cossacks galloping off to join the Czar's army and singing an old Ukranian song. I was on a plane riding over Ohio to sing for some college students, and I pulled out those three lines. I was kinda sleepy and this is where your sub-conscious goes to work and the song, 'Where Have All the Flowers Gone?', was put together in twenty minutes. The line, 'Long time passing', had been with me for several years. I had wanted to use it in a song, but hadn't figured how."

The Kingston Trio established "Where Have All The Flowers Gone?", but the most poignant interpretation comes from Marlene Dietrich, who sings it in English on one side of her single and in German on the other.

A grandmother, Malvina Reynolds, wrote a song about the effects of a nuclear disaster, "What Have They Done To The Rain", which became a hit for the Searchers in 1964. Quite appropriate that Skeeter Davis should sing about "The End Of The World", although in her case, it was a love affair. Maybe it's better to be like Cliff Richard, who was happy to be a Bachelor Boy - and still is.

1963 - BLOWIN' IN THE WIND (Bob Dylan)

BBC withdraws ban on mentioning sex, religion, politics and royalty in comedy programmes - Profumo resigns - President Kennedy visits Berlin - Philby discovered in Moscow - Martin Luther King's "I have a dream" speech - Great Train Robbery - Alec Douglas-Home becomes PM - de Gaulle says "Non" to UK entry into Common Market - President Kennedy is assassinated.

BOB DYLAN

If I was asked to nominate the Songwriting Year of the Century, I'd chose 1963. I come from Liverpool and I was 18 at the time, so it is a highly emotional choice, but it is the year that transformed popular music, if not the whole of popular culture. Both the Beatles and Bob Dylan came to the fore and the combination of their very different talents and objectives was a very engaging mix. For good or for bad, nearly every performer or group thought they should be writing their own material, and the downside is thousands of substandard and derivative songs. It would be interesting to know what Lennon, McCartney or Dylan thought about their responsibility for this, or indeed, if they even thought about it at all.

Bob Dylan's first album, released in 1962, was largely a collection of folk songs, but two of his own compositions, "Talkin' New York" and "Song To Woody", offered a taste of what was to come. However, no-one could have predicted the extraordinary power of "The Freewheelin' Bob Dylan", an album which is equally compelling today. Every track is superb, and five songs have become standards in their own way - "Girl From The North Country" (with a melody leaning heavily on "Scarborough Fair"), "A Hard Rain's A-Gonna Fall" (Dylan's response to the Cuban missile crisis), "Masters Of War" (Dylan at his most venomous), "Don't Think Twice, It's Alright" (a bittersweet love song) and "Blowin' In The Wind".

The young Bob Dylan was performing a black spiritual, "No More Auction Block For Me", around Greenwich Village. He took the spiritual, reworked it and wrote the bitter, anti-war song, "Blowin' In The Wind". In the liner notes to his second album, the freewheelin' Bob Dylan wrote, "I'm only 21 years old and I know that there's been too many wars. You people over 21 should know better." For all that, "Blowin' In The Wind" does not sound like a man on a soapbox. Considering the length of most of his songs, "Blowin' In The Wind" is simplicity itself. The lyric only consists of nine questions about peace and civil rights, and the morose answer to each is "blowin' in the wind", which may be no answer at all. One question relates to Civil Rights, which led to the song becoming the anthem of the movement in America.

If Dylan is writing about the crises facing politicians in 1963, you might wonder why he refers to "cannonballs" flying. Why should he use such antiquated imagery? The answer, my friend, is that it gives a sense of history, a theme he developed in "With God On Our Side" the following year.

A British folk singer, Sydney Carter, took the melody from a Shaker hymn of 1778, "Tis The Gift To Be Simple", and wrote "Lord Of The Dance". Like Dylan's work, it seems a protest song, but, primarily, Carter is protesting about the stuffiness of church services.

He sees Jesus as a Pied Piper, but "It's hard to dance with the Devil on your back". "Lord Of The Dance" hardly sounds controversial, but consider the climate in which it was written. The Bishop of Woolwich was branded as a heretic for merely saying in his book, "Honest To God", that God was not an old man in the sky.

All of the A-sides of the Beatles' singles in their heyday featured bright and bouncy, energetic melodies and their early hits played with personal pronouns - "Please Please Me", "From Me To You", "She Loves You" and "I Want To Hold Your Hand". They wrote some good ballad B-sides in 1963 ("Thank You Girl", "I'll Get You", "This Boy"), some brilliant album tracks ("I Saw Her Standing There", "All My Loving") and hits for other performers ("Do You Want To Know A Secret?", "Bad To Me", "I'll Keep You Satisfied", "Hello Little Girl", "I'm In Love", "I Wanna Be Your Man"). Even though some had been written during their formative years, this was a remarkable achievement - and the Beatles had hardly started. There is, however, none of the political awareness of Dylan in their songs: if they had been interested in social commentary, they could have written about Rachmanism or Profumo.

Two girls, Christine Keeler and Mandy Rice-Davies, unwittingly brought about the downfall of a cabinet minister (John Profumo), a Prime Minister (Harold Macmillan) and, in 1964, a Government (the Conservative administration). Ms Rice-Davies made a pop record, "A Good Man Is Hard To Find" although, on reflection, it should have been called "A Hard Man Is Good To Find", while Joyce Blair as Miss X made the charts with "Christine". No songwriter wrote seriously about the Profumo affair - that was left to Dusty Springfield with the Pet Shop Boys' "In Private" in 1989.

On a UK concert tour, Roy Orbison held his own with the Beatles. He was top form with the descriptive "Blue Bayou" and "In Dreams" with its beautiful opening image, "A candy-coloured clown they call the Sandman."

His compadre in dramatic high endings, Gene Pitney, wrestled with his conscience in Burt Bacharach and Hal David's intense "24 Hours From Tulsa". Jack Nitzsche and Sonny Bono wrote "Needles And Pins" for Jackie De`Shannon, which was covered, or rather copied, by the Searchers. The phase, "needles and pins-er", turned a good song into a great one.

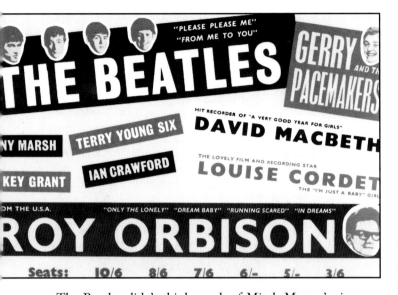

The Beatles didn't think much of Mitch Murray's singalong pop, but he wrote very good, Bobby Vee-styled material. He scored with "How Do You Do It?" and "I Like It" for Gerry and the Pacemakers and "You Were Made For Me" for Freddie and the Dreamers, although he had intended it for the Searchers. Phil Spector had developed his Wall of Sound and he had the good sense to start with good songs from the Brill Building - "Da Doo Ron Ron", "Then He Kissed Me" and "Be My Baby". Charles Aznavour scored with "La Mamma" in France, which, translated by Don Black, became "For Mama" for Matt Monro in 1964. Hank Cochran's publisher told him that "Make The World Go Away" was the worst song he had written, but he soon changed his mind.

In the West End world, Leslie Bricusse followed Lionel Bart by turning to Charles Dickens, whose work was conveniently out of copyright. Bricusse's version of "The Pickwick Papers", "Pickwick", featured Harry Secombe, a case of perfect casting, although the musical had been intended for that gap-toothed cad, Terry-Thomas. When Pickwick is mistaken for a parliamentary candidate, he sang "If I Ruled The World", which is now associated with Tony Bennett.

TONY BENNETT

The poetess, Patience Strong, was 20 years too early with "A Quiet Hour", an album which foreshadowed New Age music. Oh, and the top new classical piece from 1963 - Sir William Walton's "Variations On A Theme By Hindemith". Anyone remember that?

1964 - THE PROMISED LAND (Chuck Berry)

Cassius Clay (Muhammad Ali) becomes world heavyweight champion - Dr Beeching closes railways - Radio Caroline starts broad casting - Nelson Mandala starts prison sentence - Khrushchev toppled in coup by Brezhnev - Harold Wilson becomes Prime Minister - Mods and rockers clash at Brighton - UK abolishes capital punishment - Films include "A Fistful Of Dollars" and "Mary Poppins" - The Moog synthesiser goes on sale

While Chuck Berry was doing time for procuring girls, he asked a guard for a map of America. The prison authorities thought he was planning his escape but he wanted to write a song. In his take on "Route 66", an impoverished, probably black kid in Norfolk, Virginia travels to California, Chuck's idea of the Promised Land. The song recounts his adventures along the way - he runs into conflict in downtown Birmingham, but some friends in Houston buy him a silk suit and put some luggage in his hand. When he reaches his Canaan, he rings home,

"Take the folks back home,
This is the promised land calling,
And the po' boy is on the line."

When Chuck was released in 1964, he found his songs had a fresh popularity because of the British beat groups, and he recorded new ones that were equally good - "The Promised Land", "Nadine" ("I was campaign shouting like a southern Diplomat"), "You Never Can Tell" ("700 little records, all rock, rhythm and jazz") and "No Particular Place To Go" ("I couldn't unfasten her safety belt"). He started 1965 with the deplorable "Dear Dad" and since then, he has hardly written anything decent. Pity 'cause lap-dancing, the Internet and indeed, prison life would be ideal subjects for Chuck Berry's shrewd observations.

Numerous artists have recorded "The Promised Land" including Freddy Weller (a US country hit in 1971), Elvis Presley (a singles hit often performed in concert), James Taylor (doing James Taylor) and Johnnie Allan (with an excellent cajun take on the tune), and it has even been the foundation for a BBC Radio 2 series with Andy Kershaw. Not all the artists can be bothered to learn the words and, indeed, Chuck sings so fast it can be hard to catch them. No-one, though, has topped the Rolling Stones' 1964 take on "Route 66" in which Mick Jagger either places Moscow in the middle of America or else they are taking an extraordinary detour. Still, they probably never thought that their record would be heard outside the UK.

The Nashville songwriter, Curly Putnam, was moved by the country boy in the 1950 gangster film, "The Asphalt Jungle", who dreams of going back home, and when he gets there, he dies. It inspired "Green Green Grass Of Home", which is the perfect country song - it mentions the old hometown, mama, trains, a girl called Mary, a preacher, death and a funeral - and it includes a narration. You could argue that it was crossword puzzle writing, that it was simply getting everything to fit within the framework of a three minute song, but I love the song precisely for that reason.

"Green Green Grass Of Home" was first recorded by Johnny Darrell in 1964, then Jerry Lee Lewis and from there, Tom Jones, who heard it as the opening cut on Jerry Lee's album, "Country Songs For City Folks". A BBC-TV documentary about Tom Jones' roots showed you the old oak tree in Pontypridd as though it was a part of the song. It wasn't. Spare a thought for Johnny Darrell who also beat Kenny Rogers to "Ruby, Don't Take Your Love To Town" and O.C. Smith to "The Son Of Hickory Holler's Tramp", but lost out in the gold disc stakes.

It was a good year for show tunes, "If I Were A Rich Man" (from "Fiddler On The Roof,") "Hello, Dolly!" (although its melody was based, probably unknowingly, on a 1949 Frank Sinatra hit, "Sunflower") and "People" (from "Funny Girl"). Bob Merrill wrote "People" with Jule Styne: if he was capable of writing such great ballads, why did he only give novelties to Guy Mitchell?

Mary Wells established Tamla-Motown in the UK with "My Guy" and Astrud Gilberto sang the sensuous rhythms of "The Girl From Ipanema". Betty Everett was the first to record "The Shoop Shoop Song (It's In His Kiss)". Burt Bacharach and Hal David wrote the underrated "A House Is Not A Home" for Brook Benton as well as "(There's) Always Something There To Remind Me" and "Walk On By", both originally recorded by Dionne Warwicke. The Swingle Singers made an impact with their album, "Jazz Sebastian Bach", and Phil Ochs offered the poignant "There But For Fortune". The best Lennon and McCartney song of the year was the ballad, "And I Love Her" from the film, "A Hard Day's Night". No sooner had they written it than Mick and Keith had "As Tears Go By" ready for Marianne Faithfull.

Charles Aznavour sang "Hier Encore", which, in 1969, became "Yesterday When I Was Young". Aznavour said, "I wrote my first song about being old when I was 18. The songs I wrote many years ago haven't dated at all, although my way of singing them, my interpretation, has become sweeter."

Dave Berry performed Geoff Stephens song, "The Crying Game" slowly, sinuously and sensually. John Braine borrowed the title for a novel and then, in 1992, a new version by Boy George was the title song for a film about gender, race and Northern Ireland starring Stephen Rae and Jaye Davidson.

See the film "Little Voice" for Michael Caine's remarkably funny take on Roy Orbison's "It's Over". That was written by Roy Orbison and Bill Dees, who had a curious way of working together. Roy would go on tour and when he returned, Bill would play him his new compositions. Roy would say, "I like this bit" and "I like that bit", and he would take those sections and develop them. We once had Bill as a house guest and he bombarded us with old, new and half-completed songs. He had a song for every occasion and if he hadn't one, he'd write it on the spot. Despite his warmth, his generosity and his friendship, three days of song after song after song was too much and we needed a month to recover. We still talk about when Bill came to stay and it gave us a good insight into how he wrote with Orby - and why Orby had to go on tour.

Also in 1964, Roy and Bill wrote "Oh Pretty Woman" and Bill told me, "Roy's wife, Claudette, said, 'Give me some money, honey' and it was a very flirtatious scene as he said, 'What for?' and she replied, 'I've got to go to the store'. I said, 'A pretty woman don't need no money' and he started singing, 'Pretty woman, walking down the street'. He sang while I was banging my hands on the table and by the time Claudette came back, we had the song. The 'yeah, yeah, yeah' in 'Oh Pretty Woman' probably came from the Beatles."

1965 - YESTERDAY
(John Lennon - Paul McCartney)

Death of Winston Churchill - Cigarette ads no longer allowed on TV - President Lyndon Johnson sends marines to Vietnam - Brady and Hindley arrested for the Moor Murders - Pizza Express opens - Miniskirts in fashion.

Paul McCartney awoke one day with the music for "Yesterday" in his head. It had come so naturally that he was convinced it was some song he'd remembered. He put a dummy lyric to it about scrambled eggs, and played it to the other Beatles and George Martin, but no-one could identify it. "I thought it can't have come to me in a dream," he said, "It's like handing things in to the police - if no one's claimed it after two weeks, it's yours."

It's never been said before but I think "Yesterday" does have a link to a previous song, namely, Nat "King" Cole's hit, "Answer Me".

> *"You were mine yesterday,*
> *I believed that love was here to stay."*

Both the lyrical content and its execution are close to "Yesterday" and the melody is not far away. McCartney's song is not a steal, but if someone had pointed out the similarity to him, would we have even heard "Yesterday"?

The lyric is straightforward enough. Through a careless mistake, Paul has lost his girlfriend and he wants to put the clock back. We never find out what happened - "I did something wrong" - but that mystery only adds to the universality of the song.

George Martin realised that this song could have been written at any time during the 20th century and to give it a sense of timelessness, he suggested a string quartet, that is, two violins, cello and viola. "Yesterday" was included on the "Help!" LP, but not in the film. Because the other Beatles were not featured, it was never intended to release the song as a single in the UK.

Paul offered it to Billy J. Kramer, who told Paul that he would prefer "a real headbanger". He now includes the song, with this anecdote, in his cabaret act. "Yesterday" was a chart hit for Matt Monro, whose version was produced by George Martin, and Marianne Faithfull. Paul's version was a single in the US where it became the Beatles' 10th No 1. It has since become the most covered song in the world with over 2,500 versions available. They include Frank Sinatra, Elvis Presley, Ray Charles, Otis Redding and Cilla Black. I never have an urge to sing "Scrambled Eggs, Oh baby how I like your legs" to the music but I find myself recalling Spike Milligan's interpretation on a BBC-TV chat show:

> *"Yesterday,*
> *Someone came and took the stove away."*

I have no idea why I found that hilarious, but that brief moment has amused me for 35 years.

Billy J. Kramer rejected "Yesterday" but his hit of the year was hardly "a headbanger". He covered Burt Bacharach and Hal David's "Trains And Boats And Planes" and because of its usefulness for travel programmes, this has become one of their most enduring songs. Bacharach and David also wrote the score for "What's New, Pussycat?" The film was written by Woody Allen, who had overheard Warren Beatty on the telephone using the chat up line, "What's new, Pussycat?"

"You've Lost That Lovin' Feelin'" was written by Barry Mann and Cynthia Weil with Phil Spector. Barry and Cynthia told me how it came about:

Cynthia Weil: "We were living in New York and we went to California to write with Phil. He had found these two guys out of Orange County whom he thought were terrific and he played us 'My Babe' and 'Little Latin Lupe Lu'. They were incredible and we thought they should do a ballad, I don't know why in hell we thought that. We started to write 'You've Lost That Lovin' Feelin'' and we called Phil and played him the verse and the hook, and I said, "'You've Lost That Lovin' Feelin'" is not the right title, we'll get something better," and he said, 'No, that's the title,' and we finished it with him. That whole middle section was Phil's idea. We played it for Bill Medley and Bobby Hatfield, the Righteous Brothers, and Bobby was not happy because Bill had the whole first verse. He said, 'What am I supposed to do while the big guy's singing?' and Phil said, 'You can go to the bank!'"

Barry Mann: "We knew we had written a great song. The production was so great that I had a feeling that nothing could stop this record. When Phil played it for us over the phone, I kept yelling at him, 'It's at the wrong speed.' It was a long record for those days. It was over three minutes but Phil put 2'58" on the record as he wanted airplay."

Cythnia Weil: "That record had Phil Spector's touch, he created a whole new sound. We just knew that this was somebody who had a vision."

Barry Mann: "It's the perfect combination of a great production, great artists and a really great song. BMI had a press release last year which said it was the most-played song of the 20th century!"

Although there were many political events to write about, notably the growing trouble in Vietnam, Bob Dylan shunned political songwriting. His 1964 song, "My Back Pages" cryptically tells how he was feeling, and Phil Ochs was both disappointed by his stance and eager to

fill his shoes.

Sam Cooke, who was shot in 1964, was justly proud of his own comments on Civil Rights in "A Change Is Gonna Come", and a surfing songwriter, P.F. Sloan, who thought he would write a protest song, succeeded first time with "Eve Of Destruction" for Barry McGuire. Paul Simon sang of alienation in "The Sound Of Silence" and wrote about touring the UK folk clubs in "Homeward Bound", which he completed in Widnes. The big show song was "The Impossible Dream" from "Man Of La Mancha", while the music for an Alka-Seltzer commercial became "No Matter What Shape (Your Stomach's In)" for the T-Bones. Much more impressively, Pete Seeger was inspired by the Book of Ecclesiastes to write "Turn! Turn! Turn", a US No 1 for the Byrds. Gosh, the words are even older than Cliff Richard's "Millennium Prayer".

THE RIGHTEOUS BROTHERS

In the cinema, the tills are alive with "The Sound Of Music". When Bob Dylan comes to Liverpool, the marquee at the Odeon says, "2.30 The Sound Of Music, 7.30 Bob Dylan." Overheard as I leave: "Beats me how he can remember all those words", "Beats me how he can write them."

Bob Dylan's new, largely electric material was stunningly unique and the album, "Bringing It All Back Home", was a treasure of delights. He rewrote Chuck Berry in the spirited "Subterranean Homesick Blues", gave us a tour of "Maggie's Farm" (later taken as a song about Mrs Thatcher!), lampooned journalists in "Ballad Of A Thin Man", took a magic trip with the mysterious "Mr Tambourine Man" and concluded with the touching "It's All Over Now, Baby Blue", a combination of Rolling Stones and Gene Vincent titles. And who was the poor girl who bore Bob Dylan's anger in "Like A Rolling Stone" or the even more unfortunate person depicted in "Positively Fourth Street"? "Highway 61 Revisited", his second album of 1965, concluded with the twelve stunning minutes of "Desolation Row". When Dylan arrived in the UK for a concert tour, he told the "Melody Maker" writer, Ray Coleman, that the secret of success was to "keep a clear head and always carry a light-bulb."

1966 - ALFIE (Burt Bacharach - Hal David)

State opening of Parliament televised - Britain's first credit card, the Barclaycard, introduced - England wins the World Cup - Aberfan disaster - China's Cultural Revolution.

Burt Bacharach's music is filed under "Easy Listening" in record stores, but it really is "Queasy Listening". His sparkling, pretty melodies are usually underpinned by lyrics that make you wonder if Hal David wrote them with his analyst. Such songs include "24 Hours From Tulsa", "Don't Make Me Over" and "Wives And Lovers", which, these days, is as politically incorrect as you could get. "Alfie" is a case in point. Michael Caine played the lad about town and the song is supposedly sung by one of his girlfriends - "Alfie, is it just for the moment we live?" We're into existentialism here.

BURT BACHARACH

Much to Dionne Warwick's annoyance, Cilla Black had covered "Anyone Who Had A Heart" for the UK market, but Burt and Hal were more pragmatic, and even offered her a new song, "Alfie". It was to be for the Michael Caine film, "Alfie", although the score itself was written by the jazz musician, Sonny Rollins. They wanted an English singer to match Caine's nationality, and there is footage of her recording the song with Burt Bacharach at the piano overseeing the arrangement and George Martin producing. Burt insists on take after take, and Cilla, fortunately, doesn't crack under the pressure. The result was a remarkable single, easily her greatest moment, but as a result of company politics, a cover version by Cher was used on the soundtrack.

By contrast, Mitchell Torok, who was writing for Dean Martin, was at the session where Frank Sinatra recorded "Strangers In The Night", originally from Bert Kaempfert's score for the James Garner film, "A Man Could Get Killed". Mitch recalls, "You got an invitation to a Sinatra or a Martin session as they liked to invite their friends to sit around the studio whle they were recording at the big Sunset Recording Studios on Sunset Boulevard. Nobody coughs, nobody drops anything, nobody sneezes. Frank was going to cut a record first and the song was 'Strangers In The Night'. Electricity went through the room when he walked in with four or five guys, and the orchestra stood up and saluted. He shook hands, took off his coat, loosened his tie and the conductor started a runthrough. When they began a take, Frank was going pretty good and then the orchestra blew it. He said, 'Okay boys, we're going to try it one more time. I'm going to sing it one more time. If you don't get it, I'm gone.' You talk about pressure, but they cut the take the world heard. He did that 'dooby dooby doo' on the end, and it gives me goosepimples just to talk to you about it. He adjusted his tie, put on his hat and said, 'We're going to eat' and with that, he was gone."

Paul McCartney's beautiful song for Jane Asher, "Here, There And Everywhere" posseses, to my ears at least, a better structure and a more original melody line than "Yesterday", and it is certainly better than the numerous songs he wrote for Linda ("My Love", "The Lovely Linda", "Maybe I'm Amazed"). I've no idea why that is: I suspect that once he left the Beatles, he left his genius behind and became instead an excellent mainstream songwriter.

McCartney's evocative picture of a Liverpool spinster, "Eleanor Rigby", was superb and to quote George Melly, "Liverpool was always in their songs but this was about the kind of old woman that I remembered from my childhood and later, very respectable Liverpool women, living in two-up, two-down streets with the doorsteps meticulously hollystoned, and the church the one solid thing in their lives. There's the loneliness of it and it struck me as a poem from the start. If you read 'Love Me Do' without the music, it doesn't mean much, but if you read 'Eleanor Rigby', it is a poem about someone, which is something unprecedented in popular song. It could have come out of a novel or been written as a poem on its own, but they found the perfect tune to go with it, and George Martin has to be given credit because he found exactly the right backing which is an extraordinary mixture of church-like solemnity and humour. It was a complete portrait, a thumbnail sketch that was as solid as a Rembrandt drawing."

Gerry Goffin and Carole King's childhood reflections went into "Goin' Back" and there is a male version recorded by the Byrds and a female one by Dusty Springfield. Dusty also sang the powerhouse ballad, "You Don't Have To Say You Love Me", which was an English lyric for an Italian hit, and Nancy Sinatra sang the S&M classic, "These Boots Are Made For Walkin'", which was masterminded by Lee Hazlewood, after he had been ordered by Frank to "write her a hit". Call it "A Man And A Woman" or "Un Homme Et Une Femme", Francis Lai's heady cocktail mixture of harpsichord, piano chords and la-la-las is familiar to those who have never even heard of the film.

Bob Dylan's double-album, "Blonde On Blonde", featured one image-laden song after another and ended with the 13-minute tribute to his wife, Sara, "Sad-Eyed Lady Of The Lowlands". Ray Davies parodied the privileged in "Sunny Afternoon", a 60s companion to Noël Coward's "The Stately Homes Of England". Ralph McTell wrote a song about the homeless in Paris, but changed it to "Streets Of London", and was performing it in folk clubs long before recording it in 1968. Strangely, he didn't think strong enough for his first album.

The Mamas and Papas were "California Dreamin'", Tim Hardin sang an engaging love song, "If I Were A Carpenter" (which Scaffold amended to "If I were a carpenter and you were Our Lady"), and John Hartford's rush of lyrics made "Gentle On My Mind" very appealing. The theme from "Dr. Zhivago" became "Somewhere My Love" and the big song from "Sweet Charity" was "Big Spender". One of the few songs to be written about the Aberfan mining disaster is Mike Hart's "Aberfan" (1969) which criticises celebrities for using disasters for self-promotion.

Ken Kesey, who wrote "One Flew Over The Cuckoo's Nest", had been touring America with his band of hippies, the Merry Pranksters, for several years, and it must have been a shock for small Texas towns to be confronted with such outrageous behaviour. Tom Wolfe wrote a tremendous book about them, "The Electric Kool-Aid Acid Test", and he says, "The idea of red rubber balls was that every Prankster should always be ready to catch the ball, even if he wasn't looking when it came at him." This concept inspired a US Top 10 hit, "Red Rubber Ball", written by Paul Simon for the Cyrkle.

1967 - A WHITER SHADE OF PALE
(Keith Reid - Gary Brooker)

North Sea oil pumped ashore - Six Day War - Biafran war - Abortion legalised in UK - Pound devalued - Christian Barnard performs first heart transplant, the patient survives for 18 days - Concorde ready at last.

Drugs had been around for years in all forms of music, especially jazz. My favourite story concerns Leonard Bernstein, who was to conduct a concert in the presence of the Queen. He used to store cocaine in his cufflinks and he would take a sniff before going on stage. He took his customary snort, the adrenalin started flowing and he was bursting to get onto the podium. Unfortunately, he'd taken it too early and Her Majesty hadn't reached the Royal Box. Apparently, he dashed on stage and the orchestra was playing "God Save The Queen" as she was walking to her seat.

By 1967, the possession of LSD had been made illegal, but that only increased its mystique. Thousands of hippies, musicians and journeymen followed Dr Timothy Leary's advice to "turn on, tune in, and drop out". For some, it was "turn on, tune in and drop dead". When I saw Bob Dylan in Liverpool in 1966, I thought he was touching genius, but listening to the tapes now and hearing his introductions, I realise that he was in anutha zone.

Few musicians will admit that drugs influenced their writing because it demeans their own contributions. However, many songwriters described the images they had seen while tripping and thus created the new, spaced-out psychedelic music. I doubt if we would have had "Sgt Pepper's Lonely Hearts Club Band" without drugs, and similarly the Rolling Stones' "Their Satanic Majesties Request", Bob Dylan's "Blonde On Blonde" (from the previous year) and almost anything by the Doors, Love and Country Joe and the Fish. Frank Zappa produced his work without artificial stimulants, but as much of his 60s output was largely parody, his albums like "We're Only In It For The Money" are the result of second-hand trips.

It is also very noticeable that when the artists became "clean", their work was much more straightforward and understandable, and generally, they also became less productive. Quite aside from whether drug use should be legalised (or perhaps not), it is undeniably true that our culture would not be as rich without them. Going back 200 years, Samuel Taylor Coleridge wrote many of his poems and essays whilst on drugs.

1967 saw the dawn of the Age of Aquarius, it was the Summer of Love and the year in which psychedelia came to the fore. John Phillips' "San Francisco (Be Sure To Wear Some Flowers In Your Hair)" and John Lennon's "All You Need Is Love" were the messages of the day, but the downside of drugs was best represented by the Beatles' "A Day In The Life", which was banned by the BBC.

The essence of 1967 is captured in "A Whiter Shade Of Pale" and the truth is not plain to see as the songwriters - Keith Reid lyrics and Gary Brooker music - have not discussed the images in their song. Even now, it sounds cryptic and mysterious and there are musical references to Bach - "Suite No 3 In D Major (Air On A G String)" and "Sleepers Awake" - and literary references to Chaucer's "Canterbury Tales". If you want to argue that rock lyrics are poetry, what better place to start? And yet only a short while earlier, the Paramounts had been an R&B band and Matthew Fisher had been playing keyboards for Screamin' Lord Sutch. Matthew himself is none too sure of the song's meaning: "Keith's attitude is

THE KINKS

that he writes the words and it's up to the listeners to appreciate them on whatever level they want."

At a guess, the lyrics refer to someone chatting up a girl at a party. His mind wanders and different images come into his head. Procul Harum now perform the song with a third verse but it doesn't make things any clearer, and a fourth, equally impenetrable verse has appeared in print. The song was both Procul Harum's strength and their weakness as they fell overselves in an effort to be obscure and hence, significant. Praise though for their follow-up single, "Homburg", with its compelling opening words, "Your multilingual business friend".

The Birmingham group, the Moody Blues, had begun as a R&B band and had topped the UK charts in 1965 with a cover version of Bessie Banks' "Go Now". Their lead singer, Denny Laine, left, and when Justin Hayward and John Lodge joined, the band's style shifted significantly. They recorded an ambitious, perhaps pretentious, album with the London Festival Orchestra, "Days Of Future Passed", and that included Justin Hayward's celebrated song, "Nights In White Satin". It has made the UK charts on five separate occasions - three times for the Moodies, once for the Dickies and once for Elkie Brooks.

In 1967 Mantovani, all at sea, commented, "Perhaps 25% of the public like the classics, 25% like the Beatles, and I aim to please the 50% in the middle." The charts were still throwing up catchy melodies with MOR appeal. Herman's Hermits' "There's A Kind Of Hush" was excellent and the Monkees, replicating the younger, more innocent Beatles, copied "Paperback Writer" with "Last Train To Clarksville", and sang Neil Diamond's "I'm A Believer" and John Stewart's "Daydream Believer". Ray Davies painted his voyeuristic "Waterloo Sunset" and Paul McCartney returned to Liverpool for "Penny Lane". David Jacobs introducing "Strawberry Fields Forever" on "Juke Box Jury" said that the Beatles had made an enormous mistake.

When Paul McCartney gave his brother Mike a Nikon camera, he responded in song with "Thank U Very Much", a song that lives forever in advertising campaigns, and that, incidentally, was one of the first misspelt song-titles. Leslie Bricusse wrote the Oscar-winning "Talk To The Animals" for another Scouser, Rex Harrison, in "Dr Dolittle". Claude François recorded "Comme D'Habitude", which would become "My Way" two years later.

Jimmy Webb wrote the restrained but emotional "By The Time I Get To Phoenix", and Mark Wirtz's "Excerpt From A Teenage Opera" was so good that everyone wondered what had happened to the rest of it. Donovan, guessing the authorities would not know what he was writing about, included a reference to vibrators ("electrical bananas") in "Mellow Yellow". You could argue that the Troggs' "Love Is All Around" was typical of the Summer of Love, but the song didn't come into its own until the film, "Four Weddings And A Funeral", in 1994.

Joni Mitchell's songs were first heard via Judy Collins, who won a gold disc with "Both Sides Now", but it was soon appreciated that Joni had a unique talent of her own. Her albums exist in their own world as she paints and designs the covers and inlays and, until her recent album of covers, "Both Sides Now", only recorded her own songs. Her songs tend to be personal and confessional, often discussing her many boyfriends, and Kris Kristofferson once said to her, "Joni, save something for yourself." "Both Sides Now" was inspired by looking through the window in a plane - "I've looked at clouds from both sides now" - but related to her background and her new life as a singer-songwriter.

Charlie, now Charles, Chaplin made a stilted film comedy of manners, "A Countess From Hong Kong", and wrote its theme song, "This Is My Song". Petula Clark didn't care for the phrase, "I care not what the world may say", and a few other lines and asked the lyricist, Jack Fishman, to revise them. Chaplin was furious: "If a single word is changed, then you don't get the song. I wrote the song and it will be sung as I wrote it." I'd argue that Jim Morrison's lyric for the Doors' "Light My Fire" was equally bad - "And our love become a funeral pyre" - but then I've never been off to see the Lizard of Oz.

Stevie Wonder had written a good tune but as he couldn't get the words right, he asked Smokey Robinson to help him. Smokey suggested a lyric based on Pagliacci, the clown who would go to his dressing-room and cry. The result was "The Tears Of A Clown", which eventually became a UK No 1 in 1970. (My "Guinness Book Of British Hit Singles" lists it as "The Ears Of A Clown".) Another Motown classic was "I Heard It Through The Grapevine", which was tried with both Smokey and Gladys Knight before its writer, Norman Whitfield, realised that its lyric was perfect for the utterly paranoid Marvin Gaye.

STEVIE WONDER

Pete Seeger commented on the Vietnam war in "Waist Deep In The Big Muddy": "I guess I saw some photographs of the American soldiers slogging through the rivers and swamps down there in Vietnam, and I thought of this line, (sings)

'Waist deep in the big muddy,
the big fool says to push on.'

I'd sung enough songs to know that was a good line but it took me two or three weeks till I finally got the song written. I'm not a quick songwriter. How I envy Bob Dylan, Woody Guthrie and Phil Ochs. They can dash off songs in a hurry, but the song finally got written and it was my big song in 1967, 68, 69, 70, 71. Finally we're out of Vietnam. I look upon the Vietnam experience as an endlessly important one for the American people. It might have been a defeat for the Pentagon, a defeat for Richard Nixon, but it was not a defeat for the American people. It was a victory for the American people to get out of Vietnam. There are only a minority of Americans who think that we should have fought harder, stayed in, dropped the bomb and so on."

1968 - CONGRATULATIONS
(Bill Martin - Phil Coulter)

"I'm Backing Britain" campaign - Assassinations of Martin Luther King and Bobby Kennedy - Luxury liner, QE2, launched - Student protest in France - Invasion of Czechoslovakia - Two-tier postal service introduced.

Phil Coulter gave his songwriting partner, Bill Martin, a new melody but Bill didn't like its title, "I Think I Love You". He said that you either loved someone or you didn't. He tried to think of a five syllable word that would fit the melody and came up with congratulations. They then realised that this could be developed into a song which would cover many special occasions. This is not the easiest of assignments as Paul McCartney wrote "Birthday" for the Beatles, also in 1968, but I have never heard it sung in place of "Happy Birthday For You". On other hand, I often hear 'Congratulations' in restaurants and at parties.

"Congratulations" is not the most sophisticated song of the year, but it is the most memorable and has a variety of uses. It was played after Charles and Diana's wedding and also when the British troop ships returned from the

Falklands. Cliff Richard has made better records ("Move It!", "We Don't Talk Anymore"), but he will be remembered most for entering the Eurovision Song Contest with this song -and losing. He lost because many voting panels thought the UK had cheated by putting an established star in the contest.

Following the Beatles, Bob Dylan and Procul Harum, many enigmatic songs were around - Jim Webb's "MacArthur Park", Leonard Cohen's "Suzanne", the Rolling Stones' "Sympathy For The Devil" and the whole of Van Morrison's LP, "Astral Weeks", which sounds like one song anyway. Even the meaning of "Stand By Your Man" wasn't clear: was the oft-divorced Tammy Wynette serious in her intent to support her man, right or wrong?

"Abraham, Martin And John" paid tribute to assassinated politicians, while the troubles of the world were glossed over in "What A Wonderful World", which was ascloseasthis to an old-time standard. The song was ideal for Louis Armstrong. The Rolling Stones responded to Martha and the Vandellas' "Dancing In The Street" (1964) with the political "Street Fighting Man". It came from the excellent, blues-soaked LP "Beggars Banquet", which was a welcome relief after "Their Satanic Majesties Request".

Les Reed and Barry Mason wrote a song full of jealous passion for Tom Jones, "Delilah". Barry Mason recalls, "I had just made it, rich and famous, after being starving for years. I was in the loo at the BBC and behind me a guy was whistling 'Delilah'. I couldn't resist it. I said, 'I wrote that song you're whistling.' He said, 'I thought Les Reed wrote it.' I said, 'Les wrote the melody, I wrote the words.' He said, 'I'm not whistling the words.'"

'Delilah' is now sung by Stoke City supporters and the whole question as to why crowds catch on to certain songs could make a book in itself. In this instance, a fan known as TJ sang it in a pub because the words, unlike most soccer songs, would not offend anyone, and it developed from there.

Broadway, and even off-Broadway, theatres tended to ignore what was happening in the outside world until it was shaken by "Hair", a hippie musical with strong language, drug-taking, an anti-Goverment stance and, most of all and only very briefly, nudity. The score by Gerome Ragni, James Rado and Galt McDermot included

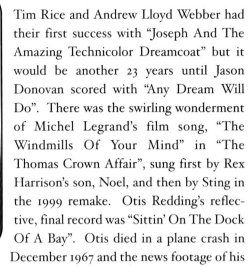

"Aquarius", "Let The Sunshine In", "Ain't Got No", "I Got Life" and "Good Morning Starshine". The songs became hits for Fifth Dimension, Nina Simone and Oliver, and, much to the authors' surprise, they found they had written MOR favourites. When "Hair" was revived in London in 1994, one critic wrote that it was as topical as "The Pirates Of Penzance".

Tim Rice and Andrew Lloyd Webber had their first success with "Joseph And The Amazing Technicolor Dreamcoat" but it would be another 23 years until Jason Donovan scored with "Any Dream Will Do". There was the swirling wonderment of Michel Legrand's film song, "The Windmills Of Your Mind" in "The Thomas Crown Affair", sung first by Rex Harrison's son, Noel, and then by Sting in the 1999 remake. Otis Redding's reflective, final record was "Sittin' On The Dock Of A Bay". Otis died in a plane crash in December 1967 and the news footage of his body being recovered from Lake Monona was more chilling than anything on the big screen.

Just as Cole Porter had written "Night And Day" for Fred Astaire's limited vocal range, Burt Bacharach and Hal David wrote "This Guy's In Love With You" for Herb Alpert to dedicate to his wife on a TV special. The Bee Gees created a standard with "Words", which, in 1999, was honoured on a postage stamp by the Isle of Man Post Office. The Brothers Gibb were born there in case you're wondering why.

1969 - SOMETHING (George Harrison)

Neil Armstrong walks upon the moon - Much violence in Northern Ireland - Charles Manson's Hollywood killings - East End gangsters, Reg and Ronnie Kray, jailed - Films include "Butch Cassidy And The Sundance Kid" (Paul Newman and Robert Redford), "Easy Rider" (Peter Fonda and Dennis Hopper) and "The Italian Job" (Michael Caine and three Minis).

It has never been clear, at least not to me, why George Harrison was excluded from the Beatles' songwriting partnership. As the years went by, he came to resent being restricted to a track or two on an album. By the time of "Abbey Road", he was able to match John and

Paul, who, for various reasons, were having difficulties writing commercial, three minute songs. Hence, "Something" is the best-known song on "Abbey Road", with George's "Here Comes The Sun" coming a close second. Frank Sinatra called it the greatest love song ever written, but, I suspect, he was trying to woo the youth market. He also attributed the song to Lennon and McCartney, which can't have done much for George's ego.

"Something" is an excellent, love song that George had written during a break for "The White Album". It hadn't gone on that album because he hadn't resolved the middle eight - see what I mean about the usefulness of a partnership - and when it was completed, he gave it to the British Ray Charles, Joe Cocker. George said, "When I wrote it, I heard Ray Charles singing it, and he did do it some years later."

"Something", for all its qualities, contains bad rhymes - "woos me" takes us back to 1900 and I hope you thought it odd when I used the word earlier. As said before, you can't copyright a title and James Taylor had previously recorded a song, "Something In The Way She Moves", and for Apple Records, as it happens. "Something" was written for Patti Boyd, who was also the inspiration for Eric Clapton's "Layla". Her sister, Jenny, inspired Donovan's "Jennifer Juniper" - quite a family.

Another excellent "Something" from 1969 is "Something In The Air" by Thunderclap Newman, a No.1 record produced by Pete Townshend. It was a very evocative song that was helped by a superb piano solo.

Although John Lennon was not at his best on "Abbey Road", he did create an anthem with "Give Peace A Chance" for the Plastic Ono Band. Pete Townshend wrote the rock opera, "Tommy", which included "Pinball Wizard". Laura Nyro wrote "Wedding Bell Blues" and raindrops were falling on Burt Bacharach's head. This jaunty song was written for the film, "Butch Cassidy And The Sundance Kid". The lyric gives the impression that

nothing is worrying Paul Newman, but you know it is really. "He Ain't Heavy, He's My Brother" sounded like a film song, but it wasn't.

Yehudi Menuhin at a meeting of UNESCO's International Music Council begged for the right to silence. He hated muzak and he objected hearing it in stores and lifts and planes, but, as he soon discovered, you can't stop the muzak. Wonder what the astronauts thought in their Apollo spaceship as they listened to muzak on their lunar cruise. David Bowie captured an astronaut's plight in "Space Oddity" and John Stewart sang of the Moonwalk in "Armstrong".

McDonald's discovered that up-tempo music encouraged fast eating and hence, fast exits, while supermarkets played slower music to encourage shoppers to linger. Serge Gainsbourg found that he had written the ultimate bonking song in "Je T'Aime, Moi Non Plus", which he originally recorded with Brigitte Bardot. Bardot, not a person known for her taste, thought the results were too embarrassing and so Gainsbourg recut it with his girlfriend, the English Rose, Jane Birkin. Their record was denounced by the Vatican, so what greater publicity can you get? It was an X-rated single to be sure, but it had a beautiful melody, which became an instrumental hit for Sounds Nice. Sounds nicer with the vocals.

1970 - BRIDGE OVER TROUBLED WATER (Paul Simon)

UK voting age lowered to 18 - Edward Heath becomes Prime Minister - Radioactive leaks at Windscale - Arab guerrillas hijack UK plane - Death of Charles de Gaulle.

The key songs of the year - the two Paul's "Bridge Over Troubled Water" and "Let It Be" - were written with Aretha Franklin in mind. Both have strong gospel overtones in their music and imagery, and Aretha was to record them to perfection.

Paul Simon's song was triggered by the Swan Silvertones' "Oh Mary Don't You Weep", and had the working title of "Hymn". He wrote it in the same house in Los Angeles that George Harrison had written "Blue Jay Way". When he told the arranger Jimmy Haskell that he had decided on a title, "Bridge Over Troubled Water", Haskell transcribed it as "Like A Pitcher Of Water". Simon wanted an arrangement that would resemble Phil Spector's "Ol' Man River" for the Righteous Brothers. He thought the first two verses should be sung solo and he later regretted giving this gem to Art Garfunkel, although he had only compliments for his performance.

Simon was never happy with his third verse - "I always felt that you could see that it was written afterwards. It doesn't sound like the first two verses." Yet isn't the line that everyone remembers from that third verse, "Sail on silver girl". It was offering some sympathy to his wife, Peggy, who had grey hairs. Simon and Garfunkel split up after recording "Bridge Over Troubled Water", so the solution offered by the song hadn't worked at all for them. It worked for many people though. Martin Amis described it as 'therapy", and Leonard Cohen said, "That might be the song that gets someone through a dark hour." If so, that's a considerable achievement.

The year also saw the inspirational feel of "United We Stand", "Spirit In The Sky", and George Harrison's "My Sweet Lord" (whose melody leant heavily on the Chiffons' "He's So Fine"). Elton John's "Your Song" (music written in ten minutes), Don McLean's "And I Love Her So" and the Carpenters' "For All We Know" were classic love songs. Then there's the sadness of James Taylor's "Fire And Rain", Kris Kristofferson's "For The Good Times" and George Jones' "Good Year For The Roses".

Pete Ham and Tommy Evans wrote and recorded "Without You" with their group, Badfinger for their album, "No Dice". It became a No 1 for Nilsson in 1972 and for Mariah Carey in 1994. In-between those successes, both Ham (1975) and Evans (1983) had hanged themselves. Maybe they should have been stronger, but their story of being constantly ripped off is told in a very well-researched book, "Without You - The Tragic Story Of

Badfinger" by Dan Matovina (Frances Glover Books, 1997).

1971 - WHAT'S GOING ON
(Marvin Gaye - Al Cleveland - Renaldo Benson)

Barriers at Ibrox stadium collapse, killing 66 - Decimal currency introduced - CAMRA formed - Internment without trial reinstated in Northern Ireland - Space Hoppers in UK stores - "Workaholics" diagnosed.

Both Stevie Wonder and Marvin Gaye had been dissatisfied with the assembly line productions at Motown, and Marvin also had his suspicions about the death of his singing partner, Tammi Terrell, and felt for his brother who was fighting in Vietnam. They wanted to create their own music and both of them were to make remarkable albums that exceeded what they had been recording with staff producers. Despite a superb ballad "Never Dreamed You'd Leave In Summer", Stevie Wonder's "Where I'm Coming From" was an album that promised potential rather than delivering goods. Marvin Gaye hit the spot first time out with the extraordinary album, "What's Going On", which, to my ears, improves with the years.

Through listening to jazz records by the horn player Lester Young, Marvin Gaye had discovered a new relaxed way to sing, and his multitracked vocals are a key feature of "What's Going On". Smokey Robinson told "Performing Songwriter" (December 1999) about the album, "At the time he was making the album, he told me that the album was being written by God. He said that he was just an instrument, and that God was writing this album because he wanted that message out. I can buy that because the message remains so significant today. I think it's the greatest album ever."

The Motown producer, Al Cleveland, and Obie Benson of the Four Tops had written a melody to suit Marvin's new vocal style. Marvin didn't listen to anything for a couple of months and then he felt he had to describe his brother's torment in Vietnam and wrote the lyrics to "What's Going On". Motown's owner, Berry Gordy, was not impressed with either the single or the album, but released them to pacify Marvin. They both almost topped the US charts, so Marvin had been vindicated. Janet Jackson has said, "He's our John Lennon. The longer he's gone, the more young people appreciate his art. 'What's Going On' was a work of genius, far ahead of its time." Outside of Motown, Isaac Hayes was also redefining black music with his powerful music for the film, "Shaft", and he became the first black musician to win an Oscar.

I have chosen "What's Going On" over "Imagine" as the song of the year, because "Imagine" is seriously flawed. However, it is an extraordinary song to write about and is the subject of a separate chapter. John and Yoko's "Happy Xmas (War Is Over)", also from 1971 and with the same message, strikes me as the better composition.

MARVIN GAYE (above) AND NEIL YOUNG (right)

"Happy Xmas (War Is Over)" delighted his producer, Phil Spector, who had made the ultimate seasonal album with "A Christmas Gift For You" in 1963. Spector brought Christmas clichés to the arrangement and recruited children from the Harlem Community Choir. As John Robertson (aka Peter Doggett) remarks in "The Art And Music Of John Lennon" (Omnibus, 1990), "This was at once a surprisingly conventional Lennon record and an altogether more thoughtful piece of work than the average seasonal offering." The single was released in the US in 1971 but its release was delayed for a year in the UK. When it came out here, it made No 2 on the NME charts. The long-haired lover from Liverpool was kept from No 1 by the "Long-Haired Lover From Liverpool".

Although the solo John Lennon was a radical songwriter, he was also competitive and, as a professional challenge, he had told Richard Williams from "Melody Maker" that he wanted to write "a classic like 'The Christmas Song', something that will last forever". In 1969 John and Yoko had begun their billboard campaign, "War is over. If you want it. Happy Christmas from John and Yoko", which became the theme for the song. He recorded "Happy Xmas (War Is Over)" in October 1971, his first record since taking up residency in America.

Don McLean's epic "American Pie" is discussed in a separate chapter. Led Zeppelin were on their stairway to heaven, Neil Young was looking for a heart of gold, Carole King and James Taylor had a friend, and Kris Kristofferson wanted someone to help him through the night. Francis Lai wrote the music for "Love Story" - well, the bits that Bach, Mozart and Handel didn't write. "Cotton's Dream" from the film, "Bless The Beasts And Children" became "Nadia's Theme" for the Roumanian gymnast, Nadia Comaneci at the 1976 Olympics where she earned seven perfect scores. "Candy Man" was the winning song from Leslie Bricusse and Anthony Newley's score for "Willy Wonka And The Chocolate Factory". The New Seekers turned their Coca-Cola ad, "I'd Like To Buy The World A Coke", into "I'd Like To Teach The World To Sing".

1972 - SONG SUNG BLUE (Neil Diamond)

"Bloody Sunday" in Londonderry - Power cuts following miners' strike - Arab guerrillas cause havoc at Olympics - The Watergate controversy - Marlon Brando stars in "The Godfather" and "Last Tango In Paris" - Dr Alex Comfort publishes "The Joy Of Sex".

Neil Diamond had seen the idyllic and romantic Swedish film, "Elvira Madigan", which uses Mozart's Piano Concerto No 21 on its soundtrack. Starting with Mozart's chords, he developed one of his catchiest tunes, "Song Sung Blue", which topped the US charts during 1972. When Neil brought it to the studio, Larry Knechtel, who had played piano on "Bridge Over Troubled Water, improvised the opening.

There's nothing wrong with "Song Sung Blue" - it has a very catchy melody (naturally) and the lyrics, for once, are not pretentious. Like "Sweet Caroline"(1969) and "Cracklin' Rosie" (1970), it is a very catchy, good-time pop record. However, there are drawbacks in having Neil Diamond as one of my songwriters of the year when so many better ones are not represented. For starters, there's his overblown score for "Jonathan Livingstone Seagull" (1973) and some of the worst lyrics ever written by a professional songwriter ("If You Know What I Mean", "Forever In Blue Jeans", and his take on ET, "Heartlight").

In "I Am...I Said", he says, "And no one heard at all, not even the chair." Did he really expect the chair to answer back? Of course not, it's lazy songwriting. Oh, and introducing this song on a live recording at the Greek Theatre in Los Angeles, he declares, "I need, I want, I care, I weep, I ache, I am, I said, I am." Wonderful! Did you ever read about a frog who dreamed of being a king and then became one? When he appeared before Bob Dylan at the Band's "Last Waltz" concert, he said, "Follow that!" to which Dylan replied, "What do I have to do? Fall asleep."

"Done Too Soon" is a meaningless jumble of famous dead people and there is such nonsense as "The Pot-Smoker's Song" and "You're So Sweet (Horseflies keep hangin' round your face)". As for "You are the words, I am the tune, play me", I ask you, although it would be better if someone else were the words. Still, you may like them and you may argue that he's parodying being a pretentious rock star. As he says, "I am an imperfect, emotional being, trying to give some substance and meaning to my life."

A HIT FOR CHARLES AZNAVOUR

By 1982 Neil Diamond had come to terms with himself after years of therapy. He said, and I'm not making this up, "I have finally forgiven myself for not being Beethoven."

Bill Withers made toilet seats for Boeing's planes and although it was a crappy job, he made many friends in the factory. The way they helped each other out inspired him to write "Lean On Me". It topped the US charts and has been a UK hit for Withers, Mud, Club Nouveau and Michael Bolton. However, everyone knows it through its appearances on TV adverts, most recently for Royal Liver's life assurance.

Another middle of the road soul song, "I'm Stone In Love With You", stems from 1972 as does that poignant ballad about a musician on the road, "Always On My Mind", which was first released by Brenda Lee. Neil Young made "Heart Of Gold" sound effortless, and his album "Harvest" is a classic, even reprised for "Harvest Moon" in 1992. The Sutherland Brothers and Quiver recorded a song that would become a No 1 for Rod Stewart, "Sailing". Lou Reed wrote the languid "Perfect Day" about taking heroin, and he didn't even include it in his book of lyrics, "Between Thought And Expression". Like many songs, it was capable of a wholly different interpretation.

Charles Aznavour sang of his loathing for disco music in the angry "Les Plaisirs Demodes". The English lyricist, Herbert Kretzmer, took a section of his song and created the ballad, "The Old Fashioned Way".

After a run of several good years, 1972 was disappointing. You can tell that by the Oscar nominations for Best Song - "The Morning After" (the winner, a love song from "The Poseidon Adventure"), "Ben" (a love song to a rat), "Come Follow, Follow Me", "Marmalade, Molasses And Honey" and "Strange Are The Ways Of Love".

1973 -   SEND IN THE CLOWNS
          (Stephen Sondheim)

          Britain joins the Common Market -
          Controversy over "butter mountains" - A new
          tax, VAT, in the UK - Princess Anne marries
          Captain Mark Phillips - General Augusto
          Pinochet seizes power in Chile and eliminates
          many of his opposition - President Nixon visits
          China - End of military action in Vietnam

When the rehearsals started for "A Little Night Music", Stephen Sondheim's musical set in a country house, he was a song short. He needed a song for the actor Len Cariou, who played the misunderstood husband of Glynis Johns. He stayed up all night and the next morning the cast gathered around his piano to hear him say, "Sorry, Len, this isn't for you. It's for Glynis." "Send In The Clowns" is about someone realising that she has missed so many opportunities in her life.

Glynis Johns said, "If you let me sing the lyrics from a piece of paper, I'll do it today." And she did. Stephen Sondheim, knowing that Johns had a small voice, had written a melody with many pauses for breath. Frank Sinatra and Cleo Laine give bravura performances, while Judy Collins is truer to the original. You have to be careful when you sing the song: if you don't pause when you sing "Don't you love farce?" it becomes "Don't you love arse?"

STEPHEN SONDHEIM

Richard O'Brien captured his love for 1950s sci-fi films in "The Rocky Horror Show", the first musical in which the audiences dress like the cast. The longevity of this ultra-camp musical has suprised everyone: let's do the time warp again, and again, and again.

Carl Davis composed stunning music for the 26-week series, "The World At War". The theme is still played today and he says, "In the title music, I tried to compose something tragic and human rather than grandiose." Barbra Streisand sang the theme from "The Way We Were" in which she starred with Robert Redford, but the most unlikely film music of the year came from Bob Dylan with "Pat Garrett And Billy The Kid", in which he also had a small role and replies in lines from his songs. The director, Sam Peckinpah, was unsure about the score as he was used to more lavish film music, but the gentle instrumentals often played with Roger McGuinn work very well. The death of Slim Pickens in the film is accompanied by one of Dylan's greatest songs and one of his greatest phrases, "Knockin' On Heaven's Door". John Martyn released his album, "Solid Air" in February 1973. It included his affectionate "May You Never", which has been recorded by Eric Clapton. In June 1973, Bob Dylan recorded his first version of "Forever Young". I can't accept that the similarity of the two songs is coincidental. Also, in 1973, Sandy Denny's first version of the haunting "Who Knows Where The Time Goes?" with the Strawbs was released, the performance dating from 1967.

Coming out of a depression, Russ Ballard wrote "God Gave Rock And Roll To You" for Argent. When Kiss revived it they ditched the reference to Cliff Richard's "Please Don't Tease". Elton John had a fine year with "Daniel" and "Candle In The Wind" and Roberta Flack sang about watching Don McLean in "Killing Me Softly With His Song". Bob Marley wanted to write about attacking the police force but thought better of it, changing his lyric to "I Shot The Sheriff".

Stevie Wonder scored with "You Are The Sunshine Of My Life" and the rhythmic "Superstition", Phil Everly was the first to record "The Air That I Breathe" and Steve Miller, determined to write a hit, came up with "The Joker". Roy Wood wrote "I Wish It Could Be Christmas Everyday" and then there's Bill Bryson's pet hate, "Merry Xmas Everybody" and mine, "Tie A Yellow Ribbon Round The Old Oak Tree".

1974 - I WILL ALWAYS LOVE YOU (Dolly Parton)

Explosion at Flixborough chemical plant kills 29 - IRA bombs at the Houses of Parliament and the Tower of London - Nixon resigns as a result of the Watergate scandal - Start of Ceefax.

Dolly Parton was part of Porter Wagoner's road show but she also made records in her own right. She became more successful than Wagoner and was determined to break away from him. On the other hand, he didn't want to ruin a very profitable relationship. Dolly disliked the way the split developed into legal wrangles and she wrote a song to tell Porter how she felt about him, no matter what. The song was "I Will Always Love You". It topped the US country charts and then again, six years later, when it was used in the film, "The Best Little Whorehouse In Texas". In 1992 the song became an international hit via Whitney Houston's recording for the film, "The Bodyguard", and wanting to reclaim the song for herself, Dolly re-recorded it with Vince Gill in 1995. It's a beautiful song for lost love that is often used at funerals.

Herbert Kretzmer wrote English lyrics for Charles Aznavour's French releases, but there was a change in approach in 1974. Herbie recalls, "LWT were screening seven different plays about women in a series called 'The Seven Faces Of Woman'. They wanted a song to link the plays and the producer wanted me to write a song for Marlene Dietrich as, at the time, she represented the ageless woman. I didn't like the idea much as if you're going to write about the mystique of a woman, then it would be better coming from a man. If she knew about her own

mystery, it would be too calculated and knowing, so I said, 'No, let's write a song about a woman as seen by a man, and what better man than Charles Aznavour, who sings about love and romance?' I brought him in on the project and it worked extremely well."

The song, "She", wasn't without its difficulties. "The first verse could only run for 35 seconds, the time before the play began, and that verse had to be complete in its own way. The song had to be stretched out for the record and yet it mustn't sound like padding. It took a few weeks to get the song together, but the instant Charles Aznavour played me that long, opening note, the word 'she' jumped into my mind, and I knew I had the song."

Alan Price wrote about his roots in a TV biography, "Between Today And Yesterday". "I had refused to write about the miners because I knew it would be controversial. The director took me to a pub that my father used to drink in before he was killed in an industrial accident. He used moral blackmail and 'The Jarrow Song' came together in five minutes in a pub in Fatfield, County Durham."

It was a year for well-crafted love songs - Olivia Newton-John's "I Honestly Love You", Diana Ross' "All Of My Life" and Barry White's "You're The First, My Last, My Everything". Abba won the Eurovision Song Contest with "Waterloo" and transformed both the event and themselves. Marilyn Sellars has her footnote in history by being the first to record the inspirational country song, "One Day At A Time".

BARRY WHITE

118

THE ANSWER TO EVERYTHING
Answer records

The easiest way to write a song is if someone else has written it before you. Sounds flippant? Well, no, during the rock'n'roll era, roughly the decade from 1955 onwards, some artists did very well by simply answering established hit records. If the record posed a question ("Are You Lonesome Tonight?, "Who Put The Bomp?"), the matter was simple: your song could be called "Yes, I'm Lonesome Tonight" or "I Put The Bomp". Jim Reeves' "He'll Have To Go" became Jeanne Black's "He'll Have To Stay". Many of the records made the US charts, and there were even answer versions to answer versions: the Drifters' "Save The Last Dance For Me" prompted Damita Jo's reply, "I'm Saving The Last Dance For You", but Billy Fury was convinced "You're Having The Last Dance With Me".

There were, it should be said, answer versions before rock'n'roll. The American soldiers responded to "It's A Long, Long Way To Tipperary" with "It May Be Far To Tipperary (It's A Longer Way To Tennessee)", and we also had "When I Met You Last Night In Dreamland", "Minnie The Moocher's Wedding Day" and "Since Bill Bailey Came Home". Hank Williams followed "Cold Cold Heart" with "My Cold, Cold Heart Is Melted Now", recorded by Kitty Wells, and he liked the new tune so much that he used it for "Your Cheatin' Heart".

Responding to "Rudolph The Red-Nosed Reindeer" is an industry in itself - "Run Rudolph Run" by Chuck Berry, "They Shined Up Rudolph's Nose" by Johnny Horton, "Rudolph The Flat-Nosed Reindeer" by Homer and Jethro, "Rudolph The Red-Nosed Redneck" by Bob Livingston, and I'm sure I once heard a record about Rudolph being breathalysed.

In recent years Bear Family have issued three superbly-packaged CDs of answer versions in their series, "...And The Answer Is" (BCD 15791/2/3), but as the CDs combine the familiar originals with their follow-ups, it is an expensive way to acquire what are, for the most part, rubbish, and I don't possess them. Still, there are some hilarious titles. Patsy Cline's "She's Got You" was answered by Judy's "She Can Have You", while Bobby Vee's "Take Good Care Of My Baby" became Ralph Emery's "I'll Take Good Care Of Your Baby".

Now, two German CDs have appeared on import in the UK, "Those Rock'n'Roll Answer Songs" (Silly Records SR 8012/3), with each volume containing 29 answer versions. Technically, they are a disaster as many tracks have been dubbed from scratchy singles. I thought something could be done about that nowadays, but the single of "Leavin' Surf City" by Dave and the Saints is in such poor condition that the track is faded out halfway through. A hi-fi magazine wouldn't look at these albums, but I draw this answering service to your attention because the CDs are packed with rare oddities.

Most artists are unknown or hide under a pseudonym - Joni Credit, the Emperor, Cook E Jarr - but there are recognisable names. In 1959 Carole King had been flattered that Neil Sedaka had dedicated "Oh Carol" to her and she responded with the Tennessee-styled "Oh Neil".

"I'd even give up a month's supply of chewing tobacky,
Just to be known as Mrs Neil Sedaccy."

She also responded to Annette's "Tall Paul" with "Short Mort", probably to amuse fellow New York songwriter, Mort Shuman. Within a few months, Carole would write such sublime songs as "Will You Love Me Tomorrow" but there's no indication of such promise here.

Ray Stevens has made several excellent comedy records including "Bridget The Midget" and "The Streak", and he responds to "Deck Of Cards" with "High School Yearbook" telling of a boy whose playing cards remind him of school. This feeble rewrite must have taken all of five minutes.

Jody Miller had some success as a pop and country singer in the 60s, recording the teen anthem, "Home Of The Brave". Her response to Roger Miller's quirky "King Of The Road", "Queen Of The House", made the US Top 20 and both songs won Grammys. "Queen Of The House" is a witty lyric in its own right, and Gloria Becker's answer to "Sixteen Tons", "Sixteen Pounds", is also about an overworked housewife.

The country singers, Sheb Wooley and Ferlin Husky, recorded scores of parodies under their alter egos, Ben Colder and Simon Crum, respectively. Wooley almost called himself Klon Dyke. Simon Crum's portrait of his girlfriend, "Enormity In Motion", is not very PC, but such reservations were unknown in 1961.

"Enormity in motion,
When we swim at school,
She cause such commotion,
She overflows the pool"

Still, it's minor league when compared to Colder's answer to "Don't Go Near The Indians", "Don't Go Near The Eskimos", not included here but a US country No 1. Homer and Jethro's daft parodies include "The Battle Of Kookamonga" for "The Battle Of New Orleans", but the collection goes with Jerry Wilson's "The Battle Of Trip-O-Lee". The US disc-jockey, Jim Nesbitt, had several minor country hits including a nudist parody of "Running Bear", "Runnin' Bare".

Sometimes the artists cut their own answer versions, the most famed example being David Bowie who updated "Space Oddity" with "Ashes To Ashes". The doowop quintet, the Bobbettes, followed their "Mr Lee" with "I Shot Mr Lee". Jan and Dean continued their 1959 hit single, "Baby Talk" 14 singles later with "She's Still Talking Baby Talk". Gary Paxton led the Hollywood Argyles through "Alley Oop" and followed it through with a solo single, "Alley Oop Was A Two-Dab Man". Pat Boone recorded a hit song about a Mexican cartoon character, Speedy Gonzales. Mel Blanc provided the one-liners and Mel himself followed "Speedy Gonzales" with "The Tiajuana Ball" in which Speedy gabbles about modern dances like "The Locomotion". In each of these cases, you wonder why they bothered.

In real life, Tom Dooley was hanged, but that didn't stop the answer versions. The Liverpool singer-songwriter Russ Hamilton's "Reprieve Of Tom Dooley" was banned by some America radio stations for mocking their history. Merle Kilgore told the story of "Tom Dooley Jr" and in this collection, we have the Balladeers copying the Kingston Trio with "Tom Gets The Last Laugh": the rope on the gallows was too long and he was able to escape. There was such a fad for Tom Dooley songs that maybe Frank Sinatra should have dedicated "A Swingin' Affair" to him. Stella Johnson continued the story of a bad gambler with "The Trial Of Stagger Lee", while Barry Frank audaciously reworked Brecht's sparkling lyric for "Mack The Knife" as "Mackie Got Married". Dudley reworked the western saga "El Paso" as an unappetising "El Pizza", but I enjoyed Bill Robinson's "Ringo's Curse" - "Who shot the guy that shot the guy that shot the guy that shot Ringo?"

Claude King's "Wolverton Mountain" is a country classic, and was quickly followed by Jo Ann Campbell, "(I'm The Girl On) Wolverton Mountain", both of which made the US Top 40. John Zacherle, a US-TV host of horror movies, had his own hit with "Dinner With Drac", but I'd never heard "I'm The Ghoul From Wolverton Mountain" before. Scary Spice is more frightening than this.

Johnny Cash's "A Boy Named Sue" is a gift for parodists, but Joni Credit's "A Girl Named Harry" adds little to the saga. Far better is Sue's songwriter, Shel Silverstein, giving his dad equal time in "The Father Of A Boy Named Sue" from his much-neglected LP, "Songs And Stories". Silverstein also recorded the hilarious song, "A Front Row Seat To Hear Ole Johnny Cash", about someone who is is prepared to go to jail to see his hero perform.

When the original is a comedy song, it should be easy to write something funny. Should be. These CDs contain Jeff Hughes' "Our Spaceman Did Come Back" ("My Boomerang Won't Come Back"), The Emperor's "I'm Normal" and Henry IX's "Don't Take Me Back Oh No" (both based on "They're Coming To Take Me Away Ha-Haaa!"), Jan and Jerry's "Bandstand Baby" ("All American Boy"), the Jayhawks' "Betty Brown" ("Charlie Brown") and Mann Drake's "The Vampire Ball" ("The Monster Mash"). Not a titter. Much better is Sandra Gould's answer to "Hello Muddah Hello Faddah" called "Hello Melvin, This Is Mama":

"Though we love you like we oughta
Don't come home because we've taken in a boarder."

The songwriter Barry Mann had a US hit with "Who Put The Bomp" and the answer version was recorded by Frankie Lymon, Morecambe and Wise, and, on this collection, Bob and Jerry. The Royal Teens' question "Who Wears Short Shorts?" was answered by another one, Cook E Jarr's "Who Wears Hot Pants?" Connie Francis' "Who's Sorry Now?" led to the Shields' apologetic "I'm Sorry Now", although the melody is different. The request to "Tell Laura I Love Her" brought forth Marilyn Michaels' "Tell Tommy I Miss Him".

The Angels' 1963 US No.1, "My Boyfriend's Back", prompted Bobby Comstock's wimpish "Your Boyfriend's Back". A punkish rewrite came from Alice Donut - "My boyfriend's back and he's going to kick your ass." Dion told of "Runaround Sue" but Ginger and the Snaps declared "I'm No Runaround" and the relationship had a happy ending as Danny Jordan sang "Runaround Sue's Getting Married". The Four Seasons' hits prompted "Jerry, I'm Your Sherry" (Tracey Day) and "Society Girl" (The Rag Dolls), and Neil Sedaka's "Making Up Is Fun To Do" (Tina Powers) and "Calendar Boy" (Stacey Ames). "Calendar Boy" is just "Calendar Girl" with a sex change. Same with Eddie Holman's update of Ruby and the Romantics' "Hey There Lonely Boy", retitled "Hey There Lonely Girl" and the best track on the CDs.

Some of the answer versions are decidedly weird. What inspired the Flying Saucers' canine reply to the Who, "My Kennel-ration"?

"You can call me stupid mutt,
Just as long as you feed my gut."

Why should the Caretakers' respond to Tiny Tim with your "Get Your Tippy Toes Off My Tulips"? "Eve Of Destruction" raised serious issues and the Spokesmen took a pro-nuke reply, "Dawn Of Correction", into the US Top 40.

Did Brian Wilson give permission for Cagle and Klender to rewrite "California Girls" as "Ocean City Girls"? Certainly, in the UK, permission has to be be sought, and the Barron Knights were turned down by the Beatles and then Tim Rice, who didn't think a lyric about vacuum cleaners suited "Don't Cry For Me Argentina". The Barron Knights also faced opposition from David Bowie's publishers but they met the Thin White Duke on "Top Of The Pops" and he okayed a feline "Space Oddity."

Stan Freberg was allowed to parody numerous 50s hits - "Heartbreak Hotel", "The Great Pretender", "The Banana Boat Song (Day-O)" - and he did them so amusingly that the artists were flattered, although Johnnie Ray disliked his "Cry". Weird Al Yankovic, a latter-day Stan Freberg, must have famous friends as he has been able to parody Michael Jackson ("Eat It") and Nirvana ("Smells Like Nirvana".)

As far as I know, no-one has answered the Spice Girls' "Wannabe", although it would be ideal. Madonna's hits have not been answered, but in this collection, the Slightly Twisted Disappointer Sisters perform "No More Madonna", based on Frankie Avalon's "De De Dinah" from 1958 with a touch of Dion's "Donna The Prima Donna". With a 27 year difference, it may be the longest time from an original to an answer version.

The 58 songs on these 2CDs include answers to "Bobby's Girl", "Duke Of Earl", "He's A Rebel", "My Guy", "There Goes My Baby" and even "Itsy Bitsy Teeny Weeny Yellow Polka Dot Bikini". They are no better than the ones I have written about, and, of course, a song called "Mrs James, I'm Mrs Brown's Daughter" couldn't possibly be any good. No matter, these question no-marks are very entertaining and I'm glad to have these CDs in my collection. I hope the vogue for answer records returns sometime, but some Beatle fans would say Oasis have already started the revival.

Lennon or McCartney?

LENNON OR McCARTNEY?

Who contributed most to the songwriting partnership?

Cole Porter, wanting to irritate Rodgers and Hammerstein, said, "How can it take two men to write one song?" But many of the best songs have been written by more than one person - usually two people, one writing the words and the other the music. In most of the relationships, the role was clearly defined, we know W.S. Gilbert, Tim Rice and Bernie Taupin wrote the words and that Sir Arthur Sullivan, Andrew Lloyd Webber and Elton John supplied the music. On the whole, Mick Jagger wrote the lyrics and Keith Richards the music.

With some relationships, the roles are less clearcut, and the most famous example of a songwriting partnership (John Lennon and Paul McCartney) is also one of the most unusual. This is because they both wrote words and music. Quite often, they would work separately and so they each have their names on songs that they did not contribute to - for example, "Yesterday" in the case of John Lennon and "I Am The Walrus" with Paul McCartney.

John and Paul decided from the outset that they would write under a "(Lennon - McCartney)" credit irrespective of who wrote the song. Have we enough information to determine what the songwriting split on each song really was and from this, can we deduce who brought the most to the partnership?

The "Lennon - McCartney" approach is still unusual. Initially, Queen credited the individual writers with their work, but once they were established they decided upon a collective Queen songwriting credit. The recent album by Yes, "The Ladder" says that all songs were "Written by Jon Anderson, Steve Howe, Billy Sherwood, Chris Squire, Alan White and Igor Khoroshev. Lyrics by Jon Anderson." Who gets what? Does Anderson get 20% or 60%?

In recent years, Paul McCartney has suggested that the credits be changed on some of the Lennon - McCartney songs, but what to? It is hard to determine what the credits should be, but McCartney can't be happy that his most famous composition, "Yesterday", also credits John Lennon and what's more, John's name comes first.

As it happens, the first single, "Love Me Do", showed "(McCartney - Lennon)": who persuaded Paul that "(Lennon - McCartney)" looked or sounded better and why did he agree? Was he even consulted?

I went to assess the proportion of each song that really belongs to each writer and draw some conclusions. I have looked for interview material where one or more Beatles tells how the song was written. Any conflicts will be noted.

The main sources are;

- "The Beatles - The Authorised Biography" by Hunter Davies (Heinemann, 1968)
- "Lennon Remembers" by Jann Weiner (Straight Arrow, 1971) (The "Rolling Stone" Interviews)
- "The Playboy Interviews" with John Lennon and Yoko Ono (Playboy Press, 1981)
- "The Lennon Tapes" by Andy Peebles (BBC, 1981)
- "The Playboy Interview" with Paul and Linda McCartney (Playboy, 1984)
- "John Winston Lennon" by Ray Coleman (Sidgwick and Jackson, 1984)
- "John Ono Lennon" by Ray Coleman (Sidgwick and Jackson, 1984)
- "The Complete Beatles Recording Sessions" by Mark Lewisohn (Hamlyn, 1988) (Contains interview with Paul McCartney)
- "Speaking Words Of Wisdom" by Spencer Leigh (Cavern City Tours, 1991) (500 quotes about the Beatles, mostly from my radio interviews: the unattributed quotes below are from this book).
- "Revolution In The Head" by Ian MacDonald (Fourth Estate, 1994) (A superb musical analysis of the Beatles' work.)
- "A Hard Day's Write" by Steve Turner (Carlton, 1994) (Where direct quotes are not available on a song, I have used this well-researched book as a source.)
- Booklet notes for "Anthology" CDs by Mark Lewisohn (1995/6)
- "Many Years From Now" by Barry Miles with Paul McCartney (Secker and Warburg, 1997) (Much of its text features direct quotes from Paul McCartney. Barry Miles also presents many of McCartney's comments and views as reported speech. As McCartney allowed this book to be an official biography, I am assuming that he agrees with all that is attributed to him.)
- "The Beatles Encyclopedia" by Bill Harry (Virgin, 2000)

Other sources are noted in the text. "Brother, Can You Spare A Rhyme?" went to print before the Beatles' autobiography was available and it may contain fresh insights into their compositions, but I doubt it - they've been interviewed so much already.

Generally speaking, John Lennon is very dismissive of much of their work, whereas Paul McCartney, ever the diplomat, hardly ever admits anything is substandard.

I wonder whether John really thought this or whether he was only showing off for journalists. Surely while writing the songs, he didn't think they were rubbish but was giving them his best shot. It's hard to believe he was saying to the public, "This isn't good enough for me, but it's good enough for you."

In the listings, each song is shown with the appropriate songwriting credit and the year it was officially released. I have graded each song from A to E according to the importance of the copyright. This is not necessarily an assessment of the song's quality, but an indication as to how valuable the copyright is with regard to repeated playing, airplay and cover versions - for example, "Yellow Submarine", which everyone knows, is Grade A and "Happiness Is A Warm Gun" is Grade D. The Grade E songs tend to be album fillers or outtakes subsequently released. Still, as most of them have been on best-selling albums, they have earned their keep.

The Liverpool Years

HELLO LITTLE GIRL (Lennon) (1963)
(First recording by the Fourmost) C
JL: "That was me. That was my first song. I was fascinated by an old song called 'Scatterbrain' and my mother used to sing that one." (Playboy)
Mitch Murray, writer of "How Do You Do It", Gerry and the Pacemakers' first record and a No 1, says, "John Lennon had written 'Hello Little Girl' and given it to Gerry and the Pacemakers. He threatened to thump me if I got Gerry's follow-up. I did get it, that was 'I Like It', and I figured it was worth a thump."

ONE AFTER 909 (Lennon) (1970) C
JL: "That was something I wrote when I was about seventeen." (Playboy)

I CALL YOUR NAME (Lennon) (1963) (First recording by Billy J. Kramer with the Dakotas) D
JL: "That was my song. The first part had been written before Hamburg even. It was one of my first attempts at writing a song." (Playboy)

I SAW HER STANDING THERE
(Lennon - McCartney) (1963) B
PM: "Originally the first two lines were 'She was just seventeen, Never been a beauty queen'. When I played it through the next day to John, I realised that it was a useless rhyme and so did John. John came up with 'You know what I mean', which was much better." (Source unknown)
JL: "That's Paul doing his usual good job of producing what George Martin used to call a pot-boiler. I helped with a couple of the lyrics." (Playboy)
Despite John's comment, the song dates back to 1961.

WHEN I'M 64 (McCartney) (1967) B
PM: "Yeah, I wrote that tune when I was about fifteen" (Playboy)
JL: "Paul's completely. I would never dream of writing a song like that." (Playboy)
The song is associated with Kenny Ball and his Jazzmen - Kenny has re-recorded it at the age of 69! - and the melody was written during the Trad boom in the early 1960s. Paul wrote the lyric around the time of his father's 64th birthday on 2nd July 1966.

A. BROWN

I'LL FOLLOW THE SUN (McCartney)
(1966) D
JL: "That's Paul again, written almost before the Beatles, I think." (Playboy)
PM: "I remember writing that in our front living room at Forthlin Road on my own." (Many Years From Now)

LOVE OF THE LOVED (McCartney) (1963) (First recording by Cilla Black) D
JL: "Paul's, written when he was a teenager." (Playboy)
Cilla Black: "Paul McCartney wrote 'Love Of The Loved'."

LIKE DREAMERS DO (McCartney) (1964)
(First recorded by the Applejacks) D
JL: "Paul's, another one he'd written as a teenager." (Playboy)

A WORLD WITHOUT LOVE (McCartney) (1964)
(First recorded by Peter and Gordon) B
JL: "McCartney, and resurrected from his past. That has the line, 'Please lock me away', which we always used to crack up at." (Playboy)
Doc Pomus told me that this was his favourite Beatles' composition.

TIP OF MY TONGUE (McCartney) (1963)
(First recording by Tommy Quickly) E
JL: "That's another piece of Paul's garbage, not my garbage." (Playboy)

YOU'LL BE MINE (Lennon - McCartney) (1995) E
An affectionate parody of the Ink Spots, attributed to both writers on "Anthology 1" as opposed to "Cayenne", which is solely McCartney.

WHAT GOES ON (Lennon - McCartney - Starr) (1965) D
JL: "That was an early Lennon, written when we were the Quarrymen. And resurrected with a middle eight thrown in, probably with Paul's help, to give Ringo a song." (Playboy)
Barry Miles in "Many Years From Now" says it is an old song written by John before they had a recording contract and which they never played live. John dusted it off and Paul and Ringo wrote a new middle eight for it. Ringo is quoted as saying his contribution was "about five words".

LOVE ME DO (Lennon - McCartney) (1962) B
JL: "Paul wrote the main structure of this when he was 16 or even earlier. I think I had something to do with the middle eight." (Hit Parader)
PM: "'Love Me Do' was completely co-written. It might have been my original idea, but some of them really were 50-50 and I think that one was." (Many Years From Now)

P.S. I LOVE YOU (McCartney) (1962) C

JL: "That's Paul's song. He was trying to write a 'Soldier Boy' like the Shirelles. I might have contributed something. I can't remember anything in particular." (Playboy)

PLEASE PLEASE ME (Lennon) (1963) B

"Bing Helps Beatles Shock!"

JL: "That's my song completely. It was my attempt at writing a Roy Orbison song, would you believe? Also, I was intrigued by the Bing Crosby song, 'Please lend your little ears to my pleas', the double use of the word 'please'." (Playboy)

ASK ME WHY (Lennon - McCartney) (1963) D

"Probably written in 1962 with John as the major contributor" (Steve Turner)

"Though awkward, its lyric shows personal traces suggesting that Lennon might have had his wife Cynthia in mind." (Ian MacDonald)

John and Paul said that they had around 100 original songs written before 1963 and considering the potential of several of them, it is surprising that they didn't play them for George Martin in 1962. We know that he considered "Love Me Do" to be mediocre and yet they had far better compositions to hand.

Mitch Murray: "I blush to say this, but George Martin liked 'How Do You Do It' and told them, 'When you can write songs as good as this, we'll record them.' I cringe just thinking of it now."

They had enough songs to make an excellent first album of original material. As well as the above, they also had "I Lost My Little Girl" (McCartney's first composition and used on "Unplugged" in 1991), "Cayenne" (a McCartney instrumental), "Cry For A Shadow" (a Lennon - Harrison instrumental apeing the Shadows), "Suicide" (a McCartney composition that he later sent to Sinatra - Sinatra thought, incorrectly, that he was taking the mick) and "In Spite Of All The Danger" (which they had recorded privately in Liverpool).

It is interesting to speculate why they agreed to a Lennon - McCartney arrangement in 1962 as many of their existing songs had been written separately. Possibly, they saw their future as writing together as a team, like Gerry Goffin and Carole King. However, there hadn't been a major songwriting team in British music since Gilbert and Sullivan! Where did this leave George Harrison - he had written with both of them individually and the material ("Cry For A Shadow" and "In Spite Of All The Danger") is nothing to be ashamed of.

The Moptop Years

George Melly: "I went along to a party given by the publishers of 'In His Own Write'. It was a literary party with people like Kingsley Amis there. I was a bit drunk and so was John. I said to him, 'Of course I can tell that you admire the great black artists, in particular Chuck Berry. 'Yeah, he's great.' 'Well,' I said, ' it must be extraordinary to be such an enormous success when they're not because these black artists are so much better than us.' I was thinking of myself in relation to Bessie Smith and of himself in relation to Muddy Waters and Chuck Berry. He wouldn't have any of it. He said, 'I could eat Chuck Berry for breakfast' in a real wide-boy, arrogant Liverpool way. I was shocked by his response and got terribly cross and we had quite a shout-up about it."

MISERY (Lennon - McCartney) (1963) C

JL: "It was more of a John song than a Paul song but it was written together." (Playboy)

DO YOU WANT TO KNOW A SECRET?
(Lennon - McCartney) (1963) B

JL: "I wrote it and gave it to George. I thought it would be a good vehicle for him as it only had three notes and he wasn't the best singer in the world." (Playboy)

PM: "A song we wrote for George to sing." (Playboy)

THERE'S A PLACE (Lennon) (1963) D
JL: "'There's A Place' is my attempt at a sort of Motown, black thing." (Playboy)
I've always thought this was one of the poorer songs, but Tony Burrows, who recorded it with the Kestrels at the Beatles' suggestion, said it was really good.

FROM ME TO YOU (Lennon - McCartney) (1963) B
JL: "We were writing it in a car and I know the first line was mine. After that we took it from there. It was far bluesier than that when we wrote it. You could rearrange it pretty funky." (Playboy)
PM: ""We wrote 'From Me To You' on the bus, it was great, that middle eight was a very big departure for us. Going to a G minor and a C takes you to a whole new world." (The Complete Beatles Recording Sessions)

THANK YOU GIRL
(Lennon - McCartney) (1963) C
JL: "That was one of our efforts at writing a single that didn't work." (Playboy)
PM: "This is pretty much co-written, but there might have been a slight leaning towards me." (Many Years From Now)

I'LL BE ON MY WAY (McCartney) (1963)
(First recording by Billy J. Kramer with the Dakotas) D
JL: "That's Paul's through and through. Doesn't it sound like him? Paul on the voids of driving through the country." (Playboy)

SHE LOVES YOU (Lennon - McCartney) (1963) A
Johnny Dean, editor of the monthly 'Beatles Book': "I got to the No 2 studio in Abbey Road, and Brian Epstein, George Martin and Dick James were waiting for the Beatles to turn up. I learned that the boys would write a song on the way to the studio. They walked in and they sang a song with acoustic guitars and with everyone cocking an ear to hear what it was like. It was 'She Loves You' and it didn't sound very impressive. The song when I first heard it and the song when they'd finished it were totally different. What they did in-between was the Beatles' magic."
JL: "It was written together and I don't know how. I remember it was Paul's idea. Instead of singing 'I love you' again, we'd have a third party. That kind of little detail is in his work now where he will write a story about someone and I'm more inclined to write about myself." (Playboy)

Author Dave Marsh: "Listen to 'She Loves You' and you'll discover a very dangerous message. 'She loves you and if you're too big a fool to respect that, I'm going to go after her'. That's what the song is really about. It's John Lennon at his slyest."
George Martin: "The 'yeah, yeah, yeah' in 'She Loves You' was a curious singing chord. It was a major sixth with George Harrison doing the sixth and the other two, the third and fifth. It was just the way Glenn Miller wrote for the saxophone."
Freddie Starr: "I remember hearing 'She Loves You' before it was released and I said, 'It's terrible, it'll never get anywhere.'"
Kenny Lynch: "I remember travelling on a coach from Warrington with them and they were singing 'Wooooooo, wooooooo' and I said, 'You can't do that. You sound like a bunch of fairies.' They said, 'The kids'll like it' and they were right."

I'LL GET YOU
(Lennon - McCartney) (1963) C
Barry Miles reports Paul as saying that this was "very co-written" in Many Years From Now.
JL: "That was Paul and me trying to write a song and it didn't work out." (Playboy)

BAD TO ME (Lennon) (1963)
(First recording by Billy J. Kramer with the Dakotas) C
Billy J. Kramer: "John gave me 'Bad To Me'."
JL: "I wrote that for Billy J. Kramer. That was a commissioned song and I remember playing it to Brian Epstein when we were on holiday in Torremolinos." (Playboy)
Mitch Murray: "I thought 'Bad To Me' was better than a lot of the songs they were writing for themselves."
Although attributed to Lennon, "The birds in the sky will be sad and lonely" sounds more like Paul.

I'M IN LOVE (Lennon) (1963)
(First recording by the Fourmost) C
JL: "That sounds like me, but I don't remember anything about writing it." (Playboy)
Dave Lovelady of the Fourmost: "We needed another song for a recording session in London the following day. John Lennon came round and sang the song into Brian O'Hara's ropey old tape recorder. John had just finished a gig, was really tired and his voice was croaky. We learnt the song in the coach going down to London."
Brian O'Hara had the tape up to his death in 1999, but he would not allow others to hear it. What will happen to it now?

I'LL KEEP YOU SATISFIED (McCartney) (1963)
(First recording by Billy J. Kramer with the Dakotas) C
JL: "Paul's." (Playboy)
Very underrated song. It would, I think, have been a huge hit for Billy J. Kramer if he hadn't blown it with a disastrous live appearance on "Sunday Night At The London Palladium".

I WANNA BE YOUR MAN (Lennon - McCartney) (1963) (First recording by the Rolling Stones) C
Ron King, the Beatles' coach driver, told Ray Coleman, "I remember John telling me that he could get ideas for songs from reading. He'd be watching television in a hotel or in a dressing-room, and suddenly he'd jump up for his cigarette packet on which he'd write a phrase or something he'd heard. Later, I'd hear it crop up in a song like 'I Wanna Be Your Man'. I thought how clever he was."
JL: "Paul had the lick and we finished it for the Stones. We played it roughly to them and then we went off to the corner of the room and finished it while they were talking. That inspired Mick and Keith to write because they thought, 'Jesus, look at that. They just went in the corner and did it!' Our version was done by Ringo, which shows how much importance we put on it, right?" (Playboy)
PM: "I wrote it for Ringo to do on one of the early albums. But we ended up giving it to the Stones." (Playboy)
Some conflict here: possibly they had written it for Ringo, and then pretended that it wasn't complete to impress the Stones

IT WON'T BE LONG (Lennon) (1963) D
JL: "'It Won't Be Long' is mine. It was my attempt at writing another single. It never quite made it. That was the one where The Times wrote about the 'Aeolian cadences', which started the whole intellectual bit." (Playboy)

ALL I'VE GOT TO DO (Lennon) (1963) D
JL: "That's me trying to do Smokey Robinson again" (Playboy)

ALL MY LOVING (McCartney) (1963) B
JL: "'All My Loving' is Paul, I regret to say, because it's a damn good piece of work." (Playboy)
PM: "It was the first song where I had written the words first." (Many Years From Now)

LITTLE CHILD (Lennon - McCartney) (1963) D
JL: "Another effort by Paul and I to write a song for somebody, probably Ringo." (Playboy)

HOLD ME TIGHT (McCartney) (1963) D
JL: "That was Paul's. Maybe I stuck some bits in there - I don't remember. It was a pretty poor song and I was never really interested in it either way." (Playboy)
PM: "I can't remember much about that one. Certain songs were just 'work' songs, you haven't got much memory of them." (The Complete Beatles Recording Sessions)
Sounds like no-one wants the credit, and yet it's not as bad as that.

NOT A SECOND TIME (Lennon) (1963) D
JL: "That's me trying to do something. I don't remember what." (Playboy)
"The Times" praised Lennon's use of Aeolian cadences, but he told "Playboy", "I have no idea what they are. They sound like exotic birds."

I WANT TO HOLD YOUR HAND (Lennon - McCartney) (1963) A
JL: "We wrote a lot of stuff together, one on one, eyeball to eyeball, like in 'I Want To Hold Your Hand', I remember when we got the chord that made the song." (Playboy)
PM: "'Eyeball to eyeball' is a very good description. 'I Want To Hold Your Hand' was very co-written." (Many Years From Now)

THIS BOY (Lennon - McCartney) (1963) C
PM: "Very co-written in a hotel room." (Many Years From Now)
JL: "Just my attempt at writing one of those three-part harmony Smokey Robinson songs." (Playboy)
Again, whom do we believe?

CAN'T BUY ME LOVE (McCartney) (1964) B
JL: "That's Paul's completely. Maybe I had something to do with the chorus, I don't know." (Playboy)

YOU CAN'T DO THAT (Lennon) (1964) C
JL: "That's me doing Wilson Pickett." (Playboy)
Ray Coleman: "The lyrics are very much John Lennon of that period. They talk of the things you can't do, which was very much a theme of John Lennon's life, things you can't do that he nevertheless did."

ONE AND ONE IS TWO (McCartney) (1964) (First recorded by Mike Shannon and the Strangers) E
JL: "One of Paul's bad attempts at writing a song." (Playboy)

NOBODY I KNOW (McCartney) (1964) (First recorded by Peter and Gordon) C
JL: "Paul again. That was his Jane Asher period I believe." (Playboy)

A HARD DAY'S NIGHT (Lennon) (1964) A
JL: "Dick Lester suggested the title from something Ringo had said. I used it in 'In His Own Write', but it was off the cuff by Ringo. Dick Lester said we're going to use it as the title, and the next morning I brought in the song." (Playboy)

I SHOULD HAVE KNOWN BETTER (Lennon) (1964) C
JL: "That's me. Just a song; it doesn't mean a damn thing." (Playboy)
PM: "'I Should Have Known Better' was one of John's." (Playboy)

IF I FELL (Lennon - McCartney) (1964) C
PM: "We wrote 'If I Fell' together but with the emphasis on John because he sang it." (Many Years From Now)
JL: "That's my first attempt at a ballad proper." (Playboy)

I'M HAPPY JUST TO DANCE WITH YOU (Lennon) (1964) D
Steve Turner calls this John's song.
Ian MacDonald says it was written by Lennon for Harrison, "the repeated notes on the verse being there to accommodate his limited range."

AND I LOVE HER (McCartney) (1964) B
JL: "Paul again. I consider it his first 'Yesterday'. I helped with the middle eight." (Playboy)
Barry Miles says that this is Paul's in "Many Years From Now".

TELL ME WHY (Lennon) (1964) C
Steve Turner says that John "knocked it off" for a concert sequence in "A Hard Day's Night".

ANY TIME AT ALL (Lennon) (1964) D
I can't trace the quote, but I know that John said somewhere that he was rewriting "It Won't Be Long". Ian MacDonald cites it as John's song but says that Paul may have helped on the chorus.

I'LL CRY INSTEAD (Lennon) (1964) D
JL: "I wrote that for ' A Hard Day's Night'." (Playboy)

THINGS WE SAID TODAY (McCartney) (1964) C
JL: "Paul's. Good song." (Playboy)
Barry Miles says that this is Paul's in 'Many Years From Now."

WHEN I GET HOME (Lennon) (1964) D
JL: "That's me again." (Playboy)

I'LL BE BACK (Lennon) (1964) D
JL: "Me completely. My variations of the chords in a Del Shannon song." (Playboy) (It's a shame that the interviewer didn't ask which one, but it's probably "Runaway".)

PM: "'I'll Be Back' was co-written but it was largely John's idea." (Many Years From Now)
More disagreement here.

FROM A WINDOW (McCartney) (1964)
(First recorded by Billy J. Kramer with the Dakotas) C
JL: "Paul's, his artsy period with Jane Asher." (Playboy)

IT'S FOR YOU (McCartney) (1964) (First recorded by Cilla Black) C
PM: "That was something I'd written." (The Complete Beatles Recording Sessions)

I DON'T WANT TO SEE YOU AGAIN (McCartney) (1964) (First recorded by Peter and Gordon) D
JL: "That's Paul." (Playboy)

I FEEL FINE (Lennon) (1964) B
JL: "Me completely, including the electric guitar lick. It's the record with the first feedback anywhere." (Playboy)

SHE'S A WOMAN (McCartney) (1964) C
JL: "That's Paul with some contribution from me on lines, probably. We were so excited to say 'turn me on' - about marijuana and all that, using it as an expression." (Playboy)
Ian MacDonald and Bill Harry attribute it completely to Paul McCartney.

NO REPLY (Lennon - McCartney) (1964) C
JL: "That's my song. That's the one where Dick James said, 'That's the first complete song you've written where it resolves itself.' You know, with a complete story. It was my version of 'Silhouettes', although I had never called a girl on the phone in my life. Phones weren't part of an English boy's life." (Playboy)
PM: "We wrote 'No Reply' together, but from a strong, original idea of his." (Many Years From Now)
Again, more disagreement. Ray Coleman calls it "the bleaker side of the Lennon persona."

I'M A LOSER (Lennon) (1964) C
JL: "That's me in my Dylan period." (Playboy)
PM: "'I'm A Loser' was pretty much John's song, but there may have been a dabble or two from me." (Many Years From Now)

BABY'S IN BLACK (Lennon - McCartney) (1964) C
JL: "Together, in the same room." (Playboy)

EIGHT DAYS A WEEK (Lennon - McCartney) (1964) C
JL: "'Eight Days A Week' was the running title for 'Help!' before they had that. It was Paul's effort at getting a single for the movie. It was never a good song. We struggled to record it and struggled to make it into a song. It was his initial effort, but I think we both worked on it. It was lousy anyway." (Playboy)
The title came from Ringo Starr and although it may be largely Paul's song, John sings the lead vocal.

EVERY LITTLE THING (McCartney) (1964) D
Barry Miles says that this is Paul's in "Many Years From Now."
JL: "'Every Little Thing' is his song; maybe I threw something in." (Playboy)

I DON'T WANT TO SPOIL THE PARTY (Lennon) (1964) D
JL: "That's me." (Playboy)

WHAT YOU'RE DOING (McCartney) (1964) D
JL: "His song; I might have done something." (Playboy)

TICKET TO RIDE (Lennon) (1965) B
Steve Turner says that this was written by John and described by him as "one of the earliest heavy metal records".

YES IT IS (Lennon) (1965) C
JL: "That's me trying a rewrite of 'This Boy'" (Playboy)

PM: "I was there writing it with John but it was his inspiration. It is a very fine song of John's." (Many Years From Now)

TELL ME WHAT YOU SEE (McCartney) (1965) D
JL: "That's Paul." (Playboy)

THAT MEANS A LOT (McCartney) (1965) (First recorded by P J Proby) D
JL: "That's Paul." (Playboy)
When I spoke to P.J. Proby, he described it as "John's song".

HELP! (Lennon) (1965) A
JL: "When 'Help!' came out, I was actually crying for help. I didn't realise it at the time; I just wrote the song because I was commissioned to write it for the movie. Maureen Cleave asked me, 'Why don't you ever write songs with more than one syllable?'. In 'Help!', there are three syllable words and I very proudly showed them to her and she still didn't like it." (Playboy)

I'M DOWN (Lennon - McCartney) (1965) C
JL: "That's Paul with a little help from me, I think." (Playboy)

THE NIGHT BEFORE (McCartney) (1965) D
JL: "That's Paul again." (Playboy)

YOU'VE GOT TO HIDE YOUR LOVE AWAY (Lennon) (1965) C
JL: "That's me in my Dylan period." (Playboy)

IF YOU'VE GOT TROUBLE (Lennon - McCartney) (1996) D
Outtake from 1965 and "written by John and Paul as Ringo's vocal offering." (Lewisohn)
Alf Bicknell, the Beatles' chauffeur: "John and Paul had written a song for Ringo to perform on the 'Help!' album, 'If You've Got Trouble'. He recorded it but they didn't think it had worked out very well."
PM: "We didn't really, until later, think of Ringo's songs as seriously as our own." (The Complete Beatles Recording Sessions".

ANOTHER GIRL (McCartney) (1965) D
JL: "'Another Girl' is Paul." (Playboy)

YOU'RE GONNA LOSE THAT GIRL (Lennon) (1965) C
JL: "That's me." (Playboy)

IT'S ONLY LOVE (Lennon) (1965) C
JL: "'It's Only Love' is mine. The lyrics were abysmal. I always hated that song." (Playboy)

I'VE JUST SEEN A FACE (McCartney) (1965) C
JL: "That's Paul." (Playboy)
Barry Miles says that this is Paul's in "Many Years From Now."

YESTERDAY (McCartney) (1965) A
JL: "I had nothing to do with it." (Rolling Stone)
The familiar story of Paul having a dummy lyric about scrambled eggs is told in the section in this book on "1965". If he was having difficulty with the lyric, why didn't he ask John for help? Did he think that John's more abrasive writing might wreck the piece?

WE CAN WORK IT OUT (Lennon - McCartney) (1965) B
JL: "In 'We Can Work It Out', Paul did the first half, I did the middle eight." (Playboy)
Playwright Willy Russell: "I particularly like 'We Can Work It Out' because it combines absolute Lennon with absolute McCartney. McCartney wrote the verses and Lennon added the middle sequence which gives the song its toughness. Paul McCartney's melodic gift with John Lennon's rough edge was an unbeatable combination."

DAY TRIPPER (Lennon) (1965) B
JL: "That's mine." (Playboy)

DRIVE MY CAR (Lennon - McCartney) (1965) C
PM: "That was my idea and John and I wrote the words, so I would go 70-30 on that to me." (Many Years From Now)
JL: "His song, with contributions from me." (Playboy)

NORWEGIAN WOOD (Lennon - McCartney) (1965) B
JL: "'Norwegian Wood is my song completely" (Playboy)
Alan Price: "I was in John Lennon's house and he played me the demo of 'Norwegian Wood'. He said that the rest of them were taking the mickey out of him because he was copying Bob Dylan. When I heard the demo, I could understand why they said that."

PM: "It's 60-40 to John because it's John's idea and John's tune, but I filled it out lyrically and had the idea to set the place on fire, so I take some sort of credit." (Many Years From Now)

Dylan took Lennon's tune and recorded his own words, "Fourth Time Around".

YOU WON'T SEE ME (McCartney) (1965) D
JL: "Paul." (Playboy)
PM: "It was 100% me as I recall, but I'm always quite happy to give John a credit because there's always the chance that on the session he might have said, 'That would be better.'" (Many Years From Now, and a most untypical remark!)

NOWHERE MAN (Lennon) (1965) B
JL: "Me, me." (Rolling Stone)
PM: "That was John after a night out, with dawn coming up."(Playboy)

THE WORD (Lennon - McCartney) (1965) E
JL: "'The Word' was written together, but it's mainly mine." (Playboy)

MICHELLE (Lennon - McCartney- Jan Vaughan)
(1965) A
PM: "I got the French off Jan, who is the wife of Ivan Vaughan and years later I sent her a cheque. I thought I better had as she is virtually a co-writer on that. From there I pieced together the verses." (Many Years From Now)

John has said that the middle section, "I love you", was his contribution and inspired by (or taken from!) Nina Simone's "I Put A Spell On You". Jan Vaughan probably did as much as he did.

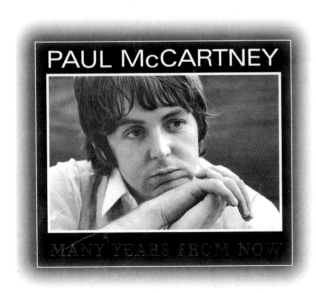

GIRL (Lennon - McCartney) (1965) C
JL: "That's me." (Playboy)
PM: "It was John's original idea but it was very much co-written." (Many Years From Now)

I'M LOOKING THROUGH YOU (McCartney) (1965) D
JL: "Paul. He must have had an argument with Jane Asher." (Playboy)
Barry Miles confirms that this is Paul's in "Many Years From Now."

IN MY LIFE (Lennon - McCartney) (1965) A
JL: "For 'In My Life' I had a complete set of lyrics. Paul helped with the middle eight musically" (Playboy)
PM: "John had the very nice opening stanzas of the song, but as I recall he didn't have a tune for it. I went down to the half-landing where John had a mellotron and I put together a tune based in my mind on Smokey Robinson and the Miracles, so I recall writing the whole melody. 'Got it, great, what do you think of it?' and John said, 'Nice' and we continued working with it from there, using that melody and filling out the rest of the verses." (Many Years From Now)
Somebody should record the original verses which refer to the overhead railway and other Liverpool landmarks. Who decided that the lyric should be more general?

WAIT (Lennon - McCartney) (1965) D
PM: "I think 'Wait' was my song, I don't remember John collaborating too much on it, although he could have". (Many Years From Now)
Ian MacDonald and Steve Turner agree that that this is a joint composition.

RUN FOR YOUR LIFE (Lennon) (1965) D
JL: "Just a throwaway song of mine that I never thought much of, but it was always a favourite of George's." (Playboy)

WOMAN (McCartney) (1966)
(First recorded by Peter and Gordon) D
Curiously, Paul McCartney, Mike McCartney and then John Lennon have written songs called "Woman". Paul wrote his song for Peter and Gordon and allegedly, he wanted to see whether his songs would sell without "Lennon - McCartney" on the label. However, Peter and Gordon had released a Lennon - McCartney composition, "I Don't Want To See You Again" as a single and very few people had bought it. Why, anyway, did Peter and

Gordon agree to such nonsense? If the song was a major hit, Paul would say, "That proves my point" and if it wasn't, it showed that Peter and Gordon hadn't got much standing on their own. "Woman" reached No 28 and I don't know whether that proved anything or not.

PAPERBACK WRITER (Lennon - McCartney) (1966) B
JL: "'Paperback Writer' is son of 'Day Tripper', but it is Paul's song." (Playboy)
PM: "John and I sat and finished it all up, but it was tilted towards me. The original idea was mine." (Many Years From Now)

RAIN (Lennon) (1966) C
JL: "That's me again - with the first backwards tape on any record anywhere." (Playboy)

The Experimental Years

ELEANOR RIGBY (Lennon - McCartney - Pete Shotton) (1966) A
The song may have started with the gravestone for Eleanor Rigby in St Peter's churchyard in Woolton where John and Paul first met, or it may be an amazing coincidence.
Lionel Bart: "'Eleanor Rigby' was originally going to be called 'Eleanor Bygraves' and I told them to change it."
PM: "I wrote that. I got the name 'Rigby' from a shop in Bristol."
Barry Miles says that the song is Paul's in "Many Years From Now".
JL: "Paul's baby, and I helped with the education of the child. The first verse was his and the rest was basically mine." (Playboy)

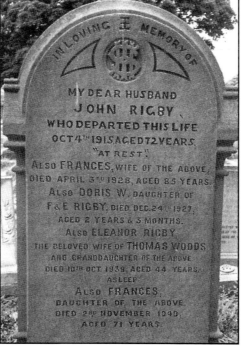

John's close friend, Pete Shotton, told me, "I took part in the writing of 'Eleanor Rigby'. The Beatles and their women, myself and my wife, were at John's this weekend. We all had dinner and as usual, the lads went upstairs, which is where John's toys were, his Scalextrix and his tape recorders and his instruments. There were five of us, we were smoking some weed, and John and Paul had guitars. Paul said, 'I've got this little tune and I've got a start to it,' and he began playing 'Eleanor Rigby'. Then we were writing it together and I'd throw words in. John was subdued during this, he didn't take much part in the writing of 'Eleanor Rigby', I did more than he did. I was

really getting into it and it was great. Paul sang 'Father McCartney' and I said, 'Hang on, Paul, you can't do that, they'll think it's your poor old dad. You've left him on his own.' Paul said, 'Shit, you're right.' We tried Father McVicar, which was quite amusing and then I asked Ringo for the phone book. I went through the Mac's and I came to 'McKenzie'. I said, 'Try that' and that's how it came about. There was a Father McKenzie in Woolton, but that was just coincidence. I know categorically that it was me who came up with the name."
JL: "I wrote a good half of the lyrics or more." (Rolling Stone)
Pete Shotton, "Paul was stuck on how to end it. I said, 'Why don't you finish it with Eleanor Rigby dying as a lonely person and Father McKenzie as a lonely vicar doing the service?' John said very sarcastically, 'I don't think you understand what we're getting at here, Pete', and I said, 'Sod you', which brought the session to an end. The next thing I heard was the record itself and of course they had that ending, and so it was John who wasn't tuned in as to what the song was about. I bumped into Paul a couple of years ago and he said, 'What was that song you really helped me with?' and I said, 'Well, I helped with quite a lot of them, you know,' and he said, 'No, there was one in particular,' and it was 'Eleanor Rigby.'"

I'M ONLY SLEEPING (Lennon) (1966) C
JL: "That's me, dreaming my life away." (Playboy)
PM: "Being tired was one of John's theme. He wrote 'I'm Only Sleeping'" (Many Years From Now)

HERE, THERE AND EVERYWHERE (McCartney) (1966) A
JL: "Paul's song completely, I believe. And one of my favourite songs of the Beatles." (Playboy)
PM: "I wrote that by John's pool one day." (Playboy)
In "Many Years From Now", Paul credits John with a few words.

YELLOW SUBMARINE (Lennon - McCartney) (1966) A
JL: "'Yellow Submarine' is Paul's baby. Donovan helped with the lyrics. I helped with the lyrics too." (Playboy)
Donovan: "The whole song was written but Paul was short of a line. I added 'Sky of blue and sea of green', not

a very difficult thing to write."

SHE SAID, SHE SAID (Lennon) (1966) C
JL: "That's mine. It's an interesting track. That was written after an acid trip in LA during a break in the Beatles tour when we were having fun with the Byrds and lots of girls." (Playboy)
Peter Fonda was taking a trip and kept saying he knew how it felt to be dead, hence the song.

GOOD DAY SUNSHINE (McCartney) (1966) C
PM: "Wrote that at John's one day - the sun was shining." (Playboy)
JL: "'Good Day Sunshine' is Paul's. Maybe I threw in a line or something. I don't know." (Playboy)

AND YOUR BIRD CAN SING
(Lennon) (1966) C
JL: "Another of my throwaways." (Playboy)
A ridiculous comment - this is an excellent song. There's a terrific version on the album, "Beatle Country", by the bluegrass band, the Charles River Valley Boys featuring Joe Val, a 1966 album now on CD (Rounder CD SS 41).

FOR NO ONE (McCartney) (1966) B
PM "I wrote that on a skiing holiday in Switzerland." (Playboy)
JL: "'Paul's. One of my favourite's of his. A nice piece of work." (Playboy)

DR ROBERT (Lennon) (1966) D
JL: "Another of mine. Mainly about drugs and pills. I was the one that carried all the pills on tour." (Playboy)

GOT TO GET YOU INTO MY LIFE (McCartney) (1966) B
PM: "That's mine; I wrote it. It was the first one we used brass on, I believe." (Playboy)
JL: "Paul's again. I think that was one of his best songs, because the lyrics are good and I didn't write them." (Playboy)

12-BAR ORIGINAL
(Lennon - McCartney- Harrison - Starr) (1996) E
Instrumental outtake from 1965. Not known what the Beatles intended to do with it.

TOMORROW NEVER KNOWS (Lennon) (1966) D
JL: "That's me in my 'Tibetan Book Of The Dead' period." (Playboy)
PM: "The title was one of Ringo's malapropisms. John wrote the lyrics from Timothy Leary's version of the 'Tibetan Book of the Dead'." (Playboy)
Ringo was a good source for song titles - "A Hard Day's Night", "Eight Days A Week" and now this.

PENNY LANE (McCartney) (1967) A
JL: "'Penny Lane' is from Paul, although it was actually me who lived in Penny Lane." (Playboy)
Roger McGough: "Liverpool didn't have a mythology until they created one."
George Melly: "The Beatles treated Penny Lane as a surrealistic thing with the nurse selling poppies and the like. I believe it caused considerable embarrassment to the local fishshop because people kept going in and ordering 'fish and finger pie'. It was typical of the Beatles to throw that in. They knew that very few would know what they were on about."

STRAWBERRY FIELDS FOREVER (Lennon) (1967) A
Co-credit for John's drug dealer?
JL: "I wrote that when I was making 'How I Won The War' in Almeria, Spain." (Playboy)
The drummer, Dave Mattacks, commented: "The first time I heard 'Strawberry Fields Forever', I thought what a great tune, that's a great song, it's got the best of everything. It changes signatures, there are odd beats and bars here and there, but you're not aware of it at the time. It's just a terrific tune with a great performance."

SGT PEPPER'S LONELY HEARTS CLUB BAND (McCartney) (1967) A

JL: "'Sgt. Pepper' is Paul, after a trip to America and the whole West Coast, long-named group thing was coming in." (Playboy)

PM :"It was an idea I had, I think, when I was flying from LA to somewhere. I thought it would be nice to lose our personalities, to submerge ourselves in the persona of a fake group." (Playboy)

WITH A LITTLE HELP FROM MY FRIENDS (Lennon - McCartney) (1967) A

Hunter Davies' book describes how they wrote the song together.

JL: "That's Paul with a little help from me." (Playboy)

LUCY IN THE SKY WITH DIAMONDS (Lennon - McCartney) (1967) B

PM: "John showed me Julian's drawing on school paper with the title, 'Lucy In The Sky With Diamonds'. Wow, fantastic title! Julian had drawn stars and then he thought they were diamonds, so we went upstairs and started writing it." (Many Years From Now)

The story of Julian's picture is definitely true, but both John and Paul denied that they realised that the song's initials were "LSD". It is hard to credit this when their friend, Jimi Hendrix, also in 1967, recorded "The Stars That Play With Laughing Sam's Dice". At a guess they both agreed to putting messages in their titles.

GETTING BETTER (Lennon - McCartney) (1967) C

Hunter Davies says it was Paul's original idea but that the song was co-written.

PM: "Wrote that at my house in St. John's Wood. All I remember is that I said, 'It's getting better all the time', and John contributed the legendary line, 'It couldn't get much worse', which I thought was very good. It's against the spirit of the song, which was all super-optimistic. It's lovely little sardonic line." (Playboy)

JL: "It's a diary form of writing. All that 'I used to be cruel to my woman, I beat her and kept her apart from the things that she loved' was me." (Playboy)

FIXING A HOLE (McCartney) (1967) D

JL: "That's Paul, again writing a good lyric." (Playboy)
PM: "Yeah, I wrote that. I liked that one." (Playboy)

SHE'S LEAVING HOME (McCartney) (1967) B

PM: "I wrote that. My kind of ballad from that period." (Playboy)

BEING FOR THE BENEFIT OF MR KITE (Lennon) (1967) D

John's, based on a Victorian circus poster he bought in an antique shop.

LOVELY RITA (McCartney) (1967) C

JL: "That's Paul writing a pop song." (Playboy)
PM: "Yeah, that was mine." (Playboy)

GOOD MORNING GOOD MORNING (Lennon) (1967) D

PM: "John's." (Playboy)

JL: "'Good Morning' is mine. It's a throwaway, a piece of garbage." (Playboy)

A DAY IN THE LIFE (Lennon - McCartney) (1967) B

This song is discussed in detail in "Many Years From Now". The idea and the first verse came from John, and they worked on the rest of the lyric together. The middle section about being on the bus comes from an earlier song of Paul's, and Paul perfected the avant-garde ending.

ALL YOU NEED IS LOVE (Lennon) (1967) A

John's first attempt at writing a message song that everybody could sing.

PM: "'All You Need Is Love' was John's song. I threw in a few ideas as did the other members of the group but it was largely ad-libs that we made up on the spot." (Many Years From Now)

BABY, YOU'RE A RICH MAN (Lennon - McCartney) (1967) D

JL: "That's a combination of two separate pieces, Paul's and mine, put together and forced into one song." (Playboy)

HELLO GOODBYE (McCartney) (1967) C

JL: "That's another McCartney. Smells a mile away, doesn't it?" (Playboy)

I AM THE WALRUS (Lennon) (1967) B

JL: "I had these first two lines on the typewriter, and then about two weeks later I ran through and wrote another two lines and then, when I saw I had something, after about four lines, I knocked the rest of it off." (Rolling Stone, 1968)

MAGICAL MYSTERY TOUR (McCartney) (1967) B
JL: "Paul's song. Maybe I did part of it, but it was his concept." (Playboy)

THE FOOL ON THE HILL (McCartney) (1967) B
JL: "Paul. Proving he can write lyrics if he's a good boy." (Playboy)

FLYING (Lennon - McCartney - Harrison - Starr) (1967) E
Instrumental for "Magical Mystery Tour" that emerged from a studio jam session.

YOUR MOTHER SHOULD KNOW (McCartney) (1967) C
JL: "Guess who? Paul." (Playboy)

STEP INSIDE LOVE (McCartney) (1968) C
JL: "Guess. Paul." (Playboy)
Cilla Black confirms that Paul wrote the song.

LOS PARANOIAS (Lennon - McCartney- Harrison - Starr) (1996) E
A jam session from 1968, not released until "Anthology 3".

LADY MADONNA (McCartney) (1968) B
JL: "Paul. Good piano lick, but the song never really went anywhere." (Playboy)
Humphrey Lyttelton: "A number of idiots came up to me and said, 'They've borrowed the introduction to 'Bad Penny Blues'. What are you going to do?' They wanted me to sue them but I told them not to be so stupid. You can't copyright a rhythm and a rhythm was all they'd used. Actually, we'd borrowed it from Dan Burley."

HEY JUDE (McCartney) (1968) A
JL: "'Hey Jude' is Paul's. One of his masterpieces." (Playboy)

REVOLUTION (Lennon) (1968) C
JL: "Completely me." (Playboy)

THINGUMYBOB (McCartney) (1968)
(First recorded by the Black Dyke Mills Band) E
TV theme by Paul McCartney (Many Years From Now)

BACK IN THE USSR (McCartney) (1968) C
JL: "Paul completely. I play six string bass on that." (Playboy)
PM: "I wrote that as a Beach Boys parody." (Playboy)

DEAR PRUDENCE (Lennon) (1968) C
JL: "'Dear Prudence is me." (Playboy)

GLASS ONION (Lennon) (1968) D
JL: "That's me doing a throwaway song." (Playboy)

OB-LA-DI, OB-LA-DA (McCartney) (1968) B
JL: "I might have given him a couple of lines, but it's his song, his lyrics." (Playboy)

WILD HONEY PIE (Lennon - McCartney) (1968) E
Fragment emerging from a singalong in Rishikesh and not related to the other "Honey Pie".

THE CONTINUING STORY OF BUNGALOW BILL (Lennon) (1968) D
John's, and based on a friend, Richard Cooke, who visited his mother while the Beatles were in India. Despite being among their more esoteric recordings, part of the melody is similar to the standard, "Stay As Sweet As You Are" (1934).

HAPPINESS IS A WARM GUN (Lennon) (1968) D
JL: "Me completely." (Playboy)

MARTHA MY DEAR (McCartney) (1968) C
JL: "Enough said." (Playboy)

I'M SO TIRED (Lennon) (1968) D
JL: "'I'm So Tired' was me in India." (Playboy)
PM: "Very much John's comment to the world."

BLACKBIRD (McCartney) (1968) C
JL: "Enough said. I gave him a line on that one." (Playboy)

ROCKY RACOON (McCartney) (1968) D
JL: "Paul. Couldn't you guess? Would I go to all that trouble about Gideon's Bible and stuff?" (Playboy)

WHAT'S THE NEW MARY JANE (Lennon) (1996) E
A psychedelic recording from 1968 that didn't come off and remained unreleased until "Anthology 3".
"The piece was John's." (Lewisohn)

WHY DON'T WE DO IT IN THE ROAD (McCartney) (1968) E
JL: "That's Paul. He even recorded it by himself in another room." (Playboy)

I WILL (McCartney) (1968) C
JL: "Paul." (Playboy)

JULIA (Lennon) (1968) C
JL: "That was mine." (Playboy)

BIRTHDAY (McCartney) (1968) C
Paul wanted to write a contemporary "Happy Birthday To You" and he had just been watching "The Girl Can't Help It" on TV.
JL: "It's a piece of garbage." (Playboy)

YER BLUES (Lennon) (1968) D
I can't find John talking about it, but the music and the lyrics sound so much like him. He had a fondness for the song, performing it on the Rolling Stones' Rock'n'Roll Circus and with the Plastic Ono Band.

MOTHER NATURE'S SON (McCartney) (1968) C
JL: "Paul." (Playboy)

EVERYBODY'S GOT SOMETHING TO HIDE EXCEPT ME AND MY MONKEY (Lennon) (1968) E
JL: "That was just a nice line which I wrote into a song." (Playboy)

SEXY SADIE (Lennon) (1968) C
JL: "That was inspired by Maharishi. I wrote it when we had our bags packed and we were leaving." (Playboy)

HELTER SKELTER (McCartney) (1968) D
JL: "That's Paul completely." (Playboy)

HONEY PIE (McCartney) (1968) C
Paul's tribute to his father, Jim. "My dad's always played fruity old songs like this and I like them. I would have liked to have been a writer in the Twenties because I like the top hat and tails thing."

CRY BABY CRY (Lennon) (1968) E
JL: "Not me. a piece of rubbish." (Playboy)
Ignore what John said in 1980. The official Hunter Davies biography finds him writing it. Typical of John to disown a song he doesn't care for.

REVOLUTION 9 (Lennon - Ono) (1968) E
Not a song but sound recordings made by John and Yoko. Adrian Henri: "William Burroughs was writing cut-up novels and I can hear his influence in that. They were disrupting reality and trying to make you see something different. It's not a revolution in the sense of throwing bombs, but a revolution in thinking and hearing and seeing."

John and Yoko released three albums of experimental sounds ("Two Virgins", "Unfinished Music No 2: Life With The Lions" and "Wedding Album") before the break-up of the Beatles and all list John Lennon and Yoko Ono as composers.

GOODNIGHT (Lennon) (1968) D
John: "Mine. Over-lush."
PM: "John wrote songs like 'Goodnight' for Ringo, which is the most sentimental ballad." (The Complete Beatles Recording Sessions)
An example of John writing in Paul McCartney mode: a reverse example is "Let Me Roll It" from Wings' "Band On The Run".

ALL TOGETHER NOW (McCartney) (1969) C
JL: "Paul. I put a few lines in it somewhere, probably." (Playboy)

HEY BULLDOG (Lennon) (1969) C
JL: "That's me, because of the 'Yellow Submarine' people, who were gross animals, apart from the guy who drew the paintings for the movie." (Playboy)
Around the release of the new print of "Yellow Submarine" in 1999, this song was reassessed, and it is much better than many people thought.

GOODBYE (McCartney) (1969)
(First recorded by Mary Hopkin) C
Paul's.

John also told "Playboy" that he "threw in a couple of one-liners to help the song along" in George Harrison's "Taxman".

The Final Years

GET BACK (McCartney) (1969) A
JL: "'Get Back' is Paul." (Playboy)

DON'T LET ME DOWN (Lennon) (1969) C
JL: "That's me, singing about Yoko." (Playboy)

THE BALLAD OF JOHN AND YOKO (Lennon) (1969) B
JL: "Well, guess who wrote that." (Playboy)

GIVE PEACE A CHANCE (Lennon - Ono) (1969) (First recorded by the Plastic Ono Band) A
JL: "No, I didn't write it with Paul; but again, out of guilt, we always had that thing that our names would go on songs even if we didn't write them. It was never a legal deal between Paul and me, just an agreement when we were fifteen or sixteen to put both our names on our songs. I put his name on 'Give Peace A Chance' even though he had nothing to do with it. It was a silly thing to do actually. It should have been Lennon - Ono." (Playboy)
But why? In 1967, Paul had already written the film soundtrack for "The Family Way" and a single for the Chris Barber Band, "Catcall", under his own name. The next Plastic Ono Band singles - "Cold Turkey" and "Instant Karma" - are attributed to John Lennon.
In 1969 McCartney wrote "Penina" for Carlos Mendes, again solely credited to him.

COME TOGETHER (Lennon) (1969) B
JL: "'Come Together' is me." (Playboy)

MAXWELL'S SILVER HAMMER (McCartney) (1969) C
JL: "That's Paul's. I hate it." (Playboy)

OH! DARLING (McCartney) (1969) D
JL: "'Oh! Darling' was a great song of Paul's that he didn't sing too well. I always thought I could have done it better." (Playboy)

I WANT YOU (SHE'S SO HEAVY) (Lennon) (1969) D
JL: "That's me about Yoko." (Playboy)

BECAUSE (Lennon) (1969) D
JL: "Yoko was playing 'Moonlight Sonata' on the piano. I said, 'Can you play those chords backwards?' and wrote 'Because' around them.'" (Playboy)

YOU NEVER GIVE ME YOUR MONEY (McCartney) (1969) C
JL: "That's Paul." (Playboy)

SUN KING (Lennon) (1969) D
JL: "That's a piece of garbage I had around." (Playboy)

MEAN MR MUSTARD (Lennon) (1969) D
PM: "Very John" (Many Years From Now)
JL: "That's me, writing a piece of garbage." (Playboy)

POLYTHENE PAM (Lennon) (1969) D
JL: "That was me, remembering a little event with a woman in Jersey and a man who was England's answer to Allen Ginsberg." (Playboy)
(That's a reference to the Liverpool poet, Adrian Henri at the Isle of Wight festival.)

SHE CAME IN THROUGH THE BATHROOM WINDOW (McCartney) (1969) D
JL: "That's Paul's song. He wrote that when we were in New York announcing Apple, and we first met Linda." (Playboy)

GOLDEN SLUMBERS (McCartney - Thomas Dekker) (1969) D
JL: "That's Paul, apparently from a poem he found in a book." (Playboy)
(McCartney found the verse in a songbook belonging to his step-sister, Ruth. He couldn't read the music, so he wrote his own.)

CARRY THAT WEIGHT (McCartney) (1969) D
JL: "That's Paul again. I think he was under strain at that period." (Playboy)

THE END (McCartney) (1969) D
JL: "That's Paul again, the unfinished song, right?" (Playboy)

HER MAJESTY (McCartney) (1969) E
Paul, in 1965, after meeting the Queen for their MBEs: "She's lovely. She was very friendly. She was just like a mum to us."
Paul had recorded this fragment to go between "Mean Mr Mustard" and "Polythene Pam" and then asked for it to be removed. The editor put it at the end of the tape and in error, it was heard on the final version of "Abbey Road". Paul decided to leave it in.

COME AND GET IT (McCartney) (1969) (First recorded by Badfinger) C
PM: "I did a demo for 'Come And Get It' for Badfinger which took about 20 minutes. It was before a Beatles session." (The Complete Beatles Recording Sessions)

ACROSS THE UNIVERSE (Lennon) (1969) B
JL: "I was a bit more artsy fartsy there. It drove me out of bed. I didn't want to write it." (Playboy)

LET IT BE (McCartney) (1970) A
JL: "That's Paul. What can you say? Nothing to do with the Beatles." (Playboy)
The author of a Paul McCartney biography, Chris Salewicz, says, "'Let It Be' was written about his mother. It was a very difficult time for Paul within the Beatles. He would lie in bed tossing and turning and trying to get to sleep. One night when he did go to sleep, he had a dream in which his mother, Mary, came to him 'speaking words of wisdom.'."

YOU KNOW MY NAME (LOOK UP THE NUMBER) (Lennon - McCartney) (1970) D
JL: "That was a piece of unfinished music that I turned into a comedy record with Paul." (Playboy)
PM: "He said, 'No other words, those are the words. I want to do it like a mantra.'" (The Complete Beatles Recording Sessions)
PM: "We had such a laugh making it. It's not a great record but I love it." (BBC Radio Merseyside)

FREE AS A BIRD

TWO OF US (McCartney) (1970) C
An ironic title this late in their career!
JL: "Mine." (Playboy)
PM: "Written about Linda" (Many Years From Now)
This is undoubtedly McCartney's song and it's curious that Lennon should want to claim it in view of his comment on "I'll Be On My Way". The song was originally recorded, but not released, by the New York trio, Mortimer, for Apple.

I DIG A PONY (Lennon) (1970) E
JL: "Another piece of garbage I had around." (Playboy)

DIG IT (Lennon - McCartney - Harrison - Starr) (1970) E
Jam session during the making of "Let It Be", only part of which has been heard.

I'VE GOT A FEELING (Lennon - McCartney) (1970) E
JL: "Paul." (Playboy)
But he's wrong - the BBC filmed him working on the middle section.

THE LONG AND WINDING ROAD (McCartney) (1970) A
JL: "Paul again. He had a little spurt just before we split." (Playboy)
Alistair Taylor, General Manager at Apple: "I was very privileged to see Paul sitting at a piano at three in the morning in the middle of the big studio at Abbey Road. He was picking out a melody on the piano and I said, 'I like that, it's a fabulous melody', and he said, 'It's just an idea'. I told him that my wife, Lesley, would love it and he told the engineer to switch the tape on. He recorded 'The Long And Winding Road' then and there, it's full of la-la's as he'd only written a few lines, and it was quite fantastic. He then gave me a copy for her."

FREE AS A BIRD
(Lennon - McCartney - Harrison - Starr) (1995) C
John's 1977 demo was augmented by the other Beatles, who also added a new section. John Lennon knew nothing of this collaboration. The next single, "Real Love", was solely attributed to Lennon.

Conclusions

In terms of quantity, Lennon and McCartney's output cannot be compared to Irving Berlin or many Broadway composers but they were performing most of the time and were recording artists throughout their time together. As a measure, Bob Dylan's 1960s output is around 200 songs and his lyrics are often substantially longer.

Still, the Beatles' output is far more impressive than contemporary bands like their acolytes, Oasis. The much vaunted view that Oasis copy the Beatles is partly true: they copy a certain type of Beatles song, usually John's and fashioned around "Dear Prudence", Don't Let Me Down," "Imagine" and a few others. If they had cribbed a few of Paul's idea, they might have made the whole world sing.

Unlike Oasis, the Beatles did not have long periods away from the recording studio. This can be partly explained by Brian Epstein's strong management, but after Epstein's death, you can see the surge in Paul's creativity as he attempted to hold the band together.

The songs can be summarised as follows:

	Liverpool Years	Moptop Years	Experimental Years	Final Years	Total
Lennon-McCartney	5	25	11	4	45
Lennon	4	28	25	11	68
McCartney	7	24	30	13	74
Total	**16**	**77**	**66**	**28**	**187**

This table shows that, in terms of productivity, McCartney is about 10% ahead: on these totals, for a typical album, you might have five McCartney, four Lennon and three joint compositions.

Note the dramatic tailing off in Lennon - McCartney compositions - effectively, nothing of consequence in the Final Years. More often than not as the years went by, John or Paul was inviting the other to improve a song that wasn't too strong in the first place.

I also graded the songs A to E according to the probable value of their copyrights. This is somewhat speculative but the results are:

	Liverpool Years	Moptop Years	Experimental Years	Final Years	Total
A	-	7	9	4	20
B	5	12	10	3	30
C	3	30	23	6	62
D	6	26	14	11	57
E	2	2	10	4	18
Total	**16**	**77**	**66**	**28**	**187**

There are 20 songs in the top category:

SHE LOVES YOU (Lennon - McCartney) (1963)
I WANT TO HOLD YOUR HAND
(Lennon - McCartney) (1963)
A HARD DAY'S NIGHT (Lennon) (1964)
HELP! (Lennon) (1965)
YESTERDAY (McCartney) (1965)

MICHELLE (Lennon - McCartney- Jan Vaughan) (1965)
IN MY LIFE (Lennon - McCartney) (1965)
ELEANOR RIGBY
(Lennon - McCartney - Pete Shotton) (1966)
HERE, THERE AND EVERYWHERE
(McCartney) (1966)
YELLOW SUBMARINE (Lennon - McCartney) (1966)

PENNY LANE (McCartney) (1967)
STRAWBERRY FIELDS FOREVER (Lennon) (1967)
SGT PEPPER'S LONELY HEARTS CLUB BAND
(McCartney) (1967)
WITH A LITTLE HELP FROM MY FRIENDS
(Lennon - McCartney) (1967)
ALL YOU NEED IS LOVE (Lennon) (1967)

HEY JUDE (McCartney) (1968)
GET BACK (McCartney) (1969)
GIVE PEACE A CHANCE (Lennon - Ono) (1969)
LET IT BE (McCartney) (1970)
THE LONG AND WINDING ROAD
(McCartney) (1970)

Of the 20 songs in the top category, seven are Lennon - McCartney, five Lennon and eight McCartney, thus showing a preference for McCartney.

The 30 songs in Grade B are:

I SAW HER STANDING THERE (Lennon - McCartney) (1963)
WHEN I'M 64 (McCartney) (1967)
A WORLD WITHOUT LOVE (McCartney) (1964)
LOVE ME DO (Lennon - McCartney) (1962)
PLEASE PLEASE ME (Lennon) (1963)

DO YOU WANT TO KNOW A SECRET
(Lennon - McCartney) (1963)
FROM ME TO YOU (Lennon - McCartney) (1963)
ALL MY LOVING (McCartney) (1963)
CAN'T BUY ME LOVE (McCartney) (1964)
AND I LOVE HER (McCartney) (1964)

I FEEL FINE (Lennon) (1964)
TICKET TO RIDE (Lennon) (1965)
WE CAN WORK IT OUT (Lennon - McCartney) (1965)
DAY TRIPPER (Lennon) (1965)
NORWEGIAN WOOD (Lennon - McCartney) (1965)

NOWHERE MAN (Lennon) (1965)
PAPERBACK WRITER (Lennon - McCartney) (1966)
FOR NO ONE (McCartney) (1966)
GOT TO GET YOU INTO MY LIFE
(McCartney) (1966)
LUCY IN THE SKY WITH DIAMONDS
(Lennon - McCartney) (1967)

SHE'S LEAVING HOME (McCartney) (1967)
A DAY IN THE LIFE (Lennon - McCartney) (1967)
I AM THE WALRUS (Lennon) (1967)
MAGICAL MYSTERY TOUR (McCartney) (1967)
THE FOOL ON THE HILL (McCartney) (1967)

LADY MADONNA (McCartney) (1968)
OB-LA-DI, OB-LA-DA (McCartney) (1968)
THE BALLAD OF JOHN AND YOKO (Lennon) (1969)
COME TOGETHER (Lennon) (1969)
ACROSS THE UNIVERSE (Lennon) (1969)

The result is again similar, nine are Lennon - McCartney, nine Lennon and twelve McCartney, giving an overall result of 16 Lennon - McCartney, 14 Lennon and 20 McCartney.

Many people believe that the Beatles were all McCartney or all Lennon, usually according to their preferences. There's a myth that McCartney couldn't write good lyrics or that Lennon good music, but the song listing shows that they could both write excellent words and music. Typically, some of Lennon's comments show him contributing to this mistaken belief by downgrading Paul's lyrical abilities, or perhaps he really thought that.

It was a partnership of equals, but in terms of both quality and quantity, McCartney has the upper hand, probably because he worked longer hours. Rather than 50-50, a fairer split would have been 55% to Paul McCartney and 45% to John Lennon. In other words, several of John Lennon's millions equitably belong to Paul McCartney. If their songwriting has been worth £400 million then John or his estate has received half of this. Possibly £20 million of that should be Paul's, and it all stems back to an adolescent agreement.

WORLDWIDE WEBB

Interview with Jimmy Webb

As a songwriter, Jimmy Webb had his finger on the pulse on the Sixties and yet his finely-structured songs contained as much craftmanship as Cole Porter's. He wrote Glen Campbell hits - "By The Time I Get To Phoenix", "Wichita Lineman", "Galveston", "Honey Come Back" - and he has maintained his friendship with Campbell, usually writing songs for each album. Glen Campbell's 1999 Australian compilation, "Reunited With Jimmy Webb" (Raven RVCD 95), has a misleading title, but it contains the whole of the "Reunion" album from 1974, along with 14 songs that Webb has written for Campbell over the years. The CD concentrates on lesser-known album tracks and is none the worse for that. I was taken by the sheer quality - as well as quantity - of their work together.

After writing several classic love songs, Webb wrote, arranged and produced the melodramatic "MacArthur Park", an international hit for actor Richard Harris in 1968. Its originality made it a song that you either love or hate, and many critics put Webb was among the worst songwriters of the decade. I loved the track myself and I admired Richard Harris for attempting something inventive: usually, the results of actors making records are no more demanding than rock stars making movies. The Richard Harris compilation, "The Webb Sessions" (Raven RVCD 52), shows that he recorded one remarkable song after another - "The Yard Went On Forever", "The Hive" and "The Hymns From Grand Terrace".

Jimmy Webb kept on going and he produced albums, usually of his own songs, for Richard Harris, Cher, Thelma

Houston and the Supremes. He played clubs and gave concert appearances, sometimes opening for Glen Campbell, but his own records have not got beyond a cult following. His singing voice is a songwriter's voice. Like Kris Kristofferson, he can perform his songs well, but invariably someone else can perform them better. Having said that, I was pleasantly surprised by "Ten Easy Pieces" (Guardian 852 8262), a 1996 CD with voice and piano versions of his own songs. He has perfected a club act in which he amusingly introduces his songs before performing them.

Although he has not written hit songs of late, the Highwaymen (that rough-voiced amalgam of Johnny Cash, Waylon Jennings, Willie Nelson and Kris Kristofferson) revived "Highwayman" and took it to the top of the US country charts in 1985. He has written new songs for Linda Ronstadt and Art Garfunkel, and a very good compilation, "And Someone Left A Cake Out In The Rain" (the "And" is the label's curious branding and not part of the lyric) was released in the UK in 1998 (Débutante DeLuxe 555 430 2). It includes Dusty Springfield, Judy Collins and Joe Cocker and is far preferable to "Up, Up And Away - The Songs Of Jimmy Webb" (Sequel NEMCD 410), released here in 1999. That curio includes the Band of Yorkshire Imperial Metals playing "MacArthur Park" and Bruce Forsyth with "Didn't We". In addition, there is Webb's own "Archive" (WEA 9548 32063 2), which includes his assessment of another Sixties songwriter, P F Sloan.

I interviewed Jimmy Webb for my BBC Radio Merseyside programme, "On The Beat", on New Year's Day, 1994. The conversation was pre-recorded and, because of time constraints, some sections were not broadcast. This is the full transcript.

Since the interview, Jimmy Webb has written a book on songwriting, "Tunesmith" (sadly, still unpublished in the UK), and embraced the Internet. His Webbsite is full of information and he invites visitors to write lyrics with him. Half the lyric is on screen, you submit the rest and he publishes the results. Last week I received a demo recording at BBC Radio Merseyside: the title is "Marble Halls, I Love You" and the writers are listed as Jimmy Webb with two Merseyside writers, Dave Howard and Brian O'Connell. Part of it at least is very good!

A stimulating fanzine devoted to Jimmy Webb and named "Bruised" is edited by Mike Howard and published from Oak Cottage, Furzen Lane, Ellens Green, Rudgwick, West Sussex RH12 3AR. Its title comes from Webb's evocative "All I Know", which was recorded by Art Garfunkel:

> *"I bruise you,*
> *You bruise me,*
> *We both bruise too easily,*
> *Too easily to let it show,*
> *I love you and that's all I know."*

I was walking along on my way to the studio and I found myself singing a line of yours, "She's called me again and I've taken all my old forgotten hopes out of the closet."

That's a line from "A Tramp Shining", a cut on the 1968 Richard Harris album called "A Tramp Shining"!

Why did you call it "A Tramp Shining"?

It was a poetic whim. It was to do with Richard's cachet at that time, he was a rapscallion. This was my attempt to put him in the spotlight as a recording artist.

A more recent quote. Your new album, "Suspending Disbelief", contains the song, "Adios" with its opening lines, "Ran away from home when I was 17, To be with you on the California coast". How autobiographical are your songs?

Well, I did leave home when I was 17 and in essence, I became a professional songwriter, really out of necessity. I found myself quite alone in California. However, I don't feel that a songwriter is under any obligation to ensure that every line he writes is the absolute, autobiographical truth. On the other hand, 90% of what I write is pretty close to my factual experiences.

I know when I interviewed Glen Campbell, he said that "Honey Come Back" was one of your earliest songs, so that would come from this period.

Yes, I remember writing it and what I was doing when I wrote it. I was working in a coffee shop in Rubidoux, California - we call it a bus boy here, the person who cleans off the tables. I wrote it as I carried the dirty dishes back and forth from the tables to the kitchen, and I washed dishes there also.

Did you write it with the narration in mind or did Glen Campbell put that in?

Oh, I did the narration bit. Do you remember a song by Bill Anderson called "Still"? (Sings) "Still, after all this time, Still, you're still on my mind." That was an absolutely beautiful country tune and it had what they call "a talking part". So there was a precedent to do that and I thought I'd try it in "Honey Come Back".

What was your first chart record?

"Up, Up And Away" with the Fifth Dimension.

Which at the time was considered a drugs song.

Well, it was definitely not about drugs because I was fresh off the farm. My father, who's a Baptist minister, got very upset about that. It was banned on a radio station in Oklahoma City, Oklahoma, and my father went down to the radio station with his Bible and preached a sermon to the programme director. Before the end of the day, the record was back on the air. It was absolutely not about drugs, it was about what it purports to be about, which was flying balloons. That was something I was doing at the time.

How did you get the song to Fifth Dimension?

I was their rehearsal pianist and arranger, which was one

of my first real jobs in the recording industry. They were known as the Versatiles then and they were signed to Soul City, a label that was owned by Johnny Rivers. Johnny had been the Male Vocalist of the Year for two or three years in a row. Johnny had signed me to his company as a writer and had gone to the San Remo Song Festival for a few weeks. He left me in charge of the group and I surreptitiously introduced my own song, "Up, Up And Away", into their repertoire. When he returned, we did the songs that we had been charged to rehearse and the group said, "Why don't we do the new song?" and Johnny said, "What new song?" When he heard it, he said, "We are going to call the album, 'Up, Up And Away'."

This all ties up as Johnny Rivers did the original version of "By The Time I Get To Phoenix". When I first heard the song here in England, I thought those place names sounded magical. Would it have the same affect on Americans?

GLEN CAMPBELL

Well, all those place names, all those small cities, are located on a very famous highway called Route 66, except that what you hear in "By The Time I Get To Phoenix" is in reverse order. The character in the song is driving back from California to Oklahoma. Usually when you hear place names in a song and they're on Route 66, those place names will be in an East /West sequence as, most often, people are moving towards that golden land of California. "Kingman, Barstow, San Bernadino, / Won't you get hip to this timely tip / When you make that California trip / Get your kicks on Route 66." (Laughs)

So you yourself like songs that contain place names.

I do, and writing that song was a very natural thing to do. I'd driven that highway dozens of times so there is nothing particularly contrived about it except in the context of creating a good song. Subsequent to that, I became involved in a game, particularly with Glen Campbell, of coming up with songs with place names in the title - "Wichita Lineman" was very definitely written for Glen Campbell as a follow-up to "By The Time I Get To Phoenix".

There was a very distinctive arrangement on "Wichita Lineman". Did you come up with that as well?

I played what we would have thought of as an early synthesiser on "Wichita Lineman", even though I didn't really have one. The only true synthesiser that was around was the Moog, but there were certain fancy organs which had special effects. I had a Gulbranson that was basically a church organ with very early digital technology. It had various bells, textures and vibrations that you could use. I hauled the organ down to the studio and I played keyboards on the record. The sound of the wires on the fade is that organ. The arrangement was done by Al De Lory, who was Glen Campbell's producer, and it was a wonderful arrangement. I couldn't have done it any better and probably would have done it a whole lot worse.

You had an American No 1 with "Galveston" for Glen Campbell, which was controversial at the time as people said, "Is it about Vietnam or isn't it?

It was about a young American soldier and as the only war we were fighting at the time was in Vietnam, the answer seems pretty obvious.

But if you had come right out and said that, I presume that you wouldn't have got much airplay.

That's right. I knew Galveston. I was raised in West Texas and I travelled around Texas with my family. More than half my young life I spent in Texas so I'm a Texoma kid. The real reasons I chose Galveston were because I wanted a place that was on the ocean and I wanted the character to be from the heartland. I didn't want him to be from the west coast or the east, and he had to be someone I could identify with.

What reaction did you get from the people of Galveston?

I went down to Galveston about three years later: they hold a big shrimp festival there and there are cajun overtones to the place with it being next door to Louisiana. It has a very unusual charisma. I was in a parade down there - I rode down the street as the guy who wrote "Galveston" and I would have to say, to be perfectly frank, that there were mixed reviews. I got some paper wads thrown at me but I was in the middle of a politically polarised situation in the States at that time. People didn't quite know how they felt about that song: is this guy a peacenik or what? The majority of people were very happy. They gave me the key to the city as they were pleased that someone had taken notice of their town.

There was a big hit in the UK by the Four Tops with "Do What You Gotta Do", but I don't think they did the original.

No, the original "Do What You Gotta Do" was recorded by Johnny Rivers, and then Roberta Flack. There's not much to say about it: it's just Jimmy Webb writing a love song.

You did a couple of albums with Richard Harris. What were your first impressions of him?

Oh, he's an incredibly seductive man, a complete charmer, so full of life, so full of energy, so full of humour and so full of warmth. He completely overwhelmed a young guy like myself, I was just 19 or 20 at the time.

Most actors go for the easy option of recording straightforward love songs, but you gave him something that required true vocal ability, "MacArthur Park". Was that your idea?

It was his choice. I was in England and I'd gone to his apartment in Belgravia. It was a lovely apartment with a grand piano and we would sit in front of the fireplace and I would play him all the songs that I knew. I had a briefcase full of them, and down towards the bottom was "MacArthur Park". I had written it for the Assocation, but they had passed on it. I remember setting it on the piano and saying, "Well, there's this one." I played through it a couple of times and he said, "We'll do it."

Did you envisage it as a seven minute single from the start?

That's the way it was written but it was never meant to be a single. As far as I was concerned, it was an experiment. It was a single that the broadcasters picked themselves. FM radio started playing it and then, slowly but surely, the Top 40 stations had to play it.

Your most famous line is "Someone left a cake out in the rain", and people ask "What does this mean? What sort of cake was it? Was it a wedding cake?" Was this something you actually saw in "MacArthur Park"?

Yes, it was, but I am dreadfully tired of talking about it. No offence intended, but I have been asked about "MacArthur Park" for years and years and years. It was meant to be an hallucinogenic image in the same style of many songs that were being written around the same time like "Nights In White Satin", "Strawberry Fields Forever" and "I Am The Walrus". They are all songs that defy precise definition.

Do you think that these songs would have been written without drugs?

I doubt it. I doubt it very seriously.

And what about the middle passage in that record? Which came first, "Classical Gas" or "MacArthur Park"?

Mason Williams is a fellow Oklahoman and I thought "Classical Gas" was a great piece. I don't know whether it preceded "MacArthur Park" or not. I know "MacArthur Park" preceded "Hey Jude" by four or five months because "MacArthur Park" was 7 minutes 20 seconds long and when "Hey Jude" came out, it was 7 minutes 21 seconds long!

You produced "MacArthur Park". Was Richard Harris surprised by the end of that session at what you had brought out on his voice?

I think he was very happy about it. He grumbled a couple of times and said that the orchestra was too loud. I was impressed by having all this amazing technology to hand. We had multiple tracks and the ability to punch in, so we could lift certain lines and combine them with others. We could have done that three years before but it would have been immensely more difficult. We had these wonderful eight-track recorders with self-synch and the ability to punch in and punch out and combine tracks and do all these wonderful things that we had only dreamed of a scant two or three years before. "Sgt Pepper's Lonely Hearts Club" was only cut on a four-track recorder! How they did that, I don't know, and it is a testament to George Martin's genius. Now suddenly we had the ability to improve a vocal performance, for instance.

So the recording studio became much more than a place where a person put down his performance.

Precisely. The recording studio became an instrument unto itself rather than just being an organ that soaked up this performance and preserved it in one fell swoop, as it were. All of a sudden, we realised that a recording studio had its own capabilities and we had albums like "Pet Sounds" which was a multi-tracking tour de force. George Martin and the Beatles were immediately aware of the possibilities and so the recording studio came into its own. Now it has completely gone away from us, the recording studio is in charge of us now, but there was a magical time when there was a symbiosis between art and the recording studio that was very important.

There are over 100 different recordings of "MacArthur Park" including another hit version from Donna Summer. Does Richard Harris' version still remain the best?

Oh yes, it is just fine. As far as I'm concerned, it does.

You followed up "MacArthur Park" with a poignant love song, "Didn't We".

RICHARD HARRIS AND JIMMY WEBB

That's a song that I wrote very early on when I was still in college - I did two years in college as a music major and I wrote a musical called "Dancing Girl" that I was trying to get performed by the drama department. "Didn't We" was the eleven o'clock number in the musical, "Dancing Girl".

Does that mean it was the last number in the show?

It's the penultimate number, the one just before the finale.

Also, on one of the Richard Harris albums is a very bitter song, "The Hive".

Yes. (Laughs) Somebody that I cared deeply about was getting married. I was completely anti-marriage, very anti-establishment. Anything to do with structured behaviour was anathema to me, and marriage was the ultimate form of structured behaviour. "The Hive" was analgous to an organisation of bees, of people doing whatever they're supposed to do whenever they're supposed to do it. That was how I saw her behaving. She was doing what she was supposed to be doing.

Another Richard Harris song which has been completely ignored is "One Of The Nicer Things". I've always thought that it had a lot of potential.

Thanks. I recorded it too, I had a single out on that song on Dunhill. I was surprised that no-one took any notice of it at the time, but I don't know how I feel about it now. It is such a long time ago. I was surprised at the time because I had written it for Ray Charles. I gave it to his people and they took a pass. I'm not very good at writing songs for individual artists and my record is very patchy in that department.

On your new album, you do "Just This One Time" and you put in the notes that you had written for the Righteous Brothers.

Yes, but at that time they had split up. I did submit it to Bill Medley. My dream project for that song would be to have Phil Spector produce it for the Righteous Brothers. I'd still like him to do that!

On your first album was a song called "P. F. Sloan", which was about the songwriter who wrote "Eve Of Destruction" and had his own minor success with "Sins Of The Family". I take it from the song

that he was getting a rough deal.

Songwriters have been getting a rough deal from the beginning - and I don't think it's changed very much! P. F. Sloan was the first guy I knew who was a pure songwriter and very successful at it. He went to the record company and told them that he wanted to make his own record and he got a tremendous backlash from them, "Why would you want to do that? You're not an artist!" You know, "artists are artists and songwriters are songwriters", this kind of robothink is still very much alive and well today.

Also in the song you refer to Roy Rogers having Trigger stuffed and to London Bridge being transferred to America. What's the connection?

Let's just say that "P. F. Sloan" is a song about disenchantment.

So was P. F. Sloan happy or disenchanted with the song you had written for him?

I guess he's happy. There have been times when I have regretted becoming so personal in my songs. There was a time when whatever I did creatively was entirely spontaneous, and I followed no rules whatsoever. Sad to say, I found myself writing about people I knew, and I knew that they would know that I was writing about them, and I intended them to. I regret that I used my talent in that way, but I was very young and I just did whatever came into my head.

So your solo albums are particularly personal albums in that they reflect your thoughts at that point in time?

I would think so, yes.

You produced an album for the Supremes in 1972, which was pretty courageous as you were taking over from the Motown producers.

Either courageous or stupid. (Laughs) I was trying to do something different for them, but also I did not have Diana Ross. I had Jeannie Terrell singing lead and it wasn't really the Supremes. They offered me the job and I thought that I could do something with them. My first job in the industry had been at Jobete, so I was a Motown writer when I started. I knew everyone at Motown, I had some emotional connection there and I am always susceptible to that and I hope I always will be. I thought it

would be great to go back and do something for Motown and hopefully be successful with it, which we weren't. I thought it was worth a try, although with all due respect, I would have preferred to have had Diana Ross in the group.

There's a song on there that could have done very well, "When Can Brown Begin?". Had you written it for them?

No, I wrote it for Sammy Davis. I was sitting with Sammy Davis in the London Palladium one night and he said to me, "Can you write a song called 'When Can Brown Begin?'" and he wrote the title on a napkin and handed it to me. I liked Sammy a great deal and I thought that I could do that. It seemed a good idea but he never recorded the song, I don't know why.

You also wrote and produced for Art Garfunkel. Did you regard him as one of the great voices in popular music?

No, I have never produced Artie Garfunkel. I have written songs for him and worked very closely with him in the studio, but I have never produced him. I have a very good idea of the territory I am working in because to be very honest and fair, I go back to the sound and the feel of the Simon and Garfunkel records and I think of that as the starting ground, even though that might not be where we end up. I am not saying for one second that I would ever try and write a song that sounds like one of Paul Simon's. It is just a very comfortable reference point. I can say, "This phrasing is comfortable for him" or "This note is comfortable for him" or "This subject matter is comfortable for him". Those early records define the characters in the play. I wrote "Skywriter" specifically for Artie, and I am very happy with it and very proud of the end result because it is in character, it is him, and I can count on the fingers of one hand how many times I have been able to do that in my life.

You wrote a song called "Highwayman" which is a song about reincarnation and...

Maybe. It started out with a dream and so I could argue with you and say that the whole thing is about a dream, that the whole song is just four dreams. Yes, I have to admit that I was considering the possibility of past lives when I wrote it. It was inspired by a very vivid dream that I had in London about being a highwayman and being pursued by cavalrymen, but after the first verse, it took a very different direction. Before I had finished with the the song, I was thinking about it in nationalistic terms. My psychic overlay of the whole tune is that it also represents the United States of America. The first verse is about an outlaw nation, a rebellious outlaw nation. The second verse is about an exploratory nation, obsessed with commerce and the sea. The third verse is about the nation that has built itself up, it has built dams and it has built buildings. The last verse looks to the future, the future not only of my country but also the future of mankind, which I believe can only lie in outer space. We must not poison this place before we have found out what else is going on in the universe. I like to think that most of my songs have at least two levels of awareness to them, and sometimes I think they have more.

That song also works as a straight country record as it has been taken up by the quartet of Willie and Waylon and Johnny Cash and Kris Kristofferson.

Apparently so, and I received a Grammy for the Country Song of the Year. When I do the song in concert myself, I kid around with the audience and say that when I won a Grammy for Best Country Song, I didn't know what country they were talking about. It seems a strange choice but then so was "MacArthur Park", and Waylon Jennings recorded it twice.

Would you like to write new songs for Willie Nelson as he has one of the greatest voices around?

I would love to work with Willie. I very much want him to record "The Moon Is A Harsh Mistress" and there are several others he could do. I think a "Willie Nelson Sings Jimmy Webb" album would be fabulous. We could definitely come up with some winners. It would be very nice for Willie to work with strings, I don't think anybody has done that properly with him.

You have a song on the new album called "Elvis And Me" and there is a song on an earlier album about Elvis as well.

Well, I used to see him all the time when I was in my early twenties and he was playing at the Hilton International Hotel. I hung out with him a lot and got to know him quite a bit. Unless you have seen Elvis close up in a real live performance, it is impossible to understand the power that he had - it was a supernatural thing. He filled the air with a strange energy which I found palpable, and

everybody felt it. He'd no idea what it was but he knew it was happening and he was amused by it, which I would have been had people being acting daft over me. There was definitely something special about Elvis, but I wouldn't have to explain it to anyone who saw him in live performance.

The song, "Elvis And Me", is really a diary entry.

It is on one level, but it is also a fan story - the fan who still believes he's alive, the fan who thinks he's sitting right over there in that empty chair, the fan who'll buy anything. In the last verse, I say, "And I know that it's wrong, but I just can't set him free", so on another level of perception, it is about the American mysticism of Elvis and the fact that every year, on the anniversary of his death, more and more thousands of people show up at Graceland, holding candles in a very eerie vigil, almost expecting a resurrection. Many thousands of Americans don't accept that the fact that he ever died, so it's a new pop theology and who knows where that leads? How will this guy be perceived 100 years from now? I see people on talk shows saying that they've seen him and playing the taped conversations. Okay, they're fakes, but it makes you think twice. The concept of Elvis being alive is more important than whether he is or not. If so many people want him to be alive, then he'll be alive. I'd love to be around in a couple of hundred years' time to see what this has mutated into. It's an amazing phenomenon and Elvis may be the leader of a new religion.

The new album, "Suspending Disbelief", was co-produced by Linda Ronstadt and she has recorded your songs in the past. Have you known her well over the years?

I have worked with her ever since "Get Closer", which was about ten years ago. I had a song on that and then we did a couple of other things together. I had four songs on her last album, "Cry Like A Rainstorm - Howl Like The Wind", and we had a Top 10 Adult Contemporary Single with "Adios", which you mentioned before. Over a ten year period you develop a relationship with somebody and when I wanted to make this record, I wanted her to do it. I can't stand rejection and it took me a long time to work up the nerve to ask her. It was a tremendous relief when she agreed because she is a kindred soul and I knew that the album would go in the right direction.

"Suspending Disbelief" is your first solo album for several years. Did you have a lot of songs to choose from?

No, I only had 14 songs at the most that I was really interested in recording. They have to be in my voice and in my character and in my way of speaking. I like to put my solo records in a kinda conversational tone.

Finally, can I just ask you about something I read somewhere, that you were in London when the Beatles were making "The White Album".

Yes, I went down to a session one night in Trident 3 where the booth is upstairs and the studio is down below. They were cutting the song that goes (Sings) "You became a legend of the silver screen."

JIMMY WEBB "SUSPENDING DISBELIEF"

"Honey Pie".

"Honey Pie", that's it. Paul was playing the piano on one side of the studio and Linda was sitting on the bench with her arms around his neck. He had a sweater tied round his neck and they looked charming. He was doing a great job playing piano. For some reason, and I will stand by this story until I die, George Harrison was playing bass and was standing in the centre of the studio, and then over on the right was John Lennon, sitting down on the floor with some candles and holding an acoustic guitar. I couldn't see Ringo as the drum booth at Trident is tucked underneath the control room, but I could hear him. It was fascinating and they played a joke on me as after they had finished a take, Paul came in and introduced me to George Martin and Geoff Emerick as "Tom Dowd from Atlantic Records". I was so terrified and so impressed by where I was that I did not correct this impression, and they proceeded to treat me as though I was Tom Dowd. They were asking me what I thought of this guitar solo and what I thought of that guitar solo and I was doing the best I could. I didn't want to disappoint them by telling them that I was only Jimmy Webb! Finally, after what I thought was entirely too much of it, George Harrison tapped me on the shoulder and said, "By the way, man, I loved those strings on 'MacArthur Park'." (Laughs)

Jimmy Webb, thank you very much.

Thank you so much.

SYLVIA'S LOVER
Shel Silverstein (1930 - 1999)

One of the most original lyricists of 20th century, and certainly one of the wittiest, is Shel Silverstein. I tried to arrange an interview a couple of times, but without any success. Dennis Locorriere told me, "Shel loved talking, but he'd talk to you about anything but his songs." I wrote his obituary for "The Independent" in May 1999 and it is reproduced here by permission. I was laughing as I wrote this obituary as snatches of his songs kept coming back to me: what a legacy to leave the world.

In his books, cartoons and songs, Shel Silverstein was known for his wry, humorous slants on life, and his own life was every bit as eccentric as the characters who peopled his work. Take the sorry tale of love not being returned in "Sylvia's Mother", an international hit for Dr Hook and the Medicine Show in 1972. "Most of the time if you tell a true story, you beef it up to make it into a song," says Ray Sawyer, the eyepatched singer from Dr Hook, "but Shel had to bring them down. The guy that ran off with Sylvia in real life was a bullfighter from Mexico, and he couldn't put that in the song."

Shel Singleton was born in Chicago in 1930 and his talents as a cartoonist and satirist were first seen while serving in Korea in 1952 and contributing to the armed forces periodical, "Pacific Stars And Stripes". Returning home, he established himself with "Playboy" and befriended the magazine's owner, Hugh Hefner. Many of his songs reflect Playboy's hedonist lifestyle and, as the record producer Chet Atkins remarked, "Ol' Shel has probably got the worst voice of anyone alive, but he's also got the run of the 'Playboy' mansion and I'm not knocking anybody with a deal like that."

Shel Silverstein's recorded "Inside Folk Music", in 1962 and some of its songs are still performed: "The Unicorn", "In The Hills Of Shiloh" and "The Wonderful Soup Stone", which was based on an Irish legend. His first children's book, "The Giving Tree", was published in 1964 and has remained in print.

In 1969 he passed Johnny Cash a poem the day before his concert in San Quentin prison. Cash asked Carl Perkins to set it to music and the result was a million-selling saga of transvestites and barroom fights, "A Boy Named Sue". Cash also sang his witty song about the condemned cell, "Twenty-Five Minutes To Go", while Loretta Lynn topped the US country chart by telling of the restrictions of motherhood in "One's On The Way" (1970). In 1970, he wrote several songs for the film, "Ned Kelly", which cast, or rather miscast, Mick Jagger as the Australian outlaw.

Silverstein met Dr Hook and the Medicine Show whilst working on a Dustin Hoffman film, "Who Is Harry Kellerman And Why Is He Saying These Terrible Things About Me?" (1971). The film was every bit as bad as its title but he realised that the outlandish hippies were the perfect mouthpiece for his material. Dennis Locorriere took the lead vocal on

"Sylvia's Mother", which he performs to this day: "I imagine I'm 17 years old again and running out of coins in a phonebox and having my girlfriend's mother telling me that she's getting married to somebody else."

Dr. Hook recorded 60 of Silverstein's acutely observed vignettes of American life and the results equal the sketches which Jerry Leiber and Mike Stoller wrote for the Coasters.. He parodied the group's desire for success in "The Cover Of Rolling Stone" and "Everybody's Makin' It Big But Me". Sample lyric:

"Elton John's got two fine ladies, Dr. John's got three,
And I'm still seeing those same old sleazos that I used to see."

The group backed the bald-headed Silverstein on his outrageous solo album, "Freakin' At The Freakers Ball" (1972), and the titles match the contents: "Polly In A Porny", "I Got Stoned And I Missed It" and "Don't Give A Dose To The One You Love Most". "We turned that one down," says Dennis, "We had enough problems with people thinking us a bunch of degenerates. We didn't want them thinking we'd got VD as well." The singer, Bobby Bare, once sang me a filthy, totally rewritten version of the country hit, "The Wild Side Of Life". "Shel wrote that", he remarked, "The wild side of life in the original was never wild enough for him."

Shel Silverstein gave Dr Hook a poignant song about the pressures of modern life, "The Ballad Of Lucy Jordan", which was also recorded very successfully by Marianne Faithfull. Dennis Locorriere comments, "'The Ballad Of Lucy Jordan' has a magical ending that never fails to excite me. His songs unfold as you sing them and he has made me so much more of a singer."

Silverstein wrote of an older man's love for his girlfriend in "A Couple More Years", which has been sung by Willie Nelson and Bob Dylan, and of the difficulties of satisfying a partner in "More Like The Movies", another hit for Dr. Hook (1978). He became a millionaire, but never owned a car and looked for bargains in flea markets. When he found an album by Bobby Gosh, he offered one of the songs to Dr Hook, namely "A Little Bit More", with the comment, "This is a great song even though no-one's ever heard it."

Taking up a challenge, he wrote an album, "Lullabys, Legends And Lies", for the country singer, Bobby Bare in four days in 1973. The classic LP included a country hit about the witch queen of New Orleans, "Marie Laveau", how you lose even when you're "The Winner" and an eight-minute picture of grotesque characters in a late-

eight-minute picture of grotesque characters in a late-night diner, "Rosalie's Good Eats Café". The album was immensely successful so Silverstein wrote two more albums for Bare in quick succession: an album of children's songs, "Singin' In The Kitchen" (1974) and "songs for the New Depression", "Hard Time Hungrys" (1975). A child comments on her father's unemployment in "Daddy's Been Around The House Too Long" and times are so hard that even God is in "The Unemployment Line".

Many other classic songs stem from the 1970s including Emmylou Harris' portrayal of a barroom prostitute, "The Queen Of The Silver Dollar", Tompall Glaser's response to Women's Lib, "Put Another Log On The Fire", and Burl Ives' touching look at old age, "Time". He commented on the hypocrisy behind Nashville's tributes to the bluegrass musician, Lester Flatt, in Bobby Bare's "Rough On The Living". ("They didn't want him around when he's living, But he's sure a good friend when he's dead.")

A restless man, he tired of writing songs and returned to children's books and cartoons. His books include "Where The Sidewalk Ends" (1974), "The Missing Piece" (1976), "A Light In The Attic" (1981) and his poems share the same anarchic views as Spike Milligan.

"Oh, if you're a bird, be an early bird,
And catch the worm for your breakfast plate,
If you're a bird, be an early early bird,
But if you're a worm, sleep late."

Many song lyrics appeared as illustrated poems in "Playboy" and were often much longer than the recorded versions. His epic poem about a bad songwriter making Faustian deals, "The Devil And Billy Markham" (1978), became an off-Broadway musical.

Shel Silverstein's heart disease made him view death as a subject for popular songs. The remarkable result, the album, "Old Dogs" (1998), performed by Waylon Jennings, Bobby Bare, Mel Tillis and Jerry Reed, happens to be the funniest album for several years. Still writing exceptional lyrics, he wrote his own epitaph: "You'd better have some fun before you say bye-bye, 'Cause you're still gonna, still gonna, still gonna die."

Shelby Silverstein, singer, songwriter and children's author,
b. 25th September 1930, Chicago: divorced, 1 son, 1 daughter: died 10th
May 1999, Key West. (My original piece gave Shel's year of birth as
1932, but his attorney and long-term friend, Sheldon Vidibor, says he was
actually born in 1930.)

MY WAY

The story of the song

Some years ago I happened to be at an audition for "Opportunity Knocks" when the producer was addressing the young (and not so young) hopefuls. "Give your music to the pianist," he said, "but please no more 'My Ways'." "My Way" is the cabaret singer's calling-card, which renders the song meaningless as any performer is, ipso facto, doing it someone else's way. "My Way" is a karaoke favourite and is the most mauled song of the century. The lyric is half-sung, half-spoken, and, to be performed convincingly, it needs an intensity that matches Al Pacino's acting. To quote an editorial in "The Times" commenting on Radio 2's songs of the century, "'My Way' may have been intended as a hymn to individuality, but paradoxically it is a favourite of the common herd."

Most people think that "My Way" is a song that Paul Anka wrote for Frank Sinatra but the story is far richer and more complex than that. Indeed, rarely have so many people been involved in one song.

The story begins in 1965 when the songwriting team of Gilles Thibault (words) and Jacques Revaux (music) wrote a pop song, a French chanson called "Comme D'Habitude". A direct English translation would be "As Usual" but the theme is different from Brenda Lee's 1964 hit of the same title. The French song is about a one-way love affair ("I touch your hair while you're asleep as usual"), while in Brenda Lee's "As Usual", the affair is definitely over.

Thibault and Revaux had written for several French artists but none of their songs was known internationally. As they were not established performers, they passed their new composition to one of France's biggest stars, Claude François. (If you want to see Revaux, he is in the 1967 film "The Young Girls Of Rochefort (Les Demoiselles De Rochefort)".

Claude François was born in Ismailia, Egypt in 1939. His father was an engineer who worked for the Suez Canal Company and who found himself without a job when the Egyptians assumed control in 1956. The promise of employment in France came to nothing and the family found themselves with little money in Monte Carlo. His father died, totally disillusioned, a few years later and, in interviews, François was very critical of the French government.

François could play drums and sing and he was determined to be a performer. He watched Frank Sinatra in rehearsal, although he had no idea that their paths would cross a few years later. François' first wife left him for the singer, Gilbert Becaud, and then in 1962 he had his first hit with a cover of Steve Lawrence's "Girls, Girls, Girls", now called "Belles, Belles, Belles". He sang twist songs and had further hits with "Si J'Avais Un Marteau (If I Had A Hammer)" and, surprisingly, Noël Coward's "Poor Little Rich Girl". He was a heart-throb and the girls called him Clo-Clo.

Claude's girlfriend was France Gall, who won the Eurovision Song Contest for Luxembourg in 1965 with a Serge Gainsbourg song, "Poupée De Cire, Poupée De Son". He was sad when they broke up, so he could identify with the latest song in his in-tray, "Comme D'Habitude". He made a few adjustments to the melody and claimed a songwriting credit. "Comme D'Habitude" stormed up the French charts.

Several songwriters including Becaud, Aznavour and Moustaki have done well in the UK, but usually their songs had been translated into English. A UK publisher was asked to supply an English lyric for "Comme D'Habitude" and find a suitable performer. The song was passed to an up and coming singer planning a cabaret act, David Bowie. He took the melody and wrote a new lyric, rather than a translation, "Even A Fool Learns To Love". A demo recording was made, but the lyric was not accepted.

Paul Anka, a pop singer with a surname made for limericks, was born in Ottawa in 1941. He found international fame when only 15 with a horny song about having the hots for his babysitter, "Diana". Over the next few years, he became Canada's greatest musical export, writing and recording such hits as "Lonely Boy", "Puppy Love" and "Put Your Head On My Shoulder". He also wrote Buddy Holly's posthumous No 1, "It Doesn't Matter Anymore", the theme for the film, "The Longest Day" and the music for Johnny Carson's long-running "Tonight Show". In the film biography, "Lonely Boy", released in 1962, Paul Anka's manager says, "God gave Paul something I don't think has been given to anyone in the last 500 years." I wonder what it was and whether Paul would share it with the rest of us.

CLAUDE FRANÇOIS

Paul Anka was, and still is, a competent, but not great, songwriter, and, unlike Burt Bacharach, he didn't have a readily identifiable style. He was a jobbing songwriter who could turn his hand to commissions for other artists, film songs and TV themes. One underrated song is "Love Me Warm And Tender", which was covered, excellently, by Arthur Alexander. In 1963 Anka recorded an album, "Songs I Wish I'd Written" and no doubt the songwriters were planning a reply, "Songs We're Glad He Didn't".

Like Neil Sedaka and Carole King, Paul Anka's ability to write hit songs faded in the mid-60s. He kept going with TV shows and appearances in Las Vegas, but his smugness prevented him from becoming a major star. His official website says that he has achieved "unprecedented success in every venue: stage, screen, television and recording", so you can see what I mean. He enjoyed working on the Strip but the button said it all, "It's Sinatra's world, we just live in it." He wanted to write for Frankie, saying "He's the only one who can put you in a mood within five seconds no matter what he's singing."

In 1968, a publisher asked Paul Anka to write an English lyric for "Comme D'Habitude", although he'd had no experience of reworking European hits. He liked the melody and he had an idea one rainy night while winding down after a performance in New York. By five in the morning, he had the lyric he wanted - "My Way". Like many adaptations of Continental songs, it bore no relation to the original lyric, but the new words said everything about Frank Sinatra's turbulent life.

Paul Anka wrote it as a journalist, writing from the standpoint of someone 30 years his senior, "I sat at the typewriter and started typing the words, 'And now the end is near...' That really got it going. The moment I got the first two lines out, I was focused entirely on Sinatra, trying to portray everything indigenous to his life and what he was about."

Everyone knew about Frank Sinatra's life - the saloon singer with the portable saloon, the rat in the Rat Pack, the Chairman of the Flawed. Counting the women in Kitty Kelley's salacious biography, "His Way", I found 60 named lovers as well as hundreds of showgirls and prostitutes. He was a man's man, who treated women appallingly (and Sammy Davis like a lackey). He beat them up, if Kelley is to be believed, and yet they loved him. Or some of them - he had lost some favourites along the way. Like his Scotch, his current marriage to the hippie actress, Mia Farrow, was on the rocks, largely because he objected to her pursuing her own career with the film, "Rosemary's Baby". Sinatra's career had the ups and downs of a roller-coaster and currently he was on top, owning his own record label, Reprise, and even appealing to teenage recordbuyers with "Strangers In The Night" and "Something Stupid" (a duet with daughter Nancy). He'd faced it all and he stood tall - you see how it is easy to associate the phrases with Frank's life.

Recognising a similar arrogance to his own, Paul Anka loved Frank Sinatra's personality. In the song, he is a driven man, often misunderstood but always true to himself, a man who can transform failure into triumph. Frank had sung about "High Hopes" but that was a children's song. Here was a lyric that got under his skin, that he could identify with in every respect. Because of his contretemps with the press, Frank Sinatra gave few interviews, and none at all which would trespass on his psyche. Instead, via "My Way", Frank could make a defiant statement to the world:

> *"The record shows I took the blows,*
> *And did it my way!"*

His way, in other words, was wholly admirable and he was to be congratulated for his independence. It was brilliant: in a few short stanzas, Paul Anka had captured the essence, the very being of Frank Sinatra.

"My Way" was a psychological Full Monty, but it was also an appalling lyric and little better than the couplets in his first hit, "Diana". I can't imagine that Sinatra's regular lyricist, Sammy Cahn, would have ever rhymed "mention" with "exemption". What does "I saw it through without exemption" mean? Possibly, I didn't neglect my duties and I got through difficult times. "I saw it through without exception" would be better, maybe even "I saw it through without convention." Or how about this, "I saw it through until my pension." Well, at least it rhymes.

Try this:

> *"Regrets, I've had a few,*
> *But then again too few for naming,*
> *I did what I had to do*
> *And saw it through without complaining."*

Also, Anka is tied to finding rhymes for "my way" itself, which leads, in desperation, to

> *"To think I did all that,*
> *And may I say, not in a shy way,*

PAUL ANKA

> *Oh no, oh no, not me,*
> *I did it my way."*

Again, how about this:

> *"To think I did all that,*
> *And rising high up in the skyway.*
> *I saw the light, I did it right,*
> *I did it my way."*

Unlike, say, Herbert Kretzmer's elegant lyric for Charles Aznavour's "She", "My Way" is not well crafted, but if Paul Anka had tinkered with it like a Paul Simon, it might have lost its potency. For all its clumsiness, "My Way" does work, and it certainly works with Sinatra singing it. Considering that Paul Anka's track record was not that great, he certainly did well with "My Way". It should be added that several well-established songs contain awkward phrasing. "And say for you that the sun don't shine" ("Streets of London"), 'Letters are written, never meaning to send' ("Nights In White Satin") and "She looks straight ahead, not at he" ("The Girl From Ipanema") spring to mind.

An Internet fad is for the lyrics of songs performed by major artists. One of Nina Simone's websites, not the official one, contains the worst transcription of "My Way" imaginable. It makes you wonder what listeners actually hear. This is a sample:

> *"Oh, I've laughed and cried, had my fill*
> *my share of losing,*
> *And now, as tears subside, counted all music*
> *To think like the old lad*
> *And may I say not in a sky away*
> *Oh no no no, you're not me, I did it my way."*

Don Costa had been the musical director on Paul Anka's hit records and now he was working for Frank Sinatra. RCA wanted Anka to keep the song for himself, but Paul passed the song to Don Costa, who noted that it had much in common with Sinatra's reflective songs from the past, "September Song", "The September Of My Years" and "It Was A Very Good Year". It was with some trepidation that he recommended "My Way" to Frank Sinatra.

Sinatra might have thought that they were mocking him.

Fortunately for them, Frank Sinatra recognised its potential, although he wasn't sure whether he wanted to expose himself in this way. In concert, Paul Anka says that he was forced to give the song to Sinatra rather than keep it for himself, but this is simply so he can follow it with a good one-liner, "I didn't want to find a horse's head in my bed."

For many years Frank Sinatra had worked with the pianist and arranger, Bill Miller. Bill's house in Los Angeles had been destroyed in a mudslide: his wife had been killed and he had been badly injured. Frank Sinatra paid the medical bills and knew that if he was to record "My Way" or anything else, he would need a new pianist until Bill recovered. He chose Lou Levy who had worked with Peggy Lee and Ella Fitzgerald.

Considering how heavily Frank Sinatra smoke and drank and the fact that he hardly went to bed (unless it was worth it), it is remarkable that he retained his voice. He didn't do vocal exercises, but somehow it stayed in shape, deeper than it had been of course, but then Sinatra was 53.

In 1967, Frank Sinatra had surprised everyone, including himself, with a light, gentle, playful album with the star composer of bossa nova music, the Brazilian, Antonio Carlos Jobim. The album, amusingly titled "Francis Albert Sinatra And Antonio Carlos Jobim", was as good as anything he had recorded. He had joked, "I haven't sung so soft since I had laryngitis."

The "My Way" session was scheduled for 30th December 1968, Sinatra's first session for six weeks and the only song he recorded on that day. Don Costa rehearsed the orchestra and Sinatra came in when he was ready. He did two takes and within half an hour, he was gone. He wouldn't record again for another six weeks.

A month later, Paul Anka got a call from Frank Sinatra. Sinatra said, "Hey, kid, listen to this," and he put the phone close to the studio speaker so that he could hear "My Way". "I cried, " said Anka, "I hadn't had a hit record or written a good song for five years. It was a traumatic period for me. I can't describe the thrill of hearing Sinatra sing that song. It was one of the milestones of my career."

"My Way", as released, was a combination of the two takes. You can hear the splice just before "I've loved, I've laughed and I've cried." Sinatra goes from a bravura voice to an intimate one and I'm told that it would be impossible to do that naturally. Even for Sinatra.

Strangely, "My Way" was not a huge US hit for Frank Sinatra, peaking at No 27. In 1970 Brook Benton took the song into the US charts but fared no better. Meanwhile, Paul Anka, reinspired, was writing songs as though they were going out of fashion. In 1971 Tom Jones went to No 2 in the US with Anka's song, "She's A Lady", and its B-side was "My Way".

"My Way" fared better in the UK. Frank Sinatra's record reached No 5. It remained on the charts for a remarkable two years, thus proving more enduring than Sinatra's follow-ups. The first was Rod McKuen's mawkish "Love's Been Good To Me" (No 8) and then Paul Ryan, noted for teenage songs with his twin brother Barry, had a fair stab at writing a song for the older Sinatra with "I Will Drink The Wine" (No 16).

Dorothy Squires was an argumentative, litigious British singer whose career had been as stormy as Sinatra's. Her show-business marriage to Roger Moore had been a disaster and she was dogged by controversy. By being written in non-specific terms, "My Way" suited her life as much as Sinatra's. Her version of "My Way" made the UK Top 30 and prompted her to book the London Palladium for a major concert return. Defying expectations, the concert sold out, and "My Way", naturally, was her show-stopper.

"My Way" achieved an additional resonance in 1971 when Frank Sinatra announced his retirement. He gave his final concert in Los Angeles. He finished dramatically with "My Way", but returned for an encore. He sat on a stool and sang the intimate "Angel Eyes" in a solitary spotlight.

It was great theatre. The final words were "'Scuse me while I disappear" and then he was gone, leaving behind his cigarette smoke. Possibly he was retiring because he couldn't grasp the changes in popular music: this man hated rock'n'roll, so what did he make of Jimi Hendrix? "'Scuse me while I kiss the sky" had become more relevant than "'Scuse me while I disappear".

In reality, Sinatra's vanishing act was more to do with his Mafioso friends than his unwillingness to perform. He was questioned by the House Select Committee on Crime and managed to control his temper. He spoke as though he was the Good Samaritan, whereas most people thought of him as a Mafia don. Introduced to the author of "The Godfather", Mario Puzo, in a restaurant, Sinatra spat in his face as he felt that Johnny Fontane had been modelled on himself. A couple of months later, he snarled at a journalist, Maxine Cheshire, "You're nothing but a $2 whore." Not much change there then.

By now, everyone wanted to sing "My Way" as their personal statement, and possibly one reason for its great popularity was that audiences also identified with the lyric: everyone wants to do things their way but most of us haven't got the nerve. Hank Snow and Don Gibson treated it as a country song, while Nina Simone and Eartha Kitt were feisty females who could identify with the lyric. Middle of the road treatments came from Acker Bilk and Mantovani. It was recorded by the Treorchy Male Voice Choir and by St Paul's Cathedral Choir, all of whom presumably believed that they were doing it their way.

David Bowie, intrigued by the impact of "My Way" and possibly thinking that his own lyric had been better, wrote "Life On Mars". Yes, you've read that right. His 1973 hit, "Life On Mars", though you'd never know it, was a parody of "My Way", and Bowie said in 1993, "There was a sense of revenge because I was angry that Paul Anka had done 'My Way'. I thought I'd write my own version. There are snatches of melody in 'Life On Mars' that are definite parodies." Bowie's fascination with Sinatra continued when he was scheduled to play him in a bio-pic. Sinatra nixed the project saying that he was not going to be portrayed by "a faggot". Judging by the closing notes on "Life On Mars", Bowie might have struggled with "My Way".

Sinatra started performing again in 1973. His new album was "Ol' Blue Eyes Is Back" and the single, appropriately titled "Let Me Try Again", was tailored by Sammy Cahn and Paul Anka. It sounded like Anka too was moving into

parody. Back on stage, Sinatra introduced "My Way" with the words, "We're about to sing the national anthem, but you needn't rise." Sinatra gave Anka namechecks but he was less inclined to mention the other writers. He would identify Anka's collaborator as General de Gaulle.

An astute reviewer for the magazine, "Woman's Wear Daily", said: "The Voice is now the void and it is a performance of self-destructive vulgarity. It is the ego-infested arrogance of a man who has made the sentiment of 'My Way' stand as his musical epitaph and he has totally surrendered any musical relevance by catering to the coarse and useless windbag within."

DONNY OSMOND

In 1974 Paul Anka recorded "(You're) Having My Baby", an international hit to be sure, but one that angered women's groups everywhere. With a few adjustments, this need not have been a controversial song at all. Perhaps Anka wanted it that way or perhaps Anka, as with "My Way", never spent enough time polishing his lyrics. Don Costa gave Anka some additional royalties by arranging a new version of "Puppy Love" for Donny Osmond, a UK No 1.

Meanwhile, Claude François, plagued by depression and insomnia, kept performing and maintained his business interests which included an agency with 40 models on its books. When his marriage to Isabelle ended, he wrote two notable songs about their relationship. In 1971 Richard Harris recorded one as "My Boy" and he had his own UK hit with the other, "Tears On The Telephone", in 1976. This prompted him to appear with his dance troupe, the Claudettes, at the Royal Albert Hall and although this was very successful, it did him little good. He died in 1978 in bizarre circumstances. He was electrocuted while changing a lightbulb in his bathroom whilst soaking wet. Presumably he had missed out on physics at school.

Gripped by the success of "My Way", many international cabaret stars wanted a song about their long and winding roads. I had assumed that Sammy Davis, typically, had followed his master's voice with "I've Gotta Be Me", but I was wrong because Davis recorded "I've Gotta Be Me" before Sinatra sang "My Way", and his record was a US Top 20 hit in January 1969. The song came from the stage musical, "Golden Rainbow", which in turn was based on the 1959 Frank Sinatra film, "A Hole In The Head"! The 1968 musical was a showcase for those singing sweethearts, Steve Lawrence and Eydie Gormé, but Davis was quick to pick up on its key song, "I've Gotta Be Me", which had the same pomposity as "My Way":

> *"Whether I'm right or whether I'm wrong,*
> *Whether I find a place in this world or*
> *never belong,*
> *I've gotta be me, I've gotta be me*
> *What else can I be, but what I*
> *am?"*

Feuds between top singers are not confined to Liam Gallagher and Robbie Williams. Johnnie Ray had recorded for Sinatra's label, Reprise, in 1966 but Ray blamed Sinatra when the recordings were shelved. He dated it back to 1952 when Sinatra was jealous of Ray's friendship with his wife, Ava Gardner. So, in 1966, Johnnie did it his way: in a fit of rage, he destroyed all his Sinatra albums. He didn't record again for several years, but he did make an album in London, "Yesterday, Today And Tomorrow", produced by Tony Hiller. One of Tony's songs was styled on "My Way" and succinctly used Ray's key word, "cry" - "I Cry In My Sleep":

> *"And what about me and what of my life,*
> *Well, I've had success, I've tasted the wine,*
> *I try to forget but your cut was deep,*
> *And God only knows, I cry in my sleep."*

The relationship between Frank Sinatra and Bing Crosby had never been perfect, but it reached rock bottom when John F. Kennedy chose to stay with Crosby rather than Sinatra in 1962. Sinatra wouldn't even speak Crosby's name and referred to him as "The other singer". Crosby wanted a "My Way" and he helped with the lyric of "That's What Life Is All About". Bing's approach to life was very different to Sinatra's and Sinatra would never

have sung the line, "I was never too courageous". The two songs, played back to back, tell us much about Der Bingle and the Hoboken Heart-throb:

> *"I've known some success, some mild acclaim,*
> *And thinking of it gives me pleasure,*
> *I've had some stress, the scars remain,*
> *When Lady Luck gave me short measure."*

Hal Shaper and Cyril Ornadel wrote "At My Time Of Life", which was sung by Sir John Mills in the 1975 West End musical of Charles Dickens' "Great Expectations". Hal Shaper recalls, "I had gone to America because we handle the publishing of over one hundred Sinatra standards, but Frank felt that the song was too old for him. When I got back to London, Bing Crosby was in town and I passed the song to his producer, Ken Barnes. They liked it enough to ask if there was anything else in the show they could do, and they cut two songs, 'At My Time Of Life' and 'Children', and they are lovely recordings."

"At My Time Of Life" is more Bing than Frank, who was 12 years older than Frank:

> *"Puffing my pipe and watching the*
> *smoke rings fly,*
> *Doing my best*
> *And as for the rest*
> *Just letting the world go by."*

DON GIBSON

One of the best "career songs" was "If I Never Sing Another Song", by the manager / lyricist, Don Black, for his artist, Matt Monro, although I don't think it's as good as Don Black thinks it is! Don Black told me, "It has nothing to do with 'My Way', nothing at all to do with 'My Way', although they are both songs for mature singers. 'My Way' is about somebody who says, 'No matter what has come along, I've been through it all the way .' 'If I Never Sing Another Song' is a story, a heartbreaking story of a singer, who has had an unbelievable share of success, looking back over a long career and trying to shrug off the fact that he is not so popular now. 'So what if I never sing another song, I'll get by,' he says, but he adds, 'I don't know how.' It's a very sensitive song and it's a million miles away from 'My Way', which is showbiz nonsense. 'My Way' is the sort of cabaret song that Americans love to sing but it doesn't bear close examination. 'I ate it up and spit it out, And did it my way', what does it all mean?" Don Black's chorus is:

"If I never sing another song, it shouldn't bother me,
I've had my share of fame, you know my name.
If I never sing another song or take another bow,
I would get by, but I'm not sure how."

The song was also recorded by Frankie Laine, who told me, "It's the same sort of song as 'My Way', although it isn't the real me speaking in those lyrics. Don Black has the singer saying, 'If I never sing another song, it wouldn't bother me.' Well, of course it would. It matters a lot and I hope that nobody thinks that I'm giving up because I've recorded that song."

Don Black continues, "I know it was Matt Monro's favourite song of all the ones that he recorded. It will become a major, major song one day. Singers keep singing it, particularly in Las Vegas. It's an anthem for someone who has been in the business a long time, and it could turn out to be a major, major copyright. As it is, Shirley Bassey and Connie Francis sing it. It suits everyone who's had a dodgy career with its highs and lows."

MATT
MONRO

There are many show songs which can be reworked as "career songs". Stephen Sondheim's superb musical, "Follies", includes "I'm Still Here", which has been associated at different times with Yvonne De Carlo, Dolores Gray and especially Eartha Kitt. It is down to Eartha as she sings:

"I've been through Reno,
I've been through Beverly Hills,
And I'm here.
Reefers and vino,
Rest cures, religion and pills,
But I'm here."

Shirley Bassey and now Helen Shapiro sing "Nobody Does It Like Me" from the 1974 musical by Dorothy Fields, "Seesaw", which also contains "It's Not Where You Start (It's Where You Finish)" which Shirley Maclaine performs. "I Am What I Am" from "La Cage Aux Folles" (Gloria Gaynor and Bassey again) was the "My Way" for the 1980s. Ms Bassey also belted out the Les Reed and Johnny Worth song, "Does Anybody Miss Me?", and Norman Newell's translation of "La Vita", "This Is My Life", and could build a whole act from career songs. You could argue, with perverse logic, that John Lennon's "Working Class Hero" was a career song and his response to "My Way".

In 1975 Jerry Leiber and Mike Stoller wrote and produced a remarkable album for Peggy Lee, "Mirrors", which ridiculously has not been reissued on CD. It's a brave singer who would cover "Ready To Begin Again":

"But I put in my teeth and I put on my hair
And a very strange thing occurs when I do,
For my teeth start to feel like my very own teeth
And my hair like my very own too."

Peggy Lee also recorded their most original song, "Is That All There Is?", a US Top 20 hit from 1969, which is, to my ears at any rate, superior to "My Way". Its jaded lyric tells how disillusioned she is with life and how nothing excites her anymore. Even when her house burns down, she says, "Is that all there is to a fire?" Curiously, the song was covered by Dorothy Squires, whose own, underinsured house had burnt down. "Is That All There Is?" has also travelled in the other direction as it has been recorded in French by Sacha Distel. Dorothy Squires recorded the masochistic "I The Chosen One" which is so full of disasters that you wonder how the singer could still be around to sing it.

As singers now want to show their youthfulness and appear younger than their years, there are few "career songs" today. When Paul McCartney sings "The Long And Winding Road", it can sound like a "career song", such was the cleverness of his writing, but I doubt that he will write a genuine one. Mick Jagger certainly won't, but I can't imagine Cliff Richard recording one either. Possibly Tim Rice will write something for Elton John, whose career has been as public and as colourful as Sinatra's, but Elt has already used the perfect title, "I'm Still Standing". For all that, the versions of "My Way" proliferate, and as I write, Jimmy Nail is rehearsing it with the Royal Liverpool Philharmonic Orchestra.

Elvis Presley was smitten with two career songs: "The Impossible Dream" from the 1965 musical, "Man Of La Mancha" and "My Way". Elvis sang "My Way" on his 1973 TV special, "Aloha From Hawaii", and some thought it was a tribute to Sinatra. In view of the tensions between them (chiefly over Juliet Prowse), I doubt that very much. Possibly Elvis wanted to demonstrate that he could sing the song better than Sinatra, and he identified with the lyric, although he spent his time doing it Colonel Parker's way. He was always looking for songs that mirrored his relationship with Priscilla: hence, his hit recording of that other François song, "My Boy".

Doc Pomus would have been the perfect lyricist for an Elvis "My Way" song, but it never happened. Elvis made do with the sentiments of the folk songs comprising "American Trilogy" while Doc, with another Doc (Dr John), wrote the staggeringly good "There Must Be A Better World Somewhere" for B B King.

> *"Flying high, some joker cuts my wings,*
> *Just because he gets a kick out of doing those*
> *kind of things,*
> *I keep on falling in space or just hanging in mid-air*
> *But I know there's just gotta be a better world*
> *somewhere."*

The most poignant version of Presley's "My Way" is also his worst. Elvis was performing until his death but his concerts had become erratic and shambolic. He struggled through songs he had sung with ease. You'll have seen him out of breath, looking as though he will never finish "My Way". Sinatra at 53 had been too young to sing, "And now the end is near, And so I face the final curtain", but Elvis at 42 was perfect.

Elvis Presley's "My Way" was the first single to be released after his death and it went to No 9 in the UK and by reaching No 22 became the highest-placed version of the song on the US chart. Curiously, another casualty, Sid Vicious of the Sex Pistols chose to spit out the words on a solo single and his version was a UK Top 10 hit in 1978, helped by a video in which he gunned down all in sight before collapsing himself. Another wrecked celebrity, Shane McGowan of the Pogues, returned the song to the Top 30 in 1996.

Leonard Cohen told Mat Snow in 'The Guardian' in 1986, " I never liked this song except when Sid Vicious did it. Sung straight, it somehow deprives the appetite of a certain taste we'd like to have on our lips. When Sid Vicious did it, he provided that other side to the song; the certainty, the self-congratulation, the daily heroism of Sinatra's version is completely exploded by this desperate, mad, humorous voice. I can't go round in a raincoat and fedora looking over my life and saying, 'I did it my way' - well, for 10 minutes in some American bar over a gin and tonic, I might be able to get away with it. But Sid Vicious's rendition takes in everybody; everybody is the mad hero of his own drama. It exploded the whole culture this self-presentation can take place in, so it completes the song for me."

Sinatra continued to perform and as he regarded his concerts as "The Main Event", it was appropriate that he should have been presented by the boxing promoter, Frank Warren, in London's Docklands in 1990. "My Way" was perfect for all his retirements and comebacks and despite an enormous repertoire, he commented that it had "done more for my career than any other song." When Mia Farrow told him about her troubles with Woody Allen, she repeated the conversation to a journalist: "Frank never lets you down. He even offered to break Woody's legs."

By then, Sinatra had become the Chairman of the Bored. He did "My Way" at every concert but because the setting for each stanza is identical, he would get lost. It was as though he was making it up as he went along. Like Elvis singing "My Way" in 1977, it became irresistible theatre. Even Luciano Pavarotti got in on the act. A fast-ageing Sinatra was in the audience when the Three Tenors belted it out and he also recorded it as a duet with Pavarotti for his eightieth birthday.

Unlike Sinatra, Paul Anka has had a happy family life. He has been married to his wife, Anne (Marie Anne De Zogheb), for over 35 years and their children are named Amelia, Anthea, Alicia, Amanda and Alexandra. (Fats Domino also gave his children names beginning with "A" - must create havoc when the postman calls.) However, Anka possesses a temper, and a tape has been circulated of him remonstrating with his musicians for playing badly. Anka says that when he is on stage, he calls the shots. Even if Jesus comes on to the stage, he says, you watch me. Really? He tells the musicians that they have to tighten up their act. "It's either 'My Way' or the highway," he says, "Take your pick."

WORKING CLASS HERO
The story of the song

"Working Class Hero" was a track on the 1970 album, "John Lennon / Plastic Ono Band". It was never one of his hits, but its anger makes it the most defiant statement that he ever wrote. However, its irony has been overlooked or misinterpreted. He told Paul McCartney, "'Imagine' is 'Working Class Hero' with sugar on for conservatives like yourself." The songs are very different but both advocate changes in society and in the ways we view each other. McCartney could never have written "Working Class Hero": it's not just the vocabulary - Paul McCartney never felt as bitter as this.

John Lennon told "Red Mole" in August 1971, "I've always been politically minded, you know, and against the status quo. It's pretty basic when you're brought up like I was to hate and fear the police as a natural enemy and to despise the army as something that takes everybody away and leaves them dead somewhere." I'm sure Aunt Mimi never thought like this.

The Plastic Beatles Band

John Lennon met the avant-garde Japanese artist, Yoko Ono in November 1966. It led to John divorcing his Liverpool wife and living with, and then marrying, Yoko. The move was unpopular with the British press and the other Beatles. John Lennon wrote about their persecution in an entertaining but messianic way in "The Ballad Of John And Yoko", a Beatles' No.1 single from 1969.

At first John had no desire to break up the Beatles. He and Yoko would release their esoteric singles under the name of the Plastic Ono Band and they recorded "Give Peace A Chance" in a Canadian hotel room with friends and hangers-on. John Lennon described heroin withdrawal in "Cold Turkey" and it's surprising that the single received any airplay at all. Thirty years on, it stands as a harrowing account of the horrors of coming off hard drugs.

Because the other Beatles had little interest in their experimental work, John told them he was leaving the group in the summer of 1969. He was persuaded to stay for "Let It Be" where his detachment all but destroyed the sessions. John and Paul made no attempt to write together: indeed, John made little attempt to write anything suitable. The Beatles' final album, "Abbey Road", was a considerable improvement and was chiefly the result of their producer, George Martin insisting that they finished positively - and with a track called "The End". Still, John's compositions ("Come Together", "I Want You (She's So Heavy)") stemmed from his personal commitments.

The splits in the Beatles were public knowledge long before the official break-up, via a Paul McCartney press release, in April 1970. The satirical American magazine, "National Lampoon", suggested that John's first solo album would be called "Fuck Me! Fuck You!" and suggested several outlandish titles. It was a very accurate prophecy.

Primal Screaming

A psychologist, Arthur Janov, heard "an eerie scream welling up from the depths of a young man lying on the floor during a therapy session. I can only liken it to what one might hear from a person about to be murdered." From this, Janov formulated primal therapy and opened his own institute in Los Angeles. He claimed that most neuroses stemmed from a lack of parental love in early childhood, and he encouraged his patients to scream at their absent parents in order to reconcile their rejection. Prior to Janov, the Beatles' track, "Yer Blues", (John Lennon of course) sounded like primal therapy, while Yoko Ono's records were one long screech. If Arthur Janov had wanted to impress John and Yoko, he could not have mixed a more potent cocktail. Primal therapy gave them the excuse to be even more self-centred than they already were.

John and Yoko read Janov's book, "The Primal Scream", and, with the arrogance of superstardom, insisted that he come to England to give them therapy. Then, to coincide with the Beatles' break-up in April 1970, John and Yoko began a four-month course in Los Angeles. John Lennon was to comment, "Janov showed me how to feel my own fear and pain. I can handle it better than I could before, that's all." He concluded, "I was never really wanted when I was a child. The only reason I'm a star is because of my repressions. The only reason I went for that goal is that I wanted to say, 'Now, Mummy, will you love me?'" Lennon may have said this, but it is nonsense. John was spoilt as a child - his Aunt Mimi doted him on him and sent him to a good school, Quarry Bank: he had, in effect, two mothers.

John and Yoko had the strangest courtship known to man, and in September 1970, they started recording "John Lennon / Plastic Ono Band" and "Yoko Ono / Plastic Ono Band" at EMI's Abbey Road studios. John's compositions, mostly of disillusionment, were the results of primal therapy. John often used the deadpan voice of "A Day In The Life" and the songs were given threadbare accompaniments. The album was co-produced by Phil Spector, but there was no Wall of Sound here. Lennon lambasted his dead mother and absent father in "Mother" and criticised his past life in "God", but no track is more spartan

JOHN AND YOKO PICTURED DURING THEIR 'BED-IN' PEACE CAMPAIGN, 1969

than the voice and guitar accompaniment on "Working Class Hero".

"John Lennon / Plastic Ono Band" was released in December 1970 and as publicity, John gave a bitter, revealing interview to Jann Wenner of "Rolling Stone", which was syndicated world-wide. The full conversation was printed in the best-selling book, "Lennon Remembers", which was published without Lennon's consent.

Class Consciousness

In the 1960s, everyone in England knew what class they belonged to. There was the upper class (for many years, the ruling class, and represented in Liverpool by Lord Derby and his friends), the middle class (itself divided into lower and upper components) and working class. Liverpool's working class men, especially the dockers, were seen as militants with strong union backing. The Prime Minister Edward Heath tried to be at one with the working classes by pointing out that his father had been a grocer, but he remained part of the establishment, a Tory grandee.

Many successful, pre-war popular songs reflected the sophisticated lifestyles of the songwriters, notably Cole Porter with his society parties. Their accurate scansion and perfect rhyming made them role models for aspiring composers. There were a few exceptions: "Brother, Can You Spare A Dime" looked at America during the Depression and Jimmie Rodgers wrote about working on the railway. Cheerful music hall songs were written for the British working classes, and this strand continued into the 1960s with records by Bernard Cribbins ("Hole In The Ground", "Right Said Fred") and Charlie Drake ("Only A Working Man"). Production lines at factories were entertained by the twice-daily radio programme, "Music While You Work", with its signature tune, "Calling All Workers". Few songs dealt with class differentials, although the classical composer Benjamin Britten wrote pieces for Communist rallies. Two years before John Lennon, the Rolling Stones wrote about working class people in "Salt Of The Earth" on their album, "Beggars Banquet". Mick Jagger, not working class himself, distances himself from them and the song is as patronising as some music hall ones.

John Lennon's estranged father, Alfred, was working class, and his mother, who wanted to pursue another relationship, placed John with her sister and her husband, who had no children of their own. They lived in comfortable, lower middle-class surroundings in leafy Menlove Avenue in Woolton, but Lennon was saddened that his mother passed him over. He failed to see, or refused to recognise, that he was treating his own son, Julian, in the same way.

John Lennon's perception of himself is worthy of a book in its own right. He hated middle class life, he hated where he lived and he thought of himself as working class. There were no blue suburban skies as he viewed his past through distorted mirrors and as he admitted in "I'll Cry Instead", "I've got a chip on my shoulder that's bigger than my feet." Like Bob Dylan, John Lennon was rewriting his upbringing, and Aunt Mimi did not find it funny. She told the "Daily Express": "I get terribly annoyed when he is billed as a street-corner boy. He had a very comfortable home in a good area."

Working Class Heroes

John Lennon's best friend, Pete Shotton, confirmed to me that John had read "The Communist Manifesto" and, indeed, Karl Marx is the only political figure on the cover of "Sgt Pepper's Lonely Hearts Club Band". In Marxist terminology, the heroes of the revolution are the tractor-drivers. Many working-class heroes like Joe Hill have been incarcerated or killed for their actions. Possibly John Lennon considered Fidel Castro, who stood up to America, and Chairman Mao, as working class heroes, but it is clear from "Revolution" that John had mixed feelings about Mao.

In the 1950s a new form of working class theatre and literature had emerged in the UK. The playwrights, John Osborne and Arnold Wesker, and the novelist John Braine, alongwith their creations, were working class heroes. However, I know of no specific use of that phrase. John, who was revisiting his past, may have had thieir kitchen sink drama in mind when he wrote "Working Class Hero". The song contains the phrase, "room at the top", a telling reference to John Braine's best-selling novel.

Many real-life working class heroes emerged during the 1960s. Fashion designers, sportsmen and pop stars had working class origins. They may lose their social class when they become celebrities, but footballers remain working class heroes. They do a physical job, they play in stadiums in working class areas, and they are also given orders by their managers. Footballers, much more than pop stars, are working class heroes.

John Lennon had been in the audience when the working class hero, Bob Dylan played the Isle of Wight in August 1969 for a much-publicised £20,000. Had this event prompted the song? If so, Lennon was being hypocritical: in January 1970, John Lennon announced that all the future proceeds from his records would go towards promoting peace on earth, but he had no intention of keeping his word. Indeed, Lennon lavished money on his own gratifications in Elton John proportions.

John Lennon could have coined the phrase, "working class hero", but it seems unlikely that such a powerful phrase was being used for the first time as late as 1970. John Lennon often gathered phrases for his songs from snatches he read or heard in the media. I've not managed to find an earlier use of "working class hero" and the most likely explanation is that he heard it during a TV discussion.

You Say You Want A Revolution

McCartney was happy regarding songwriting as a confection, fabricating "Maxwell's Silver Hammer" long after John Lennon had become introspective. Lennon realised that he only wanted to write songs when he had something to say. The plight of being in a loveless marriage and of being beseiged by fans comes out in "Help!" and "Norwegian Wood". Psychedelic drugs changed their perspective on songwriting. Lennon played with words in groundbreaking songs, which also can be linked back to the nonsense stories and poems of his youth. The drugged-up, washed-out picture of Lennon's "Strawberry Fields Forever" was coupled with McCartney's sparkling, impressionistic vision of "Penny Lane".

After this diversion, John Lennon returned to personal songwriting with a vengeance. Although criticised at the time, "I Want You (She's So Heavy)" on "Abbey Road" can be seen as the start of John Lennon's new exodus. For over seven minutes, John, perhaps the greatest wordsmith of his day, simply shouts the title line to express his love for Yoko. It marked his new phase of minimalist songwriting.

The protagonist in "Working Class Hero" starts with being born and going to school. The line about his parents having no time for him exposes Lennon's vulnerability and is pure Janov. With numbness in his voice, he describes how teachers hold pupils back and reward conformity. It is a strong concept that echoes my own school years where clever lads were hated and stupid ones were despised. Imagination has been curtailed and success is only seen in monetary terms. Lennon regards his pre-Beatle self as being as false as his Beatle one.

Lennon believes that new gods have arisen to obscure the lack of control we have over our own lives. The media (TV and newspapers), the pursuit of sex (the permissive 60s), religion (in his case, the Maharishi) and the taking of drugs blunt the appetite for social change. As he told one interviewer, "The workers are dreaming someone else's dream."

He says of "Working Class Hero", "It's a song for the revolution. It's for people like me who are working class, who are supposed to be processed into the middle class. It's my experience and I hope it's a warning to people." John Lennon was trying to impress Tariq Ali rather than absent relatives, although he wanted to be both radical and commercial. Note how on the first version of "Revolution", he can't decide whether he is to be counted in or out when it comes to insurrection.

In Y2K, it looked as though the answer was really "in" as banner headlines proclaimed that John Lennon had made a donation to the IRA. This was hardly news as John had made his feelings known in the August 1971 edition of "Red Mole" and had been photographed on a demonstration. It would be more surprising if Lennon hadn't funded the IRA and, to be fair to him, the IRA were relatively inactive at the time. In the interview, Lennon says of the British working class, "They think they're in a wonderful free-speaking country. They've got cars and tellies and don't want to think there's anything more to life. They are prepared to let their bosses run them, to see their children fucked up in school. They're dreaming someone else's dream, it's not even their own. They should realise that the blacks and the Irish are being harassed and repressed and that they will be next. As soon as they start being aware of all that, we can really begin to do something. The workers can start to take over, but we'd have to infiltrate the army too because they are well trained to kill us all."

Of his own work, he says, "The idea is not to comfort people, not to make them feel better but to make them worse, to constantly put before them the degradations and humilations they go through to get what they call a living wage."

The Beatles were far more than working class heroes: they were heroes for the whole world, irrespective of class. John regarded himself as a hero - two years earlier he had told fellow Apple workers that he was Jesus Christ returned. He was given to such remarks as "Genius is pain" (1970), but the song's title line, "A working class hero is something to be" is ironic. John is really saying, "I should not be a working class hero". Any revolution would come from the working classes and having heroes, especially superstars, are distractions. The working class are not, in effect, being anarchists and planning radical changes: instead, they are, in Lennon's words, "fucking peasants".

The reference to "the folks who live on the hill" is a songwriting cliché. The rich folks living on the hill are figures of envy in popular songs - someone with radio-controlled gates may be watched by someone in a miserable shack by the railway. Such songs include "Mansion On The Hill" and "The Folks On The Hill". Possibly, too, Lennon was taking a caustic swipe at his former partner's "Fool On The Hill".

Lennon was an instinctive songwriter and he put little gloss on his compositions. "Working Class Hero" uses basic rhymes and not always perfect ones: small/all/all, school/fool/rules, years/career/fear, TV/free/see, still/kill/hill. A top show lyricist like Tim Rice would never have left a song like that, which also explains why Rice can't write rock'n'roll. Similarly, the opening line, "As soon as you're born, they make you feel small", is a ridiculous criticism. They make you feel small because you are small! Most children, John Lennon included, receive a lot of mollycoddling so they are giving you time rather than "no time at all".

John Lennon was impressed with Bob Dylan's approach to songwriting and "Working Class Hero" can be compared to "Masters Of War", a 1963 song on "The Freewheelin' Bob Dylan". "Masters Of War" was a savage indictment of Government and big business - the holders of economic power - for promoting and profiteering from war and conflict.. Both records are guitar and voice performances, both are full of venom, and both are in 12/8 (as, incidentally, is Lennon's deliberate nod to Dylan "You've Got To Hide Your Love Away".). Both hammer words home for effect and they both sing/speak their lyrics, bringing them close to narration. On the other hand, Lennon lacks Dylan's urgency: Dylan sings as though the world is going to end tomorrow unless somebody does something about it.

The melodies are similar - possibly, Lennon started with "Masters Of War" and added his own chords. The possible plagiarism wouldn't bother Lennon as Dylan had borrowed "Norwegian Wood" for "Fourth Time Around" and besides, although Lennon might not have known this, "Masters Of War" had been based on "Nottamun Town (Nottingham Town)" from an old English mummers' play.

Expletive Deleted

Although the vocabulary of popular music became more street-wise with the advent of rock'n'roll, there was a reluctance for songwriters to use expletives to express their feelings. Many songwriters would not want to use such words, many felt they had a wider vocabulary at their disposal, and all knew that such language would restrict airplay on the BBC or US radio.

In 1969, John Lennon had included 'Christ!' in the chorus of the Beatles' chart-topping single, "The Ballad Of John And Yoko". The single would probably have been banned had it not been the latest offering by the world's leading group. Around the same time, John's exhibition of lithographs at the London Arts Gallery was raided by the police for indecency.

The word "fucking" first appeared on a commercial pop record in 1969. Leading the way was Al Stewart on the lengthy title track of his confessional album, "Love Chronicles". Country Joe and the Fish prefaced their song about the Vietnam war, "I-Feel-Like-I'm-Fixin'-To-Die Rag" with Joe's Fish Cheer ("Give me an F") for Woodstock. Arguably, Desmond Dekker was the first artist to sing "fuck" on a hit record. His No 1 record, "The Israelites" (again 1969), probably contains the line, "My wife and my kids, they fuck off and leave me", but his staccato delivery has meant that the lyrics retain some mystery.

I suspect that John Lennon was irritated that he had not got there first: he had lost the initiative, possibly because the other Beatles held him back. "Working Class Hero" contains "fucking" twice although Lennon commented that he hadn't realised that he had sung it more than once, which is unlikely. He knew what he was doing. He was furious that EMI deleted the words when printing the lyrics on the inner sleeve. It was okay to sing it, but not to print it. The expletives are essential for "Working Class Hero". If John Lennon used "flipping" or something equally bland, the song would have lost its notoriety.

Cover Versions

Many of John Lennon's songs from his solo years have been covered by other artists, notably "Imagine", "Jealous Guy" and "Give Peace A Chance". Some songs are so tied up with his persona that it is difficult for other artists to put their stamp on them without simply copying his recordings. "Working Class Hero" falls into this category, although there have been some intriguing covers.

In 1979 Marianne Faithfull included it on her album, "Broken English". Its language was mild next to a lyric from the playwright Heathcote Williams, "Why D'Ya Do It". Faithfull, from a privileged background, had suffered broken relationships and drug-abuse, and her voice, mostly through chain-smoking, had become a husky drawl. Unlike many singers, she had added, rather than removed, rough edges. This proved ideal for her love of German cabaret songs, but it also works with "Working Class Hero", which she performs to a throbbing, tension-packed accompaniment. Faithfull omits the coda, "If you want to be a hero, well, just follow me."

"Working Class Hero" has also been recorded by the Alarm, John Fiddler (of Medicine Head), Terry Hall, Richie Havens, and David Bowie as part of Tin Machine. Cyndi Lauper, at the John Lennon tribute concert held at the Pier Head in Liverpool, pranced through "Working Class Hero", holding the lyric in her hand, but Dave Edmunds' edgy arrangement suited the song. The Seattle band, Screaming Trees, performed the song on "Working Class Hero - A Tribute To John Lennon", a 1995 album in which contemporary acts performed Lennon's songs. Mark Lanegan, the lead vocalist, effects a deadpan Lennon expression and the only jarring note is when Van Connor joins him for the title line and turns it into a Spinners singalong.

The phrase, "working class", has little application in the US, where class structure is different and the phrase,

DAKOTA BUILDINGS, NEW YORK CITY

"blue collar worker", is used. Some songs, mostly country, have been written about working men - for example, "A Working Man's Prayer" and "Working Man Blues". Surprisingly and cheekily, new songs have been written using John Lennon's title and recorded by Tommy Roe and Alan Jackson.

If You Want To Be A Hero, Then Just Follow Me

Like the Maharishi and several other interests, Arthur Janov did not stay the course and John Lennon moved onto another fad. He settled in New York and his songs tended to reflect American life. He never returned to the primal screams of "John Lennon / Plastic Ono Band" and, irony of ironies, he kept in his bedroom a chest marked "Liverpool", which was full of his adolescent possessions. If he had remained alive, he would have been a stimulating guest for Anthony Clare's radio programme, "In The Psychiatrist's Chair".

I am sure that "Working Class Hero" will grow in statue with the years, but that applies to everything connected with John Lennon. I have seen a 20-volume set of everything George Orwell wrote on sale for £750. I can envisage a similar collection for John Lennon in years to come where every scrap of paper he wrote on will be analysed. His original drafts for "Working Class Hero" might be even more vitriolic than what was recorded.

One final point: despite his identification with the working man, John Lennon never did a day's labouring in his life.

IMAGINE
The story of the song

The music polls indicate that "Imagine" is certainly the song of the 70s, arguably the song of the century and possibly even the song of the millennium. To thousands if not millions of people, "Imagine" is John Lennon's finest hour and when you consider the strength of his other compositions, that in itself is an extraordinary achievement. Why has "Imagine" captured the public's imagination? What is so exceptional about it?

"Imagine" is John Lennon's declaration of hope for himself and the world. Raymond Froggatt, one of Britain's best song-writers, says, "The pièce de résistance of John Lennon's songwriting is 'Imagine'. What greater contribution could you leave to the world than a lovely song like that? If I could write a song like 'Imagine', they could bury me tomorrow and I'd die a very happy man."

On the other hand, Albert Goldman wrote in his notorious book, "The Lives Of John Lennon", that "Imagine" was "a hippie wishing-well full of pennyweight dreams for a better world - a far cry from the searing vision of the Primal Scream album. 'Imagine' suffers from a piano accompaniment as monotonous as a student in a practice room and a vocal delivery with a hook-shoulder turn as feeble as a hymn sung in a Quaker parlour."

The revelation from those comments is that Goldman praised something from John Lennon, namely "the Primal Scream album", which was officially known as "John Lennon / Plastic Ono Band" and was his first solo album since leaving the Beatles, released in December 1970. It was as unique and as unexpected as "Sgt Pepper's Lonely Hearts Club Band", but the stark music was hard to take. Following analysis with Dr Arthur Janov, John screamed his way through songs with such direct titles as "Mother", "Isolation" and "God".

"John Lennon / Plastic Ono Band" didn't sell like the Beatles' records (or even Paul McCartney's), but that this uncompromising record sold at all is an achievement. Especially when it was released for the Christmas market! "John Lennon / Plastic Ono Band" should be on any list of essential albums but it is an album to own rather than to play. John Lennon bares his soul to such an extent that the album can hardly be heard for pleasure. Great as it is, I wonder why he felt compelled to record it in the first place.

For all their avant-garde aspirations, John and Yoko knew how to manipulate the media: bed-ins, acorns for peace and performing in a bag were just three eccentric events. More low-key was the publication of Yoko Ono's poetry book, "Grapefruit", in 1970. The introduction was from John Lennon: "Hi! My name is John Lennon. I'd like you to meet Yoko Ono."

The I-word, "imagine", recurred in Yoko's poems with such instructions as "Imagine one thousand suns in the sky at the same time." This intrigued John Lennon and shortly before his death in 1980, he told Andy Peebles for BBC Radio 1: "'Imagine' should be credited as a Lennon / Ono song. A lot of the lyric and the concept came from Yoko, but those days I was a bit more selfish, a bit more macho and I omitted to mention her contribution, which was right out of 'Grapefruit'. She's just the wife and you don't put her name on it, right?'"

The song was written on Yoko's piano. John had given it to her as a birthday present and the inscription read, "This morning a white piano for Yoko." The white piano was in keeping with their love of white rooms and, even now, you never see Yoko in anything but black or white clothes.

John completed the songs for his second studio album, which was eventually called "Imagine". The songs shared the honesty of "John Lennon / Plastic Ono Band" with confessional titles such as "Crippled Inside" and "Jealous Guy". However, they were more melodic and more positive, causing Paul McCartney to remark to "Melody Maker":

STRAWBERRY FIELDS, NEW YORK

"'Imagine' is what John is really like. There was too much political stuff on the other album." Lennon didn't want McCartney's patronage or condescension and he snidely retorted, "So you think 'Imagine' isn't political. It's 'Working Class Hero' with sugar on for conservatives like yourself."

The songs for "Imagine" were recorded at home - John called it the "Ascot Sound" - and the title track featured John on piano, Klaus Voormann on bass and Alan White, now with Yes, on drums. John's rudimentary playing was supplemented by Nicky Hopkins' electric piano. The producer, Phil Spector, made satisfactory mixes and took the tapes to New York, where he added echo and strings (The Flux Fiddlers). These were no full-blooded Wall Of Sound strings though and the sympathetic arrangement on "Imagine" emphasises that the song is a solemn hymn - Albert Goldman was right there. John regarded the album as "electric 20th century folk music" and "Imagine" itself has become a folk anthem alongside "All You Need

Is Love", "Give Peace A Chance" and several Bob Dylan and Pete Seeger songs.

Because John was not a gifted pianist, "Imagine" had an elementary tune, and the piano sounds off-key at the beginning. Presumably it sounded fine to Oasis, who copied it for the opening of "Don't Look Back In Anger". How many listeners hearing those notes on the radio think they are about to hear "Imagine"? Oasis also comment on Lennon's philosophy in "Some Might Say":

"Some might say they don't believe in heaven,
Go and tell it to the man who lives in hell."

The minimalist arrangement on "Imagine" is in keeping with the lyric. The words are basic, the rhymes even more so and it is as though one of the world's finest wordsmiths couldn't be bothered - try/sky, do/too, can/man and one/one, which isn't a rhyme at all. It is a short lyric (three verses and a coda), but seems longer because it is sung slowly and hypnotically.

The song opens with the words, "Imagine there's no heaven". John then tells us to imagine no hell and then "no religion too". Many churchgoers have been disturbed by these remarks. The country singer, George Hamilton IV, told me, "When I first heard 'Imagine', I loved its melody and started to learn it. When I considered the lyrics more closely, I realised that I didn't agree with its theology. He says, 'Imagine there's no heaven' and 'Imagine there's no hell.' It's all very well to dwell on peace-and-beauty-and-I-love-you-and-let's-not-harm-each-other, but I feel very strongly that there is a heaven and a hell and that Jesus Christ died for me. That's important to me, so if 'Imagine' means what I think it does, then I don't agree with it."

Elvis Presley nearly joined the Blackwood Brothers Gospel Quartet. Billy Blackwood, the son of a founder member and a fine gospel singer himself, told me, "'Imagine' seems to be saying that if you could do away with all the restraints, then there would be a freedom available to human beings which would increase the quality of their lives. John Lennon might have looked at religion and seen bonds and burdens, but he failed to realise that God said, 'He who knows the Son will be free. The Truth will make him free.' There is a freedom in Christ to help us with the ills of the world and the consequences of our mistakes. The casting off of restraints does not lead to freedom, and psychologists know that we need guidelines and parameters within which to lead our lives. If we do away with those, we overdose on freedom, and we would soon find out that it is not the freedom we long for."

Nevertheless, "Imagine" is sung in churches and it was performed in July 1997 at the service in St Peter's Church, Woolton to celebrate the day that John Lennon had met Paul McCartney 40 years before. I asked Canon John Roberts if it was absurd to sing "Imagine there's no heaven, no religion too" in a place of worship. "Oh no," he replied, "John made a mistake, he got it wrong, but I can forgive him for that."

Actually, John is not saying that there is no heaven or religion - he is saying "imagine it". He regards religion as being responsible for ills of the world and without it, we would have "nothing to kill or die for". But is that true? Many wars have nothing to do with religion at all - surely the biggest conflict has been between the rich and the poor - and in any event, John's own futile assassination had nothing to do with religion.

Also, you could argue that John is describing heaven in his song. The only difference between heaven and his utopia is that you are also worshipping God in heaven. In another sense, John may have been poking fun at the religiosity of Paul McCartney's "Let It Be".

"Imagine" is sometimes described as a Marxist song but Lennon is not Lenin. Marxism is about class struggle, which is not alluded to in the song. It could be an oversight on Lennon's part as it was central to "Working Class Hero" and the 1975 UK hit single of "Imagine" cleverly combined the two sides. "Imagine" has been described as "the Communist manifesto set to music", but this is wrong. If Lennon really was marking his Red card, it would not have been on the short list of songs to be played when the Queen opened the Millennium Dome. In the end, "Imagine" was beaten by an earlier Lennon song, "All You Need Is Love".

In place of religion, John conceives a Brotherhood of Man. He was echoing, possibly copying, Charlie Chaplin's thoughts of being a world citizen without boundaries or differences, and "Imagine" decries religion, nationalism and capitalism.

John does not say how this Brotherhood of Man will be achieved. Even if everyone is helping everyone else, there have to be leaders for organisation. Hence, all people will not be equal. Furthermore, it is unlikely that John Lennon, who at times had a messianic complex, saw himself the same as others. Possibly he decried religion because he couldn't accept a being superior to himself. In a memorable but ridiculous statement, he declared, "We're all Christ and we're all Hitler", and during 1969, he called a meeting at Apple to declare he was the reincarnation of Jesus Christ. John was nothing if not inconsistent. Above the front door of his Tittenhurst Park mansion, he had a sign, "This is not here."

John speaks like the leader of a cult. The song is addressed to everyone and not single individuals and, as in "Working Class Hero", he wants others to join him. Then "The world will be as one." The concept mirrors "All You Need Is Love", where the love in that song is some kind of universal love.

Lennon favours "living for today", which suggests an epicurean existence. Everyone would be eating and drinking and being merry with no thoughts for the future. This would be stifling. There would no research and little creativity, so the world would not progress. "Zardoz" is only trashy but this 1973 film starring Sean Connery and Charlotte Rampling shows how the world could become a wasteland if such ideals were followed and how immortality would not bring happiness.

Mick Groves, who included "Imagine" in the Spinners' repertoire and latterly has been a Labour councillor, sees it as a socialist song. "'Imagine' is a peace song so it interests me greatly. I sing in the last verse, 'Imagine all the people sharing all the wealth', although on the single, John sings 'the world'. I remember him doing a television show for Lord Grade from America. Lennon's band was the highlight of the cabaret and they came on stage wearing back-to-front masks. He sang, 'Imagine all the people sharing all the wealth' to these people covered in jewels. That appeals to me, you see, being a socialist."

In October 1971, the "Imagine" single entered the US charts and went to No 2 but at the time it was not released as a single in the UK. The LP topped both the US and UK album charts. John was set to become a major international solo artist but, in typical fashion, he blew it with his next release, "Sometime In New York City", regarded at the time as a double-album of banal political songs lacking in melody and charm. Again, it was a curious move. Why did he move to America if he was so dissatisfied there? One song, "Sunday Bloody Sunday", considers Ireland but Paul McCartney, following Lennon's agitprop, put the position more succinctly in "Give Ireland Back To The Irish".

"Imagine" was released as a UK single in 1975 and it climbed to No 5. The single created controversy as it was backed by "Working Class Hero" from the first solo album. Because of its vocabulary, it was argued that children who bought "Imagine" might be corrupted by the other side.

After John Lennon's assassination in 1980, the public felt compelled to buy his records. "(Just Like) Starting Over", which was going down the charts at the time of his death, started over and soared to No 1. It was replaced by St Winifred's School Choir, surely a similar reaction to the Singing Nun topping the US charts after the assassination of President Kennedy in 1963. After that, John Lennon returned for four weeks with "Imagine". That, in turn, was replaced by another track from John and Yoko's "Double Fantasy", "Woman", a love song with the fragility of "Imagine". Graham Lyle, the Scottish songwriter who has written for Michael Jackson and Tina Turner, says, "I thought John Lennon wrote some amazing stuff on his own. Songs like 'Imagine' and 'Woman' went beyond the Beatles for me and, tragically, the songs he was writing at the time of his death were amongst the best he ever did."

The Lennons continuously documented their lives on tape and film. Endless rehearsals by John Lennon have been released or broadcast, and the making of the "Imagine" album is included in the 1988 film, "Imagine: John Lennon". In the video for "Imagine" itself, Yoko sits dutifully next to John at the piano, her piano, at Tittenhurst Park. She opens the shutters in the white room, letting in the daylight, which is corny symbolism but memorable. The video was included on the CD reissue of "Imagine" in December 1999. Cliff at No 1 was telling us that there was a heaven, John at No 3 was telling us there wasn't and in between the hapless Emil was dying in "Seasons In The Sun".

"Imagine" is one of the few songs from John Lennon's solo career that has become a standard and, surprisingly perhaps, most covers are from Easy Listening artists.

Petula Clark, Nana Mouskouri, Des O'Connor, Peters and Lee, and Roger Whittaker have recorded vocal versions, with instrumental ones from Acker Bilk, Chet Atkins with Mark Knopfler, and the Shadows. Other versions come from Randy Crawford (the only other interpretation to make the UK chart), Diana Ross, Joan Baez, Elton John and Gerry Marsden. When John Lennon scored with Ben E. King's "Stand By Me", King responded by recording "Imagine" with the Average White Band. The song's use at the end of "The Killing Fields" echoed "They Didn't Believe Me" at the conclusion of "Oh What A Lovely War!". At the all-star "Imagine - John Lennon" concert in Liverpool, Yoko Ono decided that the song would only be performed on film by John himself. Perhaps we were deprived of the duet version by Kylie Minogue and Lou Reed, who knows?

It is not worth analysing "Imagine" too closely as it is a mass of contradictions, both within itself and with Lennon's own life. Lennon was hardly a man with no possessions, although the very person he criticised, Jesus, lived that way. Also, he had written his plea for universal peace only three years after advocating revolution in a song called, well, "Revolution". And, for that matter, wasn't Jesus a revolutionary? In 1998 the UK churches had posters of Jesus Christ as Che Guevara for their Easter message: the text was "Meek. Mild. As if."

From time to time, John approved of insurrection and he did bankroll, and was interviewed for, Tariq Ali's radical magazine, "Red Mole", for the Workers Revolutionary Party. He was wanting to appeal to student protesters, and his interviews of the time do not ring true. He says that he was "brought up to hate and fear the police". Who by? Aunt Mimi?. I suspect that Yoko Ono was encouraging this stance and you could argue, quite forcibly, that, artistically, they were not good for each other.

The idea of leading a cult appealed to John Lennon, at least part of the time. He would have loved a doctrine named after him like Thatcherism, although of course, her ideals were very different from his. He would never have been a follower himself and, ironically, he might have frowned upon anyone accepting his leadership. His infamous remark about the Beatles being more popular than Jesus meant that the media overlooked a much more revealing comment in the same interview: "Jesus is all right, but the disciples were thick and ordinary." A comment on Beatlemania perhaps? Imagine that.

AMERICAN PIE
The story of the song

In their later years, the Beatles filled their songs with unusual imagery but there is little mystery about them because both John Lennon and Paul McCartney answered reporters' questions. The songwriters, Don McLean and Jimmy Webb are equally eloquent but they have decided not to answer detailed questions about "American Pie" and "MacArthur Park", respectively. Freddie Mercury never explained "Bohemian Rhapsody", and who can say what "A Whiter Shade Of Pale" is all about?

Originally released in 1971, "American Pie" caught the imagination of rock fans and pundits on both sides of the Atlantic. It was obvious to most listeners that the song was inspired by the death of Buddy Holly, and that much of the song's symbolism embraced the 60s heroes, Bob Dylan and the Beatles. But after that, as the song says, we were on our own, as McLean retained a dignified silence.

Thirty years on and revived in a very palatable, electronic way by Madonna, "American Pie" retains its mystique, although John Walsh, writing in "The Independent", was unimpressed: "The lady wiggled her expensive tush in front of the Stars and Stripes and displayed as much comprehensive of the song as if she'd been reciting the Bhagavadgita."

Madonna, who recorded the song at Rupert Everett's suggestion, truncated its lyric, commenting with some surprise that the original lyric was too long and that it didn't use the same melody in each verse. Didn't she realise that Don McLean was really a folkie? It was her 50th hit and her ninth No 1 coming from the soundtrack of her film,

"The Next Best Thing". Don McLean didn't quite reach No 1 as Nilsson's "Without You" was too strong. Madonna's producer, William Orbit, who also produced All Saints' "Pure Shores", replaced himself at No 1.

The Internet offers endless analysis of the song but, as anyone can publish anything they like on the Net, dodgy explanations abound. One combines Bobbie Gentry's "Ode To Billie Joe" with "American Pie" and has Billie Joe throwing a pink carnation off the Tallahatchie Bridge, where it is caught by a drunken McLean wandering on the levee below.

Here's my take on "American Pie" and even if I'm wrong, Don McLean isn't going to say so. All he says about "American Pie" is that "It means I don't have to work if I don't want to." He adds that he may go public on an 0891 number when he is poor and old, but that's unlikely as the royalties from "American Pie" are a secure pension. It's coincidence, I'm sure, but Fellini's most enigmatic film is "8 1/2" and "American Pie" is 8 1/2 minutes long. God, I'm sounding like one of those idiots on the Net.

It would be wrong to say that Don McLean has never spoken about "American Pie". He gave this insight to "New Musical Express" on 18th March 1972. "'American Pie' was an attempt to use metaphors the best I could to describe a certain loss that I felt in American music. Buddy Holly's death, for me, was a symbolic death that virtually all the characters in the song suffered. The music never dies, though, and all I was saying in the song was that people lack the basic trust to believe the music will happen again." That, clearly, has to be my starting-point.

Don McLean was born in New York in 1945 and, in the first verse, he is a 13 year old paper boy, loving rock'n'roll and dreaming of being a performer himself. In February 1959, the headlines tell of the death of Buddy Holly, the Big Bopper and Ritchie Valens in a plane crash. Holly had only recently been married, hence the reference to a "widowed bride". Some have said that the verse relates to the assassination of John F. Kennedy in 1963, but why should Jackie Kennedy be a "bride" and besides, would McLean have been a paper boy when he was 18? The reference in the chorus to "This'll be the day when I die" echoes Holly's own "That'll be the day when I die", and McLean himself has recorded several of Holly's tunes including "Everyday", "Fool's Paradise" and "Maybe Baby".

In the chorus, the 1971 Don McLean realises that his ideals have been shattered by various aspects of 1960s culture - drugs, psychedelia, race riots and the Vietnam war - all of which are referred to in subsequent verses. As John Lennon sang on his first solo album, released a few months earlier, "The dream is over". McLean wants to return to the innocence of the 1950s, which might have continued if Buddy Holly had not died. Today's music is tarnished ("the levee was dry") and he hides his sorrow by drinking.

In 1958 the doowop group, the Monotones, sang:

> *"I wonder, wonder, wonder, wonder who,*
> *Who, who wrote the book of love?"*

McLean is referring to a record he loves and then makes a reference to the "God is dead" debate from late 60s America, "Do you have faith in God above?" He contrasts this with the children's rhyme, "Jesus loves me this I know, 'Cause the Bible tells me so."

"Do you believe in rock'n'roll?" pays homage to the Lovin' Spoonful's "Do You Believe In Magic?", another song praising the glories of the Elvis years. "Can you teach me how to dance real slow?" is McLean wondering how he can enjoy spaced-out psychedelic music. McLean returns to 1958 and high school dances - the "pink carnation" relates to Marty Robbins' hit record, "A White Sport Coat (And A Pink Carnation)". "We both kicked off our shoes" refers to "sock hops" where kids would dance in their socks to avoid damage to the gym's floor. He describes the exhilaration of rock'n'roll, "but I knew I was out of luck the day the music died."

"For ten years we've been on our own" refers to the decade following Holly's death when, for various reasons, the leading rock'n'rollers - Elvis Presley, Chuck Berry, Little Richard, Jerry Lee Lewis - lost their creativity. A rolling stone gathers no moss, but here "Moss grows fat on a rolling stone". This is a critical comment on the Rolling Stones or Bob Dylan, who recorded "Like A Rolling Stone", or perhaps a punning reference to them both.

Then, in the third verse, we meet a cast of characters. The Jester is Bob Dylan, who had assumed James Dean's mantle ("a coat he'd borrowed from James Dean"). Many criticised the Rebel with a Cause's singing voice, but his "protest songs" echoed what 20-somethings were thinking. Elvis, acknowledged as the king of rock'n'roll, was making inconsequential beach movies, but who is the queen? I like to think it's Little Richard. Dylan has stolen Elvis' "thorny crown" - a Christ-reference here - and is accused of theft, but McLean can't decide whether or not he has been good for the music. The final part of the verse refers to the Beatles. The quartet practising in the park may be "Sgt Pepper", but John Lennon has become involved in radical politics and is reading "a book of (Karl) Marx".

The fourth verse allows McLean to comment on the late 60s. Charles Manson and his so-called Family committed atrocities and murders, notably of the actress Sharon Tate, in Hollywood. Manson claimed he had been motivated by hidden messages in the Beatles' "Helter Skelter". The "summer swelter" refers to the unrest following the Watts race riots in Los Angeles, admittedly in 1965, four years before Manson.

The Byrds, who recorded "Eight Miles High", were at the forefront of psychedelia and many like-minded rock musicians were busted for possession of marijuana - "it landed foul on the grass". The musicians looked to Bob Dylan for direction but he suffered a motorcycle accident in 1966 and returned with songs of domesticity ("Nashville Skyline"). "The half-time air was sweet perfume" is marijuana again, as the Beatles become Sgt Pepper's Lonely Hearts Club Band. The lines could also be about Vietnam and the US hit single, "The Ballad Of The Green Berets" by S/Sgt Barry Sadler, but I prefer the Beatles' interpretation as they remained on top. ("The marching band refused to yield"). The answer to McLean's question, "Do you recall what was revealed the day the music died?", is that music is meant to be entertaining. ("We all got up to dance, Ah, we never got the chance"), something often forgotten in the late 60s.

Things get worse in the fifth verse and it's like Kris Kristofferson's parody, "Blame It On The Stones", but this time for real. "A generation lost in space" are the 400,000 stoned hippies at the Woodstock festival. In 1966, the Beatles gave their last concert at Candlestick Park, San Francisco, and the Rolling Stones became the greatest touring rock band. In McLean's opinion, Mick Jagger ("Jumping Jack Flash") had been consumed by devil worship ("Their Satanic Majestic Request", "Sympathy For The Devil") and everything culminates in the disastrous Altamont festival. The Stones ridiculously allowed Hell's Angels ("no angel born in Hell") to act as security and they killed a concertgoer, Meridith Hunter.

ROBERT & JOHN F. KENNERDY

In the final verse, Don McLean runs into Janis Joplin (" a girl who sang the blues"). McLean tries to rekindle the music he loves, but no-one is interested. "In the streets the children screamed" relates to that appalling picture of the children running away from the danger in Vietnam. The returning American servicemen are not given a hero's welcome ("The churchbells all were broken"), although this could again refer to the "God is dead" controversy.

We reach the song's final lines - and here McLean must be thinking of the Kennedy and Luther King assassinations - Jack (1963), Bobby (1968) and King (1968). It would be inane to regard Holly, Valens and the Big Bopper as "the Father, Son and Holy Ghost", and why should they be "the three men I admire most"? "They caught the last train for the coast" harks to the gospel songs linking railways with death, although when I heard McLean in concert, he changed the reference to "the last bus".

Where does that leave "American Pie"? Without doubt, it's a negative song about 60s culture, which is why Don McLean has not spoken about it. It would hardly improve his street cred to tell the world that he hated nearly everything about the sexiest decade of the 20th century - unless, of course, he did it in a cryptic song.

And he could have added new verses to "American Pie" as the years went by. As it turned out, he didn't like the 70s anymore than the 60s. Reacting to a bad review in "Melody Maker" in 1978, he wrote, "Cynical rags like 'Melody Maker' continue to sell the disco junk and glitter trash that make the commercial music scene the perverted cesspool it has become, awash with no-talent clowns who do anything to sell records, except make decent music." Sounds like the start of another verse...

MICK JAGGER

AS TIME GOES BY

Part 4   1975-1999

1975 - BOHEMIAN RHAPSODY (Freddie Mercury)

Moorgate tube disaster - Inflation hits 25% - Equal Pay Act - Sex Discrimination Act - Jack Nicholson stars in "One Flew Over The Cuckoo's Nest" - First episodes of "Fawlty Towers".

Queen's album, "A Night At The Opera" included "Bohemian Rhapsody", which is in held in the same mysterious reverence as "A Day In The Life" is to "Sgt Pepper's Lonely Hearts Club Band". In "Bo Rhap", Freddie Mercury wanted to combine a rock ballad with heavy metal, opera and camp theatrics. Queen's producer, Roy Thomas Baker, had the difficult job for fulfilling his requirements. A backing track of piano, bass and drums was recorded first, and, over a three week period, everything else was added. There are 180 vocal overdubs in the "Galileo" section alone, and even Phil Spector's Wall of Sound wasn't as powerful and grandiose as this.

EMI wanted to edit the six minute song for single release but Kenny Everett played it in full on Capital Radio and, from the reaction, EMI realised it was a winner. The stunning video, which made such good use of their faces, was put together quickly and cheaply, and is regarded as the breakthrough in rock videos.

FREDDIE MERCURY

Freddie Mercury never discussed the meaning of his outlandish song, apart from admitting that it was personal. For example, he refers to "Bismillah", which is Islamic for the word of God and something he knew from being raised in Zanzibar. Freddie said, "It's one of those songs which has a fantasy feel about it. People should listen to it, think about it and make up their own minds as to what it says to them." Although this is hardly a song for pub singalongs, so many of its parts of it are well-known. People like to make fun of it, and there are cod lyrics on the Internet as well as novelty versions by Rolf Harris and Frank Sidebottom. The major performers stay away, no doubt realising that no version could compete with

Queen's, which returned to No 1 following the death of Freddie Mercury in 1991.

Another song featuring the phrase "mamma mia" and this time called "Mamma Mia" was a hit for Abba. Roger Whittaker sang "The Last Farewell", Roxy Music declared "Love Is The Drug", 10cc were not in love, and Jackie De Shannon wrote and first recorded "Bette Davis Eyes" in 1975, which was a hit in 1981 for Kim Carnes. Bob Marley took reggae into the mainstream with his childhood memories of living in the government yard in Trench Town in "No Woman, No Cry". The US film composer, John Williams, not to be confused with the English classical guitarist, wrote the tension-packed score for Steven Spielberg's "Jaws". Pete Townsend, mortified at turning 30, wrote "The Who By Numbers" about the problems of being an ageing rock star. One of the lighter moments came with the accordian - based "Squeeze box".

In 1975 the songwriter, David Martin, went to collect his wife, Debbie, from her greetings card shop. When he walked in, she handed him a plain card with a badge and a tear coming down from it. The message was "Can't Smile Without You", and David knew instantly that he had a song title. Martin released it himself on the DJM label and then it was recorded by Engelbert Humperdinck and the Carpenters. It became an international hit when Barry Manilow took it up in 1978.

Nothing sounds more arrogant than Barry Manilow claiming, "I write the songs that make the whole world sing," but he didn't write that song. "I Write The Songs" was written in 1975 by Bruce Johnston of the Beach Boys, who passed it first to The Captain and Tennille. It has subsequently been associated with David Cassidy, Barry Manilow and Frank Sinatra, who amended it to "I Sing The Songs". During the year, Barry Manilow did write a song that made the whole world sing, "Could It Be Magic", although its melody was derived from Chopin's "Prelude In C Minor", a slow, melancholy piece that he wrote for a funeral in 1839.

1976 - DON'T CRY FOR ME ARGENTINA
(Tim Rice - Andrew Lloyd Webber)

The Prime Minister, Harold Wilson, makes way for an older man, James Callaghan - Following sexual allegations, Jeremy Thorpe resigns as leader of Liberal Party - Drought in UK - National Theatre opens.

Following "Jesus Christ Superstar", Tim Rice had been trying to convince Andrew Lloyd Webber to collaborate on a musical about Eva Peron, the ruthless wife of a dictator. In the end, he agreed to "Evita" if Tim would work on "Jeeves". Ultimately, Andrew would work with Alan Ayckbourn on Jeeves, but "Evita" gave them their biggest success, and "Don't Cry For Me Argentina", which Eva sang to her adoring countrymen, was a No 1 hit.

In his autobiography, named after another Evita song, "Oh What A Circus", Tim Rice says, "We now had to switch from writing hats to promotion hats. Could we and the record company convince a record-buying public that had never heard of our dead Argentinean heroine to show interest in an expensive double album which we did not expect to inspire commercial radio play or a hit single?" Ultimately, "Don't Cry For Me Argentina" was so strong that it became No 1 for Julie Covington, and the song has now been recorded by many pop divas. The Shadows took an instrumental version into the Top 10, and Madonna's film version reached No 3 in 1996. (For further details, see the interview with Tim Rice.)

EVA PERON

Johnny Mathis has often recorded seasonal songs - one of his first UK hits was with "Winter Wonderland" - and his albums include "Merry Christmas" (1958), "Sounds Of Christmas" (1963) and "Give Me Your Love For Christmas" (1969). In 1976 he was given the English lyric for an Italian song, "Soleado", "When A Child Is Born" was a curious song. On first hearing, it sounds like a celebration of a baby, any baby, being born. However, the narration refers to a baby that will end misery and suffering forever, so it sounds like the Second Coming to me. Johnny Mathis had the Christmas No 1 and Alan Freeman commented, "What Mathis has done has put some reality into Christmas and made people feel religious all over again." Other versions come from Daniel O'Donnell, with a limp narration, the Fortunes, 100 Tons And A Feather, Ken Dodd, Matt Monro, Kenny Rogers and, best of all, Judy Collins.

Abba created their best-ever dance record with "Dancing Queen" and also recorded "Fernando" and "Money Money Money", which is frequently used in TV financial reports. Bonnie Tyler was "Lost In France", Chicago sang the poignant "If You Leave Me Now", Stephen Stills and Neil Young combined for the glorious "Long May You Run", and Red Sovine recorded a weepie about a crippled boy and his CB radio, "Teddy Bear". Elton John and Kiki Dee had fun with the infectious "Don't Go Breaking My Heart".

Writer/producer Tony Hiller reconstructed Brotherhood Of Man and with a new lineup resembling a British Abba, they won Eurovision with "Save Your Kisses For Me". With a payoff similar to "The Naughty Lady Of Shady Lane" (1954) and "Itsy Bitsy Teenie Weenie Yellow Polkadot Bikini" (1960), the girl in the song is a young child.

Stevie Wonder was accused of pretention with his 2 LP and an EP package, "Songs In The Key Of Life", but the music included "Sir Duke" (a homage to Duke Ellington), "Isn't She Lovely", "As", and "Pastime Paradise", reworked as "Gangsta's Paradise" by Coolio in 1996.

The songwriter, Dave Townsend, wrote "Miss You Nights", while his girlfriend was in Majorca and Cliff Richard loved the song. This superb ballad only made No 15 but it is always in the Top 10 when Cliff fans are polled for his favourite recordings.

The Eagles loved and loathed Los Angeles in equal measures in their observant songs for "Hotel California". The title song had the feel of a film script and Don Henley, who wrote most of the lyrics, said that he was evoking the spirit of Steely Dan. The album was so successful that it was impossible to top it and after "The Long Run" (1979), they went their solo ways. Like Hotel California, you can check out of the Eagles but you can't leave, and there have been reunions in recent years.

The Eagles were typical of the rock dinosaurs hated by the punk or New Wave acts. In December 1976, the Sex Pistols scored their first Top 40 success with "Anarchy In The UK". As far as popular music was concerned, there would be anarchy in the UK and it would have far-reaching effects.

1977 - SEX & DRUGS & ROCK & ROLL
      (Ian Dury - Chaz Jankel)

Start of breakfast TV - Alpha Bravo oil risk disaster - Red Rum wins third Grand National - Queen Elizabeth's Silver Jubilee - Freddie Laker's low-budget Skytrain - Search for "Yorkshire Ripper" - Deaths of Groucho Marx and Charlie Chaplin - Woody Allen releases "Annie Hall"

"I didn't think much of punk music," Ian Dury told me in 1998, " we were a heavy duty funk band with punky vocals from me. The Blockheads was next best thing to the Average White Band. We weren't really of that genre. I thought punk was a bit of a joke and it would burn out as quick as it did, but as I was 35 years old, five foot nothing, gruesome looking and couldn't sing, punk music helped me a lot. My manager said, 'You have to think of yourself as being like Muddy Waters to the Rolling Stones' and I thought, 'Bollocks to that'."

Ian Dury found himself at the front of New Wave with his album, "New Boots And Panties", which only cost £4,000 to make. He had previously led Kilburn and the High Roads, but his association with the keyboard player, Chaz Jankel, brought about the perfect setting for his witty, London-drenched lyrics. That first album by Ian Dury and the Blockheads included his comments on Essex man ("Billericay Dickie"), his stunning tribute to a rock'n'roll hero ("Sweet Gene Vincent"), the sadness of "My Old Man" and even a love song, "Wake Up And Make Love To Me". He followed the album with a great single, "Sex & Drugs & Rock & Roll":

IAN DURY

> *"Sex & drugs & rock & roll*
> *Is all my brain and body need*
> *Sex & drugs & rock & roll*
> *Is very good indeed."*

I asked Ian if he had actually coined the phrase, "sex and drugs and rock and roll", which has now passed into the language. "Yeah, I put the three things together and 'The Oxford Book of Quotations' gives me credit for it. It wasn't a major deduction, it was quite simple and bloody obvious. Another phrase is 'reasons to be cheerful', which

I also think I first structured. I wrote the song to say, 'Is that all there is?', and I said the question quite gently, 'Keep your silly ways, Or throw them out the window.' I didn't write the song as a paean to sex and drugs and rock and roll, but as soon as we started playing it, everyone started singing it. The chorus was built for group singing, and I couldn't say no to that. I can't deny the people the right to enjoy these things. So it was a dichotomy. On one side it was a question and on the other, a celebration."

Hardly surprisingly, the single was banned by the BBC but Ian Dury and the Blockheads were soon having hit singles with "What A Waste", "Hit Me With Your Rhythm Stick" (both 1978) and "Reasons To Be Cheerful (Part 3)" (1979), which was one of his many "list songs". I've always been partial to his music hall song, "England's Glory", which was recorded by Max Wall. Ian Dury titled one album after the average lifespan, "4,000 Weeks Holiday", but he didn't get that far himself and died in 2000. Luckily, he went out on a high note as his 1998 album, "Mr Love Pants", was very good indeed. There ain't 'arf been some clever bastards.

When another pub band, Dire Straits, performed "Sultans Of Swing" for Charlie Gillett on BBC Radio London in 1977, almost every A&R man in London was listening and the group was inundated with offers. With colourful, descriptive lyrics, "Sultans Of Swing" told of the joys and tensions of playing in a pub band and it became their first hit in 1979.

The 70s may be the decade that fashion forgot, but the Bee Gees' music has an enduring appeal, even if they still choose to look like relics from the 70s. Their songs are currently being revived more often than the Beatles'. The double-album for "Saturday Night Fever" sold 20 million copies and the key songs - "Jive Talkin'", "Night Fever", "Stayin' Alive" - come from the Brothers Gibb. "How Deep Is Your Love" is an excellent ballad with some killer harmonies, and it is a song that will last as long as the Beatles' work. The Bee Gees hadn't written "How Deep Is Your Love" specifically for "Saturday Night Fever": at the time, they didn't even know if there was a love scene in the script.

By 1977 Eric Clapton had already had a scattered career that took in the Yardbirds, John Mayall's Bluesbreakers, Cream, Derek and the Dominos and now solo work. He had been known from the start as "Slowhand", the title of his 1977 LP. The album included J.J. Cale's "Cocaine" and John Martyn's "May You Never" as well as his own "Lay Down Sally" and "Wonderful Tonight". "Lay Down Sally" is a cheery crowd-pleaser, but the depth of feeling in "Wonderful Tonight" gives it a resonance that grows with the decades. It's a love song to his wife Patti that also acknowledges his failings and is soaked in his blues spirit.

1999

It was a strong year for film music as Carly Simon sang the best of the James Bond themes, "Nobody Does It Better", while Barbra Streisand sang "Evergreen" in "A Star Is Born". John Williams wrote the memorable scores for "Star Wars" and "Close Encounters Of The Third Kind". Patti D'Arbanville, herself the subject of a 1970 Cat Stevens song, starred in the soft - core "Bilitis" with an appropiate score from Francis Lai. Elvis Costello's TV-spoof "Watchin' The Detectives" marked him out as someone to watch, Tom Waits mumbled his way through "Tom Traubert's Blues" which was subtitled "Four sheets to the wind in Copenhagen", Leo Sayer sang the ballad "When I Need You" and Queen wrote a football anthem, "We Are The Champions".

KATE BUSH

Fleetwood Mac were another flavour of the year but their songs were rarely strong enough to become standards - still, "Go Your Own Way" was very listenable. Talking Heads had the benefit of disturbing songs from David Byrne, especially the spooky "Psycho Killer": "Psycho killer, psycho killer, Que c'est-ce que c'est, Que c'est-ce que c'est?" It's very unhip to say this but the cover version by the acapella band, the Flying Pickets was brilliant.

Although I applauded the concept of punk and the idea of rock'n'roll becoming a proletarian music again, I didn't care for many of the records.

Malcolm McLaren brilliantly orchestrated the release of the Sex Pistols' "God Save The Queen" so that it coincided with Her Majesty's silver jubilee. The record is shown as No 2 in "The Guinness Book Of Hit Singles", although it was outselling everything else that week. The chart was fiddled - and this is true - so that Her Majesty would not be offended. How could she be offended by something as ridiculously stupid as "God save the Queen / A fascist regime"?

1978 - WUTHERING HEIGHTS
(Kate Bush)

Amoco Cadiz runs aground at Brittany - Cambridge sinks in the Boat Race - The Pole, John Paul II, is third Pope in a year and the first non-Italian in 400 years - Christopher Reeve is Superman and Robert DeNiro stars in "The Deer Hunter"

Kate Bush, who was born in 1958, wrote "Man With The Child In His Eyes", another 1978 hit, when only 14. She was discovered by Dave Gilmour of Pink Floyd when 16 and signed by EMI. In an unprecedented move, they decided not to launch her career straightaway but to wait until her talent had developed. She studied mime and dancing with Lindsey Kemp, and her first single, "Wuthering Heights", ranks among the most extraordinary debuts of all-time.

Kate Bush loved Emily Brontë's dramatic novel of passion on the Yorkshire moors, "Wuthering Heights", and she was inspired by the final page in which Cathy goes wandering on the moors looking for Heathcliff, whom she knows to be dead. Kate sang "It's me, it's Cathy, come home again" in a high-pitched, ethereal, demented voice, which emphasised her love for him. Love, it seemed, transcended everything including death. "Wuthering Heights" was promoted as a romantic single and released in time for Valentine's Day, 1978.

The album, "The Kick Inside", did equally well, but Kate was not too happy as being promoted as Britain's newest sex symbol. She said, "The media just promoted me as a female body. It's like I've had to prove that I'm an artist inside a female body". She performed live with elaborate sets the next year and for "Wuthering Heights", she wore a Victorian nightdress that she had bought on a stall in King's Road.

Kate Bush knows how to handle fame, but Gerry Rafferty has always found it uncomfortable. In the 1960s, the Paisley-born singer-songwriter toured the UK folk clubs with Billy Connolly as the Humblebums, and then made a solo album, "Can I Have My Money Back?" Moving to Stealers Wheel, Rafferty and Joe Egan recorded "Stuck In The Middle With You", a comment on their management, used to great effect in "Reservoir Dogs". Hating the deceit of miming, he refused to open his lips while the record was played on "Top Of The Pops". By 1978, after three years of litigation, he was a solo artist and had written a killer album of imaginative songs, "City To City". The key song, "Baker Street", became an international hit. It was a hit before Rafferty even sang a weary word because it opened magnificently with Raphael Ravenscroft's strident saxophone solo.

Gerry Rafferty's songs often depict the pressures of the city, and "Baker Street" tells of various characters whose dreams are shattered through living in London. Its success should have led to a slew of great albums, but Rafferty was never comfortable with the acclaim and hated press conferences, regarding them as "Fools to the left of me, jokers to the right." He has recorded fine work since "City To City", but not nearly enough of it and with very little promotion. To quote the title of a 1978 hit by Ian Dury and the Blockheads, "What A Waste".

"Grease", the Broadway musical about American teenagers in the 1950s, included "Summer Nights", but the film producers wanted more hit songs. As Olivia Newton-John was co-starring with John Travolta, her current songwriter and producer, John Farrar, was asked to write something very commercial. The former Shadow wrote "Hopelessly Devoted To You" and the duet "You're The One That I Want". Despite its frenzied pace, everyone knows the words of "You're The One That I Want", but it's the wordless "oo-oo-oo" that really makes it.

The Rolling Stones caught the moment with their disco song, "Miss You", a legendary riff that will be around a long time. Errol Brown wrote "Every 1's A Winner", a song that has a future as long as there are commercials, and Lionel Richie wrote the soul ballad, "Three Times A Lady". Warren Zevon, normally an intense singer-songwriter, had great fun with "Werewolves Of London", which was produced by Jackson Browne. Jackson Browne himself had a US hit with "Running On Empty". Elton John's instrumental for a delivery boy who died, "Song For Guy", contained more passion than his more explosive works.

Joe Walsh of the Eagles was checking out of Hotel California after trashing the rooms. His hit single, "Life's Been Good", told of the debauched life of a rock star and indicated that life wasn't good at all. Indeed, a bored rock dinosaur like Walsh was a bigger threat to a hotel's well-being than any number of punk acts. The song had a grounding in fact as his manager had, somewhat unwisely, given him a chain saw for Christmas.

1979 - I WILL SURVIVE
(Dina Fekaris, Freddie Perren)

> The Shah of Iran deposed by Ayatollah Kohmeini - Margaret Thatcher becomes UK's first woman PM - Earl Mountbatten killed by IRA bomb - US hostages held in Iran, not freed until 1981 - Rubik's cube - The winter of discontent.

Gloria Gaynor had her first hits in 1975, but she lost ground to Donna Summer, had a turbulent personal life and, after falling backwards into a monitor while performing, had spinal surgery. Her producers wrote an inspirational song which summarised her predicament, "I Will Survive", and it became an international hit, both for her and for country singer, Billie Jo Spears. "I Will Survive" is used to illustrate someone fighting adversity and it has also become a gay anthem.

Gloria Gaynor, who later recorded "I Am What I Am", says, "I don't sing these songs to myself. I sing them to my public as encouragement. I feel that a person ought to feel good about himself and if you heard one of those songs and cannot relate to them, then you ought to check out why it is that you don't like yourself, why you don't think you might survive and why you are not saying 'I am what I am' with conviction." So there.

The Bee Gees had their eyes on the disco ball with "Tragedy" and Art Garfunkel took Mike Batt's ballad about rabbits to the top, "Bright Eyes". Kenny Rogers sang the first hit song about multiple rape, "Coward of the County", Roxy Music were dancing away, and Police had a message in a bottle. Cliff Richard recorded his first anthem with "We Don't Talk Anymore" and Dr. Hook were at their most infectious with "When You're In Love With A Beautiful Woman". Brian Eno released his LP, "Music For Airports", a halfway house on the flight path to New Age music.

Paul Weller's songs for the Jam's LP, "Setting Sons", was about three lads (a businessman, a revolutionary and someone in the middle) who survive a civil war and are reunited by the end of the record. The album included "Wasteland", "Private Hell" and an incisive look at class warfare, "The Eton Rifles", and despite the Jam's contemporary edge, their love of 60s bands like the Kinks, the Who and Creation is evident. "Rolling Stone" nominated the Clash's amphetamine-driven "London Calling" as the best album of the 1980s, although it was released in the UK in 1979. The Clash revived Sonny Curtis' song for the Crickets and later the Bobby Fuller Four, "I Fought The Law" (1960), which summarised their lifestyle and proved as enduring as Joe Strummer's angry, abrasive songs.

ABBA

Pink Floyd recorded a double-album, "The Wall", and the key song was Roger Waters' "Another Brick In The Wall (Part 2)". The song was to feature a choir of schoolchildren in the background, but Pink Floyd was so impressed that the children shared the lead vocals and hence, made the point that they didn't "need no education".

Squeeze sang the quirky "Cool For Cats", which came from Chris Difford watching Benny Hill sing a nonsense song on TV. Monty Python's highly original look at the life of Christ, sorry Brian, had Eric Idle singing "Always Look On The Bright Side Of Life" while he was being crucified. The scene's black humour provided "The Life Of Brian" with a remarkable ending, although the song has become a cheerful starter for whistling football crowds.

1980 -   THE WINNER TAKES IT ALL
        (Benny Andersson - Bjorn Ulvaeus)

        Start of war between Iran and Iraq - Insider
        dealing made illegal - Lech Walesa forms
        Solidarity, an illegal confederation of trade
        unions in Poland - Sony Walkman launched -
        John Lennon assassinated.

Since winning the Eurovision Song Contest with "Waterloo" in 1974, Abba had had a succession of international hits. Björn and Benny understood the appeal of Swedish girls singing love songs in English with slight accents. The public loved their own romance as Benny and Anni-Frid were one married couple and Björn and Agnetha another. In reality, there was tension between the girls and also between all four of them and their manager, Stig Anderson.

Björn and Agnetha were constantly criticising each other and ended up destroying their love. Things came apart while they were off the road in 1978, possibly because they didn't have to wear their media faces for a while. Agnetha took up with her psychiatrist, as you do, and Björn said their divorce would not affect Abba. He can't have believed that as his writing became more intimate and, ironically, in the last months of Abba, he and Benny were at their most creative. As a Swedish proverb states, "If everything is going to hell, let there be music."

Björn wrote about the coldness of divorce in "The Winner Takes It All" and then passed the vulnerable song over to Agnetha to sing. She looked less glamorous in the video, more like someone who had been dragged through a divorce court backwards:

> *"The gods may throw a dice,*
> *Their minds as cold as ice,*
> *And someone way down here*
> *Loses someone dear."*

The tours became jaded and "Super Trouper", also 1980, made no attempt at disguising their dislike for the road:

> *"All I do is eat and sleep and sing,*
> *Wishing every show was the last one."*

The phrase, "super trouper", which came from a lighting rig, has now passed into the language.

Jona Lewie wrote a love song and included the word, "gallantry". On a whim, he changed it to "cavalry", which gave him the idea of writing about the Charge of the Light Brigade. The song, "Stop The Cavalry", also touches on the World Wars and fallout shelters. The Jam had a No 1 single with "Going Underground" with its concern for nuclear war, a considerable threat in the light of Russia's invasion of Afghanistan. Roy Orbison, asked about the sadness of his own songs, replied that he had never written anything as nihilistic as "Going Underground". Note the many references to London in Weller's songs including "'A' Bomb In Wardour Street" and "Down In The Tube Station At Midnight".

MARTIN LUTHER KING. JR.

Peter Gabriel wrote about an African leader who had died in police custody in "Biko", while Stevie Wonder dedicated his 1980 album, "Hotter Than July", to the non-violent campaigner for civil rights, Martin Luther King. In "Happy Birthday", he asked the country to adopt legislation to make King's birthday, 15th January, a national holiday and, remarkably, this has happened. How many other songs have had such consequences?

Ian Curtis, the lead singer and chief songwriter, of Joy Division was a troubled man, which brought an edge to his songs, although many of the troubles were of his own making. His health had deteriorated when "Love Will Tear Us Apart" was released in 1980, and on the verge of his greatest success, he killed himself.

When John Lennon was recording his comeback album, "Double Fantasy", he referred to "Woman" as his "1964 Beatles song". He wrote the tender song as yet another apology for his bad behaviour to Yoko Ono. Todd Rundgren wrote a whole album of Beatles-inspired songs with "Deface The Music", which he recorded as part of Utopia. Blondie were at their best with "The Tide Is High" and that orchestral man hovering in the dark came up with "Enola Gay".

1981 - GHOST TOWN (Jerry Dammers)

Former film star, Ronald Reagan becomes US president - Wedding of Prince Charles and Lady Diana - President Reagan and Pope John Paul II survive assassination attempts - 110 die when aerial walkways collapse at Kansas City hotel - Dr Owen leads the "gang of four" and forms the SDP - AIDS is first identified.

Jerry Dammers was the brainchild behind 2 Tone, the label set up for the reggae-based punk groups like Madness, the Beat, the Selecter and his own band, the Specials. He captured the unrest and unease in the inner cities in the haunting "Ghost Town", but by the time their record was released, the newspapers were full of urban violence and riots. The Specials' song, written about Coventry, articulated the feelings of many youths and acted as a warning, largely unheeded, to the Conservative government. The song still has relevance, but even if it hadn't, its chorus would still be remembered.

Two phrases from novelty songs, "Shaddup Your Face" and "The Oldest Swinger In Town", have passed into the language.

Midge Ure of Ultravox wrote and performed a killer single in "Vienna", a song that indicated that holiday romances are often just that. Smokey Robinson wrote a touching love song with "Being With You" and Diana Ross and Lionel Richie sang "Endless Love", the title song from a totally forgettable film. Bucks Fizz were at their best with "The Land Of Make Believe" and Squeeze were "Labelled With Love". Christopher Cross wrote and recorded the Oscar-winning "Arthur's Theme (Best That You Can Do)" and everything got "Physical" for Olivia Newton-John.

In New York, Dr John, then a drug addict, got together with Doc Pomus, who had jacked in songwriting for a card school. Together they wrote the best blues songs of the period, none better than an album for B.B. King, "There Must Be A Better World Somewhere". The title song is so full of feeling, and Dr John recalls, "I brought an old hymn from New Orleans, an old spiritual church hymn, and the first line was, 'This earth ain't no place I'm proud to call home,' and I forgot all about it. A couple of years later Doc says, 'You know, I finished that song.' I didn't know what he was talking about but it came out of that old hymn. When I walked in, it was finished. I put some music to it and it was a natural piece."

DR JOHN AND DOC POMUS

Instrumentals came back into fashion with ambient, synthesiser-based background music, called New Age. This hip easy listening of the 80s avoided the schmaltz of muzak but also avoided anything disturbing or even melodic. The key instrumental of the year was more dramatic, being Vangelis' theme for the true story of two runners, Harold Abrahams and Eric Liddell, in the 1924 Paris Olympics, "Chariots Of Fire". The music led to a High Court action in which Vangelis was accused of plagiarising the theme from the 1975 Greek TV series, "City Of Violets". Vangelis won the case as the judge accepted that the four-note melody found in both pieces of music was common to Greek music: "Any resemblance in the use by both composers of a sharp fall and rise in the music was coincidence."

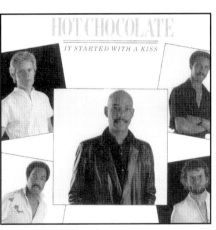

HOT CHOCOLATE

1982 - SHIPBUILDING
(Elvis Costello - Clive Langer)

Falklands war between Britain and Argentina - Princess Grace dies in car crash - Brezhnev dies - First CD players on sale - Mexico defaults on loan, highlighting the problems of Third World debts - "E.T." - Poland lifts martial law.

To everyone's surprise, Britain found itself at war with Argentina over the Falklands and the conflict would have tragic consequences for both sides. Considering the vehemence of some of Elvis Costello's political songs, he wrote about the conflict in a surprisingly subdued way with "Shipbuilding". In the song, a father appreciates that there may be more work in his area if the shipyards reopen, but he could be making the ship in which his son would be killed. Elvis Costello gave the lyric to the producer, Clive Langer, who had Robert Wyatt's high-pitched delivery in mind when he wrote the melody. Robert Wyatt recorded the song for a remarkable single with Langer on organ and Steve Nieve, piano. It became a hit on its reissue the following year when Cruise missiles came to the UK. (There is an interview with Elvis Costello later in this book.) Another hit song about the Falklands war is "Glad It's All Over", a chart entry by Captain Sensible.

"I love 'It Started With A Kiss'," says Hot Chocolate's Errol Brown, "It's a lovely pop song. I woke up with the idea and thought it was a tremendous title. I wrote it about my first love at school when I was seven. Her name was Barbara Blackwood." The infectious song was a big hit and once again, it has been taken up by commercials. Errol Brown has seen a surge of interest in his own work following Hot Chocolate's inclusion on "The Full Monty" soundtrack with 1975's "You Sexy Thing" and when he makes concert appearances, the audience cries, "Get your kit off." Inevitable really: it started with a kiss is bound to lead to the Full Monty.

Marvin Gaye was at his sensual best with "Sexual Healing", but his lifestyle was making him unreliable. Stevie Wonder teamed up with Paul McCartney for "Ebony And Ivory", oddly enough stemming from a Spike Milligan TV sketch about segregated pianos. The combination of Crystal Gayle and Tom Waits for the film soundtrack, "One From The Heart", was inspired and the songs, especially "Take Me Home", were very good. Irene Cara sang the disco classic, "Fame", and it was a good year for key songs from leading groups: Pete Wylie led the Mighty Wah! through "The Story Of The Blues", Madness wrote "Our House" because most of them had come from broken homes, and Culture Club were at their catchiest with "Do You Really Want To Hurt Me?".

Kevin Rowland of Dexy's Midnight Runners loved Squeeze's record, "Labelled With Love", but thought that the line, "drinks to remember I'm me and myself" was "drinks to remember Eileen and myself". When he learnt the right lyric, he resolved to put the name, Eileen, into his own song. "Come On Eileen" is intriguing with its opening line, "Poor old Johnnie Ray" and its "too roo loo ay a" chorus.

STING AND THE POLICE

Mick Jones of the Clash says that "Should I Stay Or Should I Go" was "a good rocking song, our attempt at writing a classic." Like "Louie, Louie", it has a killer riff and indeed, you could imagine it being recorded by a doowop group in the 1950s. The song made the UK Top 20 but it went to No l on the back of a jeans commercial in 1991.

Bryan Ferry, a man who doesn't know what a bad hair day is, wrote about the King Arthur fantasy in "Avalon", and Avalon is reputed to be on the site that is now Glastonbury. The LP, "Avalon", could have been a concept album but it wasn't. Ferry says, "I've often thought that I should do an album where the songs are all bound together in the style of 'West Side Story', but it's always seemed like too much bother to do it that way."

1983 - EVERY BREATH YOU TAKE (Sting)

Soviets shoot down straying passenger plane from South Korea - Successful moon walk and first US female astronaut - Lech Walesa award ed Nobel Peace Prize - £2.6m in gold stolen from Heathrow

Many of the performers who became successful during the punk years were musically accomplished. Right from the start, Sting showed a flair for fusing words and music, and Police featured himself (a former jazz singer and bassist), and two other experienced musicians, Andy Summers from Soft Machine and Stewart Copeland from Curved Air. Sting's talent so overwhelmed the Police that their own songs were reduced to album fillers, which led to enormous tensions. In 1983 they released their fifth, and what was to be their final, album, "Synchronicity". As usual, Summers and Copeland had to fight for their tunes and the album was dominated by Sting's lyrics, melodies and voice - and, let's face it, Andy Summers' "Mother" is the worst song on the album.

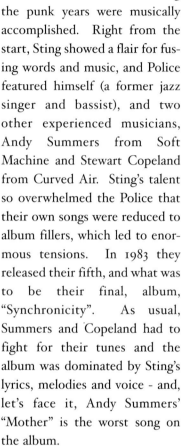

Sting had taken time off to write the songs for the album by renting a house in Jamaica. This was no ordinary house but Goldeneye, a house built by Ian Fleming, James Bond's creator. He sat at Fleming's desk to write his lyrics and he played Noël Coward's piano, which was also in the house. Unable to sleep one night, he want to the piano and within minutes, he was writing 'Every Breath You Take'. Sting has said that the riff was a homage to the Hungarian composer, Béla Bartok, but it also reflects the end of his marriage to the actress Frances Tomelty: it is, if you like, Sting's "Yesterday".

In interviews, Sting didn't want to discuss his marriage but he did add, "My personal life is in my songs. Many of them seem quite contradictory and I seem to be two people: on the one hand, a morose, doom-laden character, and on the other, a happy-go-lucky maniac." "The Times", in reviewing "Every Breath You Take", called it,

"A couple of bars' worth of music, a strong central thought and two minutes with a rhyming dictionary producing a perfect pop construction."

It was one of the most sinister songs to top the UK charts, an anthem for a stalker. Sting said, "I consider it a fairly nasty song. It's about surveillance and ownership and jealousy."

"Every Breath You Take" won a Grammy as the Song of the Year and somewhat incongruously, John Denver accepted the award on Sting's behalf. Sting reworked the song as an anti-nuclear ballad and added a coda to "Love Is The Seventh Wave" (1985) of "Every cake you bake, every leg you break."

The feud between the rap singers, 2Pac and the Notorious B.I.G, resulted in both their deaths. The producer, Puff Daddy, was horrified to see his friend, Chris Wallace (alias B.I.G), die in front of him and he recorded a tribute single with B.I.G's wife, Faith Evans. Called "I'll Be Missing You", it featured new lyrics to Police's "Every Breath You Take", and so the melody went to No 1 for the second time in 1997. Considering that we are dealing with tough, streetwise rappers, it's ironic that the new lyric was more tender than Sting's original.

You are not, incidentally, going to find much about rap in these pages. This book is concentrating on hit songwriting and so many rap songs, by their very nature, have little or no melody. I don't care for the exhibitionism of the performers, the persistent bad language and, indeed, the whole aggressive lifestyle. For all that, Grandmaster Flash and Melle Mel's 1983 hit, "White Lines (Don't Don't Do It)" is unquestionably powerful and is rap's finest moment.

It's fascinating to watch Yes in concert. Their lengthy songs ramble away from the main theme and yet for all their meandering, the musicians come back together at precisely the right moment. They have never shown much interest in writing three-minute commercial singles and their chart successes have been largely by chance. However, everything came together for one of their catchiest tunes, "Owner Of A Lonely Heart", a US No 1, which was produced by Trevor Horn and marked the return of their high-pitched lead vocalist, Jon Anderson, in 1983. With a few changes, "Owner Of A Lonely Heart" could just as easily been a Bee Gees hit.

Frankie Goes To Hollywood took their name from an illustration by Guy Peellaert in his 1974 "Rock Dreams" book showing Frank Sinatra going to Hollywood. The BBC ban helped of course, but "Relax" would have reached No 1 without the controversy as it was a remarkable pop record. The suggestive song, written by three of the band, was given a bulldozing production by Trevor Horn. Mike Read criticised the song on his breakfast show for its message of gay sex and the record, which had been on the Radio 1 playlist, was banned. It spent 48 consecutive weeks on the charts and thereby outlasted the follow-ups, "Two Tribes" and "The Power Of Love", which returned to the charts in 2000. The two million UK sales were helped by a brilliant but cynical marketing campaign which involved numerous remixes, T-shirts, slogans and an infamous video.

But does the song's origin go back to 1602 with "Hamlet" as Shakespeare wrote:

"Young men will do't
If they come to't
By cock,
they are to blame."

Another over the top production, "Total Eclipse Of The Heart", gave Bonnie Tyler her first No 1 and the Eurythmics had their first Top 10 hit with "Sweet Dreams (Are Made Of This)". Billy Joel played homage to the Four Seasons with "Uptown Girl", Joe Cocker and Jennifer Warnes were "Up Where We Belong", Roberta Flack and Peabo Bryson were celebrating their love, and Kenny and Dolly found islands in the stream. Michael Jackson was outselling everyone with "Billie Jean", "Beat It" and several others from his "Thriller" album.

Performers like songs they can identify with, hence the popularity of "The Wind Beneath My Wings", which was written by Larry Henley, formerly of the Newbeats, and dealt with the problems faced when one partner is far better known than the other. That kind of confessional songwriting was nothing compared to Loudon Wainwright's "Fame And Wealth", which was self-revealing even by his standards. He told of a drunken night in "April Fool's Day Morn" without revealing any positive side to his personality.

I knew that Willy Russell wrote songs as I had seen him in the early 1970s, but I was amazed by the quality of his work on the first night of "Blood Brothers" with Barbara Dickson at the Liverpool Playhouse. The leading role has since been played by Stephanie Lawrence, Carole King, Petula Clark, Kiki Dee and Helen Reddy, and "Tell Me It's Not True" has become a standard. The song about Marilyn Monroe is fragmented in the musical and hence, on the albums, and if it were put together as a continuous whole, it could still be a major song. Willy Russell has written occasional TV or film themes since "Blood Brothers" (eg Rebecca Storm's "The Show" for "Connie" in 1985), but he has not written a second musical.

The troubles in Northern Ireland were captured in U2's "Sunday Bloody Sunday":

> *"The trenches, deep within our hearts,*
> *And mothers, children, brothers, sisters, torn apart."*

Bono waved a white flag on stage and said, "I'd like to see a united Ireland but I don't believe that you can hold a gun to someone's head to make him see your way."

1984 -   DO THEY KNOW IT'S CHRISTMAS
          (Bob Geldof - Midge Ure)

          Andropov dies - Soviets withdraw from
          Olympics - Assassination of Indira Gandhi,
          succeeded by her son, Rajiv - Landslide
          victory for President Reagan - Gas leak at
          Union Carbide in India kills and maims
          thousands.

All-star charity singles date back to the 1950s but Bob Geldof of the Boomtown Rats recorded one on an unprecedented scale. He saw a TV report of the famine in Ethopia and he determined to do something straight-away. "I'm not interested in the bloody system", he said, "Why has he no food? Why is he starving to death?' He and Midge Ure wrote a song about their plight and they asked current UK chart artists to record it with them. Bob Geldof asked the stars to "leave their egos outside the studio" and recorded the song with no hassles. The Band Aid single sold 3.5m copies in the UK and in 1989, the song was revived by a new crop of chart stars as Band Aid II. Outside of the public spiritedness, it shouldn't be overlooked that Bob Geldof and Midge Ure wrote a classic Christmas song.

Stevie Wonder's "I Just Called To Say I Love You" came from the Gene Wilder film, "The Woman In Red", while I've heard Ray Parker Jr's theme for "Ghostbusters" belted out by the Royal Liverpool Philharmonic Orchestra. Lionel Richie said "Hello" and Willie Nelson said hello to Julio Iglesias as "To All The Girls I've Loved Before", was made to establish Julio in the US. Bruce Springsteen attacked the treatment of American vets in "Born In The USA", which was misunderstood by President Reagan, who, with Rambo mentality, quoted it as a patriotic song.

Chaka Khan had a No 1 with "I Fell For You" and Madonna had her first hits with "Holiday", "Lucky Star", "Borderline" and "Like A Virgin". Because of all the publicity surrounding Madonna, the media has been overlooked the fact that she is a very good songwriter and has written most of her hit singles.

The Smiths recorded "Heaven Knows I'm Miserable Now" and Morrissey said, "When I had no job, I could pinpoint my depression, but when I did get a job, I was still depressed." It is a repetitive lyric but it hangs together very well.

George Michael and Andrew Ridgeley were having hits with the rhythm-based duo, Wham!, and they had decided that "Careless Whisper", a ballad George had written in 1979, would not be suitable. By 1983, George was thinking in terms of a solo career and he recorded the song, first in America with Jerry Wexler, and then more to his own satisfaction with himself. For all that, it was not a song that had taken long to write. He said, "It disappoints me that you can write a lyric very flippantly and it can mean so much to so many people." "Careless Whisper" is a very good song, certainly the equal of the ones that George has sweated over, but for someone who is regarded as a major league singer-songwriter, he has published less than 100 songs over the years.

1985 -   WE ARE THE WORLD
(Michael Jackson - Lionel Richie)

Gorbachev becomes Russian leader and promises reforms, known as "Glasnost" - Several skyjacks make Americans uneasy - Heysel and Bradford disasters - Start of "EastEnders" - Formation of Red Wedge..

America responded to the Band Aid single with USA For Africa. After three days of individual preparation, Michael Jackson and Lionel Richie wrote the song in a few hours - "I'd throw out a line and Michael would come back with a greater one," said Lionel. Unlike the sadness of the British entry, "We Are The World" could be regarded as tub-thumping for America.

The song was recorded after the Grammys ceremony. There were so many stars that Bette Midler, Smokey Robinson and Waylon Jennings were not even given solo lines. The video itself is a remarkable piece of pop history and as Ben Elton remarked, "You must know who Bob Dylan is. He's the one who can't sing in the 'We Are The World' video." Like "Do They Know It's Christmas", "We Are The World" is a chant that everyone knows. The Canadian Band Aid single, "Tears Are Not Enough" by Northern Lights (Neil Young, Joni Mitchell, Bryan Adams et al), was not released as a single in the UK, although it is an excellent song.

It was also the year of the Live Aid concert. Two good but somewhat critical songs on this subject are "Hard Day On The Planet" (Loudon Wainwright) and "July 13th 1985" (John Wesley Harding).

Frankie Goes To Hollywood and Huey Lewis and the News had had hits with different songs called "The Power Of Love", but another song of the same title and performed by Jennifer Rush was even more successful. "Material Girl" (Madonna), "Easy Lover" (Philip Bailey and Phil Collins), "Saving All My Love For You" (Whitney Houston) are enduring songs, and so too, in a quirky way, is "Life In A Northern Town." (Dream Academy). The rumbling tension of Richard Thompson's "When The Spell Is Broken" is as good as anything he's written, and the whole album, "Across A Crowded Room", was one of his best. Prince's "Nothing Compares 2 U" was released by The Family in 1985 and later became a hit for Sinead

O'Connor. Fairport Convention regrouped and recorded an excellent Ralph Mc Tell song, "The Hiring Fair", which could have been written 200 years earlier.

The lead singer of Marillion, Fish (real name, Derek Dick, so why did he change it?) loved Clifford T. Ward's song, "Home Thoughts From Abroad", with its many references to domestic life. He put his own spin on the idea in "Kayleigh", the title being a reference to his former girlfriend, Kay.

Mark Knopfler walked to the TV and electrical section at the back of a store in New York City. There was a wall of sets, all tuned to MTV, and the shelf-stacker was leaning on his trolley and telling the customers his views of the videos. Knopfler was so amused that he sat in a kitchen display in the window and wrote the song, "Money For Nothing". At the time, many artists did trailers for MTV saying, "I Want My MTV" and Knopfler asked Sting to sing those words to the title line of his hit, "Don't Stand So Close To Me". He ended up with 20% of the publishing for this. The song appeared on Dire Straits' best-selling album, "Brothers In Arms", and was also a top selling single. It has been misinterpreted as many have thought that Knopfler was expressing his own views and not those of the warehouse man. "Gay News" attacked him, but Knopfler retained his humour, playing guitar on a spoof version by Weird Al Yankovic.

MARK KNOPFLER

The concept of Red Wedge, formed in 1985, was to encourage young people to vote, although its very name, which came from Billy Bragg, suggested that the vote should be Labour. Paul Weller, Jimmy Somerville and Tom Robinson joined Bragg on a Red Wedge tour in 1986. The in - your - face campaigning was unintentionally patronising and as Bragg wrote in 1988's "Waiting for The Great Leap Forwards":

*"Mixing pop and politics, he asks me what the use is
I offer him embarrassment and my usual excuses,"*

By 1996, Bragg was not happy with new Labour:

*"Where are the principles of the friend
I thought I knew
I guess you let them fade from Red to Blue."*

("From Red To Blue")

1986 - SOMEWHERE OUT THERE
(James Horner - Barry Mann - Cynthia Weil)

Duvalier flees from Haiti to France - Return of Halley's Comet - Desmond Tutu made arch bishop in South Africa - Controversial US arms sales to Iran and Nicaraguan Contras - The Mexican wave is established.

The songwriter, Cynthia Weil, told me how a new outlet for pop songs arose. "This was long before the Disney films and animation had made their comeback, and once again, Steven Spielberg was ahead of his time. He was very attracted to the story in 'An American Tail' but we thought it would be a little mouse movie that only kids would see. There was no pressure on us to come up with a hit song. The script said, 'Fievel and his sister on opposite sides of the city look out of their windows and sing a song called "The Mouse In The Moon".' And I said, "Do I have to call it this song, 'The Mouse In The Moon?'" They said, 'No, that's just a thought, write whatever you want to,' and so we wrote 'Somewhere Out There'. When Steven Spielberg heard it, he said, 'Oh, I'm so glad you've written a hit.' I thought, 'What is he talking about? This is not a hit song, this is just a beautiful little ballad and it is never going to happen.'. I couldn't have been more wrong. 'Somewhere Out There' works on many levels although I wasn't thinking of anything but the movie at the time. Someone wanted to use it for an organisation for adopted children as it could mean so much to a kid who didn't know where his birth parents were. Now, they have the idea that every animated movie should have a hit song!"

For many years, Chris de Burgh had only a cult following. Relatively few people in the UK bought his albums and he had never had a hit single. All that changed when he wrote a song for his wife, Diane, "The Lady In Red", and he said, "It's about being at a dance or a disco where the girl you're with is surrounded by admirers. You're standing watching, stunned by the fact that she's looking incredibly beautiful." It became Fergie's favourite song, perhaps because she regarded it as a paean to red hair. Rather foolishly, de Burgh wrote about his feelings for the babysitter, "Blonde Hair Blue Jeans", in 1994 and had to work hard to save his marriage.

The songwriter, Dennis Morgan, found himself at Salisbury Cathedral and he prayed that he could have a good song to take to MIDEM, a musical festival in Cannes. He was writing with Simon Climie of Climie Fisher, and they came up with "I Knew You Were Waiting (For Me)". Not surprisingly, it has a Christian feel and is a song of hope. At Cannes, Dennis Morgan pitched his song to Clive Davis at Arista, who saw it as a duet for Aretha Franklin and George Michael.

Among the hits of the year were "Chain Reaction" (Bee Gees for Diana Ross), "Addicted To Love" (Robert Palmer), "Higher Love" (Steve Winwood), "Take My Breath Away" (by Berlin for "Top Gun")., "Kiss" (Prince) and "Papa Don't Preach" (Madonna). Suzanne Vega recalled a Dietrich poster in "Marlene On The Wall".

Paul Simon created controversy by playing with South African musicians on "Graceland", but the subsequent controversy centred on just how much he had taken from them. Whatever, it was a trendsetting album with "You Can Call Me Al", "Diamonds On The Soles Of Her Shoes", "The Boy In The Bubble" and the title track, which told of his visit to Elvis Presley's home.

1987 - (SOMETHING INSIDE) SO STRONG
(Labi Siffre)

Stock market crash - Klaus Barbie, the "butcher of Lyon", given life imprisonment by French court - PEP's introduced - Oliver North whistle-blowing on arms to Contras - Earthquake in Los Angeles.

Labi Siffre saw a TV report about some killings in Africa and saw one of the perpetrators smiling. Furious that people were being treated worse than animals, he put his feelings into "(Something Inside) So Strong". He passed it to a major artist - he wouldn't tell me who! - who thought it was too controversial. Another artist turned it down for being one-sided. In the end, Labi Siffre recorded the song himself and had a Top 10 hit. The chorus is so powerful and is often used to highlight atrocities in TV documentaries. Siffre, a gay artist, says that the song can relate to any form of injustice and hence, it is also a gay anthem.

Freddie Mercury admired the Spanish soprano, Monserrat Caballé, and when they met, they sang with Freddie at the piano for several hours. He wrote a piece, "Exercises In Free Love", which she first performed at a London concert in his presence. They resolved to record an album together and several noted pop composers were asked to supply songs for the record, which was named after her home town of Barcelona. He called Caballé "La Superbra", but the song, "Barcelona", describes his admiration for her and her native city. He recorded the backing and his vocals, adding her part in falsetto. When she put her voice onto the tape, Freddie cried, "This is it! I have got it! I have got her voice on my tape!"

Jefferson Airplane reinvented themselves as Jefferson Starship and then Starship and had a UK No 1 with "Nothing's Gonna Stop Us Now", which was written by Dianne Warren and Albert Hammond. Not to be outdone, the Grateful Dead made a commercial record and found themselves in the US Top 10 with "Touch Of Grey".

Madonna wrote a lament for a little island, San Pedro, in "La Isla Bonita", but you won't find it in any atlas as it only exists in Ms Ciccone's imagination. She also had a No 1 with her self-penned title song from the film, "Who's That Girl". Other songs of the year include "Never Gonna Give You Up" (written and produced by Stock - Aitken - Waterman for Rick Astley), "You Win Again" (Bee Gees), "Living In a Box" (by Living In A Box!)

MADONNA

and Black's "Wonderful Life", which is used in insurance commercials. Suzanne Vega scored with "Luka" and "Tom's Diner" but her self - absorbed songs were criticised by some. She had a champion in Leonard Cohen: "With all the legions of Satan and forces of evil flourishing on this planet, I think it's hardly fair to pin the destruction of the western world on Suzanne Vega. She's a delightful young woman who sings beautiful songs."

1988 - FIRST WE TAKE MANHATTAN
(Leonard Cohen)

George Bush becomes US President - Benazir Bhutto, first woman Prime Minister in Pakistan - Lockerbie bomb kills 270, Libya hands over suspects in 1999 - Yasser Arafat acknowledges existance of Israel.

"I'm Your Man" was Leonard Cohen's most consistent album since "Songs Of Love And Hate" in 1971: the songs were good, very good, the arrangements were beautifully crafted, and his voice was deeper and more musical, but maybe that's the technology. To his amusement, he won a Canadian music award as the vocalist of the year. As he sings:

"I was born like this, I had no choice,
I was born with the gift of a golden voice."

Although Cohen's songs can be gloomy and depressing, this album is uplifting and the many witty lines bear repetition:

"Well, my friends are gone, my hair is grey,
I ache in the places where I used to play."

The meaning of "First We Take Manhattan" is elusive, and this is what makes the song so intriguing. At times I have thought it was about the fashion world, at others that it describes him on tour, or again it might be a view of world history - does the "birthmark on your skin" refer to being Jewish?

The song was originally called "In Old Berlin" and Jennifer Warnes sings different words but that doesn't make the meaning any clearer. When asked about the song, Cohen said it was about anything that had no ambiguity about it like "extremism, terrorism, fundamentalism". "I'm Your Man" was Cohen's best-selling album, but in his normal perverse way, he has only released one album since and hardly ever tours. He has been living in a retreat studying Za-Zen, which may be to his spiritual satisfaction if not to ours. Much more than Frank Sinatra, Leonard Cohen has been doing it his way for years.

Superstar sessions can be disappointing, but "Traveling Wilburys Vol 1" was a revelation, full of entertaining, good-time songs and strong performances. The three superstars (George Harrison, Bob Dylan, Roy Orbison) and two stars (Jeff Lynne, Tom Petty) clearly enjoyed working together. Bob Dylan teased Bruce Springsteen with "Tweeter And The Monkey Man", Roy Orbison soared on "Not Alone Anymore", and George Harrison wrote his best song in years with "Handle With Care". "Rattled" was top class rockabilly and "Dirty World" was hilarious. Had Roy Orbison not died, they might have continued in this vein and given some entertaining concerts.

ROY ORBISON

"Sweet Child O'Mine", Axl Rose's song to his girl-friend, Erin Everly, daugh-ter of Don, was heartful, but he could not control his jealousy. They parted when he thought David Bowie was being fresh with her. The Guns N' Roses sin-gle ends with the words "Where do we go now?" "Nowhere" was the answer.

No one would ever think so but Don Black has written more songs with Andrew Lloyd Webber than Tim Rice. Although it must be galling for Don Black, Andrew Lloyd Webber is seen as the dominant partner: the musicals are his projects and he hires lyricists as the occasions arise. "Aspects Of Love" is not regarded as a success (it only ran in the West End for three years!), but it contained the worldbeating "Love Changes Everything", in which Black, an experienced lyricist, put words to Webber's music. Deliberately, it is an old-fashioned ballad and it could have been written in any year this century.

The production team of Stock - Aitken - Waterman had hit after hit and Kylie Minogue topped the charts with their "I Should Be So Lucky". "Perfect" was as exhilarating as a fairground attraction. Cliff Richard had a No 1 "Mistletoe And Wine", originally sung by Twiggy in a TV musical play "The Little Match Girl", Bobby McFerrin accompanied himself on the slap happy, "Don't Worry Be Happy", and one of the best country ballads was "When You Say Nothing At All", a UK No 1 for Ronan Keating in 1999.

1989 - THE LIVING YEARS
(Mike Rutherford - B. A. Robertson)

Death of Emperor Hirohito - Fatwa against Salman Rushdie for "The Satanic Verses", lifted 1998 - Berlin Wall knocked down - Death of Liverpool FC fans at Hillsborough - Exxon Valdez spills load in Alaska - The rave culture takes hold - Tiananmen Square massacre.

Largely because of the demands of Phil Collins' very busy solo career, Genesis was no longer a full-time working band. Their bass player, Mike Rutherford formed an occasional group, Mike and the Mechanics, recruiting Paul Carrack of Ace and Squeeze and Paul Young of Sad Café. They were a solid, commercial band with the emphasis on hit singles, scoring in 1986 with "Silent Running", the theme to the film, "On Dangerous Ground".

When Mike Rutherford's father died, he regretted the lack of communication between them. He told the songwriter, B.A. Robertson of his feelings and they wrote "The Living Years". Robertson, who is known for knockabout songs with clever wordplay, excelled himself, and then found himself collaborating with Burt Bacharach, although nothing from their partnership has emerged. Many people identified with the situation in "The Living Years". I put it alongside "My Old Man" (1980) by Lou Reed and "Scraps Of Paper" (1982) by Eric Bogle, who only discovered his father's sensitivity after his death.

KYLIE MINOGUE

Chris Rea was on the M4 and his car hadn't moved for an hour. Someone in the back of the car said, "It's the upwardly mobile freeway" and Rea replied, "It's the road to bloody hell." He had written "The Road To Hell" by the time he'd reached home. The guy in the song is stuck in a traffic jam and he sees the ghost of his mother in the windscreen, who asks him what he is doing there. You see, you can write a song about anything.

Elton John included a heartfelt ballad, "Sacrifice", on his new album, "Sleeping With The Past". In 1990 he released it as a single for AIDS charities and it gave him his first solo No l. It was far from being his best song and it raises the question as to how well some singles would do without the charity tag.

Madonna topped the charts with "Like A Prayer" but its video was condemned by the Vatican for combining reli-

JON BON JOVI

gion with eroticism, and I bet they didn't go much on her name either. Following this, Pepsi-Cola cancelled a sponsorship deal, but no doubt Madonna had anticipated this uproar and knew that it would help her career.

Frank Zappa was well capable of writing commercial songs, but that never interested him and he had a highly productive, 25 year career in which he pursued his own interests. His most accessible album was "Broadway The Hard Way", which he hoped to convert to a New York show. It included "Elvis Has Just Left The Building" and, as usual with Zappa, an attack on TV fundamentalists, "Jesus Thinks You're A Jerk". Lou Reed, who also did things his way, found critical acclaim and mass acceptance with an album about his home city, "New York", which included "Dirty Blvd".

Lisa Stansfield, the biggest star from Rochdale since Gracie Fields, topped the charts with "All Around The World", and back in 1957, Gracie had been in the Top 10 with "Around The World".

LISA STANSFIELD

Phil Collins showed social concern on "Another Day In Paradise". Cher said "If I Could Turn Back Time", though, judging by her looks, she was doing well, the Bangles sang the ballad, "Eternal Flame" and Beautiful South had their first hit with "Song For Whoever". The charts were dominated by Stock - Aitken - Waterman productions: they had six No 1 records and they held that top spot for 13 weeks.

1990 -   BLAZE OF GLORY (Jon Bon Jovi)

Nelson Mandela released - Iraq invades Kuwait and starts Gulf War - Poll Tax demonstrations in UK - Margaret Thatcher replaced by John Major - Breakthrough in Channel Tunnel.

It is often said that the western is dead but every few years, "The Outlaw Josey Wales", "Dances With Wolves" or "Unforgiven" comes along. In one sense, it is a Hollywood pantomime, giving actors a chance to dress in costume and the plots can be equally nonsensical. The story of Billy the Kid no doubt appeals to young stars. Billy himself knew how to manipulate the media and, as with James Dean and Buddy Holly, he died young. He was also a homicidal maniac, but most films gloss over this. Joe Ely's perceptive song, "Me And Billy The Kid", captures his nature more accurately.

In 1988 several Brat Packers shone their spurs in "Young Guns" and it was so successful that it spawned a sequel, "Young Guns II", in 1990. Both films starred Emilio Estevez, Kiefer Sutherland and Lou Diamond Phillips. Jon Bon Jovi was a close friend of Estevez, who wanted to use a 1987 Bon Jovi hit, "Wanted Dead Or Alive" on the soundtrack. Bon Jovi said that the lyric was too modern and he would write something more appropriate. He came up with "Blaze Of Glory", a terrific rock song but totally unsuitable for a film set in the 1880s. No wonder "Variety" described "Young Guns II" as "a slick, glossy MTV-styled western". It became a US No l and also did well in the UK.

The human cartoon film, "Dick Tracy", starred Warren Beatty and Madonna and the deliciously camp score was by Stephen Sondheim. He won an Oscar for his torch song, "Sooner Or Later (I Always Get My Man)" and Madonna had a No 1 hit with "Vogue", a savage look at the fashion world.

George Micheal sang about the Gulf War in "Praying For Time", but unlike Dylan in the 60s, did anyone notice what the song was about?

The songwriter, Dewayne Blackwell, was at lunch with a fellow songwriter, Bud Lee, and they found that neither of them had any money. "Never mind," said Bud, "I got friends in low places. I know the cook." They developed the idea into a song and asked a friend, Garth Brooks, to cut a demo for them. He told them that he had cut his first album with Capitol Records and they should have given him the song earlier as he loved it. When he cut his second album, "No Fences", he revived Dwayne's old hit, "Mr. Blue" as well as the new song, "Friends In Low Places" "I guess he wanted to show he had friends in low places," said Bud. There is a rude third verse which Garth Brooks sings in concert.

The album, "No Fences", which also included "The Thunder Rolls", "Unanswered Prayers" and "Two Of A Kind, Workin' On A Full House", has become Brooks' best-selling album, clocking up 16 million sales. He has now sold over 100 million albums, far surpassing the sales of Hank Williams or Johnny Cash, and yet he has had never had a UK Top 10 single.

Morrissey, no longer with the Smiths, recorded "November Spawned A Monster", about the plight of the disabled. As the title suggests, this was not a politically correct song, though it was still sympathetic. Morrissey made the point that because someone is disabled it will be harder to win his love, but he is repulsed by himself because of that thought.

1991 -   TEARS IN HEAVEN (Eric Clapton)

Cease-fire in Gulf War - South Africa repeals apartheid laws - Rajiv Ghandi assassinated - Terry Waite freed from captivity - Gorbachev replaced by Yeltsin - Mystery of Robert Maxwell's death.

By the late 1980s, Eric Clapton was free of alcohol and drug addiction and his career was at an all-time high. He was working hard and then in March 1991, his four year old son, Conor, was killed when he fell out of the window on the 53rd floor of an apartment block. To take his mind off the disaster, Eric Clapton went into the studio to mix a live album, but he hated everything he heard. He went on holiday with an acoustic guitar and he started to write songs for an album to Conor. He soon realised that one song stood out among the rest, "Tears In Heaven". The song was both a requiem for his son and an acknowledgment that, despite all the odds, he had survived himself. Clapton said, "I have an absolute belief in music as a healing force. It's proven to me."

Strangely perhaps, Clapton included the highly personal "Tears In Heaven" in his score for the cop movie, "Rush", which starred Jason Patric and Jennifer Jason Leigh. Clapton has since written and recorded "Circus Left Town" about the last night he spent with Conor and "My Father's Eyes" which also relates to him never knowing his own father.

ERIC CLAPTON

The Australian band, INXS, scored with a song for Andrew Farriss' daughter, "Baby Don't Cry", which was written by Farriss with Michael Hutchence, and recorded with a full orchestra. The band had been well known for some years, but Hutchence's much-publicised romance with Kylie Minogue put them in the tabloids.

R.E.M. had the title of the year with "Losing My Religion", but despite a reference to confessions, it seemed to be the story of love going wrong.. Stipe said that "losing my religion" was a local phrase which meant being about to crack up. However, Stipe's grandfather had been a preacher and Stipe himself was rumored to be HIV positive, so other interpretations could be put on the lyric. The song came from their smoothest album to date, "Out Of Time", which also included the hit singles, "Shiny Happy People" (shades of the Mamas and the Papas), "Near Wild Heaven" and "Radio Song".

Kevin Costner followed "Dances With Wolves" with a romp through Merrie England, "Robin Hood: Prince Of Thieves". Michael Kamen had had the melody for 25 years and he would improvise around it when he played on stage as part of the New York Rock'n'Roll Ensemble. When asked to score "Robin Hood: Prince Of Thieves", he saw the scene where Maid Marian stumbles across Robin Hood bathing naked under a waterfall, and the melody came back to him. Robin asks her to take a message for the King and she says, "I'll do it for you." The melody was used whenever they were together and then at the end it becomes the hit song "(Everything I Do) I Do It For You", with Bryan Adams' lyric. It topped the charts for 16 weeks, beating the record set by Slim Whitman with "Rose Marie" in 1955.

Chris Isaak assumed Roy Orbison's mantle for "Blue Hotel", and Marc Cohn evoked Elvis' memory in the touching "Walking In Memphis". Hale and Pace introduced us to "The Stonk", although the word had first been used on "Sex With Paula Yates" in 1987. Right Said Fred took their name from a 1962 novelty hit by Bernard Cribbins, and their slogan song, "I'm Too Sexy", had a very attractive, surreal element to it. On a more dramatic note, Tori Amos relived an adolescent rape in "Me And A Gun".

Paul McCartney had moved into classical music with his "Liverpool Oratorio", cowritten with Carl Davis. Dame Kiri Te Kanawa sang one of the roles, but I couldn't see why McCartney, the greatest melodist of his generation, didn't write decent tunes. After all, classical orchestras play "Yesterday" and "Hey Jude", so why not give them some new gems? I find it hard to take conversational English ("sagging off", "nothing on my plate") in an operatic setting, although I know that was the point.

PHIL COLLINS OF GENESIS

Dame Kiri Te Kanawa, of all people, was also recruited to promote rugby and her "World In Union" was the TV theme music. Its melody was taken from Gustav Holst's "The Planets", a distinction shared with "Joybringer", a 1973 hit for Manfred Mann's Earthband.

1992 - ACHY BREAKY HEART (Donald Von Tress)

> World Wide Web established - General Noriega of Panama jailed in US for drug operations - President Clinton inaugurated - EuroDisney opens.

The Chippendales never made anything worth hearing, but a country singer with Mel Gibson looks and the body of a Chippendale, the ponytailed Billy Ray Cyrus had an international hit with "Achy Breaky Heart". It was an update of an earlier song by the Marcy Brothers, "Don't Tell My Heart", which had a witty, novelty lyric, and its new title was a nod to an old George Jones record, "Aching, Breaking Heart". Cyrus pumped up a Rolling Stones-styled beat and it was so infectious that chart placings were inevitable.

But "Achy Breaky Heart" was much more than a hit record. Cyrus added a dance, the Achy Breaky, which was demonstrated on the video. Just like Chubby Checker with the Twist, Billy Ray Cyrus had started a new trend, this time for line dancing. Even people who hated country music found themselves line dancing, and its very nature meant that it could be done by children and pensioners alike. Quiet village halls were soon living it up with their weekly sessions. Country artists, and some rock ones too, found that they were deliberately making records for line dancers. Others like Travis Tritt denounced Cyrus for ridiculing country music.

As long as you don't hear it too often, "Achy Breaky Heart" is a fine record, but it stopped Cyrus, a fine artist, from being heard in the way that he wanted. Strong albums like "Trail Of Tears" (1997) have not had a fair hearing. He remains a country star but after that initial breakthrough, I'm sure that he was hoping for better things.

By way of contrast, Genesis had a hit helped by a new video declaring that they couldn't dance. Bruce Springsteen brought car and female imagery together in a fine song, "Human Touch" and also recorded the incisive (and very true) "57 Channels (And Nothin' On)".

Shakespears Sister topped the charts with "Stay". k.d. lang wrote all the songs on her engaging "Ingénue", which included "Constant Craving" and "Miss Chatelaine". Shamen went to No 1 with an appalling dance record, "Ebeneezer Goode", which seemed to have only been written to convey the message , "E's are good".

Staying with country music, the beautifully-observed "He Thinks He'll Keep Her" was written and recorded by Mary Chapin Carpenter. She says, "It's not as simplistic as my guy left me and I'm sitting in the bar playing the jukebox. The issues are edgier and more compelling, and to me, that's real life." The British country singer, Charlie Dore, wrote Jimmy Nail's hit, "Ain't No Doubt".

1993 -   FIELDS OF GOLD (Sting)

Yeltsin crushes rebels in Russian parliament - China breaks nuclear test moratorium - The start of the Information Superhighway - Siege of religious cult in Waco, Texas ends in fire, which kills 72.

In 1991 Sting was walking on a beach in Malibu, reading a copy of "Country Life" and talking to his accountant. As you do. He pointed to a page in the magazine and told his accountant, "That's the house I want." The house was Lake House on the River Avon, a sixty-acre estate built by a wool merchant in 1578. It cost Sting £2m and he joked, "I got it for a song, literally."

It was an idyllic time when Sting took occupancy in the summer of 1992. The fields were ripe with crops, there were orchards, and the swans swam in the river. Throughout the summer, Sting wrote and developed the songs that formed the album, "Ten Summoner's Tales", the title evoking Chaucer's "Canterbury Tales" as well as his real name, Gordon Sumner. The melodic songs contained as many time signatures as a Dave Brubeck album, yet it was still very commercial.

Sting had moved into Lake House with his girlfriend, Trudie Styler, and their children. She desperately wanted to be married for their children's sake, but Sting didn't, and she gave him an ultimatum which he transformed into a song, "Seven Days". They were married at a lavish, medieval ceremony in St Andrew's, which was across the river from Lake House. He sang in 'Fields Of Gold':

> "I never made promises like these
> There have been some that I've broken,
> I swear in the days still left,
> We will walk in the fields of gold."

This paean to his new home and his wife only made the UK Top 20, but it has the makings of a standard. The song was beautifully but more plaintively recorded by Eva Cassidy at a live concert in 1996, which became the album, "Live At Blues Alley". With Tantric yoga, Sting said that he could sustain his lovemaking for five hours at a time. Now, when is he going to write about that?

The dance duo, Peter Cunnah and James Petrie, better known as D:Ream, had a Top 30 hit with "Things Can Only Get Better" in 1993, but it was re-mixed and went to No 1 in 1994. They had written the song of hope after the frustations of Tory rule, and it proved to be that rare occasion where rock and politics worked together. Taking a lead from America, New Labour needed a trendy, cool sound with the right message for their election campaign in 1997 and "Things Can Only Get Better" was perfect. It has been used on numerous occasions since then.

"The Perfect Year" was the hit song from "Sunset Boulevard" and Ace of Base performed the hypnotic "All That She Wants". Meat Loaf returned, bigger than ever but somewhat slimmer, with "I'd Do Anything For Love (But I Won't Do That)". John Michael Montgomery made the country charts with "I Swear", later a UK hit for All-4-One.

The most intriguing lyric of the year belongs to Marc Cohn who looked at genetics in "The Things We've

Handed Down", which has also been recorded by Art Garfunkel:

> *"You may not always be so grateful*
> *For the way that you were made.*
> *Some feature of your father's*
> *That you'd gladly sell or trade."*

2Unlimited's "No Limit" is often cited as having the worst lyric of any No 1, but 1993 was a bad year. The worst hit record of the century was "Mr Blobby" by Mr Blobby.

1994 - CAN YOU FEEL THE LOVE TONIGHT?
(Elton John - Tim Rice)

Massacre in Rwanda - South Africa holds first multiracial elections, Mandela elected president - Death of Jackie Kennedy.

There have been numerous Disney hits throughout the years, but no film and no score has had the impact of "The Lion King", their first cartoon feature to be based on an original story. It begins with the animals welcoming the birth of Simba with "Circle Of Life", but the key song is the ballad, "Can You Feel The Love Tonight?", which, like all good musical songs, works effectively outside the film.

Elton wrote the music for Tim Rice's lyrics while his boyfriend, David Furnish, was planning a documentary about his life, "Tantrums And Tiaras". If you see the documentary, which is unintentionally hilarious, you wonder how Elton got anything done, especially a Disney score which calls for constant rewrites. The project took so long that Tim Rice had to defer his stage musical of "Heathcliff" for a year.

Was it worth it? Julie Burchill in "The Sunday Times" called the songs "Rice puddings" and added, "We're not just talking Eurovision standard; we're talking bottom third of Eurovision." This is the minority view. "The Lion King", which has now been converted to a lavish musical will run on Broadway and in the West End, for years and years.

NOEL GALLAGHER OF OASIS

Damon Albarn was living in Notting Hill and when he decided to write about it, he read Martin Amis' "London Fields" for inspiration. The result was a terrific Blur single, "Parklife", which featured the Cockney actor, Phil Daniels, and sounded like an update on Ray Davies. Blur's 1995 No 1, "Country House", was even more like Ray Davies.

Kurt Cobain of Nirvana was influenced by Neil Young and he left a note containing a snatch of Young's lyrics ("It is better to burn out than to rust") at the scene of his suicide. Neil Young was very disturbed by this and he wrote "Sleeps With Angels" for him.

1995 - COMMON PEOPLE (Jarvis Cocker - Russell Senior - Steve Mackey - Nick Banks - Candida Doyle)

5,000 die in Japanese earthquake - Russian space station welcomes American astronauts - O J Simpson found not guilty of murdering wife and her friend, found liable in civil suit, 1997 - Ceasefire in Bosnia - Israel's prime minister Yitzhak Rabin, killed by Jewish extremists - Camelot starts National Lottery, the first since 1826.

There was chart rivalry between Blur and Oasis as their records, released on the same summer day, competed for No 1. Blur's "Country House" beat Oasis' "Roll With It", though neither group was at their best. The Manchester group next released their best-ever single, the anthemic "Wonderwall". Better than anything by Blur or Oasis though was Pulp with "Common People".

Yorkshire-born Jarvis Cocker, a Jonathan King lookalike if there was one, had been trying to establish his group, Pulp, for over ten years and they had had a few minor chart entries. Jarvis disliked the way the media wrote about low-rent and low-life people and he thought he would write a bitter-sweet song about the emptiness of their lives:

> *"Dance and drink and screw,*
> *'Cause there's nothing else to do."*

Both Jarvis and his musicians handled the song with the right measures of warmth and sadness, and it was a true fanfare for the common man. The single was helped by an impressive video featuring Jarvis in a shopping-trolley, and as Jarvis said, the single was saying the right things at the right time. The following year Jarvis did his bit for the common people by protesting against Michael Jackson's messianic performance at the Brits, and then a media poll on Radio 1 acknowledged "Common People" as the most significant single of the decade.

Not far behind "Common People" in its uniqueness was Joan Osborne's "One Of Us":

"What if God was one of us
Just a slob like one of us."

"One Of Us" was a million-selling single, also featured on her CD, "Relish". Unlike most of the songs, she didn't write it but it was written by her guitarist, Eric Brazilian. Some considered the song blasphemous but the concept of Christ returning as a tramp has been around for years. The song had a witty coda inferring that the only person who might contact him was the Pope. Joan Osborne's career faltered because the mandolin-based "St Teresa" was the wrong follow-up and rather than issue new albums, she chose to reissue her old ones. Like Kim Carnes, Joan Osborne has a versatile voice and she could be around a long time, providing she can find the right songs.

Ralph McTell recorded the best album of his career with 'Sand In Your Shoes'. The variations that he structured around the shortest verse in the Bible, "Jesus Wept", were both masterful and plausible. "Jesus Wept" is an ingenious song, almost on a par with Dylan's 'With God On Our Side'.

In "You Oughta Know", Alanis Morissette pre-empted Monica Lewinsky by discussing fellatio in public. Perhaps she wasn't the first - it depends whether you count Clinton Ford's "My Baby's Wild About My Old Trombone" (1968) or not. The song contained some memorable lines:

"Everytime I scratch my nails down someone else's back,
I hope you feel it."

THE SPICE GIRLS

It is still not known what happened to Richey Edwards, the lead singer of the Manic Street Preachers. Is he dead or did he do a Reggie Perrin? The group carried on without him and the first single, "A Design For Life" showed that they were right to do so. The song, very much in the Jam tradition, dealt with the pride of the working class and the patronising attitudes of the middle class. What other song has an opening line comparable to "Libraries gave us power"?

When I had interviewed Cliff Richard in the mid-70s he told me, "I would love to play Heathcliff. I know I could hate like that, be jealous like that, be vindictive like that. I know because I have been all of these things." It seemed to me that a production starring Heathcliff Richard would be doomed to failure, but I was wrong as "Heathcliff", which was written by Tim Rice and John Farrar, did extremely well. "Misunderstood Man" and "Be With Me Always" were good singles, but I preferred Cliff's spontaneous rendition of his old hits at the Centre Court at Wimbledon in 1996.

1996 - WANNABE (Victoria Caroline Adams - Melanie Janine Brown - Emma Lee Bunton - Melanie Jayne Chisholm - Geraldine Estelle Halliwell - Matthew Paul Rowbottom - Richard Frederick Stannard)

Global warming at all-time high - Suicide bombings in Sri Lanka and Israel - Divorce of Prince Charles and Lady Diana - BSE discovered in British cows - Thousands of refugees in Rwanda and Burundi abandon camps.

Girl power started in summer 1996 with five loud, cheeky, disparate girls - Posh, Baby, Ginger, Scary and Sporty Spice - and a very catchy song, "Wannabe". Since that time, their songs have fallen well into one pop tradition or another - the big ballad or the disco dancer - but "Wannabe" was genuinely fresh, and the phrase, what you "really, really, really want", is heard everyday. One thing is a little disconcerting about that record: how do seven people write a song?

The Spice Girls have been interviewed so often, you might think there was nothing more to say, but you'd be wrong. They rarely talk about how their songs are created, and they never answer such questions in any depth. Do the Spice Girls really, really, really write their songs? Are they part of the songwriting process or is the credit a cut-in that the true writers have to accept?

George Michael returned to music with "Jesus To A Child", Oasis had another anthem with "Don't Look Back In Anger", and Gary Barlow said "Forever Love", although his solo career has lacked the Williams panache.

Up to 1996, all the official football songs had dwelt on why their team was so special and how they were going to take on all comers and win with ease. This approach had a hollow ring with our national teams and some of the records, notably Rod Stewart and the Scottish World Cup Squad ("Olé Ola", No 4, 1978), have had a much better result than the matches. Praise then for two comedian fanatics, David Baddiel and Frank Skinner, and the Lightning Seeds, who decided that the 1996 Official Song of the England Football Team,

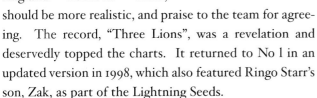
MICK JAGGER AND KEITH RICHARDS

should be more realistic, and praise to the team for agreeing. The record, "Three Lions", was a revelation and deservedly topped the charts. It returned to No 1 in an updated version in 1998, which also featured Ringo Starr's son, Zak, as part of the Lightning Seeds.

1997 - BITTER SWEET SYMPHONY
(Richard Ashcroft -
Mick Jagger - Keith Richards)

Tony Blair and New Labour swept to power - Tornadoes in US - Hale-Bopp Comet - Gianni Versace murdered - First pictures from Mars - Death of Princess Diana - Carlos the Jackal convicted of murder.

Comics regard Wigan as a joke, but George Orwell wrote a novel about the place and Buddy Holly played there. Despite a few minor successes, it looked as though the Verve were going nowhere and then their vocalist,

Richard Ashcroft, wrote "Bitter Sweet Symphony". His best idea was also the worst as he sampled Andrew Loog Oldham's very middle-of-the-road arrangement of the Rolling Stones' "The Last Time" at the start of the record. It meant that Ashcroft had to share songwriting credits with the Stones and settle with Oldham, thereby losing £1m. in royalties. As he sings:

"Trying to make ends meet,
You're a slave to money, then you die."

I'd highly recommend Ed Jones' book about his days with the Wigan band the Tansads, "This Is Pop" (Canongate, 1999), which includes much about the Verve's early years.

Normally prolific, Bob Dylan had been suffering from a writer's block for five years. He came through it by writing gloomy, personal songs about growing old. The album, "Time Out Of Mind", promised to be as much Prozac as muzak, but it was much better than anyone expected, and Dylan received some of the best reviews of his career. The writing was focused, the images rich and the melodies strong but the songs were still elusive. Take "Tryin' To Get To Heaven", what does "I've been to sugar town, I shook the sugar down" mean? The song contains one of Dylan's greatest lines:

"When you think that you've lost everything,
You find out that you can always lose a little more."

With its full title line, "Tryin' to get to heaven before they close the door", the song must be intended as a companion to "Knockin' On Heaven's Door", but what is Dylan saying? Does he think that God only lets a certain number into heaven and that the quota may be reached before he dies? Who knows, but I do know that the song will perplex me for decades to come. Both Billy Joel and Garth Brooks have included Dylan's "Make You Feel My Love" on big-selling albums. Sooner or later, somebody will have a Top 10 hit, if not a chart-topping single, with this song. For a full analysis of this album and admittedly he likes it less than I do, read Michael Gray's definitive

Song And Dance Man III - The Art Of Bob Dylan" (Cassell, 1999).

Paul Simon too was back in the news with his musical, "The Capeman". He picked a difficult subject (a true story of a Puerto Rican boy being convicted for a mindless murder), but that hasn't stopped musicials being successful before. Simon's problem was his arrogance in thinking that Broadway people would bow to his wishes, and they closed ranks against him. Paul Simon had given up performing in public, but when the musical only lasted a few months, he went on tour with Bob Dylan, both to restore his bruised ego and to repair his bank balance. For all that, "Songs From The Capeman" is an excellent CD, showing there was little wrong with the music itself.

1997 was a productive year for the old-time singer-songwriters as James Taylor released his best-ever album, "Hourglass". The opening song, "Line 'Em Up", was a comment on Nixon leaving the White House, but he told audiences that the rest of the song was "typical James Taylor introspective shit". His song for a friend's funeral, "Enough To Be On Your Own", is both polished and perceptive.

U2 wrote "Please" around the breakdown of the peace talks in Northern Ireland. It is a conversation with a hardline member of the IRA and refers to "Your sermon on the mount from the boot of your car". The Scottish band, Texas (!), paid tribute to 60s Motown with "Black Eyed Boy", although Sharleen Spiteri's song about how a woman can have a more positive perspective of a situation than a man is hardly a Motown theme.

JAMES TAYLOR

Robert E. Smith of the Cure wrote a song around a phone call he had had in New York, "Wrong Number". Other songs include "Bitch" (Meredith Brooks), "Men In Black" (Will Smith) and "Tubthumping" (Chumbawamba, who thought it was funny rather than pathetic to douse John Prescott in water at the Brits.) What could be more banal than the computer pop of "Barbie Girl"? I know, "Teletubbies Say Eh-Oh!" The Country was going la la.

1998 - MY HEART WILL GO ON
(James Horner - Will Jennings)

> Iraq blocks UN weapons inspection - Monica Lewinsky shows that some people will swallow anything - Viagra available - Good Friday agreement in Northern Ireland - Former Chilean dictator, General Pinochet, arrested - Air strikes on Iraq.

Isn't it odd that disaster movies have love themes? "Love Theme" from "The Towering Inferno" sounds ridiculous, but such things exist. The film composer, James Horner, asked the lyricist, Will Jennings, to hear some of his music for the forthcoming film, "Titanic" and see some of the footage. Jennings loved the idea of the Rose character and it reminded him of an old potter he had met, Beatrice Wood, who had been the lover of the French painter, Marcel Duchamp. The director, James Cameron, later told him that the character of Rose had been inspired by that same old woman. She died just before the Oscar ceremony at the age of 104.

Celine Dion's single flooded the charts for what seemed liked forever. This First Class song is typical of the inspirational ballads that come with lavish stage or film productions, and is little different from what Shirley Bassey has been doing for years. In a similar vein, LeAnn Rimes did a Celine Dion with "How Do I Live" - its songwriter Dianne Warren is hailed as the new Carole King but she has yet to come up with anything truly distinctive.

When Boyzone asked Andrew Lloyd Webber for a song, they didn't expect something from a new musical he was writing with Jim Steinman, but "No Matter What" was a very commercial hit single that fit perfectly into the show, "Whistle Down The Wind". Andrew Lloyd Webber has often been accused of ransacking the classics but this time he borrowed a song title from Badfinger. Boyzone's record company wanted to end its long run at the top so that they could promote a new single, so they cut the price to £1.79 (as only £1.99 singles are eligible for the chart) and hence, it slipped back. Some might argue that it was overpriced at even £1.79.

Neil Hannon of Divine Comedy paid tribute to the nationwide bus service, "National Express", which is appropriate here as so many of the early songs of the century were about transport. The numbers using public transport have risen by 7% during the year and so we are witnessing a new interest in trains and boats and planes, especially the Titanic.

Two musicians from the 1970s UK group, Dave Curtiss and the Tremors, wrote "Sepharyn". One of the musicians, the late Clive Muldoon, had a niece, Christine Leach, who heard a William Orbit backing track and she started singing "Sepharyn" over the top of it. Madonna was impressed and she renamed the song from a phrase in its lyric, "Ray Of Light".

This was Robbie Williams' year but "Angels" was a warmed-up Elton John song and, as with "Bitter Sweet Symphony", the most memorable part of "Millennium" came from another composer, in this case John Barry writing for James Bond. Elvis Costello and Burt Bacharach released a superb but morose album of new material, "Painted From Memory", while George Michael was writing about his court appearance in "Outside". Catatonia could hardly have been more contemporary. First, a homage to "The X-Files", "Mulder And Scully", then Cerys' tribute to a refashioned 60s icon, "The Ballad Of Tom Jones", and a song based on the phrase of the year, "Road Rage", and containing the line, "I still want to cut off your nuts". Lauryn Hill left the Fugees and merged reggae, rap and soul in a stunning solo album, "The Miseducation of Lauryn Hill".

Cher returned to the top with "Believe" but with her voice so processed that she sounded like a mellotron. It was further proof that the computers are making the music and the artists are becoming automatons. I wonder if computers will soon be combining every possible combination of notes so that by, say, 2020, every possible tune will have been written. Certainly, it is harder for a new composer these days as so much has already gone before him. This may explain why the 1990s has been so derivative - tribute bands, (Björn Again, Bootleg Beatles), bands

basing themselves on successful acts (Oasis and the Beatles) and the relentless sampling (why is Fatboy Slim different from Jive Bunny?).

Everyone thought the Spice Girls had had it when 5 became 4 (with the simply red girl leaving) and they sacked their manager (No more, Mr Spice Guy). They quickly showed, with great resilience, that it didn't matter and defying expectation, they have had five years at the top. Most critics thought that the two Mels had the best voices in the group, and no one gave Geri Halliwell's solo career much thought. Except Gerry, and possibly the other Spices who referred to her as "a little girl with a big imagination" in their chart-topping "Goodbye".

ROBBIE WILLIAMS

1999 - LIVIN' LA VIDA LOCA
(Robi Rosa - Desmond Child - Randy Cantor)

US relaxes restrictions on Cuba - Deaths of King Hussein of Jordan and Joe DiMaggio ("Where have you gone, Joe DiMaggio?") - Nonstop balloon flight around world - Nelson Mandala retires - Rampages in several US cities bring further calls for gun control - London train crash - Microsoft said to have monopoly - Tobacco companies accept that smoking can kill you - Self-rule in Northern Ireland suspended and then reinstated in 2000 - "Walking With Dinosaurs" is a TV sensation - George Harrison is wounded in a break-in at his home.

At the age of 89, Edmundo Ros was a guest on Ned Sherrin's "Loose Ends" in March 2000. He had promoting Latin-American music since the 1940s and now it was an international phenomenon, he said he was too old to do anything about it! However, the most rewarding aspects of the music surround the Buena Vista Social Club, veteran Cuban musicians well past retirement age who find themselves on the world stage. I saw them in Liverpool and they were wonderful. The pianist, Rubén Gonzáles, was 80 and frail, but you could tell that he was leading the band, and every piece ended with a coda from him. Although bent over with arthritis, he could still play magically, and percussively.

He was followed on stage by 73 year old Ibrahim Ferrer who regards himself as an old man living a young man's dream. These musicians must give Mick Jagger encouragement.

Like blues musicians, they are too old to have more than a cult following, admittedly a pretty large cult. The commercial version owed as much to Tom Jones as Latin-American music as the phenomenon of 1999 was the 28 year old, Puerto Rican Ricky Martin, who sang the World Cup Theme Song, "La Copa De La Vida", in 1998 and then "Livin' La Vida Loca" in 1999. He followed four Spanish albums with his first English language album, "Ricky Martin", in 1999, which contained both an English and a Spanish version of "Livin' La Vida Loca". Even his name been anglicised as he is really Enrique Martin Morales IV. He is eye candy, but he has a good voice - he was in the Broadway production of "Les Misérables" - and "Livin' La Vida Loca" is a great dance song. It has an infectious rhythm and a title line that makes dancers shout out. The lyrics are fun too:

> *"Her lips are devil red*
> *And her skin's the colour of Mocha*
> *She'll wear you out*
> *Livin' la vida loca.".*

DEBBIE HARRY OF BLONDIE

Madonna, shrewdly, was a guest artist on Ricky Martin's album and as well as the genuine article, UK and American mainstream musicians have been incorporating Latin sounds into their records. Gloria Estefan was born in Havana and there are many Latin influences in her records, which are often sung in Spanish. Geri Halliwell's cod Latin chart-topper, "Mi Chico Latino", lacked depth but was still entertaining. And in Y2K, the Manic Street Preachers' went to No 1 with 'The Masses Against The Classes' and a CD sleeve featuring the Cuban flag.

As soon as I heard Blondie's comeback single, "Maria", I realised it would be a great, stonking No.1 and a superb return to form, although it could have been written by their keyboard player, Jimmy Destri, the first time round. Admittedly, Deborah Harry is singing a man's song and this "Maria" is not as classy as the one from "West Side Story", but it's a great pop record.

The phrase, "Tender is the Night" comes from Keats' "Ode To A Nightingale", and Blur's Damon Albarn used the phrase in "Tender", which he wrote after splitting up with Justine Frischmann from Elastica. Many songs on Suede's first album were about Brett Anderson losing Frischmann.

So far no-one has written a decent song on GM crops. It will come but surely the most appropriate little has already been used, "Blowin' In The Wind".

Shania Twain may or may not be a country singer, but either way, in the words of her most successful song, "That Don't Impress Me Much". Nor does the Eclipse, nor does the Millennium, the two most overhyped words of the year. The dreaded M word led to all manner of polls. Vera Lynn was named the personality of the century and some of her artefacts have been sealed in the Millennium Vault 2000 in the grounds of Guildford Castle. It will not be opened until the year 3000. How will they respond to Dame Vera singing "We'll Meet Again"?

If I owned a record label and had lots of money, I would have invited some great, socially-aware songwriters (Bob Dylan, Joni Mitchell, Elvis Costello, Tom Waits, Ian Dury, Jarvis Cocker) to record a song about the new century. Nobody asked them and none of the artists did that individually. Why should they? After all, when Britain's greatest living playwright, Harold Pinter, was asked to comment on the new year, he said, "I have no millennium message to give to the fucking world."

CANADIAN SUNSET
Interview with Gordon Lightfoot

*"If you could read my mind, love,
What a tale my thoughts could tell"*
(Gordon Lightfoot, 1970)

In 1981 I saw Gordon Lightfoot on stage at the Liverpool Empire. I thought he'd be great, but his performance was, to be kind, dull and lack-lustre - the songs were excellent of course, but his heart wasn't in it. He was annoyed that the house was half-empty, that no-one was buying his records, and as he told us, "I'd rather be back in Toronto" - in other words, he was insulting the hapless thousand or so who had bought tickets. It was hardly surprising that he wasn't giving interviews and, to my knowledge, he did not return to the UK.

Fast forward 18 years. I'm planning a short trip to Toronto and, via the Internet, I e-mailed Gordon Lightfoot's management office, Early Morning Productions, to request an interview. To my surprise, a date is agreed and on 15th September 1999, I find myself walking down Yonge Street to Gordon Lightfoot's office.

One of the tracks on Gordon Lightfoot's most recent album, "A Painter Passing Through" (Warner/Reprise), is "On Yonge Street" and the street has shaped his career. He made his first impression at Steele's Tavern, which is next to the gaudy shopfront for Sam The Record Man. He won first prize in a music festival in Massey Hall when he was 13, his 1969 album, "Sunday Concert", was recorded there, and he has played the theatre annually ever since. I pass the posters for his concerts in November.

I arrive at Early Morning Productions and the notice on the door says "No agents, peddlers or solicitors". Not falling into any of these categories, I walk in. There are three rooms, each furnished with Gord's gold and other awards. His manager, Barry Harvey, says that Gord will be with me in a minute and that he rarely gives interviews. "You're lucky," he says, "You gave us so much notice we could hardly say no."

I know I'm lucky. My press cuttings on Gordon Lightfoot point to him being shy and reluctant to discuss his career in any detail. Allan Jones ("Melody Maker", 1975) said he had "the belligerent manner of a drunk in some late night bar", which presumably means that he was a belligerent drunk in some late night bar, and that's the most complimentary part of the feature. As it turns out, Gordon is very friendly: he shakes my hand and says, "Welcome to Canada and have a blast while you're here. I'm very glad to talk to you." He asks me about Liverpool - I decide to leave that concert performance until later.

Celebrities are nearly always smaller than I think and Gordon Lightfoot with his thin wiry body is no exception, but I hadn't expected him to look his age. He is 60 now and the children's toys alongside his desk look incongruous.

I lob him an easy one for starters. "In your song, you say that Yonge Street is the longest street in the world, is it?" "That's what they say," he replies, "If you take it as Highway 11, it goes all the way from here to the border of

Ontario and Manitoba." Later I ask a cabdriver if he would take a fare from one end of Yonge Street to the other. "That's 700 miles," he replies, "it would take all day."

Back in Gordon's office, I comment that his career has revolved around Yonge Street. "Yeah, there were many so clubs on Yonge Street in the early days. Most of the people that I know well got their practice and workout here: Robbie Robertson, Levon Helm, Ronnie Hawkins, David Clayton-Thomas, oh, there are so many of them."

Gordon adds, "Did you see The Second Cup coffee-houses? There's a couple in Yonge Street and they're all over town. I went to the opening of a rehabilitation centre for alcoholics five years ago and one of my fellow sponsors owned The Second Cup. He said, 'I got the idea from your song, "Second Cup Of Coffee".' I said, 'I am so honored, I am so pleased.'"

Surprisingly, "Second Cup Of Coffee" from his 1972 album, "Don Quixote", is not included in the new 4-CD set, "Songbook". This immense package contains

THE AUTHOR PICTURED WITH GORDON LIGHTFOOT, 1999

five hours of Gordon Lightfoot's music over 88 different tracks. It's a measure of its strength that such good material as "Second Cup Of Coffee", "Daylight Katy" and "I'm Not Supposed To Care" are not included. I recommend "Songbook" very highly, but shop around. The UK prices vary from £40 to £50, but even in Canada, the price is $75. Still, it is the equivalent of eight vinyl LPs with a hardback CD-sized book of memorabilia and recording details as well.

Instead of the missing tracks, we have 16 previously unissued songs. "I was wary about the anthology at first.," Gordon admits, "Rhino wanted to release the unpublished stuff and I thought that the songs wouldn't be good enough. There were good reasons why we didn't release them at the time! In the end, I was pretty pleased with what we found. There's a lot more good ones than I expected. I'm doing the rehearsals for the tour right now and we're including a couple of the rarities in the show. I'm getting a lot of comments on 'Heaven Don't Deserve Me' and I'm hoping the boys can learn it fast." I say it's

as fine as fine can be and I wonder why Gordon hadn't released it in 1972. He replies, "I didn't like it."

The singer-songwriter, Phil Ochs, wrote a highly complimentary profile of Gordon Lightfoot in the folk magazine, "Broadside", in July 1965. Quite prophetically, he said, "Lightfoot, aside from having the greatest last real name of anybody in folk music, is destined to become a pivotal figure in bridging the gap between folk music and country and western." Did Gordon feel the same way about his surname? "Yes, and I would add that it's a Scottish name. My ancestors are from the north of England and Scotland from as far back as I can figure out, so I'm as British as you are, brother (Laughs)." Are there traces of that in your work? "Most definitely, and our down east traditional music, which has also been an influence, originated in Britain."

As it happens, Gordon Meredith Lightfoot was born on 17th November 1938 in Orillia, Ontario, a small town by the shores of Lake Couchiching. He refers to the Second World War in "Drink Yer Glasses Empty". "We had a German prison camp in Orillia, just 80 miles north of Toronto. They used to bring those guys across the pond and keep them in captivity in Camp Borden. I was four or five years old, but I knew something was going on. The aircraft would fly over our street and I remember the coupons we had for milk and beef."

Just as Guy Clark returns to adolescent memories, Gordon Lightfoot does the same. "Yes, certain scenes and certain settings, and it's not just the wilderness I remember. I often recall the parking lot at the golf club in the town where I grew up and where I worked as a caddy on the putting green. It was a very rustic golf course and it wasn't an asphalt parking lot. The parking lot, the trees that surrounded it, the putting green and the clubhouse. It seems the most unlikely setting and yet I have referred to it hundreds of time when I've been searching for the right things to say."

In a delightful, unissued cut on "Songbook", "Mama Said", Gordon sings, "Mama didn't care when I never came home, She learned how to cope with the end of the phone." It indicates that Gordon's mother supported his interest in music. "Both of them did - Gordon Snr and Jessica - they were both very supportive. supportive. They knew that there was nothing else that I was cut out for! During the summer vacations, I would be working at a day job and working with a band at night. It did get pretty tiring doing the two things and I did crash a truck in my last year."

One song, "Did She Mention My Name?", finds him asking about an old girlfriend. Is that how it happened? "Yes, Orillia was a very small town - maybe 15,000 people - but it had all the things that are mentioned in the song like the hockey team, the music and the social life. It's changed now because our town has become a gambling Mecca with the big Rama casino. The guy is asking about his old girlfriend but he knows he will never get her back."

Gordon taught himself guitar before going to California in 1958 to study orchestration and musical theory. He returned to Toronto two years later, determined to become a professional musician. Soon he was in the chorus for CBC-TV's "Country Hoedown". In 1962 he made an album, "The Two Tones At The Village Corner", for Chateau Records with his friend and performing partner, Terry Whelan. Two solo singles were released on Chateau, "Remember Me (I'm The One)" and "It's Too Late, He Wins", both recorded in Nashville and produced by Chet Atkins. The songs sound like demos for Jim Reeves, and Gentleman Jim could have done much worse than "Remember Me (I'm The One)", only the third song that Lightfoot had written. The B-side of "It's Too Late, He Wins", a protest song called "Negotiations", sounds embarrassing today although it was ahead of its time.

On "A Painter Passing Through", there's a narrative song, "I Used To Be A Country Singer", although Gordon didn't write it. "No, that was written by Steve McEown, who is part of Even Steven, who are based in a town close by here. I've heard them doing that song for twenty years and I thought it was time that somebody took the thing and got it done. I'm hoping that somebody do a real professional country job on it and get it off the ground as it is such a good song."

In 1963 the owner of Chateau Records recommended Gordon Lightfoot to BBC-TV and he came to the UK to compère an eight-part series. "George Innes was the producer and it was called 'The Country And Western Show', but it wasn't country and western, more a variety show. I made a lot of friends like Lonnie Donegan and Frank Ifield, who had a couple of real good ones on the charts. Frank was unlucky because Tom Jones came along and knocked his socks off. I liked 'Gossip Calypso' and I was singing that for a while. It was interesting to watch the Beatles and the Rolling Stones coming along. I loved 'From Me To You' and 'She Loves You' and later I thought 'Revolver' had real good songs on it."

Gordon married the Swedish publicist, Britta Olaisson, and they settled in Toronto. Back at Steele's Tavern on Yonge Street, Gordon befriended the Arkansas wild man, Ronnie Hawkins, also making Toronto his home. "He was buying an expensive car and I happened to be tagging along. The salesman did not expect a person who looked like the Hawk to be able to buy one of those things. It turned out that he had the cash on him and I put a song together the next day called 'Talkin' Silver Cloud Blues'. I never recorded it but we played it live around town." The song was recorded by John D. Loudermilk on his album, "A Bizarre Collection Of The Most Unusual Songs".

It was in Steele's Tavern and other Toronto clubs that Lightfoot wrote the songs that established his reputation. "I was working for some time in the bars and lounges and I regard them as 'paid rehearsals'. Ian and Sylvia came to Steele's Tavern to hear what I was doing. Ian told me that they were making an album and wanted to record a couple of my tunes. They went right ahead and did that." "For Lovin' Me" and "Early Morning Rain" are featured on Ian and Sylvia's 1965 album, "Early Morning Rain" and shortly afterwards, the songs were US hits for Peter, Paul and Mary. Were Ian and Sylvia cut up about that? "Not at all. It was Ian who played the songs to Peter Yarrow in the first place!" Gordon has repaid the compliment by recording one of Ian's songs from the "Early Morning Rain" LP, "Red Velvet": "It's a song about a guy left alone, out there in the middle of nowhere."

Like many of his songs, "For Lovin' Me" was intensely personal. "I didn't know what I was doing when I wrote that song. All I knew was that my marriage was breaking up, it didn't break up until five years later but I knew it was breaking up, and some songs predict your own outcome."

At the time "For Lovin' Me" was regarded as a strong folk-pop song, but now it is loathed in feminist tracts on rock. It is the classic example of the songwriter as a male chauvinist pig, and is Gordon amused at the way it has been interpreted? "Not amused, no, I don't want to come off like a male chauvinist pig at all! Now when I listen to it, I think, 'My god, did I said that?' The line, 'I got a hundred more like you' indicates that I was a pretty busy guy. I was known to court more than one woman at a time. It led to confusion and deceit and I gave it up when I was 45. You have to tell too many lies when you are going with too many women at the same time."

As Gordon calls his company, Early Morning Productions, I presume he regards it as his key song. "'Early Morning Rain' has to be pivotal. It was written in an afternoon but it took me five years to write. I was thinking about it for a long time and it happened fast when I finally clicked in. John Denver did 'Leavin' On A Jet Plane' so then there were two songs which dealt with commercial airline travel. There are two ways of doing 'Early Morning Rain'. George Hamilton IV did it my way as did Judy Collins. Peter, Paul and Mary used the changes that Ian and Sylvia had and Elvis Presley followed

that. If a song is recorded by Elvis Presley, then it has to be pivotal! He did a wonderful job on it by the way. It's on an album called 'Elvis Now'."

George Hamilton IV has recorded many of Gordon Lightfoot's songs. "Yes, and he also did a wonderful version of 'Early Morning Rain'. He's been one of my biggest boosters. I love George, he is a great guy but I haven't seen him for years. He invited me to Nashville and I played guitar on some of his sessions although I am not much of a guitarplayer - Chet Atkins was producing and it was well done stuff. I played on 'Ballad Of The Yarmouth Castle', which was about a boat, and a couple of others but I forget what they are right now."

CHET ATKINS

Is this false modesty? Does Gordon not rate his own guitarplaying? Surely his 12-string guitar is one of the most distinctive features of his recordings. "Well, I was working as a single performer for a long time and I used a 12-string for variety as you can get an extra sound out of it. It's a good instrument to play as a soloist, but I have no illusions about my abilities. Did you ever hear Trevor Lucas? God, he's good. And so are Glen Campbell and Roger McGuinn. They play a whole lot better than me."

Gordon also wrote "Ribbon Of Darkness", a No 1 country hit for Marty Robbins in 1965. "That was the biggest surprise of my life. I got a chance to sign with a really good publishing company, Witmark Music in New York, and I had to break a contract to get there and get a release from BMI. They were great songpluggers and they plugged that song right through to Marty Robbins. It came as a complete surprise to me, as did most of the other cover recordings. I loved Marty Robbins, he was the greatest and when he got a hit with that song, I was so thrilled. Then I got to meet him and I was thrilled again."

When I saw Peter, Paul and Mary in Liverpool around 1965, they were praising this new songwriter, Gordon Lightfoot. Some demos for Warner Brothers had led to only one single, but with the same management as Bob Dylan and Peter, Paul and Mary, Gordon signed with United Artists and recorded his first solo album, which emerged in 1969 under the title of "Early Lightfoot" As well as hit songs, there was the genial "Steel Rail Blues" and another chauvinistic song, "I'm Not Sayin'", which was recorded by Nico.

CBC-TV invited Lightfoot to write about the railways for Canada's centennial. He wrote a dramatic six-minute song about the building of the lines, "Canadian Railroad Trilogy", which remains an important part of his stage show. "I've always listened to other performers. I love Bob Dylan and Kris Kristofferson and Tim Hardin and Ramblin' Jack Elliott. I loved the way Bob Gibson strung three Civil War tunes together and that inspired my 'Canadian Railroad Trilogy'. They've put the first version of 'Canadian Railroad Trilogy' in 'Songbook', but we do it a whole lot better now."

"Canadian Railroad Trilogy" was the key song on his second album, "The Way I Feel", and Gordon started having hit singles in Canada with "Spin Spin", "Go Go Round" and "The Way I Feel" itself. Also on that album was another Lightfoot classic, "Song For A Winter's Night", "which I wrote in Cleveland during a summer thunderstorm!". Then came the LP, "Did She Mention My Name?", which included "The Last Time I Saw Her", "Wherefore And Why" and the idyllic "Pussywillows Cattails" as well as the powerful protest song, "Black Day In July".

His 1968 album, "Back Here On Earth", was mostly written in London and includes two songs, "Bitter Green" and "The Circle Is Small", which have become folk club favourites. His final album for United Artists was "Sunday Concert". All his albums have aged well and the 2-for-1 compilations on BGO Records are attractively priced.

Some Gordon Lightfoot songs that I have known for thirty years still mystify me. "Give me an example," he says, "and I'll tell you what it means." I cite the line "And she gave me her presents of paper and tin" from "Affair On 8th Avenue", another song from "Back Here On Earth".

"What do you think it's about?" he asks.

I say, "Is it to do with your marriage breaking up? Two of the early anniversaries are known as paper and tin."

"No," he says, "Think of tin foil. She is giving him a who-knows-what. Maybe it's a sniff, maybe it's a snort. I don't touch cocaine myself but that's what it means."

He adds as if to say I'm not entirely wrong, "Sometimes something can mean more than one thing and can be symbolic, but there is nothing that I write that hasn't got a reason for being there."

"And does it bother you when people can't pick up on things?"

"Not at all because there isn't that much. Most of what I write is pretty straight ahead."

Although Gordon Lightfoot's six albums for United Artists sold well, his flowering as a record artist came when he signed to Frank Sinatra's label, Reprise, in 1970. The first album was called "Sit Down Young Stranger" and I ask Gordon why he chose that for the title song. "I liked what 'Sit Down Young Stranger' had to say as the Americans were bogged down in Vietnam. I was not an American but the song was ambiguous enough to work. It was a good statement and so I made it the title song of the album."

But not for long. A few months later, another track, "If You Could Read My Mind", became a hit record. "The record company asked me to fly to Los Angeles and I said okay. I got out there and they said, 'We want to change the title of the album', and I was in my proud, inflexible days, 'You don't mess with my art' and all that, so I said, 'No, you can't.' We talked for an hour and they explained it algebraically. They said, 'We can sell X but if we change the title, we can sell 7X.' I said, 'I understand, okay.'"

Is "If You Could Read My Mind" a personal statement? "Yes, it was, it's very personal. My marriage had almost ended and and my wife took the song very personally too. I've changed a line in it now. I had written 'the feelings that you lack', which was my chauvinism again. My daughter took issue with me on that, she's 34 years old now and she said, 'Why do you keep saying that about mom all the time?' and so I've changed it to 'the feelings that we lack.'" Gordon and Britta were divorced in 1973 with Britta obtaining custody of their children, Fred and Ingrid.

As Reprise was owned by Frank Sinatra, I wonder if Gordon Lightfoot had met him. "I was signed by Mo Ostin who was Sinatra's right hand man in that department. Sinatra almost did some of my tunes but it didn't work out. I was at the session when he did Stevie Wonder's 'You Are The Sunshine Of My Life', which

I thought he did great but he didn't like it. He then threw 'If You Could Read My Mind' on the floor and said, 'I can't sing this.'"

Gordon Lightfoot was among the first to recognise Kris Kristofferson's talent as "Me And Bobby McGee" is also on that first Reprise album. Around the same time, he recorded "On Susan's Floor". "Yes, I've just put that back into the act. I was at the James Robertson Parkway Inn in Nashville with Waylon Jennings, Shel Silverstein, Vince Matthews and Bob Neuwirth and some other people. Everyone was getting together to play their songs including writers coming in off the pavement to perform. Waylon played 'On Susan's Floor' which Vince and Shel had written and I thought, 'That's a nice song.' Shel was a cartoonist for Playboy magazine but when he met people like Ramblin' Jack Elliott and Bob Dylan, he wanted to be a songwriter."

The second album, "Summer Side Of Life", included some classic Lightfoot compositions including "Cotton Jenny", "Ten Degrees And Getting Colder" and "Same Old Loverman". A previously unreleased song from the same period, "Too Much To Lose", is included in the 4-CD Songbook on Rhino Records. "I like that. I wrote that for the Paul Newman movie, 'Cool Hand Luke', and when they didn't want it, I didn't want it either."

However, when "Don Quixote" was turned down for the Michael Douglas film, "Hail, Hero!", he didn't let the song pass by. It was released as a single and became the title track of a 1972 album. The album also includes "Beautiful", "Alberta Bound" and "Christian Island" and features Ry Cooder, but largely uses his road musicians - Red Shea, Terry Clements and Rick Haynes.

Gordon received a setback when he contracted Bell's Palsy, which paralysed part of his face. His face is partly in shadow on his fourth Reprise album, "Old Dan's Records", because it had not yet returned to normal. "Old Dan's Records" - a pun on "old dance records" - features some of his strongest songs - "That Same Old Obsession", "Hi'Way Songs" and "Can't Depend On Love", and his musicians are enhanced by the bluegrass brothers, Bruce and Larry Good

In 1974 Lightfoot released his most commercial album, "Sundown", with its famous title song. I ask if the song had come easily. "I had a stray girlfriend and although I was a stray myself, I was not feeling good when I wrote that. It was round about the end of our three year relationship. She was out at the bar meeting one of my competitors. When I'm in a relationship and there is infidelity, I find I can make it work for me in songs."

Why did he decide on the title, "Sundown"? "Because it worked. We lived on a farm and we came out of the house into this glorious ball of sun in the west. If you've got the sundown, the worry about a girl, a guitar and some booze, 'Sundown' is the kind of tune you're gonna come up with. 'Sundown' is the biggest selling song I've ever had. I was in Northern Ireland when it hit No 1 in Billboard and they announced it on stage in Belfast. I knew it was No 3 but McCartney was in first place and I didn't think I would top him."

From the same album, "Carefree Highway" also made the US Top 10. That was about an old flame. "She turned up at one of the Massey Hall concerts. I don't think she knew the song was about her and I didn't tell her."

In 1975 Gordon recorded an album, "Cold On The Shoulder", which included a Valentine to his audience, "All The Lovely Ladies", and a song for his daughter, "Fine As Fine Can Be". Mostly though the songs are about love going wrong with "Rainy Day People" standing out.

I tell Gordon that I love the way he plays with words. "Ribbon Of Darkness" is a superb expression and "Cold On The Shoulder" contains several of my favourite examples such as 'high-steppin' strutters' in "Rainy Day People" and that hilarious image, 'She was all decked out like a rainbow trout', in "Rainbow Trout". "Yeah, it's nice to keep the lyrics interesting. I've always had a facility with words and I like them to flow well. I like to include humour if I can, I'm always trying to do that. 'She was all decked out like a rainbow trout' refers to the record parties out in Los Angeles and the way the girls dress right to the roof. Believe me, I've seen some girls like that. (Laughs)"

The breezy title song about rural life, "Summertime Dream", was one of several excellent songs on Gordon's next album. It included his US hit, "The Wreck Of The Edmund Fitzgerald". "The boat actually sank in Canadian waters, it sank on the Canadian side of the line that runs through Lake Superior. It was a good-sounding record but it was six minutes long, and the record company shortened the instrumentals and got it down to 4 minutes 35 seconds for the single. We play it everywhere we go and we love playing it. The people we have met through the song is a story all unto itself. Several events have taken place and I support a scholarship at Western Michigan University, which has a maritime academy. By the way, there's a Woody Guthrie reference in that song where the old cook says, 'It's been good to know you.' It's a tribute to the great songs that he wrote."

Another mysterious line now. In "I'm Not Supposed To Care", Gordon Lightfoot sings, "I'll give you the keys to my flying machine if you like." Is that a reference to his private jet? "Yes, but don't get me wrong. I don't own one of those things, you just rent them. It's the only way to do it, it's been the only way to do it for 25 years and probably people will read this and say 'Isn't that decadent?' and yet it's not, it's the only way to do it."

Gordon's 1978 album, "Endless Wire", included one of his best-known songs, "Daylight Katy", but the sales were starting to fall. The songs on his first digital album, "Dream Street Rose" (1980), are known only to Gordon Lightfoot fans, while "Shadows" (1982) has the worst LP cover I've seen from a major artist. Still, the album included "14 Karat Gold" and "Baby Step Back" ("My previous brother-in-law used to say at the first tee, 'Either you step up or step back.'"), although the album is ruined by some mumbled vocals.

It was around this time that I saw Gordon Lightfoot at the Liverpool Empire. A disastrous performance and he didn't seem happy. "That was a rough time," he admits, "I didn't even finish my show at the Dominion Theatre in London. It was my own fault and it was the last of my drinking days. I gave it up for good in 1982. That was

17 years ago, and I could go back anytime and do a great show now." Did your voice improve after the drinking? He laughs, "No, but my attitude improved a whole lot after the drinking stopped."

His drinking affected all areas of his life. Gordon and his girlfriend, Cathy Coonley, had a son, Eric, but she left him because of his alcoholism and that, combined with a drink-driving conviction, made him break his habit in October 1982.

Gordon Lightfoot's 1983 "Salute" is a neglected album, containing fine songs of Canadian life like "Knotty Pine" and "Whispers Of The North", as well as "Someone To Believe In" and "Broken Dreams". Despite poor sales, his position in Canadian music was assured and he sang the opening lines of Canada's famine relief single, "Tears Are Not Enough". Its producer, David Foster, then wrote a beautiful song with Gordon, "Anything For Love." "That was a collaboration at the suggestion of my Warner/Reprise producers at the time. He wrote the melody and I added the words, and I tried to make it nice, I tried to make it good. It took us four days to record it in LA and he taught me so much that I breezed through the final months of 'East Of Midnight' with no problem at all. There was a song that I just wanted to do with machines and he showed me what to do."

Unfortunately, "East Of Midnight" is another of those forgotten albums but surely "Anything For Love" has the makings of a standard. "I hope so. I heard a country demo on it but they didn't get into the essence of the song."

The 1990s have seen a change in Gordon Lightfoot's lifestyle. He and his second wife, Elizabeth, have two young children, a son Miles and a daughter Meredith. "I used to work all night and sleep all day and I did that for years and years. When I got married, the whole thing turned round and now I go to bed real early. Benjamin Franklin said, 'Early to bed, early to rise, makes a man healthy, wealthy and wise.' I don't know about that, but it's good working early in the morning."

In 1993 he released "Waiting For You" with his declaration of affection, "I'll Prove My Love", and a Bob Dylan song, "Ring Them Bells". "I like 'Ring Them Bells' and we do it well, me and my little band. He was here and I told him that we were doing it and he said, 'Play it for me', and I had to sit right there and play it for him, which I was quite nervous about. I've been to see him five times and he's been to see me once, which is the correct balance. I love that country soundtrack he did for 'Pat Garrett And Billy The Kid' with Bruce Langhorn on guitar. That's fantastic."

"A Painter Passing Through" in 1998 was Lightfoot's first album for five years and only his second album of the 1990s. "With my marital situation and two young children, I don't have the time to do the songwriting anymore. After my first marriage, I didn't get married for 19 years - and that's when I did the bulk of my work. You need peace and quiet to write songs and you don't get peace and quiet when you have a family. I can still play well - we can all still play well - and as long as the health of the group holds, I can keep playing for quite some time, but it remains to be seen whether I will make any more albums. It takes me five years to write enough songs for an album."

ON YONGE STREET

He adds, "I renewed my contract twice during the time I was with Warner Brothers and the one that I made last year was the 14th and last one under the contract, so I have no obligations to make any more albums. I don't have to worry about coming up with new songs."

It sounds as though Gordon Lightfoot is retiring but surely not. I throw out suggestions. In the 1970s, he wrote a delightful children's song, "The Pony Man", so couldn't he write an album of children's songs? He laughs. "That's not an easy option. Children's songs take as long as any other if you want to get them right."

A second suggestion - an album of covers. "I've thought about doing that and I'd enjoy picking the songs. It's not just well-known songs as I get a lot of good stuff submitted to me. There are always four or five songs sitting on the back burner that I might get into at some point."

What about a live album, another Sunday concert from Massey Hall? "We've thought about that too. There is live stuff on the Internet right now that can be downloaded if people want it."

Another choice is to write for other artists. Could he write for the stars emerging from Nashville? "It's hard for me to compare my songs with theirs. I watch the CMT channel and it's real good, although the turnover is tremendous. There's a tremendous talent of talent out there and it's good and solid with a definite style." But, I say, there aren't many good songs anymore. "Oh, I disagree. The songs are there, the competition is there, and country music is alive and well as far as I can see."

Gordon Lightfoot will keep playing 40 or 50 dates a year. "Our drawing power has improved over the past seven or eight years and there has been such an improvement in musical delivery since I have stopped drinking. We have a real powerful show now and it rotates as I change the songs around. We always stay within a framework of two hours and twenty minutes. We play all over North America and we'd love to come to Britain if we could get the time and get it organised, but I don't know how big the demand is there now." I tell him that James Taylor has made a spectacular comeback in the UK and is now regarded as an elder statesman. "That comparison suits me fine. I see us in the same category, Adult Contemporary."

As I leave his office in Yonge Street, I thank him for the interview and also 35 years of great music. "Thank you. I am not a boastful person, and I have difficulty in accepting praise, but thank you for the compliments."

A DATE WITH ELVIS
Talking to Elvis Costello

On 14th April 1999, I was in BBC Radio Merseyside, editing on headphones a concert we had recorded with Julie Gold, who had written "From A Distance". Suddenly, I was asked, "Spencer, do you want to interview Elvis Costello?" "Sure," I said enthusiastically, "When?" "In 15 minutes' time at the Royal Court," I was told, "Steve Caddick is already there setting up his camera. Diane Oxberry can't get over from Manchester for 'NorthWest Tonight'." "What do you want me to ask him?" "Ask him about his album with Burt Bacharach and something about playing in Liverpool."

I put away what I was doing and made the short walk to the Royal Court. I scribbled down a few notes. I had no idea how much time I would have with him but I wanted to make the best of it. God give me strength.

Like many regional theatres,the Royal Court has made mixed fortunes, but we should be glad it's still there. It was rundown following political wrangles and, indeed, was almost demolished for market stalls in the early 80s. Now it is a listed building, and so it should always be there. It is solidly built on steel frames, but the heating, encased in the walls, imploded in the 80s and caused enormous damage. The theatre is getting back to the way it was. The Queen Mary Suite, which was featured in "Chariots Of Fire", has been restored to its former glory. It's hard to believe it was under four feet of water.

My first memory of the Royal Court is seeing Tommy Steele in pantomine in 1957. My mother, highly suspicious of rock'n'rollers, was sure she wouldn't enjoy it. Tommy

Steele came down from the roof, floating down on ballons and flashing his million watt smile. "But he's so clean," exclaimed my mother, visibly surprised.

On another occasion, Wilfrid Hyde-White, appearing in a crime drama, came on stage after 15 minutes, acknowledged the audience's applause, sipped some sherry from the wings, and then said, "Ah, the play", and returned to character. How the rest of the cast must have loved him. Another week, Brian Epstein went nearly every night to see Vivien Leigh in "A Streetcar Named Desire".

Elvis Costello likes playing the Royal Court because his mother, worked there. He was in the star's dressing-room. Or rather, Julie Goodyear's dressing-rooom. She agreed to star in panto if the dressing-room met her specifications. She wanted a bath and there can't be many theatres where you can take a bath. Steve Caddick set up the camera in the dressing-room and had a chair for Elvis and a chair for me. Elvis came in, wearing a black leather jacket and a black leather trilby, and looking very friendly.

I remarked on the health-food buffet laid out on the table. "Oh, we always had that in the dressing-room," said Elvis, "but we used it to throw it at each other back in those days."

I'd been asked to record a five minute interview for "NorthWest Tonight", but Elvis was in no hurry and Steve was happy to record everything we got and give me the soundtrack for my radio programme. Elvis gave us 40

A Date With Elvis

ANTHONY BROWN

minutes, and as he thinks and talks fast, this is an hour with anyone else.

There was only one camera and so when the interview was done, Steve adjusted the camera position for some reverse doubles and I had to do some noddies. Your nod can then be inserted at appropriate points during Elvis' answers. We went on stage to film some of the sound-check. I looked out at the auditorium from the per-former's viewpoint: 1,500 seats and a beautiful ceiling. Elvis could play somewhere bigger, but he feels at home here.

I had no idea that I was going to be talking to you today but I was entering your records on my PC last night and found that I had got 446 tracks of yours.

Good grief, that must be most of them.

I was prompted to do it by seeing you on "TFI Friday" dismissing a lot of your old albums.

No, I thought I was doing quite the opposite! That was what Chris Evans was expecting as when I reissued them on CD a couple of years ago, I was quite truthful in my assessment of them. It was a good opportunity to tell the story and if you're going to ask somebody to buy a record that is a few years old, you have to be prepared to tell the background story. Inevitably, that invites a degree of self-criticism. Even so, I think there is plenty of good music in those records.

No-one seems sure whether to include you as a Liverpool artist or not. Do you count yourself as being a Liverpudlian?

The situation is confusing. I was born in London but I was christened in Birkenhead. My mother's from Liverpool and my father's from Birkenhead, so I don't know what that makes me. I went to school in London for most of my life, but my last two years in school were here in Liverpool. All my holidays were on Merseyside, so I can understand the confusion. Whenever I'm doing anything good, I am appropriated as one of the Liverpool artists and when I'm bad, I get the opposite treatment - "Blooming southerner coming up here, trying to sell a

load of old rubbish to us." It's always going to be like that, and it's the same in Ireland with my dad's family coming from Ireland. I'm an honorary Irishman when I'm doing well and if I'm doing badly, I'm a Brit.

I have an album of your dad's where he is singing Elvis Presley's hits.

Yes, he made a lot of records in the 60s and 70s, mostly cover records. He made some records under his own name and he had a No 1 hit record in Germany, but most of his work was on radio with the Joe Loss Orchestra. He had a very broad repertoire and most of his recordings were on little EPs where people used to cover the hits of the day.

Did he find that frustrating?

I don't know, you'd have to ask him. It was a money-making thing and I know he found it a lot of fun when he had to recreate some bizarre record that had made the charts. The Joe Loss Orchestra kept pace with the sounds of the day more than you would imagine for a big band line-up. They had four or five saxes, trumpets and trombones, and they managed to play the hits of the day very credibly. My record collection bears witness to that because I used to get the demonstration records that my dad was given to learn the songs. That's why I know so many more songs than lots of people my age. I was coming across them all the time as I was growing up.

I heard of someone in the Merseysippi Jazz Band called Wally Fisher who had punched your dad in the 1950s as he wasn't singing the material that he liked.

(Laughs) I don't know anything about that, but it sounds entirely probable.

How big an influence was your father on your musical tastes?

Both my parents were a very big influence on me, and not just in music. I had the example of my father going to work and the discipline of going to work as well as the less glamorous aspects of when I went to rehearsals and saw a lot of people sitting there in shirt-sleeves. It's not all one big party, and I was aware of that very early on. There's a lot of hanging around, a lot of time in dressing-rooms and a lot of draughty theatres. I used to go with my dad to the Hammersmith Palais on a Saturday afternoon while my ma was getting some peace and quiet, and I would see the band perform for a sparse crowd. People would practise their ballroom dancing, so it was a weird glimpse into another world.

And what about your mother's influence?

My mother worked for several music stores, Rushworth's amongst them, and there was a lot of responsibility to know the catalogue and to be informed. You couldn't look it up on a computer, you had to know the catalogue and you had to have an opinion. Records were fragile and expensive, and people would ask, "Is this version of Beethoven's 5th or this one the one that I should be buying?". She developed a very broad taste in music, even broader than my father's really, embracing the be-bop that they grew up listening to and the ballad singers that I have loved all my life like Frank Sinatra, Mel Tormé and Peggy Lee. She has also kept pace with modern sounds and with classical music, I got this aural education before I ever thought of putting a note on the page.

Have you ever thought of doing an album of songs for dancing, either for yourself or by producing your father?

I have performed with my dad on a couple of occasions and we did "At Last", the Glenn Miller song, which was a big tune for him. I enjoyed singing it with him but I don't have a special talent for singing that kind of music. Maybe one day I'll do an album , I don't know. There's no saying what I might do. I have touched on so many different types of music over the years and there's no saying what might become part of it. It's all in my head somewhere and I can sing hundreds of songs that were written

IN "NO SURRENDER"

before the rock'n'roll era. I don't know all the changes and I couldn't play them all the way through, but I do know a surprising amount. I have absorbed them somehow and it must be through repetition and constant exposure to them.

You have sung with Tony Bennett. Were you apprehensive before you sang with him?

I was the first time. The first occasion was in 1982 for an American television show and it was with the Count Basie Orchestra so it was a remarkable invitation to get. I'd had a fair degree of success on my own but I was only five years into my professional life. It was only six months before Count Basie passed away and just to stand up in front of that band was amazing. Unfortunately, I had a terrible sore throat on the night and it became a nightmare. A few years ago I got an invitation to sing with Tony Bennett on his "Unplugged" show and I guess he had a less critical memory of my first appearance than me. I made a better show of it the second time.

The first time I came across you was as part of a duo called Rusty with Allan Mayes and it was in some Liverpool pub. From what I remember, he had the dominant role in the partnership.

Yeah, that is probably right. Allan was a year older than me and he was more familiar with the way things work. He'd played in other bands and I'd just come up from London to live here in 1970. I had only started playing in public in 1969. I joined his current group, a four-piece, when I came to Liverpool. I don't know if it tells you anything about me but within six months we were down to a duo. He had the contacts and he drove the car - I only learnt to drive when I was 35 - and so I was relying on him to get to venues. We played on slow nights at the Yankee Clipper and the Temple Bar. They were happy to let you play there as they thought we might attract a few more drinkers. I'm not sure that the people who came to hear us play were very heavy drinkers. (Laughs) There was a divide at the time between traditional and contemporary folk evenings, and if you played guitar, no matter what music you listened to privately, you were branded either traditional or contemporary folk. A friend of mine, Vin Finn, had a couple of clubs around town based on people writing their own music, but really the audiences didn't want to hear people playing their own songs.

I can recall Paul Simon doing clubs on Merseyside and people thinking that he was wrong for the clubs because he was doing his own material.

Yes, there was a lot of that. There was a songwriters' club in Bold Street that lots of us played at. The clubs staggered from crisis to crisis as none of them made any money. They were put on by dedicated people and they would thrive in one venue for a while, like the Remploy Club over in Wallasey and the British Legion on the north side of the park in Birkenhead.

So lots of people in Liverpool will have seen you in the early days.

Oh yes, people may see me on TV tonight and think, "That looks like the guy I saw years ago" and they're probably right. God knows what I was like, probably terrible, but it's all part of learning how to play. In the end, Allan and I did a residency at the Crow's Nest out in Widnes on a Friday night. That was playing in a pub and so you had to make a lot of noise to be heard, which was a good introduction to rock'n'roll really. I'd never played in a rock band and I didn't do that until I started to live in London. I played an acoustic guitar in Widnes but I have always had a loud voice.

You called yourself Elvis Costello. Everybody knows where the "Elvis" comes from, but is the "Costello" because of Abbott and Costello?

No, no, no! It's my great-grandmother's name and it's an Irish name. I'd always been known by my initials, "D. P.", so it was pretty easy to go to another name. Declan was a difficult name for people to grasp as it is not very common in England, and MacManus made it even more difficult. If I rang someone up to say I was coming down to play, they could never grasp my name, so I needed something a little easier on the ear. I picked something from the family rather than something out of thin air. My first manager chose the Elvis part which was a double dare - you look people straight in the face and say, "I am called Elvis". It was outrageous but it was not as much a liability as being called "Sid Vicious".

The most amazing thing about Elvis Presley is that Elvis Presley is his real name.

Yes, I don't think anyone knows of it existing before that. I thoroughly recomend Peter Guralnick's books about Elvis - there are two volumes, "Last Train To Memphis" about his early life and "Careless Love" from the time he came out of the army until his death. They are the best books about Elvis that you can read and you will find the history of his family there. All his family had names that look like anagrams! Some of them may have suffered from being spelt wrong on electoral registers. He had lots of relations with very unusual names but maybe a lot of people in the south did.

Well, his second name, "Aron", was spelt wrongly.

Right and you get that a lot in America. People came over to America with Irish and Hungarian names and they either wrote them down incorrectly or deliberately changed them as they would be easier to assimilate.

You took the name "Elvis Costello" before Elvis Presley died.

It seems a good while before, but maybe it was only six months. I was putting out records at the back end of 1976 while I was still in a day job. As soon as the first album came out, I had to take the plunge and go professional. A week later I was on the cover of "Melody Maker" and it was like five years' rehearsal for overnight success.

Well, very few people are true overnight successes.

Yes, they have usually had some sort of apprenticeship. When you first start out, it is in your best interests to speak only of the thing of the moment as that is what you want to impress upon people. If you show too much sentiment for all those faltering steps, it diminishes the impact. Once you've established yourself, you can go back and look at it with any affection that you have for it. I don't have tremendously nostalgic feelings for those earlier days. I have friends from that time but then there are lots of people I haven't seen for years.

Did you feel that it might go terrifically wrong for you when Elvis died and that your name would look like a sick joke?

Only for a brief time. It was a good education into the ways of the music business. I'd had one through being with my father but I hadn't had any exposure into the way the media interacted with music. It was obvious to me then how very insubstantial a lot of the attention was, it was down to people wanting to speak to you on the basis of a novelty. I didn't have much respect for that, so I kept myself out of the way. When somebody dies, they are sincere for a while and then they look at it from other angles as they are trying to make the story go on for a bit longer. We had American companies offering to put me on national television and make me some sort of freak show, and I wouldn't have anything to do with it. I was never a huge Elvis Presley fan but I certainly had more respect for him than some of the media

had. I knew his life meant a lot to other people and I had friends who were very upset when he died. I wasn't going to play in that game, and as I was going for a completely different audience, the comparison never came up again. Nobody ever thought that I was an Elvis impersonator as I had established my own identity fairly quickly.

I've loved your albums over the years and I've always enjoyed your bonus songs: you've done songs by the Merseybeats and the Escorts. Were these records which you'd loved in the past?

Yes, some of them I remember from the 60s and some from a record label that I co-owned, Demon Records. We were reissuing some of the best stuff from the 60s and 70s. Usually, I would have heard one or two singles by the groups and I would find that we would be releasing a whole album. I was discovering some fantastic tracks. The Escorts were a great group and I've always loved the Merseybeats. I saw the Merseybeats play when they were guests on the Joe Loss Pop Show on the BBC when I was on my school holidays. I saw them carrying in their amplifiers at nine in the morning, so that was another glimpse into the less glamorous side of pop music. (Laughs)

Paddy Chambers of the Escorts was down on his luck at one stage and he was made up that you had recorded "Night Time".

That's a great song. It's like an Impressions song. The Escorts also cut the Smokey Robinson song, "From Head To Toe", and I think they did a better version than the Miracles. I was paying tribute to their version and it was great to do. It was music that I liked when I was growing up, and I loved rediscovering these tracks when I was with Demon. It was a nice avenue to pursue for a while.

The groups did quite a few Burt Bacharach and Hal David songs like the Merseybeats with "It's Love That Really Counts".

Yes, and people living in England had an advantage over other countries in that some of those songs were hits twice. They were hits for the local artists like Zoot Money and the Merseybeats and Cilla Black and Dusty Springfield, and then you would hear the originals by Dionne Warwick or Jackie deShannon, and some of those would be hits as well. We had the benefit of getting steeped in those songs. That's why I thought it was extraordinary that people were surprised that I should like Burt Bacharach. That must be in the minds of people who only know his music from the Carpenters. In the 60s his music was very intertwined with beat music, and a lot of beat groups played his songs even though they struggled to play them correctly because they didn't have the same orchestration. His songs had an R&B feel about them and the Beatles recorded "Baby It's You".

I love "Painted From Memory" but I was surprised that you didn't write any modern R&B songs together.

Well, Burt was very anxious that we should look forward. There are some R&B tinged songs on the record but it is very difficult to go back to those rhythms, they sound arcane now and it would be like playing Dixieland to be-bop lovers in the 50s. If you said to them, "Let's play like Jelly Roll Morton", they would say, "Are you kidding?" Now we are 70 years away from Jelly Roll Morton, we can listen to it and say, "Wasn't that hip?" It's much harder when you are only a few years away. You can't have the same affection for it and you want to move on and create new songs.

Burt Bacharach wrote most of his best-known songs with Hal David. Hal David wrote very edgy, neurotic lyrics, and there is an element of that in your own work, isn't there?

I'm glad that you've pointed that out because people miss that Hal David's words are sometimes very torrid, and Burt's melodies mirror that, especially his harmonies with the little jumps that are made rhythmically. I cannot understand the description of Burt Bacharach's music being "Easy Listening". It may be rhythmically gentle in its expression but it is very dramatic and it has such strength.

How did you work together?

We wrote the music for the album together - some people assume that I wrote the words and he wrote the music, but we wrote the music together. Sometimes he led the way and other times I led the way. I may have written a larger proportion of the music of some of them, but we always worked on them together, and there would always be a crucial structural change made by one examining the other's composition. Sometimes we would write bar by bar and note by note, sitting at the piano together. That was very difficult, but we managed it. Then I would write the text and I learnt from the example of Hal David, without ever wishing to copy him, that I should never take away from the drama of the music by having the words draw attention to themselves. The text should reflect what is going on in the music. Some of my own songs are elaborate lyrically, but I didn't need to do that with these songs because the music was already telling the story. I just had to underline it with the words. In that way, the two pieces of the composition fitted together much better.

But the songs, like your own songs, have to go somewhere. They have to say something, don't they?

We wrote our first song together for a movie, "Grace Of My Heart", and that was "God Give Me Strength". From writing that, we had a theme of lost love, something which is in everybody's life and experience. It wasn't difficult to develop that theme and have an album that stayed in that mood. The experience that you often have on modern albums, and my own in particular, is that they jump around all over the place. Sometimes it's hard for people to believe that the same person created the songs. On this album, we stayed in the same world emotionally, but there's enough substance in those ideas to sustain at least one album's worth of material. Songwriters have been writing songs of lost love for hundreds of years, so we weren't going to run out of topics!

Was Burt Bacharach demanding in the studio when it came to recording your vocals?

I think we were both very demanding of the circumstances. I've seen the film of him pushing Cilla Black for endless takes on "Alfie", which is presumably what you are referring to, but we rarely went past six takes on a song. We were trying to cut live vocals with the tracks. Sometimes we would recut the track because we weren't happy with the playing, not the singing. We recut two songs on other days. I did some vocals again, but some of the best vocals are live and a couple are first takes. I'm not suggesting that Burt has lowered his standards, but I am a different kind of singer from the singers who have worked with him in the past. I have an edgier voice and I am going for emotion and not perfection. There are flaws in all of my records, technically speaking, but what are you comparing it to? I sing like me, I don't sing like other people. I was trying to represent the truth of these songs, and I believe I achieved it.

Why did you choose to write about Toledo?

Paris, Texas has already been done in a movie, but it's one of those names where there is a very splendid place in Spain and a rather dismal, industrial town in Ohio. I wanted the contrast. The song is about a man who has been unfaithful and he has to face his wickedness and confess. He will do anything to excuse himself and delay the moment when he has to confess, so it's a roundabout way of saying that the grass is always greener on the other side. That is really the rhyme that he invents around the comparison of the two Toledos.

You must have been delighted with its reception because the critical response has been great and you have won a Grammy.

Yes, it's been great. We've had a lot of attention for the record from all over the world and from some countries that I am very fond of like Italy, Sweden and Holland. It reintroduced me to the Australian audience as I hadn't been there for seven years and it has done very well here too. It's been a difficult time for the record company that released it because as soon as it was released, the record company got taken over, but I always have bad luck with these things. That makes it very difficult for people to do their jobs as they are nervous about their own future inside the new company. I'm on the road now with Steve Nieve and that gives people the opportunity to have a second look at it. A single, "Toledo", is being released and Steve and I are out doing these concerts. Central to the repertoire are the songs from "Painted From Memory".

And you have done several concerts with Burt Bacharach himself.

Oh yes, we did six concerts and a television show and it's been great - a 30 piece orchestra, strings and vocalists - but it is very risky to take that on the road. You have to be certain that there will be an audience that will fill the hall to the rafters in every town. It's also very demanding for Burt who will not delegate, which means that he rehearses up to five hours a day and then does a two hour show. I would love to persuade him to do more because it is great fun, but the songs were originally written at the piano and so a different light is shone on them when you hear them in piano and voice performance. You hear the raw composition and Steve played an understated role on the record. He played second keyboards, so hearing him interpret the songs is another pleasure for me. I am feeding off that in the concerts we are doing at the moment.

Have you and Burt thought of writing new songs for Dionne Warwick?

No, but if she were to like any of the songs on "Painted From Memory", I would be delighted if she would record them. She is someone that I have always admired. She works with Burt intermittently, but I don't think I would write something specifically for her. That would be trespassing on Hal David's territory a bit too much. They are already some covers from "Painted From Memory". Charles Lloyd, the jazz saxophonist, has recorded "God Give Me Strength" and there will be several vocal covers over the next few months. A whole album of instrumental versions of the songs from "Painted From Memory" is coming out under the direction of the guitar-player Bill Frisell.

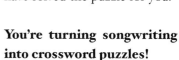

A few years ago you wrote some songs with Paul McCartney and it seemed to me that you were trying to get him back to his Beatle roots.

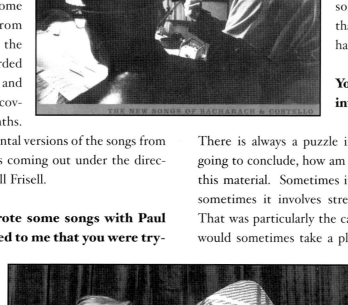

BURT BACHARACH AND ELVIS COSTELLO

Well, there were certain cadences in the songs that appealed to me and he didn't object, though he would give me a sideways look sometimes. I can't sing up above him as his voice is so high so I would end up below him, which is a relationship he was familiar with from the Beatles. We wrote a bunch of really good songs and a couple of them were big hits - "Veronica" was a big hit for me and "My Brave Face" was a Top 20 hit in America for him. A couple of songs have stuck around in my repertoire, "So Like Candy" and "That Day Is Done", which is a song I'm very fond of. It was great working with him and also to record with him. Of course it was. I was thrilled.

So you like both writing on your own and with other people.

Yes, you can't compare them because you give up certain things when you write with someone else. You might see a way that this puzzle of music and words could work out, but because you have to accommodate this other person, you can't have it that way. That's what you give up. What you gain is that unexpected thing when someone suggests something that didn't occur to you. They have solved the puzzle for you.

You're turning songwriting into crossword puzzles!

There is always a puzzle in writing music: how is this going to conclude, how am I going to get the best out of this material. Sometimes it involves another statement, sometimes it involves stretching the original material. That was particularly the case with Burt Bacharach. He would sometimes take a plainly phrased piece of music and then break up the metre to make it more characteristic. With Paul McCartney, it was more spontaneous, it was batting ideas back and forth until something emerged. I have written with a number of other people, I have written with my wife, I have written many songs on one-off occasions over the years, but the complete freedom of writing to my own criteria is something that I am much more familiar with. I have written 250 songs on my own, so by far the largest proportion, I have written on my own.

What is a Lennon and McCartney song where you really appreciate the craft of their songwriting?

If you're looking at songs that they actually wrote together, I would say "We Can Work It Out". That is a wonderful song but you can only guess at who wrote what. People often do that and they're wrong. People have done that with my songs with Burt Bacharach. They have told me absolutely straight-faced that they love "Toledo" because it is pure Bacharach. I don't think Burt would mind me saying that I could play you the original draft of that song, which is entirely my music, and although we did much work on it together, you would be able to recognise it as the song, "Toledo". I am not saying that I wrote that one and he didn't, but I wrote a larger proportion of the initial music, and then we crafted it together until it became more interesting. I don't think that you can make assumptions about who did what, but there are hundreds of Lennon and McCartney songs that I love.

You have just taken part in the Linda McCartney tribute concert. Did you know her well over the years?

Obviously I did, yeah. We did a Concert For The People Of Kampuchea at the end of 1979 with Wings. Later, we were working in adjacent studios around the time of "Tug Of War" and "Imperial Bedroom". Paul and Linda were always really friendly, and then the most important time was when I was working with Paul on the songs for "Flowers In The Dirt" and the other songs that came out of those sessions. Linda was tremendously welcoming and put myself and my wife very much at ease. That isn't a trivial thing when you are dealing with someone who, no matter how much self-confidence you have, is still the person that he is. It's bound to be intimidating. She was full of affection and good spirit and she always encouraged our collaboration. She was a lovely person who stood up for what she believed in and often got a lot of flak for it. Not to mention her beautiful artistic eye as a photographer.

Most of the flak was because Paul had her in the band.

That criticism is real stupidity and I could never understand it. People were judging them by the wrong criteria. They were saying, "This isn't the Beatles, this is what we want." It was just a different way to approach playing.

How did you decide what to perform on the tribute for Linda McCartney?

I think everybody wanted to sing songs that would resonate through the evening. I sang one of Paul's songs, a very beautiful ballad, "Warm And Beautiful", with an arrangement by Mike Thomas whom I worked with in the Brodksy Quartet. I performed it with just piano and the Duke Quartet who augmented the Pretenders for much of the evening. I did "That Day Is Done" with piano, which is one of the songs from "Flowers In The Dirt" that Paul and I wrote together, which is like a spiritual, you might say. Then I did the Nick Lowe song, "What's So Funny About Peace, Love And Understanding?" using the Pretenders for a little rock-'n'roll, and then later on, in the finale, I played rhythm guitar and sang harmony with Paul for "Lonesome Town" and "All My Loving". It was a gas to do "All My Loving" with him. We did a smashing version at the soundcheck as a combo, but inevitably everybody runs onto the stage at these sort of events as they wanted to wish him well. Someone was yowling out of tune. For those who hear the harmony on TV, that wasn't me singing out of tune, I was dead in tune!

It was clearly a very emotional night for Paul McCartney.

Yes, he went on stage to acknowledge the audience, to thank everyone who had attended in honour of Linda and to thank all the musicians, but I don't think that anyone was certain that he would perform until the moment actually came. That was a very difficult moment for him. He did it with tremendous grace and tremendous composure. The papers said he was tearful but he was full of emotion and I saw somebody speaking with a lot of love about somebody he adored. It was an uplifting and rather exhausting evening, not just because it was physically long but because those sentiments are very draining on you. I felt like I'd done a three-hour show and I'd only sung five songs.

It also must be frustrating because once you've done a few songs, you've got to get off.

Yes, Steve Nieve said that our three songs were over like a flash, but everyone came along with the right attitude and with good songs to sing.

Over the years you have written political songs like "Peace In Our Time" and "Shipbuilding". Have you thought of writing about Kosovo?

It's not a songwriter's responsibility to comment on everything that happens. So many conflicting thoughts come to mind in times like these, and I don't think so much of my own view of the world that I have something unique to say. Something may emerge but it doesn't always work like that. It isn't - "Something happens and I must write about it." - a unique train of thoughts has to come out of the event, and that was the case with "Tramp The Dirt Down", "Shipbuilding" and "Pills And Soap", which are the strongest of those songs. I don't want to be knee-jerked into doing something about it. You have to wait to how it works out and see who's responsible in the long run.

How did you come to write "Alison"?

I picked up a guitar one day and it came out. It is very hard to remember how songs came out, especially when it is 23 years ago. I had in mind the Detroit Spinners' song, "Ghetto Child", which doesn't have anything to do with the song lyrically, but that was the song it was modelled on musically. I often model a song on something I like and then it comes out all different. Some of my most original songs have been when I have been trying to copy somebody and got it wrong!

You had your first major cover with Linda Ronstadt's version of "Alison".

Yeah, that made me a ton of money, not that I was very grateful. It made the difference between having to do what record company people said and being able to go my own way, so that cover brought me a bit of liberty.

And what about "Watching The Detectives"?

I used to read a lot of Raymond Chandler's books and I was trying to write a mystery story in a song. There are certain reggae records that I took ideas from, and "Down By The River" by Neil Young is in there somewhere., you know, in terms of the rhythm guitar part. There's also the guitar theme for "Man Of Mystery", certain spooky Bernard Herrmann themes for Hitchcock's films, and the music for "The Twilight Zone"! I was trying to incorporate all that, but I didn't have access to an orchestra and it was done with a combo band. That's the way a lot of pop music works, you're trying to evoke things that are done with much grander sounds, and you end up doing them with old tin cans and elastic bands.

You did some concerts with Bob Dylan. Did you discuss songwriting with him?

Not really, but I've had some really interesting conversations with him as our paths have crossed a number of times. They are unique and private conversations, but I don't think there has been anything profound. I enjoyed playing those concerts with him. I had never supported anybody before. I went along with my guitar and as I was unexpected on the bill, I could play whatever I wanted. Nobody was going to shout for "Oliver's Army" or anything like that. I had the licence to do whatever I wanted, which turned out to be new songs.

Do you like the way he constantly revises his own songs?

I think he is absolutely fascinating, constantly fascinating. There is nobody like him, at least there is but not in music. He is much closer to Picasso.

Elvis Costello, thank you very much.

Thank you.

THE LINE KING
Interview with Sir Tim Rice

Sir Tim Rice's autobiography had been expected for some years and the first volume, "Oh, What A Circus", was published in 1999. The 450 pages cover his life up to and including the opening of "Evita", effectively 1944 to 1978. He and Andrew Lloyd Webber transformed British musical theatre and made it a world force with "Joseph And The Amazing Technicolor Dreamcoat", "Jesus Christ Superstar" and "Evita". It was a partnership of equals and they showed that musicals could cover controversial material and did not need spoken dialogue.

Since his partnership with Andrew Lloyd Webber, Tim Rice's career has been patchy. "Blondel", which he wrote with Stephen Oliver, had some months at the Old Vic but it was not a financial success. "Chess", an extraordinary subject for a musical, was written with Björn Ulvaeus and Benny Andersson from Abba, and had long theatrical runs as well as producing the standard, "I Know Him So Well".

In recent times, Tim Rice has become an Oscar-winning Disney lyricist and his songs for "Aladdin" (with Alan Menken) and "The Lion King" (with Elton John) have been very well received. The songs from the all-star album of "Aida", again written with Elton, were intended for a stage musical, and another musical, "King David", this time with Alan Menken, has been completed. Lord Lloyd Webber - try saying that when you've had a few! - is much mocked by the media, but Sir Tim also has his detractors. The phenomenal success of "The Lion King" is no guarantee that the next project will do as well:

Tim Rice gave a few interviews for his book in between rehearsals for the London opening of "The Lion King". I was allotted half an hour which was not long enough for someone who is naturally talkative and has done so much. I would have liked his views on other lyricists and composers and how he worked with different writers. I would have liked more about his early years (when he worked at EMI and produced Scaffold) and to know whether there is any life in the first musical that he wrote with Andrew Lloyd Webber, "The Likes Of Us", which concerns Dr Barnardo and has never been produced. Maybe next time.

Most of your published works are show songs, songs written for other characters rather than yourself, and yet so many songwriters such as John Lennon and Joni Mitchell write about themselves. I wonder whether you feel cut off from this or whether, in an oblique way, you have been writing about yourself because you do you call your autobiography after one of your songs, "Oh, What A Circus".

There is an element in any writer's work of himself, however much that might not seem to be the case. I would certainly say that in some of my songs, although written for shows, there are bits of me. There's probably more of me in "Chess" than in any other show, but "High Flying, Adored" from "Evita" is a song which questions the value of fame and fortune and even "Don't Cry For Me Argentina" contains something of myself. That song was written as an insincere speech given by a political manipulator, although it was delivered deliberately as a pretty pop song in order to manipulate the audience. "Any Dream Will Do" has a few of my thoughts in it, so, by and large, I have included my personal feelings in my songs.

Could you ever imagine yourself writing a song like John Lennon's "Working Class Hero"?

Hardly, it'd be a middle class hero with me! John Lennon had an incredible ability to write incredibly personal songs. Look at "Oh Yoko!" and the fact that he mentioned Yoko by name in so many of his songs. Most songwriters might write "I love you" and it wouldn't be "I love so-and-so", if you know what I mean. I don't think that I would ever get as specifically personal as John Lennon. You can often say personal things, knowing that a lot of people won't realise that it is about yourself. It is quite nice really - you can reveal yourself to the world but only to those who want to see it. (Laughs)

That's an advantage of the lyricist over the composer of the music.

The interpretation of what the music says is often as much in the mind of the listener as it is in that of the composer. A composer can write a beautiful melody and it might mean three different things, all equally valid, to three different listeners. That doesn't happen with words, I'm not saying it can never happen, but words by their definition are much more specific. They say something straightforward or pretty definite and can only be interpreted in one way. You hardly ever get a lyricist who is a child prodigy. Nobody writes anything that is truly considered good until they are at least 17 or 18, whereas many composers have written good pieces at much younger ages. Mozart was writing beautiful pieces when he was six! You don't need as much

experience to create things with music as you do with words.

But can too much experience get in the way of a good lyric? I get the feeling that you would love to write something like "Awopbopaloobop Alopbamboom", but you are now too sophisticated to do so.

I think that's spot on. "Tutti Frutti", which you have just quoted brilliantly, is a great lyric. It's fun and it's very memorable. "Blue Suede Shoes" is a great lyric. "Summertime Blues" is a great lyric and a sophisticated lyric, and that's a straightforward rock'n'roll song. I find it very difficult to be simple, certainly these days, and some of the best songs I've written in the past - "Everything's Alright", for example - have had very simple lyrics, and often those are the ones that hit home. You can have too much experience, too much technique, and you can sometimes forget that your basic job is communication, which is the most important thing for any songwriter to remember.

Even though your songs for Disney, like the score of "The Lion King", are aimed at children, they are by no means children's songs and they are very sophisticated in many ways.

What I tried to do with "The Lion King", and indeed with "Joseph" many years before that, was to write something that would appeal to the young, the pre-teens if you like, but would not talk down to them and was not afraid to use words that were sophisticated or new to them, if they were the best words. I think too that this is one of the secrets of the success of the Harry Potter books. If a complex word is needed, the author, J. K. Rowling, will use a complex word rather than talk down and make things easy. As long as a child can understand 75% or 80%

of the lyric, they may learn and understand the other 20% and maybe learn new words in the process. In "The Lion King", I use the expression, "quid pro quo", which wouldn't be well known to anyone of eight or nine. In "Joseph", I remember some children asking me what "fratricide" meant, and having a bit of sophistication is terrific in a children's work. You shouldn't be deliberately long-worded but you shouldn't be afraid of using the right word, even if it happens to be an adult one.

That leads onto a very interesting point. I had Marianne Faithfull on the show and we got talking about Jerome Kern's "Yesterdays", which she had recorded. I was saying that even though it was by Jerome Kern, it was bad songwriting to rhyme "yesterdays" with "sequesterdays" because nobody would use that word in conversation, even at the time that he was writing the song. She disagreed, saying it was a marvellous word to sing and that it fitted perfectly into the lyric.

This is an awful admission but I don't know the song, although I've heard of it of course. I don't know if that song was written for a musical or whether it was a one-off song, but musicals tended to be more sophisticated in that way. Nowadays, you can still be sophisticated but you use more colloquial expressions like "I Don't Know How To Love Him" or "I Know Him So Well", although that doesn't mean that they are banal songs. I don't think that I would use the word, "sequesterdays", although I did make up "Machiavell-me" in "Evita", so who knows? I must just add "Yester-Me, Yester-You, Yesterday" by Stevie Wonder. That is more basic, of course, but that title works really well.

Your first staged musical with Andrew Lloyd Webber was "Joseph And The Amazing Technicolor Dreamcoat". That started as a 20 minute musical and became a two hour stage play.

"Any Dream Will Do" was in it from the beginning and yet it didn't become a hit until many years later. Didn't you realise its potential at the time?

I don't think we did immediately, but it was No 1 in Ireland and No 1 in Australia quite soon after the show was written. It wasn't until the big Jason Donovan production of "Joseph" in 1991 that it became a big bona fide hit single here. Initially, we thought of it as a show song and put it on the studio album. Sometime later, about the middle of 1969, we recorded a choirboy singing "Any Dream Will Do" for a single and I changed the lyrics, not completely but I took out the references to coloured coats and anything to do with Joseph. This was silly because that was the appeal of the song, lyrically, in the first place. I just didn't think that the song had potential as it stood as a hit single.

Something that you hardly mention in your book is the tremendous Albert Finney film, "Gumshoe", which was set in Liverpool.

I thought it was an excellent film and I saw it again on television not that long ago and I thought, "Yes, it's a good movie." If I haven't mentioned it other than in passing, it is because I didn't have much to do with it. Andrew wrote the score and I was only asked to contribute a lyric to one song, which was only heard by the hero when he is playing a record in his bedroom. It's called "Baby, You're Good For Me" and it was sung by Roy Young, who used to be with Cliff Bennett and the Rebel Rousers. It was never issued on record as there wasn't even a soundtrack LP.

No, I have a single of the song...

Sorry, yes, there are two songs actually. There is a song called "Finally", which is more or less the same tune that Andrew eventually used for "Sunset Boulevard".

It worked instrumentally very well in the film, but sticking words on it didn't work. Perhaps they were bad words. We recorded the song with Pamela Paterson, who was on "Opportunity Knocks". Andrew spotted her and thought that she would be the girl to sing the song, but the song wasn't good enough and I don't know whatever happened to Pamela Paterson. I don't think it was her fault that the single was a flop.

Back to Liverpool again and "Jesus Christ Superstar". I had always assumed that the genesis for that show was John Lennon's remark about the Beatles being bigger than Jesus Christ.

John Lennon said that in 1966, a long time before "Superstar", but the pop music that kicked me into action on "Jesus Christ Superstar" was Paul Jones of Manfred Mann singing the wonderful Bob Dylan song, "With God On Our Side" on "Ready Steady Go!". It contains the couplet:

> *"Now I can't think for you,*
> *you'll have to decide*
> *Whether Judas Iscariot had*
> *God on his side."*

Brilliant lines. Even before that, when I was at school, having been to a couple of very religious schools, I thought that Judas Iscariot and Pontius Pilate were two people who were permanently condemned for their part in the destruction of Jesus. I wondered how I would have felt if I had been around at the time, would I have believed Jesus to be anything other than a man. I was preoccupied with these thoughts, and thought that one day I would write a book or a play or an article about it. I know now that these were not particularly original thoughts. When I met Andrew and I found myself moving down the path of musicals, it crossed my mind, after seeing Manfred Mann, that maybe Judas' story could be a musical. We were going to call it "Judas Iscariot", which would have been a good title, and then we thought we would call it "Jesus Christ" and then finally, "Jesus Christ Superstar".

You did give Judas the best songs, somewhat better than Jesus' songs.

I think you're right, but then I identify with Judas far more than with Jesus - I think of myself as being human rather than as a god! It was easier to write more natural, human songs for Judas, although the "Gethsemane" song that Jesus has is strong. Also, Judas tended to be ranting and raving and attacking and pushing the action along, whereas Jesus, at that stage in his life, was very passive and waiting for it to happen. He was coming to the conclusion that this was his destiny. "Gethsemane" has him asking, "Should I fight it one more time or should I accept the hand I have been dealt by God?" Jesus is tortured and beaten and tried by Pilate and, as in the Bible, he doesn't put up much of a fight. He only has an intellectual response, and he doesn't say, "Right, lads, get the swords out, let's attack." He doesn't try to escape.

Around that time, the Lord Chamberlain's office had been abolished so what you could do on the stage was much freer. Five years earlier, "Jesus Christ Superstar" could never have been staged.

I have never really thought about that until you said it, so there's always something new. The Lord Chamberlain had the power to cut, alter or stop a production, and "Hair" was the first musical to be staged after the post was abolished. Robert Stigwood, who produced "Hair", very craftily got a lot of publicity. He said, "I'm delaying the opening of 'Hair' because otherwise the Lord Chamberlain would stop me as it contains nude people and rude words. Even though I have signed up the cast and booked the theatre, I am going to keep it dark until we can run it without the Lord Chamberlain." It was wonderful publicity and six weeks of nothing took place, except for lots of publicity about how terrible this show must be. "Jesus Christ Superstar" followed on three years later and now you mention it, I guess it would have had trouble. We would have had to alter it enormously.

It would have been under the cosh so much that it would have effectively destroyed it.

Did you like Tom Paxton's parody, "Jesus Christ, S.R.O."?

I don't remember particularly liking it if I'm honest, but I don't mind being parodied. I've got the record and I know I played it at the time. I was flattered that someone as distinguished as Tom Paxton should consider us worthy of parody but I don't recall the record being that good.

I was struck by the original cast album of "Jesus Christ Superstar". You had Murray Head, Ian Gillan of Deep Purple, Paul Raven who became Gary Glitter, and Mike D'Abo from Manfred Mann. Yvonne Elliman sang "I Don't Know How To Love Him" brilliantly.

Yvonne Elliman is quite wonderful and she did "I Don't Know How To Love Him" beautifully the first time she was asked to record it. She also sang her other parts on the record brilliantly and then went into the show on Broadway. Sometime later, she asked, "Why does Jesus' mother sing 'I Don't Know How To Love Him'? Why would his mother feel this way?" She genuinely thought that the part she was playing, Mary Magdalene, was Jesus' mother. She was confused and it's very understandable. She had a Japanese mum and she didn't know that much about the Christian story. She sang the song so beautifully and yet no director had felt it necessary to explain who Mary Magdalene was. Everyone wrongly assumed that she would know who she was as the story was so well-known. This goes to show how motivation and dramatic art and all that stuff that directors come up with is a complete waste of time. In musicals, you either sing in tune or you don't, and that's almost all that matters.

TIM RICE PICTURED WITH ANDREW LLOYD WEBBER

In a musical you decide on the characters you are going to have and then you decide on what they are going to sing, and in some musicals, a main character may not get a song. For example, Bill Sikes doesn't sing in Lionel Bart's "Oliver!", presumably because Lionel Bart couldn't come up with anything suitable. Similarly, the narrator in "Blood Brothers" only pushes the plot along and could do with a decent song.

Yes, you have to tell the story and get all the dramatic moments you need without worrying unnecessarily whether each character has got enough good songs or whether each character has got the right balance of songs. As you pointed out earlier, maybe we should have given Jesus a couple more in "Superstar" but in a way, it is Judas' story and perhaps the title is misleading. And "Blood Brothers", I have always regarded as a brilliant play with songs rather than a musical - it's that way round, I think. It's difficult - Mary Magdalene in "Superstar" has one and a half great songs in the first half and none in the second. Because of this imbalance, we decided to add a new song, "Could We Start Again Please", and that has helped as it meant that her character didn't disappear. It doesn't matter so much on a record because you can always put the track on again.

I expected to read a lot about your disagreements with Andrew Lloyd Webber in the book, but you are very kind to him. You do mention his tantrums from time to time and you do mention people becoming "non-persons" with him. Did you ever become a "non-person"?

No, I don't think I have done. We have had major rows where a conversation might not then take place for two or three months, but I have never felt that it was permanent and we didn't have a dramatic break-up, we just drifted apart. You can easily go for three or four months without seeing someone if you're not working with them. There were a few tantrums in the early days but nothing too serious. He would get very depressed before the opening of a show or before the launch of a new project and he would say it was terrible and was never going to work. This can be contagious. The first time was with "Joseph" but we all believed it was terrible. He wanted to call off "Superstar" with only three days to go and I went along with this for a while. I thought, "Oh my god, he's probably right." He was the same with "Evita", but this time I was wised up and I said, "No, this is actually very good, don't worry."

And now you are working with Elton John who is famous for his tantrums!

(Laughs) Yes, composers must be a sensitive lot! I've never seen one of Elton's tantrums. He has always behaved impeccably with me. [*Note: Since this interview, Elton has stormed out of the Broadway opening of their musical, "Aida", so possibly Sir Tim got more than he bargained for.*]

Were you disappointed that Julie Covington didn't want to play the lead role in the first stage production of "Evita"?

I think we were at the time, yes, no question of that. Julie had done a wonderful job in the studio and she seemed extremely keen on the whole project and then suddenly, towards the end of 1976 when the single began to show signs of being a hit, she got less and less interested in the project. She backed away from it and began to feel that it was a fascist plot, that we were exploiting the workers. I'm exaggerating a bit but she definitely disapproved of the success of "Don't Cry For Me Argentina". She did turn down the part of Evita and we were concerned because we hadn't found anybody else who could do it. We began auditioning and we still couldn't find anyone. We thought that Julie might relent, we couldn't believe that she would turn the part down. In the end, we found Elaine Paige who was perfect for the role, and I think, with great respect to Julie, probably better. She was a better musical actress than Julie and she had a much more powerful voice. She could hit the back of the stalls, she had all the range of emotions and she was also a brilliant actress. We didn't think that we would find someone as good as Elaine until we found her. Julie is astoundingly

good but she didn't have the stamina or the desire to belt out a huge part in a huge musical night after night after night. She was a straight actress who happened to have a beautiful voice, which worked wonderfully in the studio. Eventually she came round and accepted that she had made a contribution towards a bit of theatre history.

Finally, Tim, I know that you wrote Elvis Presley's final record.

Elvis was a hero to both of us and we always hoped that Elvis would sing one of our songs. He was doing covers towards the end of his life - in fact, he did covers for most of his life - and we thought it would be terrific if we would cover something of ours. We sent him the "Joseph" LP, but we never got any response. We knew the publisher, Freddy Bienstock, who controlled his recording output to a certain extent, and Freddy said, "If you have a couple of original songs for Elvis and if Elvis' company has the publishing of these songs," - that is, owns the copyright - "there's a good chance that Elvis will record them." I thought, "Great. Publishing is a small deal and Elvis can have my house and car if he records something of mine." Andrew and I wrote a couple of songs and one of them was "It's Easy For You". We sent it to Freddy in the middle of 1974 and we kept hearing, "Yes, he's going to record it, he's going to record it", but nothing happened until 1976, one of his last sessions at Graceland, and again nothing happened again for quite a while. It was the final track on the album, "Moody Blue", and I had two days of listening to this wonderful voice making a reasonable fist of our nice but lightweight song, "It's Easy For You". I was holding the album in my hands and I was so pleased that Elvis had done one of our songs, that Elvis had actually spent five minutes learning our song and recording it. Then Elvis moved to that great jukebox in the sky, and I had the last track on the last side of his last album while he was still alive. About the same time, I had the last track on the last side of the last album of Bing Crosby before he died which was a song I wrote with Marvin Hamlisch called ironically "The Only Way To Go", and I thought, "Oh my goodness, there's a curse here." When Whitney Houston recorded "I Know Him So Well" as the last track on one of her albums, I thought I hope she doesn't pop off now! Luckily, she's survived.

Tim Rice, thanks very much for talking to us.

Thank you, Spencer, you've been a gent.

WE CAN BE HEROES JUST FOR ONE DAY

Tribute songs

I have written about Elton John's double-tribute "Candle In The Rain" separately, but it is by no means unique in eulogising a 20th century icon. In this chapter, I look at some other tribute records and in order to form my Top 40, the following rules applied, although I occasionally break them:

(1) The subject should be dead, or at least inactive, when the song was written. Hence, songs to Nelson Mandela are ineligible, and similarly discarded are the tribute to Don McLean, "Killing Me Softly With His Song", John Stewart's powerful song about the moon landing, "Armstrong", and David Bowie's "Andy Warhol".

(2) The song has to be complimentary, so songs about Adolf Hitler are excluded.

(3) The subject must have died this century as otherwise, we'd be weighed down with songs about Jesus Christ and, for that matter, Jesse James. And, of course, Don McLean's "Vincent".

(4) By and large, the subject is not to be a musician as there are hundreds of tributes to Hank Williams, Elvis Presley and John Lennon and really the singers are only praising their own kind.

I haven't included any classical compositions in the list, but one of the most intriguing is Charles Koechlin's "Seven Stars Symphony", which was written in 1933.

STEPHEN BIKO (1946-1977)
Activist who founded the South African Students' Organisation and worked hard to establish black pride and consciousness. Arrested, he died during a hunger strike and probably at police hands. The issues are confronted in the film, "Cry Freedom".

(1) THE DEATH OF STEPHEN BIKO -
TOM PAXTON
(Vanguard VS 5009, 1978)
The adjective that fits so much of Tom Paxton's work is "worthy". He wrote about injustice so poignantly in "The Death Of Stephen Biko", and he told me, "Stephen Biko's death was despicable and I'd wanted to write about it for some months. The 'New York Times' then gave all the details including some things that the South African Government cannot have wanted to make public. I knew then that I no longer had any excuse for not writing that song." "The Death Of Stephen Biko" is intense and very moving, but I am sorry that it was not covered by a major artist - Paxton doesn't have the voice for the chanting refrain of "Ah, ah, Africa". The more restrained version on "Politics - Live" (Flying Fish FF 70486, 1989) is more suited to his style.

(2) BIKO - PETER GABRIEL
(Charisma CB 370, 1980, No.33)
Peter Gabriel had been moved at the time of Biko's death and later, when he was researching African rhythms, "it seemed appropriate to write the song." It contained the memorable lines, "Outside the world is black and white /

A man is only one colour dead." Gabriel performed "Biko" at Nelson Mandela's 70th Birthday Concert at Wembley, and Simple Minds were so impressed that they recorded their own version.

AL BOWLLY (1899-1941)
Bowlly, who was raised in Johannesburg, came to London in 1928 and became the UK dance-band crooner to challenge Bing Crosby. He was killed when a German bomb exploded outside his flat and his best-known recordings are "The Very Thought Of You" and "Goodnight Sweetheart".

(3) AL BOWLLY'S IN HEAVEN - RICHARD THOMPSON
(From "Daring Adventures", Polygram POLD 5202, 1986) "That was a voice and that was a band," sings Richard Thompson in his poignant tribute to Al Bowlly, although the song is chiefly about the rehabilitation of disabled servicemen after the war - "Al Bowlly's in heaven and I'm in limbo now". In a brilliant line, he evokes one of Bowlly's greatest hits, "Once in a blue moon, you might find a job." Richard Thompson told his biographer, Patrick Humphries, "I quite like Al Bowlly, but I don't think he's Bing Crosby or anything. He was the Great British Hope, but what else did we have? And he died, that's always useful. Perhaps he was the 40s' Nick Drake."

TARA BROWNE (1945-1966)
Tara Browne was a member of the Guinness family and heir to a fortune. He was killed when he drove his sports car into the back of a van, and his girlfriend said that he had swerved the car to protect her.

(4) A DAY IN THE LIFE - THE BEATLES
(From "Sgt Pepper's Lonely Hearts Club Band", Parlophone PMC 7027, 1967) Tara Browne was friendly with both John Lennon and Paul McCartney and he visited the McCartney family home on the Wirral. John Lennon read about the accident in the "Daily Mail" and incorporated the story into the second verse of "A Day In The Life". Marianne Faithfull has said that Tara Browne took acid, which possibly explains the line, "He blew his mind out in a car". Another item in the "Daily Mail" referred to 4,000 holes in the road in Blackburn, Lancashire.

LENNY BRUCE (1925-1966)
Quickfire American comedian who broke taboos by discussing religion, sex and drugs, liberally sprinkling his performances with four- and twelve-letter words. He was imprisoned for obscenity (1961), deported from the UK (1963) and died of an overdose (1966). His records sound tame in the wake of Billy Connolly and Ben Elton but he opened the door.

(5) LENNY BRUCE - BOB DYLAN
(CBS A1460, 1981) Dylan only met Bruce once - they shared a taxi - but it is intriguing to hear one iconoclast paying tribute to another. Dylan addesses himself with the line, "He was an outlaw, more than you ever were."

KURT COBAIN (1967-1994)
Leader of grunge band, Nirvana, whose bursts of rage included the anthem, "Smells Like Teen Spirit", although the lyrics are indecipherable.. Plagued by drug abuse and conflicts with his wife Courtney Love, he blew his head off with a shotgun.

(6) SLEEPS WITH ANGELS - NEIL YOUNG
(From "Sleeps With Angels", Reprise 9362-45749-2, 1994) Neil Young was one of Kurt Cobain's role models, and he left a suicide note quoting Young's "It's better to burn out than to rust." from "Rust Never Sleeps". Young resolved never to sing the song again and recorded this moving tribute. Ironic that it should be released on Reprise, which was founded by Frank Sinatra who had vowed that he would never have rock'n'roll on his label.

KURT COBAIN

BOBBY DARIN (1936-1973)
Multi-talented singer-songwriter with hits in many styles - "Splish Splash", "Mack The Knife", "If I Were A Carpenter". Grew up not knowing his mother was his sister, married film star Sandra Dee, and died as a consequence of having rheumatic heart disease as a child.

(7) BORROWED TIME - BILLY KINSLEY
(From "Many Happy Returns" by Class of 64, Holley FAB421338, 1977)
The song concentrates on Darin's heart disorder and the compulsion he had to live life to the full - "He always knew he'd pay the toll, / For living on borrowed time." Kinsley was, indeed still is, a member of the Merseybeats and Liverpool Express, and the song is written by two former Merseybeat musicians, Frankie Connor (Hideaways) and Alan Crowley (Tuxedos). Billy sings the song well, but it is perfect for Dion.

JAMES DEAN

1996

JAMES DEAN (1931-1955)
Dean had the shortest career of any major film star - "East Of Eden", "Rebel Without A Cause", "Giant", a few bit parts, and that's it. He embraced Method acting and lived his role in "Rebel Without A Cause". The extent of his troubled personality has only been recognised in recent years. Died while driving his Porsche at high speed.

(8) JIM DEAN OF INDIANA - PHIL OCHS
(From "Phil Ochs' Greatest Hits", A&M AMLS 973, 1970)
One of Phil Ochs' best jokes was to release an album of new songs called "Greatest Hits". It included his forlorn, five-minute tribute to James Dean. At first hearing, it is impossible to decipher the first lines which must have cost the song its listeners. Ochs was obsessed by Dean, often copying his looks, stance and speech patterns. One big difference: Dean was a rebel without a cause: Phil Ochs was a rebel with far too many.

(9) JAMES DEAN - THE EAGLES
(From "On The Border", Asylum ASY 9016, 1974)
High-energy tribute songs are unusual but this is in keep-ing with Dean's life - and death. It contains the much-quoted line, "Too fast to live, too young to die, bye-bye." Considering the composing pedigree - Jackson Browne, Glenn Frey, J.D. Souther and Don Henley - it has to be a good song, but surely they could have improved upon "Along came a spider, Picked up a rider, Took him down the road to eternity."

AMELIA EARHART (1898-1937)
Aviator who became the first woman to cross the Atlantic in 1928. In 1937 she and her co--pilot disappeared on a round-the-world flight.

(10) AMELIA EARHART'S LAST FLIGHT -
PLAINSONG
(From "In Search Of Amelia Earhart", Elektra K 42120, 1972)
Andy Roberts of Plainsong recalls, "I found this book, 'In Search Of Amelia Earhart' by Fred Goerner, and I passed it round the band and we were knocked out by it. It estab-lished that she was a political martyr rather than just this strange, lone, lady flier who had disappeared through some aeronautical accident in 1937. She was flying round the world but also was spying for the American government in the Pacific. She crash-landed on a Japanese-held island and her co-pilot was executed by the Japanese, while she died of dysentery. Ian Matthews wrote a song about it, 'True Story Of Amelia Earhart', and then we found a contemporary song by Red River Dave, 'Amelia Earhart's Last Flight', and it seemed a good idea to put them together, although it wasn't meant to be a concept album." Red River Dave often chronicled his-torical and contemporary events and he wrote "Amelia Earhart's Last Flight" in 1937. Two years later, he per-formed it on the first television broadcast from the World's Fair.

(11) AMELIA - JONI MITCHELL
(From "Hejira".(Asylum AS 53053, 1976)
"Hejira" was released at the height of Joni Mitchell's con-fessional songwriting. While praising the aviatrix, she confesses, "Maybe I've never really loved / I guess that is the truth, / I've spent my whole life in clouds / At icy

ALBERT EINSTEIN (1875-1955)
German-born American physicist and mathematician, who published the Theory of Relativity when only 26 years old. Won Nobel Prize for Physics and revolutionised the way scientists - and the world - thought about matter, space and time.

(12) EINSTEIN-A-GO-GO - LANDSCAPE
(RCA 22, 1981, No.5)
No record can do justice to Einstein's genius, but Landscape recorded the catchiest version of the Relativity equation set to music that I know. Another is "E Equals MC Squared" by Big Audio Dynamite (CBS A6963, 1986, No.11), whose lyric is as complex as the formula - and don't overlook "She Blinded Me With Science" by Thomas Dolby (Venice In Peril VIPS 104, 1982, No.49).

ERROL FLYNN
(1909-1959)
Good-looking actor who appeared in such swashbuckling epics as "The Charge Of The Light Brigade", "The Adventures Of Robin Hood" and "The Sea Hawk". The publicity from his numerous love affairs led to the phrase "In like Flynn" and his autobiography was called "My Wicked, Wicked Ways". When he died in Canada at the age of 50, the coroner believed he was examining the body of a much older man.

(13) ERROL FLYNN - AMANDA McBROOM
(From "Live From The Rainbow And Stars", DRG 91432, 1995)
David Bruce was a supporting actor in several Errol Flynn films and was one of his drinking partners. His daughter, Amanda McBroom, wrote a touching song about their relationship and how Flynn led him astray. Full of perceptive lines especially "Luck kisses some and she passes by others, / Disappointment and bourbon are hard on the heart."

ANNE FRANK (1929-1945)
Part of a German family which fled to Amsterdam to avoid Nazi persecution. The family lived in sealed-off rooms from 1942 and Anne kept a diary of events. Her chronicle of daily life was left behind when the family was discovered and Anne Frank died in Belsen. The sales of her remarkable diary are over 20 million.

ANNE FRANK

(14) SONG FOR ANNE FRANK - HARVEY ANDREWS
(From "Spring Again", Ariola 876 632, 1994)
Harvey Andrews has the best voice in British folk music, but only the converted buy his records. He can write with considerable humour, but the trilogy that encompasses the Second World War and the Berlin Wall is deadly serious and may be too earnest for some. The third song, "Song For Anne Frank", was prompted by a visit to the house where Anne Frank hid with her family: "I pause inside your room and wait for whispers / The echo of a voice that calls your name."

BETTY GRABLE (1916-1973)
Actress in film musicals whose shapely legs were insured for $1m. She married the bandleader Harry James and was the GI's No 1 pin-up during World War II.

(15) BETTY GRABLE - NEIL SEDAKA
(From "Laughter In The Rain", Polydor 2383 265, 1974)
A little-known gem, just Sedaka with his piano telling of his childhood love for Betty Grable. Grable's film career was over by 1955, and Sedaka and his lyricist Howard Greenfield describe her appearance on a TV talk show, which brings back the memories. By the time the record came out, Betty Grable had died.

JOE HILL (1872-1915)
The Swedish-born labour organiser came to America in 1901, advocating solidarity in articles and songs. Undoubtedly, he was framed for murder in 1914 and despite

pleas for a retrial, he was executed the following year. He became a martyr for the labour cause.

(16) I DREAMED I SAW JOE HILL - JOAN BAEZ From "One Day At A Time", Vanguard VSD 79310, 1970) This song was written in 1925 but was forgotten for many years. Joe Hill states his spirit is still there to fight against "the copper bosses". Bob Dylan took its lyrical construction and melody for his own "I Dreamed I Saw St Augustine" in 1968, and I assume Joan Baez was being mischievous when she recorded the original version. Nevertheless, it is a brilliant performance of a spellbinding song.

VICTOR JARA (1935-1973)
Popular Chilean singer/guitarist whose controversial material included a song about a nun's desires and a reworking of the Lord's Prayer. His "Preguntas Por Puerto Montt" accused the militia of slaughtering defenseless peasants. In 1973, he was taken to a stadium and, in full public view, had his hands broken. Then he was shot dead.

(17) VICTOR JARA - ARLO GUTHRIE (From "Amigo", Reprise K 54077, 1975) After Jara's death, his family had to flee the country and the British poet, Adrian Mitchell gave them sanctuary. He was moved by their story and wrote a lyric for his stage production, "Love Songs Of World War Three". He says, "I wrote my ballad to a tune by Woody Guthrie called 'Dear Mrs Roosevelt'. I sent it to Arlo Guthrie, hoping he'd sing it. He set it to a new tune of his own and recorded it." The ballad, with its moving refrain, "His hands were gentle, his hands were strong", is so well-constructed that you wish they had collaborated on other songs. Mitchell's TV play about Jara was never produced, but his life was emotional and controversial and would make a remarkable film.

JOHN F. KENNEDY (1917-1963)
The 35th President of the United States of America. Kennedy took office in 1960 and removed Soviet missiles from Cuba in 1962. His social reforms were packaged as the New Frontier and the project was continued by Lyndon Johnson after Kennedy's death.

(18) IN THE SUMMER OF HIS YEARS - CONNIE FRANCIS (MGM 13203 (US), 1963) Chris Evans cancelled "TFI Friday" following Diana's death, but in 1963, the satirical show, "That Was The Week That Was", changed its style overnight for a tribute to John F. Kennedy. The lyricist Herbert Kretzmer explains, "John Kennedy was shot on a Friday and the show had already been written and frozen. The news of his assassination reached us at 6pm and Ned Sherrin wanted a song for the following night. I was in tears and so was half the world, and I said, 'I can't think of a single way to express what I'm feeling in song.' He said, 'We're meeting tomorrow morning to rewrite the whole show.' I spent the night wondering how I could accomodate an event of that magnitude. Then I had the idea that it should sound as though it was written at some other time, like a folk song, but still make sense in a contemporary context. There are two kinds of American folk song - the Stephen Foster 'I Dream Of Jeannie'-type song, which was too soft and limp, and the western. I had the idea of a man riding through a Texas town and being shot down at high noon. Kennedy's death had the ingredients of a western movie and therefore the ingredients of a western song. It started, 'A young man rode with his head held high under the Texas sun, / And no-one guessed that a man so blessed / Would perish by the gun.' It did not mention Kennedy or the assassination and it could have been written at any other time. Millicent Martin sang it in the programme and the entire TW3 show was shown coast to coast in America. The song was recorded by a host of American female singers including Connie Francis, Toni Arden, Kate Smith and the great Mahalia Jackson, who only used a tom-tom and cut out the last verse, which on reflection was very wise."

(19) HE WAS A FRIEND OF MINE - THE BYRDS (From "Turn! Turn" Turn!", CBS 62652, 1966) "I wrote that song the night John F. Kennedy was assassinated," says Roger McGuinn, "You could say it is one of the earliest Byrds' songs. The arrangement used for 'Turn! Turn! Turn!' was the way I'd always sung it." Oddly enough, I don't think the Byrds got the arrangement right - the start is too jaunty, the tambourine is annoying and they suddenly finish. I much prefer the version from the Searchers' former lead singer, Tony Jackson. This was part of a Portuguese EP and not released in the UK until the CD "Just Like Me" (Strange Things STCD 10003) in 1991.

(20) THE KENNEDY MARCH - THE JOE MEEK ORCHESTRA
(Decca F11796, 1963)

The easy way to write a tribute. An instrumental can have any one of a hundred titles and Joe Meek chose "The Kennedy March" for this stirring epic. Considering what some of his nursery-rhyme lyrics were like, maybe it was just as well. If you want something more sophisticated, try Herbert Howells' classical chorale, "Take Him, Earth, For Cherishing", which also was written in the last weeks of 1963.

ROBERT KENNEDY (1925-1968)
Attorney General during his brother's presidency. Kennedy fiercely promoted the Civil Rights Act 1964 and he was the Democratic nominee when he was killed by a Jordanian assassin in 1968.

(21) THE LAST CAMPAIGN TRILOGY -
JOHN STEWART (From "The Phoenix Concerts - Live", RCA APL2-0265, 1974)

This eight-minute section from "The Phoenix Concerts - Live" combines three songs - "The Last Campaign", "Wild Horse Road" and "All The Brave Horses". In 1968 John Stewart and his wife Buffy Ford had been part of Kennedy's campaign team: "We would fly into a town with him. We would get off the plane and dash to the rally where they would be people who had been waiting two, three or four hours to see Kennedy. They were tired and restless and we'd give them a point of focus and get their energy up, so that when Kennedy arrived, they wouldn't be so splintered. It was a dog and pony show but it was politics. We were there as the court jesters if you like, the travelling band." The most poignant song contains the line, "Shoot all the brave horses and how will we ride?", and Stewart says, "It was about what we had gone through with the Kennedys and Martin Luther King and the irony that the best people are so often shot down in their prime." In 1985 John Stewart collected all his campaign songs for the album, "The Last Campaign" (Homecoming HC 00300), which is now part of the LaserLight 3CD boxed-set, "American Journey" (LaserLight 55 590).

MARTIN LUTHER KING (1929-1968)
Black clergyman leader of US civil rights movement from mid-1950s until his assassination. Noted for preaching non-violence, even in self-defence, which found him at odds with the militant Malcolm X. He was awarded the Nobel Peace Prize in 1964.

(22) WHY(THE KING OF LOVE IS DEAD) - NINA SIMONE (Live recording from 1968 now available on RCA 07863 66997 2)

An extraordinary picture of the hours after King's murder

MARTIN LUTHER KING

is given on the recent CD, "Saga Of The Good Life And Hard Times" by Nina Simone. She had thought about cancelling her concert in New York and instead included a 16-minute tribute. Songs and speech work as one as she asks, "What's going to happen now in all of our cities?" She comments, "We can all shed tears but it won't change a thing", and adds tearfully in "Why (The King Of Love Is Dead)", "They're shooting us down one by one." The concert was originally issued, sharply-edited and less provocatively, as "Nuff Said", but the full version was released in 1997 - and some shops have filed it under "Easy Listening".

(23) ABRAHAM, MARTIN AND JOHN - MARVIN GAYE
(Tamla Motown TMG 734, 1970, No.9)

King's most famous speech was "I have a dream" and many thought that the dream would become a nightmare after his death. "I Have A Dream" is a heartfelt song from soul man Solomon Burke, but it didn't have the impact of Dick Holler's simple, folk-styled tribute to Abraham Lincoln, Martin Luther King, John F.Kennedy and, although not included in the title, Robert Kennedy. Holler wrote the song on the day of Robert Kennedy's assassination. The US hit recording was by Dion in 1968 but British fans will know the poignant interpretation by Marvin Gaye. Tom Clay's version of "What The World Needs Now Is Love" includes snatches of speech from the Kennedys and Martin Luther King and has children defining "bigotry" and "segregation", which is audio-journalism at its best.

(24) HAPPY BIRTHDAY - STEVIE WONDER
(Motown TMG 1235, 1981, No.2)
Stevie Wonder dedicated his album, "Hotter Than July", to the memory of Martin Luther King, whose own speeches had been released by Motown in the 1960s. On one track, "Happy Birthday", he advocated that all Americans should remember him through a public holiday on his birthday, January 15th. I thought the possibility of having a public holiday so soon after Christmas would never be accepted but it has applied since 15th January 1986.

(25) PRIDE (IN THE NAME OF LOVE) - U2
(Island IS 202, 1984, No.3)
U2 visited the Peace Museum in Chicago and they related Martin Luther King's ambitions for a united America to their own hopes for Ireland. Their album, "The Unforgettable Fire", contained two tributes, the lullaby, 'MLK', and the Top 10 single, 'Pride (In The Name Of Love)".

CHARLES
LINDBERGH
(1902-1974)
American aviator who flew non-stop across the Atlantic in 1927 in his plane, "The Spirit Of St Louis", made to his own specifications. His son, also called Charles, was kidnapped and killed in 1932, leading to tougher legislation against kidnapping. He flew combat missions during World War II and won a Pulitzer prize for his autobiography, "The Spirit Of St Louis".

(26) LINDY COMES TO TOWN - AL STEWART WITH LAURENCE JUBER
(From "Between The Wars", EMI 7243 8 34018 2 6)
This good-time song evokes the feeling in Paris when Lindbergh landed in 1927 - "The world had grown no bigger than a pocket handkerchief." The song goes into the first person to present the happiness and relief that

Lindbergh must have felt, little realising that within five years his son would be kidnapped and killed.

L.S. LOWRY (1887-1976)
Artist noted for depicting Lancashire mill towns. Critics sneer at his work but he had a singular vision of Manchester life and is far more than a pre-war Beryl Cook.

(27) MATCHSTALK MEN AND MATCHSTALK CATS AND DOGS - BRIAN AND MICHAEL (Pye 7N 46035, 1978, No.1)
Kevin Parrott and Mick Coleman recorded this singalong tribute under the more commercial name of Brian and Michael. The record also featured St Winifred's School Choir, who later recorded "There's No-one Quite Like Grandma". As for Brian and Michael, well, I remember they were going to appear for a week at a Liverpool theatre about 15 years ago and the week was cancelled for lack of support. True, Lowry painted matchstalk men and matchstalk cats and dogs but that was as close to understanding the painter as they got.

BONNIE PARKER

BONNIE PARKER (1911-1934) and CLYDE BARROW (1900-1934)
Homicidal criminals, noted for robberies in Texas and Oklahoma during the Depression. Betrayed and killed in a police ambush.

(28) THE BALLAD OF BONNIE AND CLYDE - GEORGIE FAME
(CBS 3124, 1967, No 1)
Woody Guthrie's "Pretty Boy Floyd" outraged listeners in 1939, and many songs have glamorised outlaws. Consider "Al Capone" (Prince Buster), "The Night Chicago Died" (Paper Lace) and "Ma Baker" (Boney M). A very romantic picture of two notorious bank-robbers was given in Arthur Penn's film, "Bonnie And Clyde", which prompted Peter Callander and Mitch Murray to write "The Ballad Of Bonnie And Clyde" for Georgie Fame, again with little regard for historical accuracy.

EVA PERON (1919-1952)

Beautiful, ambitious actress who married politician Juan Peron in 1945. When he became President of Argentina, she became his chief advisor. She helped the needy, improved education and increased the role of women in society. She was Argentina's queen of hearts, but some questioned her motives as she became rich and stylish. Princess Diana's death has been grouped with Marilyn Monroe's and John F. Kennedy's but a more apt comparison is with Evita, who died from ovarian cancer when 33 and now has saint-like status in Argentina.

(29) DON'T CRY FOR ME ARGENTINA - JULIE COVINGTON

(MCA 260, 1976, No.1)

Tim Rice captured the essence of Peron's personality with "Don't Cry For Me Argentina", the key song from the musical, "Evita". In her song to the people, Eva argues that she never wanted the attention, "As for fortune and as for fame, I never invited them in... The answer was here all the time, I love you and hope you love me." This complex song was a No 1 record but Julie Covington turned down the stage role, where it proved a tour de force for Elaine Paige and then Marti Webb. Madonna, who saw echoes of Evita in her own life, starred in the 1996 film version.

'PICASSO'S LAST WORDS' BY ANTHONY BROWN

EDITH PIAF (1915-1963)

The Little Sparrow was a big-voiced singer, whose tormented private life fascinated and scandalised France. As she defiantly sang, "Non Je Ne Regrette Rien".

(30) CHOCOLATE CIGARETTES - TOM RUSSELL

(From "Hurricane Season", Round Tower RTMCD 49, 1991)

"All that smoky passion in every line of every song" is a superb summary of Piaf's work, and this evocative song was written by Tom Russell and Sylvia Tyson. Hard to believe that Edith Piaf had the control to give up her craving for tobacco by "pulling on a chocolate cigarette".

PABLO PICASSO (1881-1973)

The world's best known painter and the founder of Cubism and Surrealism, which simply means that lots of artists copied him. Unlike many modern artists, he could paint superb, conventional pictures, but as he commented, "I paint objects as I think them, not as I see them." His mural, "Guernica" (1937) commented on the bombing of civilians in the Spanish Civil War. Towards the end of his life, he would stockpile notes containing his signature knowing that they would become valuable. (He is not, incidentally, the best-known artist in the UK: one poll in 1999 revealed that was Rolf Harris.)

(31) PICASSO'S LAST WORDS (DRINK TO ME) - WINGS

(From "Band On The Run", Apple PAS 10007, 1973)

We wouldn't have this cheerful song if Paul McCartney hadn't been showing off. Dustin Hoffman was filming in Lagos at the same time as Wings were making "Band On The Run". He came round for dinner and said he'd never seen anyone write a song. McCartney took the report of Picasso's last words, "Drink to me, drink to my health, You know I can't drink anymore", and immediately wrote a song around it. Hoffman was so impressed that he went dancing round the room.

(32) PABLO PICASSO - JONATHAN RICHMAN AND THE MODERN LOVERS

(From "Modern Lovers", Beserkley BSERK 1, 1976)

This tribute flows with early pre-punk energy. Richman is attracted by the scores of young women who hung around Picasso rather than by his paintings. The song contrives to rhyme "asshole" with "Picasso".

GRIGORY EFIMOVICH RASPUTIN (1871-1916)

Mystic who acquired influence over Russian royal family. His credo was "Sin that you may obtain forgiveness", so the court parties were filled with debauchery. He was murdered as part of the revolution.

(33) RASPUTIN - BONEY M
(Atlantic/Hansa K 11192, 1978, No.2)
"Ra, Ra, Rasputin - Russia's famous love machine" is lacking in intellectual content, but then so was the Russian artistocracy, who allowed themelves to be taken in by this charlatan. Bobby Farrell from Boney M never sang on the records or on stage but he now fronts a Boney M tribute band with three girls: well, he wasn't a bad dancer.

> JIMMIE RODGERS (1897-1933)
> In his sleeve notes for "A Tribute To Jimmie Rodgers", Bob Dylan says, "Though he is claimed as the Father of Country Music, the title is limiting and deceiving in the light of today's country music." Indeed.

(34) JIMMIE RODGERS - MAX BYGRAVES
(From "Maximemories", Celebrity MAXLP 1, 1981).
This LP consists of nothing but tributes and the subjects include the Beatles, Judy Garland, Peter Sellers and Benny Hill. In a style reminiscent of Tom T. Hall, Bygraves narrates how he was turned onto Jimmie Rodgers' music by an old man in Nashville. "He made a hundred records and everyone was great," says Max. Nice to know he inspired Max as well as Bob Dylan, so why didn't Bob invite him onto his all-star "Tribute To Jimmie Rodgers"?

> NICOLA SACCO (1891-1927) and
> BARTOLOMEO VANZETTI (1888-1927)
> Italian immigrants to America who were convicted in 1921 of robbery and murder. Controversy surrounded the conviction and their electrocution did not take place until 1927. In 1977, the verdict was held unsafe because of the judge's prejudice against their anarchist views.

(35) THE BALLAD OF SACCO AND VANZETTI - JOAN BAEZ
(From "From Every Stage", A&M AMLM 63704, 1976)
Woody Guthrie was not satisfied with the songs he wrote for the record company owner, Moe Asch, about Sacco and Vanzetti. He wrote, "I'm drunk as hell today, been that way for several days. I refuse to write songs while I'm drunk and it looks like I'll be drunk for a long time." Although Guthrie did record his songs, they are not amongst his best work. Joan Baez took up the challenge and her ballad is solely based on Vanzetti's letters to his father from prison.

> BILL SHANKLY (1913-1981)
> Manager of Liverpool FC and noted for his total devotion to the game: "Football is not a matter of life and death - it's more important than that."

(36) THANKS TO THE SHANKS - LEE BRENNAN
(Garden GS 006, 1981)
Lee Brennan recorded a tribute LP to Johnny Cash for Decca, but mostly he is known around the Liverpool clubs and bars. His whisky-voiced tribute to Shankly includes references to "In My Liverpool Home" and "You'll Never Walk Alone" and ends with Lee singing "Shankly" to the tune of "Amazing Grace". It may sound naff to Southerners but this can start tears rolling in a Liverpool pub. It was included on the 1996 CD, "You'll Never Walk Alone - 24 Anfield Anthems" (Cherry Red CDGAFFER 4) and also on the CD is the narrated "Tribute To Shankly" by Shanks' Pony.

BILL SHANKLY

> WALLIS SIMPSON, DUCHESS OF WINDSOR (1896-1986)
> Edward VIII abdicated in 1936 because the Government - and indeed the people - did not think it was suitable that the King should marry an American divorcée. In particular, it was considered ill-suited to his role as Supreme Governor of the Church of England. George VI made them the Duke and Duchess of Windsor and they were exiled to France.

(37) KINGDOM FOR A KISS - CAROLYN HESTER
(From "Music Medicine", Outpost ORC 8201, 1982)
(Released in the UK on the CD, "Texas Songbird", Road Goes On Forever RGFCD 019)
The 1978 TV series, "Edward And Mrs Simpson", told their story to a new generation and this touching song is another reminder of those times. Carolyn Hester says, "I

wrote it out of my affection for England and for their story. It's a simple song and I was very pleased that Nanci Griffith invited me to sing it for two nights at the Royal Albert Hall." The Duke and Duchess' Paris home was bought by Mohammed Al Fayed and was visited by Diana and Dodi on the day of their deaths.

RUDOLPH VALENTINO (1895-1926)
Phenomenally handsome star of such silent films as "The Four Horsemen Of The Apocalypse" and "The Sheik". Died in New York of a perforated ulcer and thousands of crying women lined the streets at his funeral procession. The first superstar (outside of Jesus Christ, that is.)

(38) I'LL TAKE A TANGO - NILSSON
(From "Sandman", RCA RS1015, 1976)
The country songwriter, Alex Harvey, gave this curious song to Nilsson. It starts, "Deep down in my soul, I hate rock'n'roll" and harks back to the days of Valentino and the very stylised, romantic dance, the tango. The song was also covered by Cilla Black.

FRANK LLOYD WRIGHT

hurt. I didn't laugh / Your diaries are not a worthy epitaph.". Reed followed it with a totally affectionate album for the late songwriter, Doc Pomus.

FRANK LLOYD WRIGHT (1869-1959)
American architect, noted for his "organic architecture" in which the buildings reflect their natural surroundings. As well as many homes, he designed the Guggennheim Museum in New York.

(40) SO LONG FRANK LLOYD WRIGHT - SIMON & GARFUNKEL
(From "Bridge Over Troubled Water, CBS 63699, 1970)
Several songs ("Bette Davis Eyes", "Salvador Dali's Car") use a name in a striking way without really being about that celebrity. A fine example is "So Long Frank Lloyd Wright". Art Garfunkel planned to be an architect and the song is more a testimony to himself ("we'd harmonise 'til dawn") than to the famed architect, despite the lines, "Architects may come and / Architects may go and / Never change your point of view". By the title, Paul Simon is adjusting to the fact that the duo is on the verge of splitting up.

ANDY WARHOL (1928-1987)
New York artist famous for representing modern life - Campbell's soup cans, Coca-Cola bottles, Marilyn Monroe and Elvis Presley. Many creative, but off-the-wall, talents worked in his Factory, being involved in art, films, journalism and rock including the Velvet Underground.

(39) HELLO IT'S ME - JOHN CALE AND LOU REED
(From "Songs For 'Drella", Sire WX 345, 1990)
Two former members of the Velvet Underground, John Cale and Lou Reed, wrote "Songs For 'Drella" for a Brooklyn stage show. Lou Reed's lyric for "Hello It's Me" mixes admiration with resentment - "You hit where it

ANDY WARHOL

234

CANDLE IN THE WIND

The story of the song

In 1971, Elton Hercules John began his chart-making career with a sensitive ballad, "Your Song", but by 1973, he was out-glittering Gary with his lavish outfits and indulging in over-the-top stage antics. His album, "Don't Shoot Me, I'm Only The Piano Player", was a transatlantic No.1 and he went to Jamaica with producer Gus Dudgeon to record the follow-up. Elton and his lyricist Bernie Taupin had the songs ready, but, after various delays, the impatient singer moved to Strawberry Studios in France. During May 1973, they recorded 21 tracks and the result was the double-album, "Goodbye Yellow Brick Road".

Despite the glitz, Elton John's records have always contained some melancholia. He was a troubled man and, indeed intriguing comparisons can be made with the Las Vegas pianist-showman, Liberace. The very title, "Goodbye Yellow Brick Road", implies that Elton had been over the rainbow and found it lacking. The double-album started with "Funeral For A Friend", a sombre instrumental that Elton had written for his own demise, followed by Bernie's lyric for the end of a relationship, "Love Lies Bleeding" - "Everything about this house/ Was born to grow and die". Bernie collected Marilyn Monroe artifacts and the third song was his tribute to her, "Candle In The Wind".

Marilyn Monroe had been raised in foster homes, possibly raped as a child, endured loveless marriages and attempted suicide. She became a leading sex symbol via her giggle, her wiggle, her pout and her platinum blonde hair, all of which are present in "Bus Stop" and "Some Like It Hot". She died in mysterious circumstances in 1962, and the role the Kennedys played in her life - and, indeed, in her demise - has been debated for years. The film star became an icon largely because Andy Warhol had the vision to make a silksceen of her face.

Bernie had felt compelled to write about her. "I wanted to say that it wasn't just a sex thing, that she was someone everybody could fall in love with. I could never come up with the right approach." The right approach came when Bernie read Ralph J. Gleason's obituary to the hard-drinking, hard-living Janis Joplin in "Rolling Stone". It was entitled "Another Candle Blown Out" and Gleason, in turn, quoted a poem by the Pulitzer prize-winner, Edna St. Vincent Millay:

> *"My candle burns at both ends;*
> *It will not last the night;*
> *But, ah, my foes and, oh, my friends,*
> *It gives a lovely light."*

Although Gleason did not use the phrase "candle in the wind", he wrote, "God knows, that blazing candle did cast a lovely light, even though from time to time it flickered and the light dimmed, and the looming face of tragedy appeared."

Bernie wrote the lyric for "Candle In The Wind" and passed it to Elton. He also adored her and was discovering the two-edged nature of fame for himself. "When I

I think of Marilyn, I think of pain," he said, "I can't ever imagine her being happy."

Talking to Paul Gambaccini in "Rolling Stone" at the time, Bernie Taupin said, "'Candle In The Wind' is the best song we've ever written. It's my favourite song, it means a lot to me. The sentiment is how I feel, and the melody really suits the mood of it. It may come across as another schmaltzy song but people can listen to it and realise what the writers feel for her."

For all that, "Candle In The Wind" was only the third single to be released from the album and, even more surprisingly, it stalled at No 11 on the UK chart. In the States, it was relegated to the B-side of the black-sounding "Bennie And The Jets", which became a US No 1. "Candle In The Wind" was not even included on the US edition of Elton John's "Greatest Hits", but Elton was so fond of the song that he gave Bernie a dress and a pair of white satin stilettos that had been worn by the film star. At a private party, Princess Margaret asked Elton to perform the song and he was so surprised that he stumbled over the words.

Elton has recorded tributes throughout his career - sometimes for old gunfighters. In 1978 he dedicated a gentle instrumental, "Song For Guy", to Guy Burchett, a 17 year old delivery boy for his company, Rocket Records, who had been killed in a motorcycle accident. In 1980 and within a day of John Lennon's assassination, Bernie Taupin had written "Empty Garden (Hey Hey Johnny)", but Elton's soulful single failed to make the Top 50. Ironically, it was followed by a single called "Princess". In 1987, Bernie Taupin recorded a tribute to Billy Fury on his own album, "Tribe".

Controversy dogged Elton, notably the untrue allegations in "The Sun", but it didn't lessen the public's affection. Generally speaking, the records that didn't sell didn't deserve to, and when he had a good song, the public bought it. In 1988, in the midst of his troubles, Elton

made the Top 5 with an orchestral "Candle In The Wind", recorded in concert in Australia.

In 1990 Elton announced that his earnings from future singles would go to charity and his generosity had a fine start when "Sacrifice" went to No 1. Strangely, the album, "Two Rooms", in which 16 performers recorded his best songs, did not include a version of "Candle In The Wind".

In 1994 Elton John and Tim Rice made themselves a fortune with their five-song score for "The Lion King". In total contrast to the Disney film, a TV documentary about Elton on the road, "Tantrums And Tiaras", was made by his companion, David Furnish. Evidently, Elton worked himself into frenzies over very little. Meanwhile, Bernie Taupin was quietly writing lyrics in California and, judging by the film, it was no wonder that they worked in two rooms. Elton's next album, "The Big Picture", was being released on September 22nd 1997, and a single from it, "Something About The Way You Look Tonight", was scheduled for September 8th.

The previous December Elton and Luciano Pavarotti made the Top 10 with "Live Like Horses". Elton, looking at a photo of the two of them, remarked with customary candour that "Eat Like Horses" was more appropriate - and Elton's hairstyle looked as though it might be given a saucer of milk at night. Both Elton and Pavarotti were very friendly with Princess Diana, and they were clearly platonic friendships. However, Elton disagreed with her over a charity commitment and they wrote each other letters that they later regretted.

In January 1997, Elton John was depicted as the new Gianni Versace supermodel in an hilarious photospread in "The Sunday Times Magazine". He was heartbroken when the designer was assassinated and Princess Diana comforted him at the funeral, thus renewing their own friendship.

Princess Diana died on 31st August, and many show-business names were invited to the funeral in Westminster Abbey. Pavarotti was too griefstricken to sing, but Elton John accepted. I questioned the wisdom of this decision - he had broken down at Versace's funeral and those TV tantrums were only a year ago. Nevertheless, the Queen allowed him 3 minutes 45 seconds, such is the precision timing on these occasions.

Elton John had three choices:

Firstly, he could sing an old favourite just as it was. "Don't Let The Sun Go Down On Me" was a possibility, but it takes an eternity to get to the chorus. The most suitable candidate was "Your Song", which Diana had loved. Some lines were eminently suitable - "Yours are the sweetest eyes I've ever seen" - but one line, "I'd build a big house where we both could live", would have to go.

Secondly, Elton and Bernie could write a new song. Could they come up with something in six days - and would it be any good? Elton's singles had been rather hit and miss and of late, rather more misses than hits.

Thirdly, Elton could amend an existing song. Diana loved "Candle In The Wind", probably because she identified with the lyric - "They made you change your name", "Never knowing who to cling to when the rain set in" and "Even when you died, the press still hounded you". Such lyrics would never have been allowed

at the Abbey, even though they would have complemented Earl Spencer's speech.

Elton decided to revise "Candle In The Wind", so he was taking a song that been written for someone in particular and rewriting it for someone else. Or rather Bernie Taupin was. He called Bernie Taupin in California and within an hour, Bernie had faxed him some new words. Emma Forrest in "The Guardian" called it "drive-thru grief". "'Her footsteps on England's greenest hills...' in Versace stilettos? Diana was always in London. She hated the countryside. What are you talking about, Elton?" The journalist had missed the point. The line has a resonance surely to William Blake and "Jerusalem".

Criticism of the opening line, "Goodbye England's rose", might be more pointed. How did the people of Scotland and Wales view that, and she was, after all, the Princess of Wales? Nevertheless, she was born in Sandringham, Norfolk, so the farewell made sense.

Sadly, Bernie Taupin had removed the irony and anger from the song, but one line was stunning, up there with his best work - "You were the grace that placed itself where lives were torn apart." I read the Poet Laureate, Ted Hughes' lines about the nature of grief and those of other professional poets and realised that Bernie said it better.

On September 6th, I felt sorry for Elton John. He had to perform in front of the biggest audience in his life, the biggest audience in anyone's life - and he had Lord Attenborough sitting next to him. That's enough to put anyone off. Also, or so I am told by a musical friend, the piano was slightly out of tune.

Tony Blair read the lesson and Elton moved to the piano. As soon as he sang the first line, I knew he was going to make it, that something inside him would pull him through. After 24 years of singing a different lyric, he feared that he might lapse into the old one but if he used his teleprompter, I didn't notice. His voice cracked with emotion and he sang with such warmth that everyone everywhere must have applauded. Even in the Abbey, the applause from the crowds watching on giant screens filtered through the windows and doors.

The service had a UK audience of 31.5 million - ten million more than Diana's wedding. The broadcast was conveyed to over 200 countries and the total viewing figure exceeded 2,500,000,000. The service had not only united the nation - it had united the world. When the procession reached the Princess' resting place, the BBC ended its coverage by repeating "Candle In The Wind".

By then, Elton John had gone to a recording studio where George Martin was waiting for him. The 71-year- old producer had assembled woodwind and a strings quartet for his final recording. A lesser producer would have overloaded the song, but George Martin gave it a quiet, sensitive arrangement - not unlike "Yesterday" for Paul

SIR ELTON JOHN

McCartney. Elton was technically perfect on the second take, but he couldn't match the emotion of that live performance before billions. Still, if people wanted the original performance they could buy the CD or cassette of the funeral. What a morbid lot we are.

In my view, "Candle In The Wind 1997" should have been the lead track on the single and the other tracks should have been instrumentals - "Funeral For A Friend" and "Song For Guy" would have been ideal. Indeed, a song for Di and a song for Guy on the same CD would say something about the grim equality of death.

Instead, "Candle In The Wind 1997" was placed in-between two new songs: "Something About The Way You Look Tonight" and "You Can Make History (Young Again)". Presumably this was because "Something About The Way You Look Tonight" and "Candle In The Wind 1997" could be shown as a double-header on the chart. "Something About The Way You Look Tonight" wasn't a bad song and wasn't unsuitable, but it was derivative of Rod Stewart and Berlin's "Take My Breath Away" At one stage, Elton strains like Joe Cocker, perhaps an indication of the way his voice is heading He had, after all, reached 50.

The intention was to get 1.5 million singles pressed for Saturday. The single was released in France on the Friday and at midnight there was a queue at Tower Records in London for the first UK copies. They sold 1,500 copies that night and their entire 5,000 stock by midday. We may no longer have a singles-buying culture, but another million copies were pressed over the weekend. Shops had to limit purchasers to three copies, especially when it was discovered that some no-marks were buying handfuls and offering them at higher prices in the streets.

People of all ages wanted the single. The pricing was sensible - £3.99 for CD and £1.99 for cassette. Many older people don't have CD players, so pensioners could purchase the song for £2. Even people who thought Elton John totally naff were buying the single and some, in true record collecting spirit, were putting them aside as momentos for their grandchildren. Paul Gambaccini has suggested that people transferred their grieving from giving flowers to buying CDs, which accounts for some people buying 40 or 50 copies. Whatever, millions were raised for the Memorial Fund and even the Chancellor, Gordon Brown waived the VAT, something that wasn't done for the Band Aid single.

BERNIE TAUPIN & ELTON JOHN

BERNIE TAUPIN

That first Saturday night Elton John appeared on the Lottery programme. Bob Monkhouse told him that the record had already sold a million copies - "And that's just in Portsmouth", quipped Elton. As Elton never intended to sing the song again, he performed "Something About The Way You Look Tonight".

The next day Elton John was No 1 on the new chart. A recent No 1 has been Puff Daddy's tribute to the murdered rock star, Notorious B.I.G., "I'll Be Missing You", which is based on Police's "Every Breath I Take". Like "Candle In The Wind 1997", it removes the darker side of the original song.

The worldwide sales of the single were colossal. Israel, for example, has only a small recordbuying market. The country concentrates on albums, and because "Candle In The Wind" was such a momentous event, it became the first single to be released there. If you grew sick of hearing the single, spare a thought for like-minded Canadians. The new version of "Candle In The Wind" topped their charts for over a year.

Did "Candle In The Wind" become the biggest-selling single of all-time? Possibly, but it depends on what it has to beat. "The Guinness Book Of Records" places Bing Crosby's "White Christmas" at No 1 with sales of over 150 million, which beggars belief. 150 million people have never gone into a store to buy "White Christmas". The sales must include all the Bing Crosby and seasonal compilations which include "White Christmas". Many purchasers will already own the track so they are buying the record in spite of, rather than because of, "White Christmas". Bing has 60 years' start on Elton, and Elton can only topple him if his version is included on numerous compilations. It's possible. The crash will be remembered for years - and its repercussions will haunt the Royal Family forever.

One final piece of synchronicity: only minutes before the tragedy, Bob Harris on BBC Radio 2 played a listener's request for Paul Anka's "Diana". A few records later he played Queen's "Heaven For Everyone". Maybe Whispering Bob has more powers than Diana's own psychic.

songs to die for

ANTHONY BROWN

SONGS TO DIE FOR

The modern way to say goodbye

"One foot in the grave, one foot on the gas,
Got an angel at the wheel and I'm goin' home fast.
I can't take it with me so I'll do the next best,
I want a rock'n'roll funeral when they lay me to rest."
("Rock'n'Roll Funeral" - Jerry Lee Lewis, 1986)

By including a rock song in its order of service, Princess Diana's funeral was said to break with tradition. Certainly, this was remarkable for something akin to a State Funeral, but similar examples take place everyday throughout the UK. Even as you read this, someone is being laid to rest to Elvis Presley's "The Wonder Of You" or "Until It's Time For You To Go".

The Church of England is portrayed as stick-in-the-mud but ministers are flexible about the funeral service and agree it should reflect and celebrate the deceased. On the other hand, despite the fact that so much great popular music has been composed by Jewish songwriters, the deceased's family are unlikely to hear his favourite record in a synagogue.

Most funerals are for the elderly and without doubt, Mario Lanza is Top of the Funeral Pops. His interpretations of "I'll Walk With God", "The Lord's Prayer" and "Ave Maria" are much requested. Another favourite is Daniel O'Donnell singing "The Old Rugged Cross", a record deserving to be buried alongside the departed.

The mourners at one Merseyside funeral requested that their 92 year old friend be remembered by "Telstar" by the Tornados. The minister told me, "Before the service, I thought it was an odd choice, but when I asked the congregation to remember him while they listened to the record, it was perfect." Mrs Thatcher's favourite record is "Telstar", so that could be her choice too.

Often the record will be chosen by those who remain. A favourite with the elderly is "Bless You For Being An Angel" by the Inkspots, while all generations go for "You'll Never Walk Alone", Gerry and the Pacemakers style, "Softly As I Leave You" by Matt Monro and "Amazing Grace" by Judy Collins. Popular sentimental songs include "Annie's Song" (which doesn't mention Annie by name so can apply to anyone), "I Will Always Love You" "Lean On Me", "The Living Years", "Look For Me In Rainbows" (a lovely song from Vicki Brown) and, coming up fast, Charlie Landsborough's "My Forever Friend". One family pallbearer requested the Hollies' "He Ain't Heavy, He's My Brother".

Thirty-somethings do not expect to die and may have left no wishes as to the record they want. Their partners have chosen such records as "Nothing Compares 2 U" (Sinead O'Connor), "The Power Of Love" (Jennifer Rush), "The Best" (Tina Turner), "You're In My Heart" (Rod Stewart) and "Your Song" (Elton John). Ministers dissuade mourners from selecting "Bridge Over Troubled Water" by Simon and Garfunkel as it is five minutes long. An intriguing choice, and entirely appropriate, was Black's "Wonderful Life" at the funeral of a loner.

Sometimes the genre is more important than the song or its message, and this is particularly true of country music. Many Liverpool fans have been buried in their cowboy boots and at a Norris Green funeral, you can't go wrong with "Blue Eyes Crying In The Rain" by Willie Nelson.

When celebrities die, there may be some acknowledgment of their work. The congregation applauded when the Drifters' "Save The Last Dance For Me" was played at the funeral of the crippled songwriter Doc Pomus. His partner, Mort Shuman, was to die within the year and he had written a very witty song about hypocrisy, "Funeral Tango", which was unsuitable for any funeral. According to Roger Lewis' biography, "The Life And Death Of Peter Sellers", the actor had a premonition of his death and even visited Golders Green Crematorium to inspect the ovens. And maybe the sound system. Within a week he was cremated to the sounds of Glenn Miller's "In The Mood".

SANDY DENNY

One minister, asked to play a cassette as the body was being cremated, heard Frank Sinatra singing, "And now the end is near, And so I face the final curtain". At least it wasn't "Light My Fire".

Strangely enough, the record may not be in the deceased's collection and ministers may have to scurry around to find a copy. An enterprising record company could release an album of songs for matches, hatches and dispatches.

Some songs have a dual purpose - Jennifer Rush's "The Power Of Love" is as popular at weddings as it is at funerals.

When I was at school, the maths master kept a list of the hymns that he wanted at his funeral in his wallet. The selections would change from time to time but "Fight The Good Fight" was always the rousing opener. Record collectors should do the same - what is the song that you would most like to be associated with? Leonard Cohen's "Closing Time" or Bruce Cockburn's "Lord Of The Starfield" would be good choices, but I'll select Sandy Denny's "Who Knows Where The Time Goes?", which is certainly the story of my life. I would prefer live music to a record and so I hope that the golden-voiced Chris While and Julie Matthews, who live nearby, would perform it. Now that I've put the request in print, they can hardly refuse, but I'm not planning on going for some years yet.

Make sure you stipulate which version of a song you want. "Isn't She Lovely" is often requested for christenings and one minister found himself in deeper water than the font provided because he had brought along David Parton's version, which omits the baby's cries. If your favourite record is "I Believe" by Frankie Laine, you might be mortified to find that your final statement to the world is via Robson and Jerome. Of course, your loved one might nix the choice entirely and play "I'm glad that you're dead, you rascal you." or "Just a perfect day".

THE MILLENNIUM PRAYER
The story of the song

Chart music, by and large, is for the young, and older people buy albums. Young recordbuyers buy records by young performers and so the average age of the Top 10 artists will generally be in the early 20s. Artists such as Bryan Ferry, Van Morrison and Elvis Costello may still release singles, but usually they are to promote their new albums.

Cliff Richard and Status Quo have been reluctant to relinquish their place in the charts. They have condemned the BBC's playlists for being ageist. Status Quo haven't had a sizeable hit in five years and in 1998, Cliff Richard, in order to establish his point, issued "Can't Keep This Feeling In" to radio stations as a 12" dance single under the pseudonym of Blacknight. It made some playlists (even on black community stations) but when Cliff announced that he was Blacknight, the record was quickly dropped.

Cliff Richard's interview with Chris Evans on "TFI Friday" went well, but Evans, ever the opportunist, was soon deriding Cliff. He banned Cliff Richard records from the building and used the controversy to promote his own programme on Virgin Radio. Similarly, Billy Butler, then a veteran DJ on Liverpool's commercial station, Radio City, was suspended for playing the record. This did Cliff no harm at all and "Can't Keep This Feeling In" became his first Top 10 hit in five years.

The radio stations didn't recognise the singer of "Can't Keep This Feeling In" because Cliff was singing in falsetto. The whole album, "Real As I Wanna Be", was like that and despite Cliff's efforts to push it as the best record he'd made, it wasn't an artistic success and he returned to his normal singing voice for "The Millennium Prayer". Thank God for that.

I doubt if the radio stations were being ageist when they excluded Cliff from their playlists. After all, Eric Clapton, Cher and Tina Turner have no problems in getting airplay. No, the main problem is Cliff's Goody Two Shoes image, which may not sit well with the station's own image. Cliff is a self-control freak, keeping fit, helping others and showing little interest in sexual relationships. Why shouldn't he be celibate if he wants to be? If a poll were taken of the country's best-known Christians, Cliff would get as many votes as the Archbishop of Canterbury. All this is really very laudable, but it is hardly the life of a rock star. It has become a national pastime to knock Cliff: it is the same as the way politicians are always booed when they attend the Brits Awards.

Cliff has many of the same qualities as Tony Blair - that friendliness, those youthful looks, that smile, that cheerfulness, that religious conviction. Tony Blair was once in a rock band and if everything in politics had gone horribly wrong for him, he could have fronted a Cliff Richard tribute band. It is like having a Cliff impersonator in Downing Street, and wouldn't Cliff have been an ideal candidate for London mayor?

Cliff has been making religious records for many years. Back in the 1960s he was including "When I Survey The

Wondrous Cross" in his cabaret act at the Talk Of The Town and he has often organised gospel tours. In 1982 he made the Christmas charts by giving "O Little Town Of Bethlehem" a new melody. In 1990 he had his first No.1 with a religious song, "Saviour's Day".

Many artists have recorded rock versions of biblical text, the most famous example (and the best) being Pete Seeger's glorious "Turn! Turn! Turn!" for the Byrds, which is taken from Ecclesiastes. Jimmy Webb recorded Psalm 150 and Bono adapted Psalm 40 for U2's closing number, "40". John Otway, of all people, revived William Blake's "Jersualem" for a single, "The New Jerusalem", in 1986. Sister Janet Mead had a US hit with her version of "The Lord's Prayer", while Funkadelic recorded "The Lord's Prayer". Siouxsie and the Banshees played only "The Lord's Prayer" at their first gig. Whenever you see Joe Brown, he performs an instrumental version of the hymn, "All Things Bright And Beautiful".

"Auld Lang Syne" is no stranger to the pop charts. It was incorporated in the G-Clefs' hit single, "I Understand", which was covered by Freddie and the Dreamers. Many singers have incorporated "Auld Lang Syne" into their versions of the standard, "What Are You Doing New Year's Eve?" Dan Fogelberg has released "The Same Auld Lang Syne".

The Lord's Prayer can be taken as a message from one millennium to another. It is generally acknowledged that there was a historical figure called Jesus Christ, but no one has been able to establish the authenticity of what has been attributed to him. The Lord's Prayer is in both Matthew and Luke's gospels, with the form in Matthew being universally used by Christians. The prayer begins with an address to God and the first three sections emphasise his greatness. Then, four petitions relate to man's physical and spiritual needs. The doxology was added later to some gospel manuscripts and is used elsewhere by Roman Catholics. The church has always regarded the Lord's Prayer as sacred but it has been rewritten from time to time, with Cliff combining various versions for his text.

On the day of Princess Diana's funeral in 1997, the songwriter Paul Field found himself on a motorway with very few cars on it. When he pulled into a service station, he found everyone was watching the funeral on a large screen. As "The Lord's Prayer" was said, the viewers joined in. Paul realised that although this was a secular

age with falling church attendances, everybody knew "The Lord's Prayer".

The prayer, once set to music, became the main theme for a production featuring songs, dances and sketches and called "Hopes And Dreams". The musical was written for Methodist churches to encourage them to become positive forces in their communities. A CD was recorded in Blackpool for the Kingsway label and because "Auld Lang Syne" was being used for "The Lord's Prayer", it was felt that a Celtic feel should be added. The producer, Nigel Wright, had seen a bagpiper busking on the Prom and he was added to the mix.

Paul Field knew Cliff Richard as Cliff had recorded his song, "Thief In The Night". He also had a new song, "All That Matters", which Cliff had recorded for the tribute album for Princess Diana. He told Cliff about "A Prayer For Our Time", as it was then called, and asked Cliff to add his vocals. Cliff did this in a Wimbledon studio in June 1998. No one at the time saw it as a potential single. Except Cliff.

The radio comedy programme, "I'm Sorry I Haven't A Clue", regularly asks the panelists to sing the words of one song to another. You get some outrageous mixes and it is very amusing. However, the most biting parody came when the Communist Manifesto was set to music under the title of "Workers Of The World Unite" on the National Lampoon album, "Lemmings".

Generally the lyrics fit their new setting very well, and so it was with Cliff. Athough "The Lord's Prayer" is by no means a perfect fit, he's a decent singer and he makes it sound better than it is.

Early in 1999, many plans were being announced for the millennium. Many events had gargantuan prices and some were later cancelled or greatly reduced because of this millennium greed. Cliff Richard, speaking in March, said, "I hope that people will not rip this country off because it's the millennium. I don't think we should capitalise on it."

Cliff wanted to appear at the opening concert for the Millennium Dome and when that wasn't forthcoming, he organised his own week of concerts at Birmingham NIA. Cliff has such a staunch body of fans that the tickets sold out within days including £100 tickets for New Year's Eve itself. That final concert would be for Children's Promise, an affiliation of seven children's charities, in which people were asked to dedicate the proceeds of their final hour of work in this century.

By now, Cliff had realised that "A Prayer For Our Time" could be retitled "The Millennium Prayer" and would be perfect for the New Year celebrations. "The Lord's Prayer" celebrated Christmas and "Auld Lang Syne" the turn of the year, so what could be better than combining them? He re-recorded the song for a single with his label, EMI. Bagpipes were out and trumpets were in. Cliff commented, "I hope in some small way to offer an anthem for us all as we leave one millennium and look forward to the next."

Cliff would add the royalties from "The Millennium Prayer" to Children's Promise and he asked EMI, his record label for 40 years, to release it. They refused. It is assumed that they refused because they thought it was a naff idea, but this hardly makes sense. Many substandard singles are released during the year and EMI would normally humour an artist of Cliff Richard's calibre. I suspect they refused because there would be no profit for themselves. Whatever the reason, this would prove to be one of those great moments in pop history.

Cliff was determined to have the single released and he went to a small independent label, Papillon,

CLIFF RICHARD

which had released a new CD by Jethro Tull. The single was released on 15th November and was turned down by BBC Radio 1 (obviously) and BBC Radio 2 (not so obviously). Radio 2's motive may have been misunderstood, possibly deliberately. They might have classified it as a Christmas single and hence, decreed that, in line with their custom, it could not be aired until 1st December. Whatever, it was seen as a blanket ban by the Beeb.

And everyone said Cliff hadn't a prayer.

Papillon hired a PR company to promote the record, taking the line that Cliff was being victimised. This time it wasn't ageism (well, it might have been that too), but the ban was decrying the very meaning of Christmas, the very meaning of the millennium. After all, it's because of the baby Jesus that we have the numbering that leads to year 2000. Making 'The Lord's Prayer' to the tune of 'Auld Lang Syne' seem an act of rebellion was a major PR stroke. However, Andy Kershaw in "The Independent" said the record was not on the BBC's playlist because it was "sanctimonious old shite".

The PR company mailed churches and asked them to publicise the record. Johnny Kennedy writing in "Catholic Pictorial" said, "I've met Cliff. I spent an hour with him once, and he's a thoroughly decent man. There's never been a breath of scandal connected with him, he's never taken drugs and he does his best to help people. Maybe that's why the radio stations don't like him." Interestingly, Johnny Kennedy used to work for the aforementioned Radio City. If he'd still been there, would he have played the record?

Did this call to Christians sell the record? I'm not sure. After all, millions of UK Catholics ignore what their church leaders and newspapers are telling them about contraception.

It was a real Cliffhanger to wonder how the single would fare, and in the face of apathy and hostility from radio stations, the single sold. Brave souls were prepared to face sniggers in HMV or Virgin as they went to the counter with a copy of the single. Over 60,000 copies were sold in the first week and it entered the charts at No 2 without any airplay. Cliff performed it on the ITV show, "An Audience With Cliff Richard" in which he assumed the same crucifixion pose as Michael Jackson at the notorious Brits Awards. Cliff was also added to the Royal Variety Performance and appeared after the star attraction, Barry Manilow, to finish the show. The following week, Cliff was No 1 and selling 160,000 in one week. This was also the first time that a song in blank verse had made No 1, although the standard, "Moonlight In Vermont" also has no rhyming lines.

Christmas is the silly season for popular music as all manner of records are released in the hope of capturing the Christmas market. Clive Dunn's 'Grandad' (1970) and St Winifred's School Choir with 'There's No One Quite Like Grandma' (1980) were enormous Christmas hits when they mightn't have even made the Top 20 at another other time of the year. That's because they are ideal gift opportunities: it's difficult to know what to give your grandparents: here's the perfect gift - it's cheap and they might even like it.

The race for the Christmas No. 1 in 1999 was particularly tough as that single would also be the Millennium No 1. The competition was fierce, although the Spice Girls could only be found on a "Perfect Day" workout of the Rolling Stones' "It's Only Rock'n'Roll". The serious money was on the Irish boy band, Westlife, a junior Boyzone and managed by Boyzone's Ronan Keating. The 19 year olds were trying for their fourth No.1 with their fourth single, a remake of Abba's optimistic "I Have A Dream", which admittedly was backed by the gloomy Jacques Brel song, "Seasons In The Sun".

Then there was John Lennon, who was born a week earlier than Cliff, but no-one mentioned ageism there. "Imagine" had won so many polls as the song of the century and it was skilfully packaged with "Happy Xmas (War Is Over)", "Give Peace A Chance" and a CD-Rom video of "Imagine".

The main Christmas turkeys were yodelling, dancing hampsters, a cynical dance record masterminded by Jonathan King, and 'Mr. Hanky The Christmas Poo", which, literally, was full of shit. Also rockin' around the Christmas tree and in the same vein as Cliff, two French

monks had a dance version of "The Hallelujah Chorus" and Wild Willy Barrett produced an American preacher intoning St John's words, "I am the good shepherd", over a disco beat. The Christmas rapping was "Street Preacher" by Denver Boot if anyone's interested.

Then came the celebrity knocking, First, surprisingly, was Gaby Roslin during the Children In Need telecast. Then George Michael, co-hosting a breakfast show on Capital FM, called it "vile and exploitative". Ant and Dec knocked the single on "CDtv" and their guest, Mel C, agreed, calling it "a complete pile of shit. It's been put together very cheaply and it's ripping off fans."

George Michael mocked Cliff by calling him "The Vicar" and added, "I think everyone listening to this show should buy 'Imagine' just to make sure they don't have that heinous piece of music on the radio as we go into the millennium."

George Michael had public sympathy when he was hounded by the LA police, but his outburst was regarded as out of order here. I was in a bank queue where the teller, who didn't know me at all, asked me what I thought of "The Millennium Prayer" and said how "vile" she considered George Michael to be. Vile, no. Hypocritical, yes. In 1996, this man returned to recording after a long absence with "Jesus To A Child".

Rev Kyle Paisley wrote to the letters page of the "Daily Telegraph": "George Michael's attack on 'The Millennium Prayer' is blasphemous and hypocritical. While the setting of 'Auld Lang Syne' may not be to everyone's taste, to describe it as 'vile' is insulting - insulting to God Himself." Eternal's Louise, joining in the fun, chastised her neighbour, Mel C, and commented, "It's certainly nothing to be ashamed of."

Alan Clarke of Hoylake, writing in the "Liverpool Echo", said "Cliff Richard had made a mockery of the Lord's Prayer for financial gain - and this from a so-called Christian."

George Michael's words, or Alan Clarke's come to that, were not well chosen. How can a Christian message and a charity single be 'exploitative'? Cliff's Birmingham concerts were already sold out and then he was taking time off to go round Australia in a bus - reliving "Summer Holiday" no doubt. He had already been knighted, so he wasn't

doing it for public acclaim. You could argue that the single wasn't completely for charity as a purchaser might buy a Cliff CD at the same time but that's clutching at straws. Cliff was not even jumping on the bandwagon as he often been in the running for the Christmas No 1 winning with "Mistletoe And Wine" (1988) and "Saviour's Day" (1990).

"The Millennium Prayer" stayed on top for three weeks, but it didn't make the Millennium No 1. That went to Westlife with "I Have A Dream". The Spice Girls and their friends could only manage No.19 with their charity single, "It's Only Rock'n'Roll". So at No 1 we had "Our father, who art in heaven", at No 2 "Adieu, Emil, my

CLIFF RICHARD ON STAGE IN BIRMINGHAM
AT THE TURN OF THE MILLENNIUM

trusted friend" and No 3 "Imagine there's no heaven." Cliff was also doing well in the calendar stakes, outselling both Boyzone and Michael Owen.

Cliff caught 'flu and had to cancel one of his Birmingham shows, but otherwise his millennium week went well. His record touched a chord and his popularity has soared: even those who can't stand him have applauded the way Cliff has stood up against the big companies and the system. Like Paul McCartney promoting his return to the Cavern at the same time, he can show the younger acts a lot about self-promotion. What, I wonder, will he do for an encore as Cliff will surely want further hit records?

Cliff Richard helped to make pop fun again - and at the same time, let's not forget, he rasied over £1m for the Children's Promise, handing the cheque over at the Millennium Dome in March 2000. "The Millennium Prayer" wasn't wonderful, nor was it rubbish. It really boiled down to the anti-Cliff brigade. Cliff, like the previous Tory government, had just been around too long and people were heartily sick of him. It's remarkable that a man so close to the state retirement age should make the most rebellious record of the year, but would it have had the same reaction if Cliff had said, "This is my last record before I retire." No chance of that though.

And whatever your religious belief, no-one can deny that they are wonderful words. They are very noble, beautiful words. No yodelling hampster could come up with them. Nor George Michael. What was that he wrote? "Wake me up before you go-go / Don't leave me hanging on like a yo-yo."

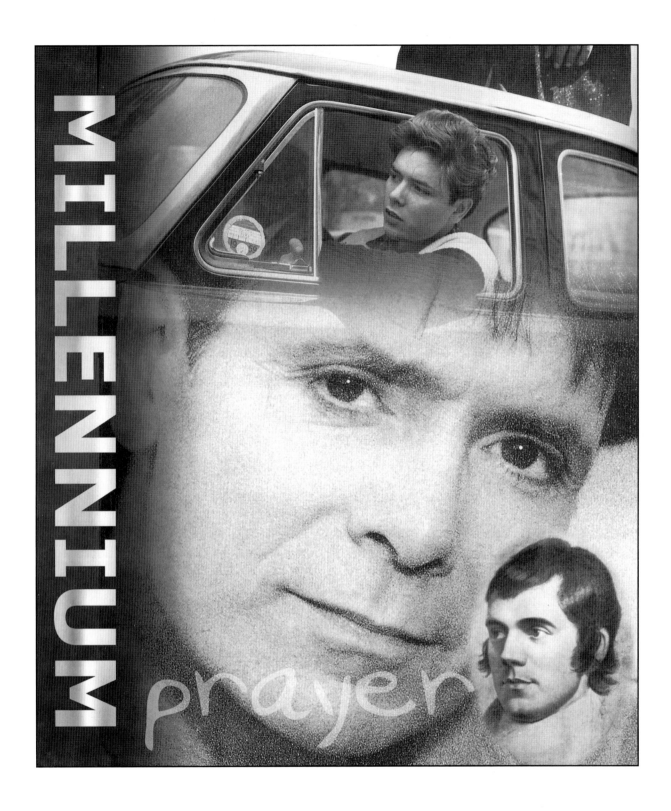

1999 - THE YEAR OF THE LIST

Favourite songs of the century

Unquestionably, 1999 was officially the Year of the Rabbit but it was really the Year of the List (or possibly the Year of the Anorak). Journalists and TV and radio presenters have reviewed the past decade, century and millennium to arrive at the best or worst in any given category - sporting moments, politicians, films, TV, plays, books, poems, art, cars, restaurants, toys and pin-ups (now known as "babes"). The lists have continued into Y2K and I wonder how editors are going to fill their pages come 2001. Maybe the passion for lists has gripped us so tightly that they will continue unbounded, with the lists for the Music of the Millennium being replaced by the Music of the Last Fortnight. (Oh sorry, aren't they the same thing?)

Some lists have been ridiculous: Muhammad Ali was deservedly the BBC's Sports Personality of the Century, but how can he also be, as some suggested, the Sports Personality of the Millennium. Who can say who was the leading sportsman in 1307 or 1451? Well, it probably was an archer in 1066. Similarly, "The Stage" polled its readers to ascertain the millennium giants in theatre and entertainment and found that William Shakespeare was having to beat off a challenge from Noel Edmonds. Among the more preposterous polls was the millennium's top explorers - Christopher Columbus, Captain Cook, Neil Armstrong, Marco Polo and Shackleton.

Often, the lists are to demonstrate how much we have progressed, but have any authors bettered the writers of the Bible in Y0K? The start of St John's Gospel is among the most beautiful passages ever written, while Revelation has as much psychedelic imagery as anything from the late 1960s - and what a bad trip it was. St Paul may be the world's best letter writer, although I'm not sure how the Corinthians, the Romans or the Ephesians responded to them. "Oh, here's another letter from St Paul telling us that we must pray all the time, we must not sin and we must not fornicate." What a bundle of laughs he was - and did anyone take any notice?

The music lists were an industry in themselves as there were so many of them. The most significant one for the purposes of this book is the BBC's poll for the Songs of the Century and it was broadcast by Paul Gambaccini on Radio 2 in April 1999, thereby assuming that nothing important would emerge in the final months. The Top 100, together with the 50 bubbling under, are given on BBC Online. The Top 25 are as follows:

BBC Radio 2 - Songs Of The Century

Title	*(Composers)*	*Year*
(1) Yesterday (John Lennon, Paul McCartney)		(1965)
(2) Stardust (Hoagy Carmichael, Mitchell Parish)		(1929)
(3) Bridge Over Troubled Water (Paul Simon)		(1970)
(4) White Christmas (Irving Berlin)		(1942)
(5) Unchained Melody (Alex North, Hy Zanet)		(1955)
(6) Imagine (John Lennon)		(1971)
(7) My Way (Claude François, Jacques Revaux, Gilles Thibaut, Paul Anka)		(1969)
(8) Summertime (George Gershwin, DuBose Heyward)		(1935)
(9) Over The Rainbow (Harold Arlen, E Y "Yip" Harburg)		(1939)
(10) As Time Goes By (Herman Hupfeld)		(1931)
(11) Smoke Gets In Your Eyes (Jerome Kern, Otto Harbach)		(1933)
(12) You'll Never Walk Alone (Richard Rodgers, Oscar Hammerstein II)		(1945)
(13) Candle In The Wind (Elton John, Bernie Taupin)		(1973)
(14) Rudolph The Red-Nosed Reindeer (Johnny Marks)		(1949)
(15) Hey Jude (John Lennon, Paul McCartney)		(1968)
(16) In The Mood (Andy Razaf, Joe Garland)		(1939)
(17) Alexander's Ragtime Band (Irving Berlin)		(1910)
(18) Bohemian Rhapsody (Freddie Mercury)		(1975)
(19) Rock Around The Clock (Max C Freedman, Jimmy De Knight)		(1953)
(20) Ol' Man River (Jerome Kern, Oscar Hammerstein II)		(1927)
(21) Ev'ry Time We Say Goodbye (Cole Porter)		(1944)
(22) Blowin' In The Wind (Bob Dylan)		(1963)
(23) We'll Meet Again (Ross Parker, Hugh Charles)		(1939)
(24) I Heard It Through The Grapevine (Norman Whitfield, Barrett Strong)		(1967)
(25) When I Fall In Love (Edward Heyman, Victor Young)		(1952)

Every song in that list - and indeed in the whole 100 - is a classic but there are many intriguing aspects to the selections. "Yesterday" at No 1 is hardly a suprise, but is "Hey Jude" really the Beatles' second best song? I doubt it.

Only two songs from the 1990s made the Top 100 - both film songs, "(Everything I Do) I Do It For You" and "My Heart Will Go On" (from "Titanic") - and just "Fields Of Gold" is bubbling under. Gambaccini commented that the art of songwriting was effectively dead: "This art form doesn't exist for young musicians today. They are making records, rather than songs to be sung by other people." This is mostly true, but even with sampling, you can have worthwhile material. Gabrielle's "Rise", a

No 1 in February 2000, sampled Bob Dylan's "Knockin' On Heaven's Door", but it would have held its own as a good song without the sample.

We all know the regurgitated thank you speech for the TV Awards ceremonies: "This award means a lot to me because it was voted for by you, the public." The BBC took a similar line with their Songs of the Century. The votes had come from the public.

So far so good, but Paul Gambaccini added that it was compiled from public voting together with an analysis of radioplay and record and sheet music sales, plus, most significantly, the opinions of a panel of experts . How the weighting took place was not explained and, in theory at least, the whole thing could have been as biased as the choosing of the New Labour's mayoral candidate for London.

Look at the Top 3. Does anyone seriously think that if you went onto the streets of a city and asked people to name their favourite song that many of them would think of "Stardust"? It is a great song to be sure, but there hasn't been a hit version or a popular version since Billy Ward in 1957. I see the hand of the experts in this high placing. The BBC's Songs of the Century is still an excellent and important chart, but it would be nice to know how Paul Gambaccini and his producer, Kevin Howlett, put it together.

As well as publishing the Top 100, the BBC also published some of the experts' individual choices and they too made good reading:

Elton John - "Bridge Over Troubled Water" (No 1), "Crazy", "Ol' Man River", "Imagine", "Blowin' In The Wind", "I Say A Little Prayer", "River Deep - Mountain High".
Tim Rice - "Smoke Gets In Your Eyes" (No 1), "Bridge Over Troubled Water", "Yesterday", "White Christmas".
Neil Tennant - "As Time Goes By", "Non, Je Ne Regrette Rien", "Night And Day", "I Will Survive".
Billy Bragg - "Garageland", "The Anthem Of The Union Of The Soviet Socialist Republics". (Clearly Billy Bragg is the ideal man to run the disco at your party.)

National Public Radio - America's 20th Century Greats

In a similar way to the BBC, National Public Radio in America compiled a list of the 100 most important American musical works of the 20th Century from the votes of 14,000 listeners entering their website, their own staff and a panel of musicians including Isaac Hayes, Kathy Mattea, Michael Feinstein and Wynton Marsalis. It was a strange listing, where songs were next to shows, singles, albums and classical works. "Warner Bros. Cartoon Music" by Carl Stalling (1936 to 1958) is a curious choice as is "Back In The Saddle Again", a 1939 record by cowboy actor, Gene Autry. A TV

performance of Billie Holiday singing "Fine And Mellow" is also selected. Again, the full list, given alphabetically, can be found online.

"Peggy Sue" by Buddy Holly, "Rapper's Delight" by the Sugarhill Gang and "Smells Like Teen Spirit" by Nirvana are more records than songs. The compositions that are purely listed as songs are:

Title (Composers)	Year
We Shall Overcome (Charles Tindley, Zilphia Horton, Frank Hamilton, Guy Carawan, Pete Seeger)	(1903)
Give My Regards To Broadway (George M. Cohan)	(1904)
Alexander's Ragtime Band (Irving Berlin)	(1910)
King Porter Stomp (Jelly Roll Morton)	(1923)
Stardust (Hoagy Carmichael, Mitchell Parish)	(1928)

Mack The Knife (Bertolt Brecht, Kurt Weill, Marc Blitzstein)	(1929)
I Got Rhythm (George Gershwin, Ira Gershwin)	(1930)
As Time Goes By (Herman Hupfeld)	(1931)
Dream A Little Dream Of Me (Gus Kahn, Wilbur Schwandt, Fabian Andre)	(1931)
Night And Day (Cole Porter)	(1932)
Take My Hand, Precious Lord (Tommy Dorsey)	(1939)
Goodnight Irene (Huddie Ledbetter, John Lomax)	(1936)
My Funny Valentine (Lorenz Hart, Richard Rodgers)	(1937)
This Land Is Your Land (Woody Guthrie)	(1940)
'Round Midnight (Bernard Hanighen, Thelonious Monk, Cootie Williams)	(1944)

The singles, which put the songs with the performers, are,

St Louis Blues - Bessie Smith	(1914)
West End Blues - Louis Armstrong	(1928)
Wildwood Flower - Carter Family	(1928)
Mood Indigo - Duke Ellington	(1930)
Hellhound On My Trail - Robert Johnson	(1937)
One O'Clock Jump - Count Basie & his Orchestra	(1937)
Sing Sing Sing - Benny Goodman & his Orchestra	(1937)
All Or Nothing At All - Frank Sinatra with Harry James & his Orchestra	(1939)
Back In The Saddle Again - Gene Autry	(1939)
Body And Soul - Coleman Hawkins	(1939)

In The Mood - Glenn Miller & his Orchestra (1939)

Take The "A" Train - Duke Ellington & his Orchestra (1941)

White Christmas - Bing Crosby (1942)

(Get Your Kicks On) Route 66 - Nat "King" Cole Trio (1946)

Foggy Mountain Breakdown - Flatt and Scruggs (1949)

I'm So Lonesome I Could Cry - Hank Williams (1949)

Blue Moon Of Kentucky - Bill Monroe & his Blue Grass Boys (1954)

Hoochie Coochie Man - Muddy Waters (1954)

Rock Around The Clock - Bill Haley (1954)

Maybellene - Chuck Berry (1955)

Blue Suede Shoes - Carl Perkins (1955)

Ain't That A Shame - Fats Domino (1955)

The Great Pretender - Platters (1956)

Hound Dog / Don't Be Cruel - Elvis Presley (1956)

I Walk The Line - Johnny Cash (1956)

Great Balls Of Fire - Jerry Lee Lewis (1957)

Peggy Sue - Buddy Holly (1957)

Tom Dooley - Kingston Trio (1958)

His Eye Is On The Sparrow - Mahalia Jackson (1958)

La Bamba - Ritchie Valens (1958)

Take Five - Dave Brubeck Quartet (1959)

What'd I Say - Ray Charles (1959)

Crazy - Patsy Cline (1961)

Blowin' In The Wind - Bob Dylan (1963)

Hello, Dolly! - Louis Armstrong (1963)

My Girl - Temptations (1964)

Like A Rolling Stone - Bob Dylan (1965)

Papa's Got A Brand New Bag - James Brown (1965)

Good Vibrations - Beach Boys (1966)

Light My Fire - Doors (1967)

Purple Haze - Jimi Hendrix Experience (1967)

Respect - Aretha Franklin (1967)

(Sittin' On) The Dock Of The Bay - Otis Redding (1967)

Stand By Your Man - Tammy Wynette (1968)

Coal Miner's Daughter - Loretta Lynn (1970)

Fire And Rain - James Taylor	(1970)
Oye Como Va - Santana	(1970)
Let's Stay Together - Al Green	(1971)
Theme From "Shaft" - Isaac Hayes	(1971)
What's Going On - Marvin Gaye	(1971)
I Wanna Be Sedated - Ramones	(1978)
Rapper's Delight - Sugarhill Gang	(1979)
Once In A Lifetime - Talking Heads	(1980)
Smells Like Teen Spirit - Nirvana	(1991)

Nothing by Paul Simon or Bruce Springsteen amongst the solitary songs but their albums, "Graceland" and "Born To Run" were listed. George Gershwin fared the best of all composers with entries for "Porgy And Bess", "Rhapsody In Blue" and "I Got Rhythm". Missing without action were the Eagles, the Byrds, Michael Jackson and Crosby, Stills and Nash. Perhaps CSN were omitted as Nash was British, but that didn't stop National Public Radio from listing "Mack The Knife", which is a German composition given an American lyric.

HMV / Channel 4 - Music Of The Millennium

Both the BBC and National Public Radio polls used the public's votes and adjusted them in some way. The Music of the Millennium shows what happens when you present the votes without adjustments and how ridiculous voting can be.

In essence, it was a very good idea. HMV, Channel 4, Classic FM, "The Guardian" and "The Independent" combined to ask the public to vote in 10 different categories. 80,000 people cast over 500,000 votes, which is very impressive. The winners of the ten categories are all reasonable choices:

Best Song (Title / Artist) - "Bohemian Rhapsody" (Queen)
Best Album - "Sgt Pepper's Lonely Hearts Club Band"
Best Female Vocalist - Madonna
Best Male Vocalist - Elvis Presley
Best Band - Beatles
Best Songwriter - John Lennon
Best Jazz Performer - Louis Armstrong
Best Classical Composer - Mozart
Best Piece of Classical Music - "The Four Seasons" (Vivaldi)
Most Influential Musician of the Millennium - John Lennon

So why was the Saturday night given over to the awards on Channel 4 so ridiculed? The answer is that many highly-placed entries reflected that the voters were more interested in the last few months than the millennium (HMV and Channel 4 have high yoof profiles), that multiple voting and large fan bases can bias results, and that the public, for whatever reason, may cast nonsense votes. (An example of irregular voting en masse came with the "Melody Maker" Top 100 Albums poll - "Sgt Pepper", normally a frontrunner, was nowhere to be seen and the Smiths' album, "The Queen Is Dead", was No 1.)

Steps did well in the voting and Robbie Williams was ubiquitous. How can Robbie Williams possibly be more influential than Beethoven, Chuck Berry, George Gershwin or Duke Ellington, both individually and even combined? Although he didn't win any categories (he was second Best Male Vocalist), the poll was a triumph for Robbie, who would have been highly placed in the Best Female Vocalist if he'd worn a dress. The nutcase votes included someone who believed Adam Ant was the Best Classical Composer. Wonder what they did with the votes for Engelbert Humperdinck in that category.

How long can you reasonably expect a voter to consider the form? Many people will have completed the form in five minutes whilst in HMV - and did the pictures of Robbie and Madonna on the front of the form help to sway the voting? Maybe you need a couple of hours to determine your votes and to decide, for example, between Billie Holiday and Natalie Imbruglia. You may be stuck when it comes to the Best Classical Piece and so you pick "Carmina Burana", which has been heard in Old Spice ads and the film, "Excalibur".

Elvis Presley has a loyal army of fans who voted strongly for him, giving him 11% of the total vote in the Best Male Vocalist. The most glaring evidence of this comes in the Best Album category where "Aloha From Hawaii Via Satellite", never normally regarded as a top Elvis album, is at No 4.

On the other hand, Cliff Richard, who has an equally vocal fan base, only managed No 43. They all came out for "The Millennium Prayer", but possibly this event passed the fan club organisers by.

Calling one category, Best Song, was misleading as voters were asked for both title and artist - in other words, they were voting for the Best Record, which is rather different. The Top 20 positions were,

(1) Bohemian Rhapsody - Queen   (1975)
(2) Imagine - John Lennon   (1971)
(3) Angels - Robbie Williams   (1997)
(4) American Trilogy - Elvis Presley   (1972)
(5) Smells Like Teen Spirit - Nirvana   (1991)

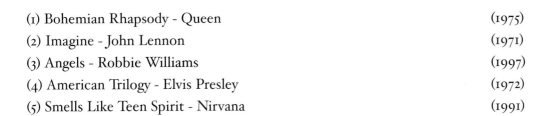

(6) Stairway To Heaven - Led Zeppelin	(1971)
(7) Millennium - Robbie Williams	(1998)
(8) Hey Jude - Beatles	(1968)
(9) Strawberry Fields Forever - Beatles	(1967)
(10) Unfinished Symphony - Massive Attack	(1991)

(11) Yesterday - Beatles	(1965)
(12) A Day In The Life - Beatles	(1967)
(13) My Heart Will Go On - Celine Dion	(1997)
(14) Heartbreak Hotel - Elvis Presley	(1956)
(15) Billie Jean - Michael Jackson	(1982)

(16) A Forest - The Cure	(1980)
(17) The Wonder Of You - Elvis Presley	(1970)
(18) Suspicious Minds - Elvis Presley	(1969)
(19) Wonderwall - Oasis	(1995)
(20) Thriller - Michael Jackson	(1983)

The Top 20 Best Songwriters were,

(1) John Lennon

(2) Paul McCartney

(3) Bob Dylan

(4) Michael Jackson

(5) Jerry Leiber & Mike Stoller

(6) Noel Gallagher

(7) Elton John

(8) Robbie Williams

(9) Cole Porter

(10) Kurt Cobain

(11) George Michael

(12) Burt Bacharach

(13) David Bowie

(14) Paul Simon

(15) Freddie Mercury

(16) George Gershwin

(17) Thom Yorke (Radiohead)

(18) Andrew Lloyd Webber

(19) Prince

(20) Paul Weller

Votes for songwriting teams like Leiber / Stoller were permitted, but there is no indication of what happened to the Lennon / McCartney votes.

Considering the wave of Abbamania in the late 90s, Benny and Björn are only No 39. Carole King only came in at No 64 and Dianne Warren fared little better at No 60.

Considering all the damaging publicity, it is an achievement for Michael Jackson that he can still be voted No 4. His tormentor, Jarvis Cocker, is only No 42.

ASCAP - Top Songs Of The Century

ASCAP (American Society Of Composers, Authors And Publishers) listed the 25 most-performed songs of the century, but did not give individual rankings. ASCAP did, however, confirm that the song with far and away the most performances was "Happy Birthday To You". How many additional public performances of this song were given without paying copyright fees? I am unsure about its inclusion in this list as surely it is no more than a jingle. There are no verses, just one short chorus.

It must be stressed that there are two main publishing organisations in the US, namely ASCAP and BMI, and composers and publishers are usually affiliated to one of them. ASCAP's list relates solely to the songs on its catalogue, and similarly with the BMI list shown later.

Title	Composers)	Year
Happy Birthday To You (Mildred J Hill, Patty Hill)		(1893)
Rhapsody In Blue (George Gershwin)		(1924)
Tea For Two (Irving Caesar, Vincent Youmans)		(1924)
Sweet Georgia Brown (Ben Bernie, Kenneth Casey, Maceo Pinkard)		(1925)
Mack The Knife (Kurt Weill, Berthold Brecht, Marc Blitzstein)		(1928)
Stardust (Hoagy Carmichael, Mitchell Parish)		(1929)
I Got Rhythm (George Gershwin, Ira Gershwin)		(1930)
As Time Goes By (Herman Hupfeld)		(1931)
Night And Day (Cole Porter)		(1932)
Santa Claus Is Comin' To Town (J Fred Coots, Haven Gillespie)		(1932)
Blue Moon (Richard Rodgers, Lorenz Hart)		(1933)
I Only Have Eyes For You (Harry Warren, Al Dubin)		(1934)
Winter Wonderland (Felix Bernard, Richard B Smith)		(1934)
Over The Rainbow (Harold Arlen, E Y "Yip" Harburg)		(1939)
That Old Black Magic (Harold Arlen, Johnny Mercer)		(1942)

White Christmas (Irving Berlin)	(1942)
The Christmas Song (Mel Tormé, Robert Wells)	(1945)
Unchained Melody (Alex North, Hy Zaret)	(1955)
I Could Have Danced All Night (Frederick Loewe, Alan Jay Lerner)	(1956)
Misty (Erroll Garner, Johnny Burke)	(1954)
Moon River (Henry Mancini, Johnny Mercer)	(1961)
I Left My Heart In San Francisco (Douglass Cross, George C Corey Jr)	(1962)
Hello, Dolly! (Jerry Herman)	(1964)
Raindrops Keep Fallin' On My Head (Burt Bacharach, Hal David)	(1969)
The Way We Were (Marvin Hamlisch, Alan Bergman, Marilyn Bergman)	(1973)

Even though Christmas songs are only played in December, there are four Christmas songs in the list, largely because the songs are perennial. The most recent composition is from 1973 - I wouldn't think the current ASCAP members would be happy about that! Neither ASCAP nor National Public Radio rank their entries. Is this some comment on the American psyche or something to do with political correctness, I wonder? Nowdays the presenters are expected to say "And the Oscar goes to…" as opposed to "And the winner is…".

BMI - Top Songs Of The Century

This BMI (Broadcast Music Inc) list was based on airplay on US radio and television only. The top song had over eight million airplays and all the songs in the listing have had over five million.

Title	(Composers)	Year
(1) You've Lost That Lovin' Feelin' (Barry Mann, Cynthia Weil, Phil Spector)		(1965)
(2) Never My Love (Donald Addrisi, Richard Addrisi)		(1967)
(3) Yesterday (John Lennon, Paul McCartney)		(1965)
(4) Stand By Me (Ben E King, Jerry Leiber, Mike Stoller)		(1961)
(5) Can't Take My Eyes Off You (Bob Crewe, Bob Gaudio)		(1967)
(6) Sittin' On The Dock Of The Bay (Otis Redding, Steve Cropper)		(1968)
(7) Mrs Robinson (Paul Simon)		(1968)
(8) Baby I Need Your Loving (Eddie Holland, Lamont Dozier, Brian Holland)		(1964)
(9) Rhythm Of The Rain (John Gummoe)		(1962)
(10) Georgia On My Mind (Hoagy Carmichael, Stuart Gorrell)		(1930)

Many commentators were surprised to find "You've Lost That Lovin' Feelin'" at No 1, but BMI is only reporting on BMI songs and so the whole of the rival ASCAP catalogue, which is much larger, has been ignored. It is another example that lists are only as good as their parameters and their guidelines, and if we don't know what they are, the results should be treated with caution.

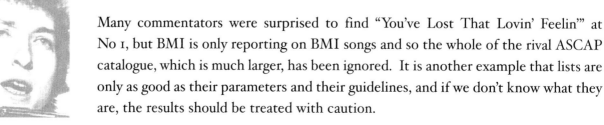

The only British song in either the ASCAP or the BMI lists above is "Yesterday". The Beatles' songs would be connected to the UK Performing Right Society (PRS) and hence would be affiliated to either ASCAP or BMI in the US. ASCAP only put American songs in their listing.

The only writers to have four songs in BMI's Top 100 list are John Lennon ("Yesterday" (3), "Michelle" (42), "Let It Be" (89), "Imagine" (96)) and Paul Simon ("Mrs Robinson" (7), "The Sound Of Silence" (18), "Bridge Over Troubled Water" (19), "Scarborough Fair" (31)). Lennon's success has a hollow ring about it as his input into those three Beatle songs was minimal. Possibly Lennon and McCartney's comparative lack of success in the poll is down to the fact that the songs are not generally available for use in commercials.

It doesn't say much for American radio if they are constantly playing "Never My Love" and "Rhythm Of The Rain", and we are not told what period this covers. And how come the first nine songs are all from the 1960s? Obviously, though, there is an inherent bias against newer songs as they have fewer years of potential airplay.

BBC National Poetry Day - Britain's Favourite Song Lyrics

Rock lyrics are poetry, maybe. In 1999 viewers were asked to nominate their favourite song lyrics. The Top 10 was quoted as a mixture of songwriters and records,

(1) Imagine (John Lennon)	(1971)
(2) Angels (Robbie Williams, Guy Chambers)	(1997)
(3) Bohemian Rhapsody (Freddie Mercury)	(1975)
(4) I Am The Walrus (John Lennon, Paul McCartney)	(1967)
(5) Millennium (Robbie Williams, Guy Chambers, Leslie Bricusse, John Barry)	(1998)
(6) Yesterday (John Lennon, Paul McCartney)	(1965)
(7) Beware Of The Flowers ('Cause I'm Sure They're Going To Get You Yeh) (John Otway)	(1977)
(8) Sit Down (James) (Timothy Booth, James Glennie, James Gott, Gavan Whelan)	(1991)
(9) Nights In White Satin (Justin Hayward)	(1967)
(10) Stardust (Hoagy Carmichael, Mitchell Parish)	(1929)

Definitely block voting in the John Otway camp, though personally, I'm delighted to see it! And all those Robbie fans again.

Millennium Dome

By the time it is through, the Millennium Dome will have cost around £1,000m and even though it holds little appeal for me, I don't resent the expenditure. True, I haven't bought a £20 ticket and gone to see it for myself, but the cost is around £20 (less the sponsorship) per person and I reckon we have all had our £20s of fun from its steady chronicle of disasters. The news hasn't been this much fun since Ken Dodd's trial.

Peter Gabriel was asked to write the music for an aerial ballet, but no Genesis song made the final list for the song to be played as we left the millennium. It had to be British and the flag-waving "We Are The Champions" (Queen) was one choice. Robbie Williams got in there with "Millennium" and even Oasis were considered with "Don't Look Back In Anger". I also think that Pulp's "Disco 2000" didn't stand much chance.

The front-runners were Lennon and McCartney's "All You Need Is Love" and Lennon's "Imagine". The upbeat optimism of "All You Need Is Love" won the day or rather the night. Her Majesty then had to endure an updated arrangement of "God Save The Queen" from Jools Holland and sung by Ruby Turner. Couldn't they have sung it to "Auld Lang Syne"?

Conclusion

Such lists may encourage readers to seek out music that they haven't heard properly before, but the results are always flawed. It is always good to seek the public's views, but it seems that you are damned if you adjust the results and damned if you don't.

If you are considering the best playwright of the millennium, William Shakespeare will come top by a substantial margin. Fortunately, the musical crown isn't so clear cut. There are no clearcut answers as to who the best songwriter of the century was or what the best songs were. Even considering the best songwriter of the 60s is a tough race between John Lennon and Paul McCartney, Burt Bacharach and Hal David, and Bob Dylan. It's better that way - it's much more entertaining when we can argue for our favourites and downgrade those we dislike.

INDEXES ♫

There are three indexes for "Brother, Can You Spare A Rhyme?". The first lists the names of persons or groups mentioned in the text. The second (page 270) lists the songs in the book and, in addition, all the songs have been dated. The third index, a general one, (page 281) covers the titles of albums, books, films, magazines, musicals, plays, and radio and TV programmes.

NAME INDEX

AFTERWORD

A few years ago I wrote a book for a major publisher and the cost of preparing an index was taken from my royalty statement. I was surprised to find that it was £500, but now, having just finished the index for this book, I realise that it was very good value indeed. Few things are more soul-destroying and time-consuming than preparing an index and yet it is very necessary for what is essentially a reference book. Still, it's done now and I'm pleased with myself.

Looking through the index, I realise that there are a few gaps in the narrative and because the pages have been designed with text wrapped around photographs, it is not practicable to make changes. Indeed, such changes might create havoc with my index! Nothing would, however, change my choice of the song of each year. Instead, I will make a few observations here and, in effect, I am writing the first review.

The blues singer-songwriter, Robert Johnson, deserves more space. I take his Faustian pact with the Devil with many pinches of salt, but he was a remarkable musician who produced remarkable music including "Rambling On My Mind" (1936), "Cross Road Blues" (1936), "Hellhound On My Trail" (1937) and "Love In Vain" (1937). He suffered an agonising death in August 1938 when only 27: some say Satan was extracting his revenge but more likely he was poisoned by a jealous husband. Whatever the truth of the matter, it is clear from his lyrics that he himself felt that he was pursued by demons ("I got to keep movin', There's a hellhound on my trail"). His recordings have influenced Eric Clapton, Led Zeppelin, the Rolling Stones and Peter Green, who has recorded his entire songbook. In June 2000 a court decided that his royalties belonged to a retired truck driver, Claud Johnson, whose mother had a brief romance with the musician in 1931. Someone testified that she

ROBERT JOHNSON

had seen them having sex! A few weeks later it was determined that the Rolling Stones had "improperly borrowed" two of his songs, "Love In Vain" and "Stop Breakin' Down", so Claud will be a rich man in his retirement.

Rock'n'roll is founded upon classic riffs - the opening of "Johnny B Goode" and the rhythms of "La Bamba", "Bo Diddley" and "Louie Louie" being among them. Although not much of a song, "Louie Louie" deserved more attention. It was written about a lovesick sailor by Richard Berry in 1957 and then became a US hit with mumbled lyrics by the Kingsmen in 1963. The lyrics were scrutinised by the FBI for obscenity, who declared that were "incomprehensible at any speed". The song has been recorded by such rock'n'roll revolutionaries as Patti Smith and Frank Zappa, and also by Julie London and the Beach Boys. The Beatles could have cut a killer version, but there is an excellent Merseybeat recording by the Southport band, Rhythm & Blues Inc.

I overlooked "The Floral Dance" - sorry about that. The origins of the melody of "The Floral Dance" are unknown, but it was arranged by Katie Moss in 1911, who also wrote the words. It became part of a celebration held every May 8th in Coinagehall Street in Helston, Cornwall. The melody is played and the dancers fill the street. "The Floral Dance" has been recorded by numerous artists, but when the leading Yorkshire brass band, the Brighouse and Rastrick, recorded the song in 1977, it became a surprise hit, making No 2. A vocal version by Terry Wogan also made the charts.

The Italian song, "Gloria", was a Continental hit for its composer, Umberto Tozzi, in 1979 but the first version to make the UK charts was in English by Jonathan King. The song was not a hit in America at the time, but it was given to a New York singer, Laura Branigan, who sang backing vocals for Leonard Cohen. She recorded it with a different English lyric as a powerful disco record in 1982, and it sold several million copies.

Because the first line-up of Foreigner in 1976 featured both British and American musicians, they thought "Foreigner" would be an appropriate name. Foreigner became a top rock act, but although successful, they were dissatisfied with their 1979 album, "Head Games". They reduced their numbers from six to four and released a new album, "4", in 1981. This best-selling album showed them with a more mellow sound, in particular with the ballad, "Waiting For A Girl Like You", which was written by Lou Gramm, the lead vocalist, and Mick Jones, the lead guitarist. As a single, the song was No 2 in the US for ten weeks without ever making the top spot.

Only Elvis Presley and Cliff Richard have had more records than Madonna on the UK charts and it is possible that she will pass their totals. Part of her success is due to her constantly-changing image, but part is also due to her being a excellent judge of songs, whether her own or other people's, as was shown with her revival of "American Pie" in 2000. The ASCAP director, John Bettis, who wrote "Top Of The World" and "Yesterday Once More" (both 1973) for the Carpenters, gave her "Crazy For You" (1985), which captured her image of a woman who knows what she wants - and gets it! I've heard Alan Parker, the director of "Evita", on "Desert Island Discs" describing her ego: "When she sings the scale, she goes 'Me, me, me, me, me.'"

Mariah Carey was writing a song about a friend who had died and she felt that she would like to record it with the top Motown group, Boyz II Men. Quite independently, Nate Morris of Boyz II Men was working on a tribute song to his road manager who had also died, and they combined their thoughts in "One Sweet Day". The single featuring the two acts was released in 1995 and it topped the US charts for a remarkable 15 weeks and made the Top 10 in the UK. It was also included on Mariah's best-selling album, "Daydream".

I could go on adding songs forever. I've just seen George Benson live and his version of "The Greatest Love Of All" was so compelling that I wondered why I'd omitted it from the text. I had it in there and then crossed it out! It comes from the 1977 film, "The Greatest Love Of All", in which Muhammad Ali played himself. In the opening

sequence, Ali is seen training while George Benson sings "The Greatest Love Of All". The song was revived with spectacular success by Whitney Houston in 1986 and it works as a superb love song, quite apart from the sporting element.

It appears that whenever I go to see someone I will regret omitting them from the text. Last week Jimmy Nail performed his bitter-sweet "Big River" with the Royal Liverpool Philharmonic Orchestra, and I loved how a song about his own town could be so specific and yet apply just as equally to Liverpool. During the same concert, the orchestra played a stunning arrangment of "Sgt Pepper's Lonely Hearts Club Band" as though it were written by George Gershwin. It suited its new "Rhapsody In Blue" arrangement and I hope that they record it.

Also, I didn't give enough attention to some American singer-songwriters from the 1970s: Guy Clark ("Desperados Waiting For A Train" and "L.A. Freeway", both 1975), Townes Van Zandt ("If I Needed You" and "Pancho And Lefty", both 1973), Jeff Walker ("Mr Bojangles", 1968, and the founder of outlaw country), Steve Goodman (that great train song, "City Of New Orleans", 1971), Butch Hancock ("She Never Spoke Spanish To Me", 1977, and the quirky "West Texas Waltz", 1978) and Chip Taylor (another killer riff in "Wild Thing", 1965, "Angel Of The Morning" two years later, and the whole of "Chip Taylor's Last Chance", 1973). Chip gave it up to become a professional gambler, made a profit each year and returned to performing in 1996. Tom Russell still seems like the new boy when compared to the above but he's been around for over 20 years, and "Gallo Del Cielo" (1979) is a compelling story-song about cock-fighting and family relationships.

The Scottish singer-songwriter, Eric Bogle, lives in Australia but he returns to the UK every other year for an extensive tour. Like Loudon Wainwright, he often writes about being a performer - "Big (In A Small Way)", "Bloody Rotten Audience" and "Just Here For The Money", but he is unlikely to surpass the poignant "And The Band Played Waltzing Matilda" (1972), which he wrote after watching an ANZAC march in Canberra.

In the text, I praised Sting's "Fields Of Gold", but I have acquired a new CD collection by the very traditional folk singer, Walter Pardon. It's called "A World Without Horses" and one track, "The Lawyer (Mowing The Barley)" has similarities to "Fields Of Gold". I would guess that Sting heard this old folk song and adopted its moods and melody for "Fields Of Gold". If that is so, he should be congratulated for spotting its potential.

I only mentioned Clifford T Ward in passing, a definite mistake, as 1973 was a golden year with him writing his hit "Gaye" as well as singles that showed his love of domesticity ("Scullery"), his love of the English vocabulary ("Wherewithal"), and his love of England itself ("Home Thoughts From Abroad"). I emjoy the cover version by Jack Jones where he asks how things are in Worcestershire.

I should have paid attention to Hubert Gregg, who presents "Thanks For The Memory" on BBC Radio 2. He wrote the wartime classics, "I'm Going To Get Lit Up (When The Lights Go Up Again In London)" (1940, but only a hit in 1943 when we looked like winning!) and "Maybe It's Because I'm A Londoner" (1944). I have mentioned "Among My Souvenirs" (1927), but its songwriter, Horatio Nicholls, a pseudonym for the publisher Lawrence Wright, called himself the Prime Minister of Melody and also wrote "That Old-Fashioned Mother Of Mine" (1920), "I Never See Maggie Alone" (1926) and "Down Forget-Me-Not Lane" (1941). He also wrote a song, "The Festival Of Britain" (1950), but I'm still waiting for Travis or Noel Gallagher to come up with "The Ballad Of The Millennium Dome".

So that he will always have a football team to support while watching a match on TV, my father-in-law always favours the one closer to his home. I'm like that myself as I love the music that is made around me in Liverpool. I've tried not to let that bias the way I have written the book, but I hold high hopes for what my friends will be doing in Y2K and beyond.

I could never like Frankie Connor's songs more than he likes them himself but the former Hideaway has recruited Merseybeat musicians to perform albums of new material, "Cavern Days" (1989) and "Many Happy Returns" (1997), written by himself with the self-effacing, former Tuxedo Alan Crowley. They are produced by Billy Kinsley. Billy Kinsley, who still performs with the Merseybeats and Liverpool Express, has been planning a solo album for years: songs like "You Are My Love" (1976) and "Chinatown" (unissued) indicate that this could be an excellent album.

Hughie Jones only wrote a few songs while he was with

the Spinners, notably "The Ellen Vallin Tragedy", but he is finding his feet and he writes very well-crafted songs, usually about the sea. Whereas Hughie's songwriting is painfully slow, Chris While and Julie Matthews, who now live in Southport, write as though there's no tomorrow. Sooner or later, they will write major hits and "Love Is An Abandoned Car" (Julie), "Every Word We Speak (Sounds Like Goodbye)" (Julie) and "Friendship Song" (Chris) are just three songs that could be recorded by major performers. Fairport Convention, always a haven for good British writers, recorded Julie's "Jewel In The Crown" as the title track of their 1995 album, while Barbara Dickson recorded their joint composition about AIDS victims, "Young Man Cut Down In His Prime" (1995).

Liverpool is called the Nashville of England and there are some excellent writers here. The best-known is Charlie Landsborough who found his niche through recording one delicate love song after another. He has a huge UK following, and such songs as "What Colour Is The Wind?" and "My Forever Friend"(both 1994) are being recorded by international acts. The other day someone asked me to play the song in which Charlie Landsborough gives his girlfriend a wash. I didn't know of any such song, but then realised it was a watch. The song, "Love You Every Second" is one of Charlie's best, but it does contain an awkward line that surely could have been improved - "I bought this small watch for to measure the time". Still the Bellamy Brothers soared high with a song that contained the appalling line, "If I was dying of thirst, would your flow of love come quench me."

Staying with country music in Liverpool, Kenny Johnson, formerly with the Hillsiders, is one of the UK's top country performers, but he hasn't produced an album of new material since the excellent "Summer Nights" in 1991. The award-winning New Country band, the Cheap Seats, have already split up, but their lead singer and chief songwriter, Ethan Allen, shows enormous promise for the future. So too does a new rock band, Pool, whose lead singer and songwriter, Gavin Skelhorn, played Billy Fury for a year on the West End stage.

There are lots of excellent songwriters on Merseyside including Ian Broudie (Lightning Seeds), Ian McCulloch (Echo and the Bunnymen) and Ian McNabb (Icicle Works). Pete Wylie has rarely had their acclaim but his recent album, "Songs Of Strength And Heartache", was as good as anything that has come out of Liverpool. His anthemic "Heart As Big As Liverpool" is sung at Anfield and is likely to be around for years. Not of course that it will supplant Pete McGovern's "In My Liverpool Home". Pete wrote the first verses in the Roscoe pub in 1961 and he's still writing them. With over 200 verses, this song is a history of post-war Liverpool.

Starting with Lita Roza and "How Much Is That Doggie In The Window?" (1952), there have now been over 50 No 1 records from Liverpool from Merseyside. It depends on how you count - Mel C comes from Widnes and Marc Almond from Southport and so the total can exceed 50 if you wish. Russ Hamilton's warm ballad, "We Will Make Love", stopped at No 2 in 1957 because the workers at the pressing plant went on their summer holidays and stocks ran out. Whatever it's roughly one chart-topper a year, which is good going, and Atomic Kitten with well-crafted pop songs written by OMD stand to increase the total.

More and more too I am finding good songs in the Top 40. Ten years ago I had lost faith with what was in the charts, but good songwriting is coming back. As I write, the Corrs are No 1 with the excellent "Breathless": their folk roots are dwindling fast and they sound like they want to be the new Fleetwood Mac.

Bob Dylan is due for a new album, and the sheer quality of his work over the last four decades has been remarkable. So often critics have derided his new albums only to find them reassessed a few years later. Even when an album has been derided ("Empire Burlesque"), it is usually the production rather than the songs that are at fault. I hope before they're finished that Paul McCartney collaborates with Bob Dylan as I think they could produce some remarkable work, and although there are major exceptions, McCartney's best work is often with others, whether it be John Lennon or Elvis Costello. At a rough guess, McCartney has written around 600 songs, which is still only a third of the output of Irving Berlin.

CDs still continue to excite me. In recent weeks, I have been enthralled by the 3 CD set by the Magnetic Fields called "69 Love Songs". In this, the songwriter, Stephin Merritt, pays tribute to the various musical styles of the 20th century and his own songs are ingenious. My current favourite is "Busby Berkeley Dreams", but the lyric writing is of a very high standard throughout. ("Reno Dakota, I'm no Nino Rota, I don't know the score.")

I thank Dennis Locorriere for the kind words in his Foreword and also for introducing me to his songwriting partner in Nashville, Michael Snow. I knew the name as he wrote "Rosetta", a 1971 hit for Georgie Fame and Alan Price, but I had no idea that he came from Liverpool. He has just released his first album, "Here Comes The Skelly", and I wish him lots more Rosettas, not to mention lots of good songs with Dennis.

My friend, Peter Doggett, wrote the CD booklet for the new Paul Simon compilation, Greatest Hits. He had to submit the notes to Simon for approval and he ended with a flourish, "Maybe the best is yet to come". Paul Simon crossed out the "Maybe". Let's hope he's right.

Thank you and goodnight or as they say in "Louie Louie", me gotta go.

Spencer Leigh
Liverpool, 13th July 2000

PICTURE CREDITS

The owners of the copyright of many of the older pictures have been lost with time. If the owner of any pictures wishes to contact me, I can give the credit in any future edition of the book.

3 BBC Radio Merseyside, Eddie Barford/Liverpool Daily Post & Echo, 6 Dennis Locorriere, 11 A&M, 12 20th Century-Fox, 13 Castle Communications, EMI, 14 Keith Prowse Music, BMG, 15 WEA, 16 Polygram, unknown, Arista, 17 EMI, 18 Virgin, WEA, 19 Polygram, BMG, BMG, Editions EG, 20 Monument, Polygram, 21 EMI, A&M, Sony, 28 Sony, 29 Francis, Day & Hunter, 36 MGM, 37 Deram, Castle Communications, 39 Carlin, 40 Ode, 42 BMG, 43 BMG, 44 BMG, BMG, 45 MCA, Belinda Music, 54 BMG, 56 Freshwater Music, 57 WEA, 59 Samuel Goldwyn, B Feldman, 61 US Postal Service, 63 EMI, 64 MCA, 65 EMI, US Postal Service, 67 EMI, 68 Del-Fi Records, 69 US Postal Service, 70 Chappell & Co, 72 MCA, MGM, 77 EMI, 78 EMI, 80 Sony, 82 EMI, 88 MCA, 91 Chess, 92 Sun, 93 EMI, 94 Sony, 95 WEA, BMG, 96 MGM, 98 Pink Paper, 99 Victoria Music, EMI, BMG, 100 Sony, 101 Ode, 102 Sony, 103 Sony, 106 EMI, 107 Phil Spector International, 108 A&M, 109 TRO-Essex, 110 Castle Communications, 111 Tamla-Motown, 112 BMG, 113 EMI/Apple, 114 Sony, 115 Tamla-Motown, WEA, EMI/Apple, 116 Chappell & Co, 118 BMG, 20th Century, 119 Silly Records, 123 EMI/Apple, 127 EMI, 128 EMI, 129 United Artists, 130 Unknown, 131 EMI, 132 Secker and Warburg, 135 EMI, 138 EMI/Apple, 139 EMI/Apple, 142 Elektra, 144 EMI, 146 BMG, 149 Elektra, 150 Flying Fish, 152 WEA, 153 Polygram (France), 157 BMG, 158 EMI, 160 EMI/Apple, 161 Hulton Getty Picture Collection, 162 EMI/Apple, 165 EMSO Arts, 166 EMI/Apple, 167 EMSO Arts, 168 EMI/Apple, 170 United Artists, 172 Second picture, Rolling Stones Records, 173 EMI, 176 Demon Records, 177 US Postal Service, EMI, 178 Rolling Stones Records, 179 Sony, 181 Sharyn Felder, EMI, 182 A&M, 183 ZTT, 184 Sony, 186 Sony, 187 WEA, 189 Mercury, Arista, 190 WEA, 192 A&M, 196 WEA, 199 Gregory Heisler/Reprise, 201 WEA, 202 BMG, 204 WEA, 205 WEA, 207 Mercury, 210 Palace Pictures, 215 Mercury (twice), EMI, 217 WEA, 219 Nigel Parry/Katz Pictures, 220 Walt Disney International, 221 David Wedgbury, 226 Geffen, 227 US Postal Service, 236 DJM, 237 Both Rocket Records, 238 Rocket Records, US Postal Service, 245 EMI, 246 EMI, 247 EMI, 284 Sony, 288 RCA.

SPENCER
LEIGH
LIMITED